Archibald Forbes

Memories and Studies of War and Peace

Archibald Forbes

Memories and Studies of War and Peace

ISBN/EAN: 9783337219253

Printed in Europe, USA, Canada, Australia, Japan

Cover: Foto ©Thomas Meinert / pixelio.de

More available books at **www.hansebooks.com**

MEMORIES AND STUDIES

OF

WAR AND PEACE

BY

ARCHIBALD FORBES

WITH PORTRAIT OF THE AUTHOR

New York

CHARLES SCRIBNER'S SONS

153-157, FIFTH AVENUE

1895

To the Revered and Beloved Memory

OF

GENERAL MONTGOMERY CUNNINGHAM MEIGS,

QUARTERMASTER-GENERAL OF THE ARMY OF THE

UNITED STATES FROM 1861 TO 1882,

HIS SON-IN-LAW INSCRIBES THIS BOOK.

CONTENTS.

MEMORIES AND STUDIES

OF

WAR AND PEACE.

I.

TEN YEARS OF WAR CORRESPONDENCE.

Skobeleff under Fire—The Ideal War Correspondent—Old and New Methods of War Correspondence—The Franco-German War—Saarbrücken—Gravelotte—An Episode of the Entry into Paris—The Starving Magistrate—Malet in the Commune-time—The Servian Campaign—A Long Ride—The Russo-Turkish War and its War Correspondence—My Comrades—The Crossing of the Danube—Tzar Alexander II.—Life on Campaign—Second Battle of Plevna, July 30th—Fighting in the Schipka Pass—My Interview with the Emperor—His Return to St. Petersburg—Telegraphy *in excelsis*—King Theebau and his Presents—Rough Surgery in Afghanistan—Mentioned in Despatches—Ulundi and the Zulu Valour—A Long Gallop with the Tidings.

IT was down by the Danube side, in the earlier days of the Russo-Turkish War. Skobeleff and myself were squatting in a hole in the ground, to escape the rain of bullets and shells which the Turks were pouring across the river on the detachment which the young general commanded.

"Here you and I are," said Skobeleff with a laugh, "like Uriah the Hittite, right in the forefront of the battle; and how strange it is that quiet stay-at-home folk all over the world, who take their morning papers just as they do their breakfasts, know ever so much more about this war as a whole than we fellows do, who are actually listening to the whistle of the bullets and the crash of the shells!"

Skobeleff did not pursue the subject further, because just then a shell exploded right in front of us, and of the mud which it threw up a splash hit him in the face and changed the current of his ideas; but all the same his remark was a

B

very true one. War correspondence and the electric telegraph have for years given the peaceful citizen the advantage, in the matter of quick and wide war news, over the soldier who is looking the enemy in the face on the actual battlefield. But this intelligence, although the peaceful citizen takes little account of the manner of getting it, and has come to look for it as a thing of course—as a mere matter of everyday routine —yet reaches his breakfast-table as the outcome only of long thoughtful planning, of arduous physical and mental exertion, of hairbreadth risks encountered. It is my purpose in this chapter to tell something of the war correspondent's working life, something of the character of his exertions to satisfy the world's crave for the " latest intelligence from the seat of war," and something of the dangers that encompass the path of his duty. If the recital of some bygone personal experiences in this field may strike the reader as involving the imputation of egotism, I would respectfully beg of him to admit the excuse that it is not easy for a man to avoid egotism altogether when he is speaking mainly of himself.

In my day-dreams, indulged in mostly when smarting under the consciousness of my own deficiencies, I have tried to think out the attributes that ought to be concentrated in the ideal war correspondent. He ought to possess the gift of tongues—to be conversant with all European languages, a neat assortment of the Asiatic languages, and a few of the African tongues, such as Abyssinian, Ashantee, Zulu, and Soudanese. He should have the sweet, angelic temper of a woman, and be as affable as if he were a politician canvassing for a vote ; yet, at the same time, be big and ugly enough to impress the conviction that it would be highly unwise to take any liberties with him. The paragon war correspondent should be able to ride anything that chance may offer, from a giraffe to a rat ; be able to ride a hundred miles at a stretch, to go without food for a week if needful, and without sleep for as long ; never to get tired—never to feel the sensation of a " slight sinking, you know ;" and be able at the end of a ride—of a journey however long, arduous, and sleepless—to write round-hand for a foreign telegraph clerk ignorant of the correspondent's language, at the rate of a column an hour for six or eight consecutive hours; after which he should, as a matter of course, gallop back to the scene of action without an hour's delay. He should be a competent judge of warfare; conversant with all military operations, from the mounting of a corporal's guard to the disposition of an army in the field. He ought to have supreme disregard for hostile fire when real duty calls upon him to expose himself to it; and his pulse should be as calm when shells are bursting around him as if he were watching his bosom-friend undergoing the ordeal of the marriage service. He must have a real instinct for the place and day of an impending combat: he must be able to scent the coming battle from afar, and allow nothing to hinder him from getting forward in time to be a spectator of it. He should be so constituted as to have an intuitive perception how the day hath gone; to be able to discern victory or defeat while as yet, to the spectator not so gifted, the field of strife seems confusion worse confounded; and so to rely on his own judgment as to venture, while the turmoil is dying away, to turn his back upon it, and ride off the earliest bearer of the momentous tidings. To potter about waiting till the last shot be fired; to linger for returns of killed and wounded, and for the measured reports of the commanders; to be the *chiffonier* of the rags of the battle-field—that is work which he must leave to his helpers, if he has any such. Alas! there never was such a man as I have ideally depicted, and there never will be such a man. I think Julius Cæsar would have been an exceptionally brilliant war correspondent, if the profession had been invented in his time, and if he could have weaned himself from the meaner avocations of commanding armies, conquering countries, and ruling nations. But the first Napoleon, if only he could have been a little truthful occasionally, would have eclipsed Julius Cæsar and knocked William Howard Russell into a cocked hat.

Before the Franco-German War there had been war correspondents, and one at least of those had made for himself a reputation to vie with which no representative of a newer school has any claim. But their work, being almost wholly in the pre-telegraphic period, was carried on under less arduous conditions than those which have confronted the more recent war correspondent. Nor was it incumbent on the former to carry their lives in their hands. Before far-reaching rifled firearms were brought into use, it was quite easy to see a battle without getting within the range of fire. But this is no longer possible, and in the future will be still more impossible. With guns of position that carry six miles, with mobile artillery having a range of more than three miles, and with rifles that kill without benefit of clergy at two miles, the war correspondent may as well stay at home with his mother unless he has hardened his heart to take his full share of the risks of the battlefield. Indeed, if he has determined to look narrowly into the turbulent heart of each successive paroxysm of the bloody struggle—and it is only now by doing this that he can make for himself a genuine and abiding reputation—he must lay his account with adventuring more risk than falls to the lot of the average soldier. The percentage of casualties among war correspondents has recently been greater than that among the actual fighting men. In the Servian Campaign of 1876, for instance, there were twelve correspondents who kept the field and remained under fire. Of these, three were killed and four wounded. Certainly not more than thirty correspondents and artists, all told, were in the Soudan from the earliest fighting to the final collapse of the Nile expedition; but on or under its cruel sands lie the corpses of at least five of my comrades. O'Donovan, the adventurous pioneer of Merv, perished with Hicks. The last hope has long faded that Vizetelly, endowed though he was with more lives than the proverbial cat, has still a life in hand. Cameron and St. Leger Herbert were struck down on the same bloody day, and rest together in their shallow grave in the hot Bayuda sand. Poor Gordon, who, like myself, had been a soldier before he became a war correspondent, died a lone death of thirst in the heart of the desert while pushing on to where his duty lay. Time would fail me to tell of those who have perished of fevers and other maladies, who have been wounded, shipwrecked, and encountered strange hair-breadth escapes; of others, again, who have come home so broken by hardship and vicissitude that what remains of life to them is naught save weariness and pain. And it is such men whom a commander who has been himself adventurous has classed with the camp-followers, and has stigmatised as " drones who eat the rations of fighting men and do no work at all "!

It was the Franco-German War of 1870 that brought about the revolution in the methods of war correspondence, although at Saarbrücken, in the earlier days of that great contest, there was as yet scarcely any perception of the opportunities that lay to our hands. But if at Saarbrücken the correspondents thus early on the war-path were still unregenerate in this respect, we had some experiences in which the comic and the tragic were curiously blended. Within two miles of the little town lay a whole French army corps, which any day might overwhelm Saarbrücken and its slender garrison of a battalion of infantry and three squadrons of uhlans. So we lived, quite a little detachment of us, in an hotel on the outskirts, ready for a judicious bolt. At this hotel there arrived one morning a young German girl who was engaged, we learned, to a sergeant of the gallant Hohenzollerns. She had come, it seemed, to say farewell to her sweetheart before the fighting should begin and he should march away, mayhap never to return. Some of the livelier spirits among us conceived the idea that the pair should get married before the farewell should be said. Both were willing. The bridegroom's officer gave him leave, on condition that should the alarm sound, he was to join his company without a moment's delay. All was in readiness and the clergyman was just about to join the couple in holy matrimony, when the sound of a bugle suddenly broke in on the stillness. It was the alarm! The bridegroom hurriedly embraced the bride, buckled on his accoutrements, and darted off to the place of rendezvous. In ten minutes more the combat was in full intensity; the French had carried the heights overhanging the town, and were pouring down upon it their artillery and mitrailleuse fire. Our hotel was right in the line of fire, and soon became exceedingly disagreeable quarters. We got the woman down into the cellar, and waited for events. A shell crashed into the kitchen, burst inside the cooking stove, and blew the wedding breakfast, which was still being kept hot, into what an American colleague called "everlasting smash." It was too hot to stay there, and everybody manœuvred strategically to the rear. A few days later was fought, close to Saarbrücken, the desperate battle of the Spicheren, in which the bridegroom's regiment took a leading part. The day after the battle I was wandering over the field, helping to relieve the wounded, and gazing shudderingly on the heaps of dead. Suddenly I came on our bridegroom, in a sitting posture, with his back resting against a stump. He was stone dead, with a bullet through his throat.

Perhaps the most thrilling episode of all that colossal struggle of 1870 was the singularly dramatic climax of the battle of Gravelotte. All day long, from noon until near the going down of the sun, the roar of the cannon and the roll of the musketry had been incessant. The deep ravine of the Mance between Gravelotte and St. Hubert was a horrible pandemonium wherein seethed struggling masses of German soldiery, torn by the shell-fire of the French batteries, writhing under the stings of the mitrailleuse, bewildered between inevitable death in front and no less inevitable disgrace behind. Again and again frantic efforts were being made to force up out of the hell in the ravine and gain foothold on the edge of the plateau beyond; and ever the cruel sleet of lead beat them back and crushed them down. The long summer day was waning into dusk, and the fortunes of the battle still trembled in the balance, when the last reserve of the Germans—the Second Army Corps—came hurrying up towards the brink of the abyss. In the lurid glare of the blazing village, the German King stood by the wayside and welcomed his stalwart Pomeranians as they passed him. High over the roll of the drums, the blare of the bugles, and the crash of the cannon, rose the eager burst of cheering as the soldiers answered their Sovereign's greeting, and then followed their chiefs down into the fell depths of the terrible chasm. The strain of the crisis was sickening as we waited for the issue in a sort of rapt spasm of sombre silence. The old King sat with his back against a wall on a ladder, one end of which rested on a broken gun-carriage, the other on a dead horse. Bismarck, with an elaborate assumption of coolness which his restlessness belied, made pretence to be reading letters. The roar of the close battle swelled and deepened, till the very ground trembled beneath us. The night fell like a pall, but the blaze of an adjacent conflagration lit up the anxious group here by the churchyard wall. From out the medley of broken troops littering the slope in front, rose suddenly a great shout that grew in volume as it rolled nearer. The hoofs of a galloping horse rattled on the causeway. A moment later Moltke, his face for once quivering with excitement, sprang from the saddle, and, running towards the King, cried out: "It is good for us; we have restored the position, and the victory is with your Majesty!" The King sprang to his feet with a fervent "God be thanked!" and then burst into tears. Bismarck, with a great sigh of relief, crushed his letters in the hollow of his hand; and a simultaneous hurrah welcomed the glad tidings.

On the 1st of March, 1871, the day of the entry into Paris of the German troops, rather a curious experience befell me. While as yet within the German *cordon* in the Place de la Concorde, I observed that I was being dogged, having been called on to answer a question asked by a German commander who was riding up the Champs Élysées. I had no sooner passed out of that *cordon* than I was vehemently assailed by an angry French mob, who insisted that I was a German spy. I made as stout a resistance as was compatible with circumstances, but at length they got me down, and then I imagined it was all over with me. But a detachment of national guards holding a police post rescued me at the bayonet point from the genial enthusiasts who were dragging me along the gutter on my back, with the expressed intention of drowning me in the basin of an adjacent fountain. A good deal of my clothing had been torn off me, but that was a trifle. Overhauling myself in the police station, I discovered that with half of my great-coat had disappeared my note-book, which was in the pocket of the missing section of the garment. This was a most serious misfortune. In those times I had accustomed myself to write out at full length in my note-book the description of scenes or events of which I was a witness, detailing in form ready for the printer the accounts of incident after incident as the incidents successively evolved themselves. From the summit of the tower overhanging the Cascade I had looked down that morning on King Wilhelm's great review of his army on the Longchamps racecourse; and my description, two columns long, of that remarkable scene was in the lost note-book. One result of this custom of concurrent writing out was that the writer's memory did not charge itself with the recollection of what had been committed to paper; and thus I had not only lost the actual "copy" already indited and out of hand, but was destitute of the power to reproduce the lost matter. While I was internally bewailing myself of this misfortune, a citizen in a fine glow of triumph rushed into the police station. "Voilà!" he shouted, as he waved aloft my note-book in one hand and my coat-tail in the other; "here is damning evidence that the prisoner is a wicked spy! Here are the villain's notes, the lies he has been writing down concerning our unhappy Paris!" I could have embraced the excited *ouvrier*, frowsy as he was; he had done me an incalculable benefit in his anxiety to have my doom sealed. His face was a study when, in the gladness of my heart, I offered him a five-franc piece. The implacable patriot accepted it.

Presently, under an escort of national guards with fixed bayonets—for the mob was still dangerous—I was marched through a couple of streets to the bureau of a sitting magistrate. My companions were a gentleman in a blouse who was accused of having stolen an ink-bottle; a tatterdemalion detected in selling a couple of cigars to a Bavarian cavalryman; and a woman whom the Paris mob had stripped and painted divers colours, because she had been caught parleying with a Prussian drummer. The magistrate was so good as to deal with me first. Fortunately I was able to produce to him my British passport and my journalistic credentials. He called in his sister, who had lived in England, to assist him in deciding as to the authenticity of those documents. She promptly pronounced in their favour, and his worship became immediately gracious. He told me that I was free, and he was good enough to lend me an old coat in which to walk to my hotel; at the same time gracefully begging me to excuse what he termed "the little inconvenience I had experienced, on account of the not unnatural excitement of the Paris populace."

The magistrate's good sister sent me to a bedroom, where I washed off the most flagrant stains of the recent unpleasantness. Outside, the mob was still howling fiercely. Time was very precious to me; I could not endure to wait indefinitely the dispersion of the gentlemen of the pavement, yet I did not care to re-offer myself to their tender mercies. The magistrate's sister in this strait proved herself a ministering angel. She said there was a door opening into a quiet side-alley, and actually offered to escort me to my hotel, which was close by. As we walked, I told the kind lady that I did not know how to thank her; had it been her servant, I could have found no difficulty in requiting the good office, but a lady—"Oh!" she broke in—"that is not so difficult; I will put my pride in my pocket. My brother has a fair salary, but he has not seen a franc of it for six months. We are gentlefolk; we cannot join the *queue* outside the baker's shop, and—and—oh, mon Dieu! we are actually starving"—and the poor lady burst into tears. "We could not take charity," she continued, sobbing—"but we have heard of that kind *don anglais* which, they say, is now being distributed freely; if only one could get a little aid from its bounty!" We had a sub-dépôt in my hotel; I myself was one of the accredited almoners; some of the commissioners were living with me. I hurried the lady into a room in which there was no one to remark her emotion; then I found John Furley, and told him the little story. Furley was a man of energy. In five minutes a big hamper had been packed full of comestibles, and a porter had it on his back, waiting for the lady's instructions. With the chivalry of a fine gentleman, Furley announced to her that one of his men was at her disposition. She came out into the hall, looked down at the big basket, whose open mouth disclosed among other things a leg of mutton, a couple of fowls, a huge honest loaf, and sundry vegetables ; then she gave a great gasp, and I feared that she was about to faint. She was anæmic from sheer want, but she rallied—tears helping her; and then she went silently away with her veil down over her wan face, and the stalwart porter tramping behind her. It was such people as those, with pride and fixed salaries which were not paid, who suffered worst during the siege ; and they, too, it was who were the most difficult to relieve when the siege was just over, but without as yet any alleviation of their misery. The women were the most stubborn and the most proud. The concierge would assure the almoner that the two old ladies on such a floor were literally starving. The old ladies, when you pushed their button, would appear, statelily gracious. " Yes, the English were a kind people, and the good God would reward them. There were some poor creatures in the roof who were in pressing need. For themselves, thanks ; but no, they could not accept charity. Merci : bon jour, monsieur !" and then the door would close on the wan eyes and hollow cheeks. Ah me, it was melancholy work !

Elsewhere in this book will be found some detailed account of the fell days of the closing scenes of the Commune, the only phase of it of which I was a witness. All that I need here say is, that in the lurid chaos which marked the ruthless stamping out of the Commune by the Versaillist army under Marshal MacMahon, the conditions under which correspondents tried to fulfil their duties were more full of peril than one could incur in any battle of which I have had experience. In a battle you know your danger. The enemy is for the most part in front, and you can either stand up and take your chance of his fire, or take cover to protect yourself from it. But in the seething turmoil of the last days of the Commune, bullets were flying from front, flanks, and rear. There was a universal raving lust for blood. As Mr. Labouchere cheerfully remarked: "They shot you first, and apologised to your corpse afterwards." The brightest feature of the grim drama which I can recall after so long a lapse of time, was the imperturbable coolness of Mr., afterwards Sir Edward, Malet. He remained in charge of the British Embassy in the Rue du Faubourg St. Honoré, when Lord Lyons and the rest of the official *personnel* migrated to Versailles. For three long days it seemed that Malet, or at all events the embassy he inhabited, was the target for the artillery alike of Versaillists and Communards. Shells bedevilled the ball-room and knocked holes miscellaneously all over the building; explosion after explosion blew down the walls of the embassy garden, through which the Versaillists were sapping their way to outflank their stubborn antagonists of the Commune. Malet, bland and cheery as was his wont, quietly and methodically performed his duties; the shell fire apparently concerning him not at all. In no conceivable circumstances could Malet look absurd ; and that surely is a great gift ! Just before the German siege began, he came out from Paris to Meaux with a communication to Bismarck. I happened to meet him near the German forepost line. His franc-tireur escort had compelled him on the previous night to sleep "under the beautiful stars ;" when I met him he was riding between two Prussian uhlans. He was perched on a great military saddle, the schabracque of which rose about him before and behind ; his stirrups were about ten holes too long, and the big troop-horse he bestrode plainly evinced dislike of his civilian rider. No concatenation of circumstances could have tended more to give a man an aspect of grotesque absurdity. But Malet did not in the least look like a guy. He had no consciousness of being ludicrous, and even at the first blush he was not ludicrous. On the contrary, he was self-possessed, easily dignified, and conveyed somehow the impression that this was precisely the mode of progression which he deliberately preferred over all other modes.

I imagine that people at home in England took but faint interest in the little war which in the summer and autumn of 1876 the petty principality of Servia was waging against its Turkish suzerain. It was, nevertheless, an interesting struggle, both in itself and as virtually the prelude to the great Russo-Turkish war of the following year. Up at Deligrad, about 140 miles from Belgrade, the capital of Servia, General Tchernaieff, with his Russian volunteers and rough Servian levies, for three months confronted the Turkish army commanded by that venal old impostor, Abdul Kerim Pasha. Our life with Tchernaieff was almost comically squalid. His headquarters were in a ruined schoolhouse, and his staff lived in holes dug out in the ground and thatched over with reeds. We lay on straw all round a great fire which was maintained in the centre, and which occasionally set light to the roof and burnt us temporarily out of house and home. One morning the Turks woke up from their lethargy, and carried with a rush the defences of the hill of Djunis which Tchernaieff had been holding so long on the swagger. I have always had a shrewd suspicion that Abdul Kerim and Tchernaieff understood each other extremely well: that the former for a price contentedly allowed himself to be amused by the latter during the summer months; and that when the order came from the Seraskierate that the immobility so long allowed to last must at length peremptorily be ended, Tchernaieff was complaisant enough not to make much more than a brisk show of resistance. The scheme, however, was in a measure thwarted by the honest and zealous fighting of General Dochtouroff heading the Russian volunteers, who died very freely in their trenches, and who had sent many Turkish souls to Hades before they accepted defeat. The Servians behaved badly; their resistance fell to pieces in a few hours; and, in the end, Dochtouroff and myself had to ride through a belt of Turkish skirmishers to escape being cut off.

Anyhow, the game was up, and Servia lay at the mercy of the Turks. I was the only correspondent on the spot, and it behoved me to make the most of this casual advantage. At five o'clock in the afternoon, when I rode away from the blazing huts of Deligrad, more than 120 miles lay between me and my point, the telegraph office at Semlin, the Hungarian town on the other side of the river Save from Belgrade—telegraphing was not permitted from the Servian capital. I had an order for post-horses along the road, and I galloped hard for Paratchin, the nearest post station. When I got there the postmaster had horses, but no vehicle. Now, if I had merely sent a courier, this obstacle would have sufficed effectually to stop him. But it was apparent to me, being my own messenger, that although I could not drive I might ride. True, the Servian post-nags were not saddle-horses; but sharp spurs and the handling of an old dragoon might be relied on to make them travel somehow. All night long I rode that weary journey, changing horses every fifteen miles, and forcing the vile brutes along at the top of their speed. At nine next morning, sore from head to foot, I was clattering over the stones of the Belgrade main street. The field telegraph-wire had conveyed but a curt, fragmentary intimation of disaster; and all Belgrade, feverish for further news, rushed out into the street as I powdered along. But I had galloped all night, not to gossip in Belgrade but to get to the Semlin telegraph-wire, and I never drew rein till I reached the ferry-boat. At Semlin one long drink of beer, and then at once to the task of writing, hour after hour against time, the tidings of which I was the bearer from the interior. After I had written my story and put it on the wires, I lay down in my clothes and slept twenty hours without awakening once. I had meant to start back for Deligrad on the afternoon of the day of my arrival in Belgrade, but sheer fatigue had caused me to lose a day in sleep. It seemed to me, however, when I recovered from my chagrin at this delay, that perhaps, after all, I was fairly entitled to a good long sleep; for I had seen a battle that lasted six hours, ridden a hundred and twenty miles, and written to the *Daily*

News a telegraphic message four columns long—all in the space of thirty hours.

At the beginning of the Russo-Turkish War in the early spring of 1877, the first great anxiety with the correspondents who were detailed to follow the Russian fortunes was to obtain an authorisation to accompany the armies in the field. Without such an authorisation the correspondent, if he gets forward at all, is liable to be treated as a spy and soon finds himself in trouble. I suppose there is no correspondent of any considerable general experience who has not been in custody over and over again on suspicion of being a spy. I have been a prisoner myself in France (made so both by Germans and French), Spain, Servia, Germany, Hungary, Russia, Roumania, and Bulgaria; and I cannot conscientiously recommend any of these countries from this point of view. The authorities of the Russian army were very fair and courteous about the authorisations of correspondents. In principle they accepted all who presented themselves accredited by respectable papers and bringing a recommendation from any Russian ambassador. There was to be no field censorship; you simply gave your honour not to reveal impending movements, concentrations, and intentions. You might, with this exception, write and despatch just what you chose; only a file of your paper had to be sent to the headquarters, and a polyglot officer—Colonel Hausenkampf by name—was appointed to read all those newspapers, and to be down upon you if you exceeded what he considered fair comment. Then you got a warning; and, if you were held to have gravely and spitefully transgressed, you were expelled.

I always pitied the unfortunate Colonel Hausenkampf from the bottom of my heart. He had to read all the letters published in all the newspapers of all the correspondents, and I predicted for him either speedy suicide or hopeless insanity. But he remained alive and moderately sane, in spite of this arduous duty and of the task which at the outset devolved upon him, of listening to every correspondent who made application for a permission. He was fearfully badgered.

One day I called on him at the headquarters in Ploesti, and found him seated in a bower in a garden, resolutely confronted by a gaunt man in a red beard and a ferocious tweed suit. " Mon Dieu!" exclaimed the Colonel to me—" will you oblige me by taking this man away and killing him ? He is a Scotsman, it seems, and I am not acquainted with the Scottish language ; he knows none other than his native tongue ! He comes here daily, and looms over me obstinately for an hour at a time, firing off at intervals the single word ' Permission !' and tendering me, as if he would hold a pistol at my head, a letter in English from a person whom he calls the Duke of Argyll—a noble, I suppose, of this wild man's country ! " It is needless to add, since the " wild man " was a Scot, that he achieved his permission and did very good work as a correspondent.

We were all numbered like so many ticket-porters, and at first carried on the arm a huge brass badge, which heightened our resemblance to the members of that respectable avocation. The French correspondents' sense of the beautiful was, however, outraged by this neat and ornamental distinguishing mark; so at their instance there was substituted a more dainty style of *brassard*, with the double-headed eagle in silver lace on a yellow silk ground. The permission was written on the back of the photograph of the correspondent to whom it was granted, which photograph was duly stamped on the breast of the subject with the great seal of the headquarters. A duplicate of this photograph was inserted in a " Correspondents' Album," kept by the commandant of the headquarters. When I last saw this book there were some eighty-two photographs in it; and I am bound to admit that it was not an overwhelming testimony to the good looks of the profession. I got, I remember, into sundry and divers difficulties through having incautiously shaved off some hair ·from my chin which was there when my photograph was taken. In vain I argued that it was not the beard that made the man ; the sentries were stiff-necked on the point of identity, and I had to cultivate a new chin-tuft with great assiduity.

My most prominent colleague in the Russo-Turkish War was Mr. Januarius Aloysius MacGahan, by extraction an Irishman, by birth an American. Of all the men who have gained reputation as war correspondents, I regard MacGahan as the most brilliant. He was the hero of that wonderful lonely ride through the Great Desert of Central Asia to overtake Kauffmann's Russian army on its march to Khiva. He it was who stirred Europe to its inmost heart by the terrible, and not less truthful than terrible, pictures of what have passed into history as the " Bulgarian atrocities." It is, indeed, no exaggeration to aver that, for better or worse, MacGahan was the virtual author of the Russo-Turkish War. His pen-pictures of the atrocities so excited the fury of the Sclave population of Russia, that their passionate demand for retribution on the " unspeakable Turk " virtually compelled the Emperor Alexander II. to undertake the war. MacGahan's work throughout the long campaign was singularly effective, and his physical exertions were extraordinary; yet he was suffering all through from a lameness that would have disabled eleven out of twelve men. He had broken a bone in his ankle just before the declaration of war, and when I first met him the joint was encased in plaster-of-Paris. He insisted on accompanying Gourko's raid across the Balkans; and in the Hankioj Pass his horse slid over a precipice and fell on its rider, so that the half-set bone was broken again. But the indomitable MacGahan refused to be invalided by this mishap. He quietly had himself hoisted on to a tumbril, and so went through the whole adventurous expedition, being involved thus helpless in several actions, and once all but falling into the hands of the Turks. He kept the front throughout, long after I had gone home disabled by fever; he brilliantly chronicled the fall of Plevna and the surrender of Osman Pasha; he crossed the Balkans with Skobeleff in the dead of that terrible winter; and, finally, at the premature age of thirty-two, he died, characteristically, a martyr to duty and to friendship. When the Russian armies lay around Constantinople waiting for the settlement of the Treaty of Berlin, typhoid fever and camp pestilences were slaying their thousands and their tens of thousands. Lieutenant Greene, an American officer officially attached to the Russian army, fell sick, and MacGahan devoted himself to the duty of nursing his countryman. His devotion cost him his life. As Greene was recovering MacGahan sickened of malignant typhus; and a few days later they laid him in his far-off foreign grave, around which stood weeping mourners of a dozen nationalities.

Another colleague was Mr. Frank Millet, who, still young, has forsaken the war-path, and appears to be on the high road to the inferior position of a Royal Academician. Millet, like MacGahan, is an American. He accompanied Gourko across the Balkans after the fall of Plevna. The hardships which he cheerily endured when men were frozen around him in their wretched bivouacs among the snow, and when to write his letters he had to thaw his frozen ink and chafe sensation into his numbed fingers, move admiration not less than the brilliant quality of the work performed under conditions so arduous. Lieutenant Greene, in his work on the campaign which constitutes its history, remarks that of the seventy-five correspondents who began the campaign only three, and all those Americans—MacGahan and Millet of the *Daily News*, and Grant of the *Times*—followed its fortune to the close. But this is not strictly correct; one other member of our profession—for that profession surely includes the war-artist—saw the war from beginning to end, Frederic Villiers, then the artist-correspondent of the *Graphic*.

The first serious fighting of the campaign occurred on that June morning when Dragomiroff's division of the Russian army forced the passage of the Danube under the fire of the Turkish batteries about Sistova. It happened that Villiers and I were the only correspondents who were spectators of that operation.

It was still dark when we threaded our way through the chaos in the streets of Simnitza, and at length made our way down into the willow grove by the Danube side, where Yolchine's brigade was waiting until the pontoon boats should

C

be ready for its embarkation. It was a strange, weird time. The darkness was so dense that scarce anything could be seen around one; and the Turkish bank was only just to be discerned, looming black up against the hardly less dark and sullen sky. Not a light was permitted—not even a cigarette was allowed to be smoked. When men spoke at all, which was but seldom, it was in whispers; and there was only a soft hum of low talk, half drowned by the gurgle of the Danube, and broken occasionally by the launching of a pontoon boat. The grey dawn faintly began to break. We could dimly discern Dragomiroff, mud almost to the waist, directing the marshalling of the pontoon boats close to the water's edge. Here come the "Avengers," a stern, silent band, the cross in silver standing out from the sombre fur of their caps. They have the place of honour in the first boats. As the leading pontoon pulls out, Captain Liegnitz, the gallant German *attaché*, darts forward and leaps into it. The stalwart Linesmen of Yolchine's brigade are manning the other boats. The strong strokes of the sailors shoot us out into the stream. The gloom of the night is waning fast, and now we can faintly discern, across the broad swirl of water, the crags of the Turkish bank and the steep slope above. What if the Turks are there in force? A grim precipice that, truly, to carry at the bayonet point in the teeth of a determined enemy! And an enemy is there, sure enough, and on the alert. There is a flash out of the gloom, and the near whistle and scream of a shell thrills us as it speeds over us and bursts among the men in the willows behind us. There follows shell after shell, from right opposite, from higher up, and from the knoll still higher up, close to where the minarets of Sistova are now dimly visible. The shells are falling and bursting on the surface of the Danube; they splash us with the spray they raise; their jagged splinters fly yelling by us. There is no shelter; we must stand here in this open boat, this densely packed mass of men, and take what fortune Heaven may send us. The face of the Danube, pitted with falling shells, is flecked too with craft crowded to the gunwale. Hark to that crash, the splintering of wood and the riving of iron, there on our

starboard quarter! A huge pontoon laden with guns and
gunners has been struck by a shell. It heaves heavily twice;
its stern rises; there are wild cries—a confused turmoil of
men and horses struggling in the water; the guns sink,
and drowning men drift by us with the current down to
their death. From out the foliage, now, in the little cove
for which we are heading, belches forth volley after volley
of musketry fire, helping the devilry of the shells. Several
men of our crew are down ere our craft touches the mud of
the Danube shore. The " Avengers " are already landed;
so is Yolchine, with a handful of his Linesmen. As we tumble
out of the boats with the bullets whizzing about our ears, and
swarm up on to the bank, we are bidden by energetic orders
to lie down. We fall prone on the damp and muddy sward
under the cover of a little bank. Already dead and wounded
men lie here thick among the living and hale. Boat after
boat has disembarked its freight. At length Yolchine thinks
he has men enough. He who, with young Skobeleff, has
never lain down, gives the word, and the two spring up the
bank; a billow of strong, supple Russian soldiers released
from restraint surges with resistless rush up the steep ascent.
The detachment of Turkish soldiers holding the position are
overwhelmed, but they do not fly. No; they die where they
stand, neither quailing nor asking for quarter. For that brave
band of Mustaphis, Abdul Kerim Pasha unconsciously furnished a noble epitaph. " They have never been heard of
since," he wrote. No, nor will they till the last trumpet
sounds!

The first time I saw close the Emperor Alexander II., so
ruthlessly assassinated a few years later, was on the day after
that June morning on which General Dragomiroff's division
of Russian soldiers had forced, with considerable loss, the
passage of the Danube. The Tzar had come to thank his
gallant troops for the exploit of fighting their way across
the great river under conditions so arduous. In front of
the long massive line drawn up on the crest of the slope
to the eastward of Sistova stood three men awaiting the

coming of the Great White Tzar—the divisional General
Dragomiroff; the brigadier, gallant old Yolchine; and young
Skobeleff, who had shown the way to all and sundry. The
Emperor, having acknowledged the salute and greeting of
the troops, embraced the divisional general in the Russian
fashion, and shook hands cordially with the cheery little
brigadier. Then he approached Skobeleff—and we all
watched the little scene with intent curiosity; for it was
as notorious that Skobeleff was in disfavour, as that his
splendid valour of the previous morning might well have
effaced any save the most obstinate disfavour. For a moment
Alexander hesitated as the two tall, proud, soldierly men
confronted each other; one could discern in the working
of his features the short struggle between prejudice and
appreciation. It was soon over, and the wrong way for
Skobeleff. The Tzar frowned, turned short on his heel, and
strode resolutely away without a gesture or a word of notice.
Skobeleff, for his part, bowed deeply, flushed scarlet, then
grew pale and set his teeth hard. It was a flagrant slight
in the very face of the army, and a gross injustice; but
Skobeleff took it in a proud silence that seemed to me
very noble. It was not long before he could afford to be
magnanimous. This despite was done him on the 29th of
June. On September 3rd Skobeleff, after having heaped
exploit on exploit, led the successful assault on the Turkish
position at Loftcha, and drove his adversaries out of that
strong place not less by the splendid daring he so con-
spicuously displayed than by the skilfulness of the tactics he
had devised. On the following evening, at his own dinner-
table in the imperial marquee at Gorni Studen, Tzar Alexander stood up and bade the company to pledge him in a
toast to "Skobeleff, the hero of Loftcha!" It has not been
given to many men to · earn a vindication so grand and
triumphant as that. Nor is it every omnipotent Emperor
who would have shown a frankness so manful. Absolute
monarchs are not addicted to constructive apologies.

In campaigning in Bulgaria we correspondents had to

rely on our own resources; it was like going a-gipsying, with now and then a battle thrown in by way of variety. When our Russian friends crossed the Danube, it became necessary for us to abandon the flesh-pots of Egypt, in the shape of the civilisation, beauty, and good cooking of Bucharest, and to depart, so to speak, into the wilderness, there to join the army. My companion in this, as in previous campaigns, was Frederic Villiers, then the artist of the *Graphic.* Villiers is an excellent fellow, but he had, like the rest of us, his weak points. Perhaps his weakest point was that he imagined going to bed in his spurs contributed to his martial aspect. He may have been right, but as I shared the bed-place on the floor of a narrow waggon, I did not see the matter quite in that light. We had for joint attendant my old Servian courier Andreas. Let me describe our travelling equipage. We had found in Bucharest a vehicle which, when covered with leather and fitted with sundry appliances, made a sufficient habitation for two men who could pack tight, and give and take one with the other. By a simple arrangement the floor of this carriage became at night a bed-place, the cushions, and the poultry which Andreas cherished, serving for a mattress. Our waggon was drawn by two sturdy grey horses, one of which was blind—a characteristic which the man who sold him to us cited as an important advantage, as calculated to make him steadier in a crowd. The vehicle I have described was not a waggon only. Cunningly contrived in a roll attached to one of its sides, we carried a sort of elementary canvas apartment. Villiers and I were "at home" in our canvas drawing-room to some very distinguished personages in the course of the campaign. If we were within there was no pleading "not at home," for, as the awning was open on at least two sides, the inmates were visible to the naked eye a long way off. Our cooking appliances consisted of a stew-pan and a frying-pan. One does not require any more weapons than these to perform wherewithal the functions of a plain cook. I am a plain cook myself; perhaps, to be more explicit, I should say a very plain cook. Of one grand discovery in culinary science I can boast. I found out in Bulgaria that when you attempt to fry lean meat without fat, lard, oil, or butter, you not only burn the meat, but you burn the frying-pan also!

In the early days of this campaign—MacGahan away beyond the Balkans with Gourko, and Millet far off in the Dobrutcha with Zimmermann—the task devolved upon me of covering Bulgaria from the right flank to the left flank of the Russian main advance; and I had to be in the saddle morning, noon, and night; for I had to try at least to see everything, and I mostly had to be my own courier back to the telegraph base at Bucharest. General Ignatieff, the famous diplomatist, was a good friend in giving me timely hints of impending events. When I was taking leave of him after my first visit, the general said: "Come to me when you want anything. I like your paper because it is a Christian paper, and I am a very Christian man; and if I am not mistaken you are so also." I regarded this last observation as strong proof of the aphorism that discerning penetration is one of the leading attributes of a great diplomatist.

Probably—*pace* Lord Wolseley—there is no harder toil than that which the zealous war correspondent must undergo in a country almost wholly destitute of communications, and when momentous events are crowding fast one on the other. The nearest telegraph office is his goal; for us in Bulgaria, the nearest available telegraph office was in Bucharest, scores of long miles distant. The supply of trustworthy couriers was very scanty, and even the best courier will not strain ardently when he is not working for his own hand. I write in constant consciousness of being over-egotistic; but one would like that the newspaper-reader at home should know under what conditions he is served with war news. To this day I shudder at the recollection of those long wearisome rides on dead-tired horses from the Lom, or the Balkans, or the Plevna country, through the foodless region down to Sistova on the Danube, where the bridge of boats was. Leaving my horse in Sistova, I would tramp in the darkness across the bridge and over the islands and flats ankle-deep in sand, the three miles' distance to Simnitza, the squalid village on the Roumanian side of the great river. I have reached Simnitza so beaten that I could scarcely stagger up the slope. Once when I got to the Danube bridge, I found that it was forbidden to cross it. Several pontoons in the centre, said the officer on duty, were under water, and there was no thoroughfare; nobody, he said, was allowed to go upon it. I respectfully represented to him that as I did not belong to the Russian army, it was nothing to him what might happen to me. He laughed; said that if I drowned it was no affair of his; and, to quote his own lively expression, that I might go to the devil if I had a mind. I escaped the devil, but had to accept a thorough ducking, and was very nearly carried down stream in the direction of the Black Sea, which might have been a worse fate than that indicated by the Russian officer. Simnitza reached somehow, there were still about ninety miles to Bucharest. Off then to Giurgevo, a fifty miles' night ride in a country rattle-trap drawn by four half-broken ponies harnessed abreast. I have been upset freely all along that dreary plain; spilt into a river, capsized into a village, overturned by a dead horse into a foul and dismal swamp. During the railway journey from Giurgevo to Bucharest it was possible to begin inditing my telegram, writing a few pages at a time when the stoppages at the stations occurred. Bucharest finally reached, I had to finish my message without delaying even to wash, that it might be in time for next morning's paper in England. I have reached Bucharest so encased with mud, so blackened with powder, so clotted with inch-deep dust, so blistered with heat, that the people of Brofft's hotel had difficulty in recognising me. The telegram finished—long or short, there was no respite till that were done—came a bath and then food—they used to charge me double price for those meals, and I rather think they lost money; and then a few hours' sleep till the evening train back to Giurgevo should start. Up and off again by it, and so back without a halt to the position which I had quitted to despatch the telegram.

Villiers and myself were the only civilian spectators of the desperate and futile attack which the Russian soldiers commanded by Krüdener and Schahoffskoy made on that lovely July day of 1877 upon the girdle of earthworks with which Osman Pasha had partly surrounded the Bulgarian town of Plevna. Up among the oak shrubs on the height of Radischevo, while the Russian cannon thundered over our heads, we watched the resolute but hopeless assaults of the Russian infantrymen on the Turkish redoubts on the gentle swell in the bosom of the great central valley. Plevna lay down yonder to the left front in its snug valley among the foliage, quiet and serene like a sleeping babe amidst a pack of raging wolves, the sun glinting on its spires and minarets. Behind us, the Russian cannon belching fire and iron. Close to us, the general with set face and terrible eager eyes, the working of his lips and fingers belying his forced composure. And at our feet hell itself, raging in all its lurid splendour, all its fell horror. A chaos of noises comes back to us in the light summer wind: the sharp crackle of the rifle fire, the ping of the bullets, the crash of near-exploding shells, loud shouts of reckless men bent on death or victory, shrieks and yells of anguish—ay, even groans, so near are we. Look at that swift rush; see the upheaval of the flashing bayonets, listen to the roar of triumph, sharpened by the clash of steel against steel! There is an answering hurrah from the Russian gunners above us, for the Russian infantrymen have carried at the bayonet-point the two nearest Turkish redoubts.

Yes; that much, it is true, was gallantly accomplished, but with a terrible loss of life and waste of blood. The struggle will bear telling more in detail. Two brigades were lying down in the reverse slope of the ridge behind the guns, and, therefore, behind us also. The order to rise up and advance over the ridge was hailed with cheers;

and the battalions, with a swift, swinging step streamed up the steep slope, the movement heralded by the artillery with increased rapidity of fire. That fire was momentarily arrested while the infantrymen crossed the ridge, breaking ranks to pass through the interval between the guns, which presently, as soon as the front was clear again, renewed their fire with feverish activity. The Turkish shells hurtled through the ranks as the Russian battalions advanced, and men were already down in numbers; but the long undulating line tramped steadily over the stubble of the ridge, and crashed through the undergrowth in which we were sitting on the descent beyond. No skirmish line was thrown out in advance. The fighting line remained the formation for a time, till, what with impatience and what with men dropping, it broke into a rapid spray of humanity, and surged on swiftly and with no close cohesion. The supports were close up, and ran forward into the fighting line independently and eagerly. It was a veritable chase of fighting men impelled by a burning desire to get forward and come to close quarters with the enemy firing at them yonder from behind the shelter of the parapet of the redoubt.

Villiers follows with his eye the fortunes of the left brigade, I concentrate my attention on the right—Tcherkoff's—brigade. Presently all along the face of the infantry advance burst forth flaming volleys of musketry fire. The jagged line springs onward through the maize-fields, gradually assuming a concave front. The roll of rifle fire from both sides is incessant, yet dominated by the fiercer and louder turmoil of the artillery above us. The cannon redouble the energy of their fire. The crackle of the musketry fire swells into a sharp continuous peal. The clamour of the hurrahs of the fighting men comes back to us on the breeze, making the blood tingle with the excitement of the fray. A village is blazing on the left. The fell fury of the battle has entered on its maddest paroxysm. The reserves which had remained behind the crest are being pushed forward over the ridge in reinforcement. The wounded are beginning to trickle back to behind the ridge —some of the poor fellows have already passed us. We can see the dead and the more severely wounded lying where they have fallen on the stubbles and among the maize. The living waves of fighting men are pouring over them ever on and on. The gunners behind us stand to their work with a will on the shell - swept ridge. The Turkish cannon fire begins to weaken from that earthwork opposite to us. More supports stream down with a louder cheer into the Russian fighting line. Suddenly the disconnected bodies are drawing together. We can discern the officers signalling for the concentration by the waving of their swords. The distance of the Russian front from the Turkish parapet is not now 200 yards. There is a wild rush, headed by the colonel of the central battalion of the brigade. The Turks in the redoubt hold their ground, and fire steadily and with terrible effect, into the rushing masses of their enemies. The colonel's horse goes down. Yes, but the colonel is on his feet in a second, and waving his sword, leads his men forward on foot. But only for a few paces. He staggers and falls; the brave colonel is a dead man.

We can hear faintly the tempest-gust of wrath, half howl, half yell, with which his men—bayonets at the charge —rush on to avenge him. They are across the ditch and over the parapet, and in among the Turks in an avalanche of maddened revenge. Not many Turks get the chance to escape from the gleaming bayonets swayed by muscular Russian arms. There was a momentary desperate struggle, hand to hand, bayonet to bayonet; and then the Russians were in possession of the Turkish redoubt No. 1, with the two guns inside it. The Turks had been hurled out, what of them lived to escape; we watched the huddled mass of them in the gardens and vineyards behind the position, cramming the narrow track between the trees to gain the cover of their second position.

The redoubt farther to the left was also captured, but, although Schahoffskoy threw in repeated reinforcements, it could not be held by the Russians, although they were loath to leave grip of it.

And now, ardent as they are, the Russians get no farther. It is but too apparent that there are not men enough for the further enterprise. Nearer Plevna, there has occurred a swift succession of furious charges and countercharges between Turks and Russians, in which, as the final issue, the latter have got the worse. See the stubborn, gallant fellows there, standing now all but leaderless—for nearly all the officers are down—sternly waiting death there for lack of leaders either to lead them forward or to march them back! Noble heroism or sheer stolidity, which? "For God and the Tzar!" is the shout of answer that comes back to us on the wind, as the gaps torn open by the Turkish fire are made good, and the ranks knit themselves the closer. The utter pity of it! A craving that is almost irresistible comes over one to abandon inaction, and to be doing something — something, no matter what, in this acme, this climax of concentrated slaughter. The mad excitement of the battle surges up into the brain like strong drink. The estimable citizen sitting at home at ease, can form no idea how hard it is, in such a convulsion of emotion, to bide at rest and write out a telegram with industrious accuracy; how difficult to compose sentences coherently when the brain is on fire and the pulses are bounding as if they would burst.

The sun sank in a glow of lurid crimson. The Russian defeat was utter. The *débris* of the attacking troops came sullenly back, companies that had gone down into the fray two hundred strong returning now by fives and tens. For three hours there had been a steady current of wounded men up from out the battle to the reverse slope of the ridge from the face of which we watched, back into comparative safety. All around us the air was heavy with the low moaning of the wounded, who had cast themselves down behind us to gain relief from the agony of motion. A crowd of maimed wretches were hustling each other round the fountain at the foot of the slope, craving with wistful longing for a few drops of its blood-stained and scanty water. Bad was their plight; but one's blood turned at the thought of the awful fate of the poor fellows who, too severely wounded to move to the rear, were lying on the maize-slopes down there, waiting for inevitable cruel death at the hands of an enemy who not only gave no quarter, but savagely mutilated before he slew.

The Turks spread over the battlefield, slaughtering as they advanced, and were threatening to carry the ridge, when the wounded who lay behind it would have been at their cruel mercy. In this hour of terrible strain Schahoffskoy proved himself a gallant and a feeling man. "Gentlemen," said he to his staff and the people about him, "we and the escort must co-operate to hold the front. These poor wounded must not be abandoned!" The bugle sounded the "assembly," but there rallied to the sound but a poor company of beaten-out men, most of whom were wounded. We extended along that grim ridge, each man moving to and fro in a little beat of his own, to show a semblance of force against the Bashi-Bazouks. Through the glowing darkness one could watch the streaks of flame foreshortened close below us; and nerves, tried by a long day of foodlessness, excitement, fatigue, and constant exposure to danger, quivered under the prolonged tension of endurance as the throbbing hum of the bullets sped through or over the straggling line. At length dragoons from the reserve relieved us; and so, following the general who had lost an army going in search of an army which had lost its general, we turned the heads of our jaded horses, and, threading our way through the wounded, rode slowly away from the blood-stained ridge. It was only to endure a night of wretchedness. No sooner had we established a bivouac, and general and aide-de-camp, Cossack and correspondent, had thrown themselves on the dewy ground and fallen into slumber, than the alarm arose that the Bashi-Bazouks were surrounding us. Again and again the little band wearily arose and struggled its way through the loose environment of the Turkish marauders. At length daybreak came, and I rode away on the journey to Bucharest, the bearer to the world of the details of the catastrophe. Mile after mile of that dreary road the good horse covered loyally, tired and foodless as he was; but I felt him gradually dying away under me. The stride shortened, and the flanks began to heave ominously. I had to spur him sharply, although I felt every stab as if it had pierced myself. If he could only hold on to Sistova, rest and food awaited him there. But some three miles short of that place he staggered, and then went down. I had to leave the poor gallant brute as he fell, and tramp on into Sistova with my saddle on my head.

The Russo-Turkish campaign had been in progress for several months before I had the honour of being presented to the Emperor Alexander II. That fell out in this wise. The Imperial headquarters were in the Bulgarian village of Gorni Studen when the fighting began in the Schipka Pass up in the Balkans. General Ignatieff gave me a timely hint, and I started immediately for the scene of action. As we rode along through the beautiful valleys that trend up into the Balkans, we met the hordes of wretched Bulgarian fugitives who had fled across the mountain chain from the fell retribution of the Turks. The whole country seemed one great picnic; but it was an indescribably mournful picnic. My artist-companion revelled in the picturesqueness of the vivid colours of the women's dresses; but he had no heart to depict the bivouacs in their profound misery. We were the witnesses, not of a few casual fugitives, but of the general exodus of the inhabitants of a whole province. There were peasants, but there were also many families of the better class —families whose women were dressed, not in dingy Bulgarian clouts or in Turkish trousers, but as the Englishwoman of the period attired herself. There were women to whom one felt it not quite the thing to speak without an introduction, yet whose only habitation was the shade of a tree, whose only means of conveyance was a miserable pony on which they sat with a child in arms and another clinging behind. Many had no means of conveyance at all; and one saw women plodding painfully, carrying children in their arms, whom they tried to shade with parasols—poor fond creatures!—the tender folly of motherhood, when homes were blazing behind them, and misery about them and before them. In war men take their chance—if they fall, they fall, so to speak, in the way of business—but the business sickens one when the rigours of evil fortune involve helpless women and children.

We reached the fire-swept pass of the Schipka on the afternoon of August 23rd, just as the Russian fortunes were trembling in the balance. There had been almost continuous fighting ever since the morning of the 21st. Suleiman's Turks were 30,000 strong. At the beginning Darozinski, the Russian commander of the force garrisoning the Schipka, had little more than 5,000 bayonets with forty guns in the defensive positions. There had come to him early on the 22nd, swiftly marching from Selvi, a strong regiment commanded by the valiant Colonel Stolietoff, who a few months later conducted a Russian mission from Central Asia to Cabul, an enterprise which gave rise to the Afghan war of the winter of 1878–79. The unequal fight of 7,000 Russians against 30,000 Turks lasted for many hours. And at length, as the shadows were falling, the Turks had so worked round on both the Russian flanks that it seemed as though the claws of the crab were momentarily about to close behind the worn Muscovites, and as if the Turkish columns climbing either face of the Russian ridge would clasp hands in rear of the Russian position.

The moment was dramatic with an intensity to which the tameness of civilian life can furnish no parallel. The two Russian chiefs, expecting imminently to be environed, had sent a last telegram to the Tzar assuring him that, please God, driven into their positions and beset, they and their soldiers would hold their ground to the last drop of the last man's blood. It was six o'clock. There was a lull in the fighting, of which the Russians could take no advantage since the reserves were engaged up to the hilt. The grimed, sun-blistered men were beaten out with heat, fatigue, hunger, thirst, and wounds. There had been no cooking for three days, and there was no water within the Russian lines. The poor fellows lay panting on the bare ridge, reckless in their utter exhaustion that it was swept by the Turkish rifle fire. Others doggedly fought on down among the rocks, forced to give ground, but doing so grimly and reluctantly. The cliffs and valleys resounded with triumphant Turkish shouts of "Allah! il Allah!"

The two Russian commanders stood on the parapet of the St. Nicholas redoubt, on the loftiest and most exposed peak of the position. Their glasses were scanning the visible glimpses of the steep brown road leading up from out the Iantra Valley, through stunted copses of sombre green and yet more sombre dark rock. Stolietoff cries aloud in a sudden access of excitement, grips his brother commander hard by the arm, and points down the pass. The head of a long black column is plainly visible against the reddish-brown bed of the road. "Now God be thanked!" exclaims Darozinski solemnly. He was a dead man thirty hours later. Both commanders cross themselves with bared heads. The troops spring to their feet; they descry the long black serpent coiling up the tortuous brown road. Through the green copses a glint of sunshine flashes, banishes the sombreness, and dances on the glittering bayonets.

Such a gust of Russian cheers whirled and eddied among the mountain-tops, that the Turkish war-cries were drowned in the welcome which the Russian soldiers sent to their comrades hurrying to help them. As the head of the column came nearer, it was discerned that it consisted of mounted men. Had Radetsky then, men asked one another, sent cavalry to cope with infantry among the precipices of the Balkans? The column halted, and from its bosom a mountain battery came into action against the Turkish position on one of the ridges. The riders dismounted, formed up, and then marched swiftly until within easy range of the Turks, when they broke and scattered, and straightway from behind every stone and bush spurted white jets of powder-smoke.

The column was a battalion of a crack rifle brigade, and the brigade was not three kilometres behind. Radetsky, down in the valley, had dismounted a Cossack regiment and taken over its ponies for behoof of the leading rifle battalion, at whose head he himself had pushed on. He marched up the pass with his staff behind him, ran the triple gauntlet of the Turkish rifle fire, and joined his two subordinate commanders on the peak. Fighting on the following morning began before dawn, and endured during the whole day. About nine a.m. General Dragomiroff came up with the Podolsk and Jitomer regiments comprising one of his divisions. With the latter he marched up towards the peak along a road every step of which was swept by bullet-fire. He had reached the central position, and was deploying the Jitomers for attack, when a bullet, passing through his right knee, brought him to the ground. The gallant old man clung to his spectacles; and when we had borne him into comparative safety, he himself ripped open his trouser-leg and bound a handkerchief round the wounded knee. Surgeons gathered around him, but, like the true soldier he was, he insisted on waiting for his turn.

It was a very bloody day; and on that exposed backbone of bare rock, commanded on either side by the Turkish fire, no man's life was worth five minutes' purchase. I was burning to get to the telegraph wire—the more eager because it seemed to me that during the day the Russians had so prospered that, although the struggle was sure to last for some time, they would be able at least to hold their own. I asked the general what was his estimate of the situation. Radetsky was oracular. "The Turks," said he, "will no doubt renew their attacks to-morrow with fresh troops, and will probably do so for a good many morrows. But," he added grimly, "I am a tough man, and, with God's help, come Turk, come devil, I shall hold on here till I am killed or ordered away." That pronouncement was good enough for me. It was already full dark when, having bidden farewell to the friendly general and to my comrade Villiers, who had determined to remain on the Schipka, I started off on the journey to Bucharest, where the nearest telegraph office was, a distance of about a hundred and seventy miles.

All night long I rode hard, having posted relays of horses;

and on the morning of the 25th, having neither eaten, drunk, nor rested since the morning of the previous day, I rode into the Imperial headquarters in Gorni Studen. The first man I met was General Ignatieff, who called out—

" Where from, now ? "

" From the Schipka," was my reply. " I left there late last night."

" The devil you did !" exclaimed Ignatieff. " You've beaten all our messengers by hours. Yours must be the last news ; and you must see the emperor and tell it him."

Now I had not been exactly brought up among emperors, but I have at least some sense of propriety, and I knew that a man ought to wait on an emperor in his Sunday clothes. I hadn't seen any Sunday clothes, or Sundays either, for three months ; and I was conscious that my aspect was eminently disreputable. I had been wearing clothes originally white for over a fortnight, night and day. The black of my saddle had come off on to them with great liberality ; and they were spotted with the blood of poor General Dragomiroff, whom, when wounded, I had helped to carry into a place of comparative safety. I had not washed for three days, and I altogether felt a humiliatingly dilapidated representative of that great empire on which the sun never sets. But Ignatieff insisted that in the circumstances the Emperor would by no means stand on ceremony. He went inside and awakened his Imperial Majesty, who had been asleep ; and he presently ushered me through the Cossack guard into the dingy alcove which formed the hall of audience. The Imperial quarters were a dismantled Turkish house, the balcony of which, where the Emperor stood, was enclosed with common canvas curtains. There was not even a carpet on the rugged boards. A glimpse into the bedroom whence his Majesty had emerged showed a tiny cabin with mud walls, and a camp bed standing on a mud floor. The Emperor received me with great kindness, shaking hands, and paying a compliment to my hard riding. He was gaunt, worn, and haggard, his voice broken by nervousness and by the asthma that afflicted him. Some months later I saw his Majesty in St. Petersburg—a

D

very monarch, upright of figure, proud of gait, attired in a brilliant uniform, and covered with decorations. A glittering court and suite thronged around the stately man with enthusiastically respectful homage. The dazzling splendour of the Winter Palace formed the setting of the sumptuous picture. And as I gazed on the magnificent scene, I could hardly realise that the central figure of it, in the pomp of his Imperial state, was of a verity the selfsame man in whose presence I had stood in the squalid Bulgarian hovel—the same worn, anxious, shabby, wistful man who, with spasmodic utterance, and the expression in his eyes as of a hunted deer, had asked me breathless questions as to the episodes and issue of the fighting.

I ventured to suggest that I could make him understand these much better if I had a sheet of paper on which to draw a plan. The Emperor said at once—

"Ignatieff, go and fetch paper and pencil."

Ignatieff went; and his Majesty and myself were alone together, standing opposite each other, with a little green baize table dividing us. Presently Ignatieff returned with a sheet of foolscap on which I rapidly sketched the positions, explaining the details as I proceeded. The emperor caught up the salient points with the quickness of a trained military intelligence.

"Mr. Forbes," said he—he spoke in English—"you have been a soldier?"

"Yes, your Majesty," was my reply.

"In the Artillery or Engineers, doubtless?"

"No, sir," said I, "in the cavalry of the Line."

The Emperor remarked—

"I was not aware that your cavalry officers were conversant with military draftsmanship."

I replied that I had served as a private trooper, not as an officer; thereby, I fear, conveying to his Majesty the impression that the honest British dragoon is habitually skilled in plan-making. When I had finished telling what I knew, the Emperor said with great graciousness—

"Mr. Forbes, I have had reported to me your conduct

on the disastrous days before Plevna, in succouring wounded
Russian soldiers under heavy fire. As the head of the State,
I desire to testify how Russia honours your conduct by
bestowing on you the order of St. Stanislaus with the
crossed swords, a decoration never conferred save for personal bravery ! "

During all the days of unsuccessful fighting before Plevna,
in the great September struggle, the Emperor was almost
continually on the field. So sure had the Russians been of
winning, and so complete had been their arrangements,
that a little observatory had been erected on a commanding
elevation, with a luncheon-table constantly spread, in a
marquee behind, which was very much frequented by the
Emperor's military *entourage.* As for the Emperor, he
neither ate nor drank. I watched him on the balcony of
his observatory on the afternoon of the fifth day of the
fighting—his own *fête* day, save the mark !—gazing out with
haggard eager eyes at the efforts to storm the great
Grivitza redoubt. As the Turkish rifle fire sheared down
his Russians while they strove to struggle up the slope
slippery already with Roumanian blood, the pale face
quivered, and the tall majestic figure visibly winced and
cowered. He stood alone and self-centred, obviously impressed with the lurid horror of the scene.

When Plevna had fallen, I accompanied the Russian
Emperor on his return to St. Petersburg, and was an eye-
witness of the fervid cordiality of his reception. From the
railway station, he drove straight to the Kazan Cathedral
in accordance with the custom which prescribes to Russian
emperors that in setting out for or returning from any
important enterprise, they shall kiss the glittering image of
the Holy Virgin of Kazan, which the cathedral enshrines.
Its interior was a marvellous spectacle. People had spent
the night sleeping on the marble floor that they might be
sure of a place on the morrow. There had been no respect
of persons in the admissions. The mujik in his sheep-
skins stood next the soldier-noble whose bosom glittered

with decorations. The peasant woman and the princess knelt together at the same shrine. In stately procession the Emperor reached the altar, bent his head, and his lips touched the sacred image. When he turned to leave the building, the wildest confusion of enthusiasm laid hold of the throng. His people closed in about the Tzar till he had no power to move. The great struggle was but to touch him, and the chaos of policemen, officers, shrieking women, and enthusiastic peasants swayed and heaved to and fro; the Emperor in the midst, pale, his lips trembling with emotion —just as I had seen him when his troops were cheering him in the battle-field—struggling for the bare ability to move, for he was lifted clean off his feet and whirled about helplessly. At length, extricated by a wedge of officers, he reached his carriage, only to experience as wonderful a reception when he reached the raised portico of the Winter Palace. As for his daughter-in-law, the Tzarevna of the period, now the Empress Dowager, her experiences were unique. As her carriage approached the terrace, the populace utilised it as a convenience whence to see and cheer the Emperor. Men scrambled on to the horses, the box, the roof, the wheels; progress became utterly impracticable. A bevy of cadets and students who lined the foot of the terrace, were equal to the occasion. They opened her carriage-door by dint of great exertion, they lifted out the bright little lady who clearly was enjoying the fun greatly, and they passed her from hand to hand above their heads till the Emperor caught her, lifted her over the balustrades, and set her down by his side on the terrace. I saw the metal heels of her remarkably neat boots sparkling in the winter sunshine over the heads of the throng.

In many respects the monarch whom the Nihilists slew was a grand man. He was absolutely free from that corruption which is the blackest curse of Russia, and which still taints the nearest relatives of the Great White Tzar. Alexander had the purest aspirations to do his duty towards the vast empire over which he ruled, and never did he spare himself in toilsome work. He took few pleasures; the melancholy of his position made sombre his features and darkened for him much of the brightness of life. For he had the bitterest consciousness of the abuses that were gradually alienating the subjects who had been wont from their hearts to couple the names of " God and the Tzar." He knew how the nation writhed and groaned; and he, absolute despot though he was, writhed and groaned no less, in the realisation of his impotency to ameliorate the evils. For, although honest and sincerely well-intentioned, Alexander had a taint of weakness in his character. True, he began his reign with a show of self-assertion, but then unworthy favourites gained his ear, his family compassed him about; the whole huge stubborn *vis inertiæ* of immemorial rottenness and tenacious officialism lay doggedly athwart the hard path of reform. Alexander's aspirations were powerless to pierce the dense solid obstacle; and his powerlessness to do this, with the disquieting self-consciousness that it behoved him to do it, embittered his whole later life. In the end, the man who was once a reformer, died a tyrant.

One of poor MacGahan's most sanguine beliefs was that a time would come, if the Millennium did not intervene, when the war correspondent should overhang the battle-field in a captive balloon, gazing down on the scene through a big telescope, and telegraphing a narrative of the combat as it progressed, through a wire with one end in the balloon and the other in the nearest telegraph office. I don't profess to be very sanguine myself that this elaboration of system will ever be carried into effect; and I think, on the whole, I should prefer, were it attempted, that some one else should conduct the aërial service. But I remember once beating time, or at least apparent time, in a curiously remarkable fashion, in the transmission across the world of war news by means of the telegraph wire. In the early morning of November 22nd, 1878, a column of British troops gained possession of the fortress of Ali Musjid, up in the throat of the Khyber Pass. I rode

back ten miles to the nearest field telegraph office at
Jumrood, and sent the tidings to England, in a short
message bearing date 10 a.m.   There is five hours' difference of time between India and England, in favour of the
latter; and newspapers containing this telegram, dated
10 a.m., were selling in London at 8 a.m.—two hours of
apparent time before it was despatched.   Nor was this all.
Owing to the five hours' difference of time between London
and New York, it was in time for the regular editions of
the New York papers of the same morning.   The message
was immediately wired across the American continent; and
owing to the difference in time between the Atlantic coast
and the Pacific slope, the early-rising citizen of San Francisco purchasing his morning paper at 6 a.m., was able to
read the announcement of an event actually occurring two
hours later in apparent time 15,000 miles away on the
other side of the globe from the fair city inside the
Golden Gate.   Puck professed his ability to put a girdle
round the earth in forty minutes: but this telegram sped
some two-thirds round the earth in two hours less than no
time at all.

During a lull in the fighting in Afghanistan in the
winter of 1878–79, I made a hurried run across the Bay
of Bengal to Burma, and ascended the river Irrawady to
Mandlay, the capital of native Burma, for the purpose of
learning something of the now dethroned King Theebau,
who had then recently succeeded to the titles of Lord of
the White Elephants, Monarch of the Golden Umbrella, and
all the rest of it.   Theebau, when I worshipped the Golden
Feet, had not yet begun to massacre his sisters and his
cousins and his aunts, who were all kept in durance waiting
for their doom in a building within the palace enclosure.
He courteously postponed that atrocity until I had
quitted his tawdry capital, but perpetrated it before I had
reached Calcutta on my return to India.   It was said, I
question if truthfully, that he had subsequently taken to
drink and became bloated, under the provocation of what

may be called a double-barrelled mother-in-law, for the unfortunate Theebau was married to both the lady's daughters; but when I had the honour of making his acquaintance, he looked a manly, frank-faced young fellow, with a good forehead, clear steady eyes, and a firm but pleasant mouth. He received me, not in state, but quite informally in a kiosk in the garden of his palace, dressed in a white silk jacket, and a petticoat robe of rich yellow and green satin. A herald, lying prone on his stomach, introduced me in the following portentous apostrophe—

"Archibald Forbes, a great newspaper teacher of the *Daily News* of London, tenders to his Most Glorious Excellent Majesty, Lord of the Ishaddan, King of Elephants, Master of many White Elephants, Lord of the Mines of Gold and Silver, Rubies, Amber, and the noble Serpentine, Sovereign of the Empires of Thunaparanta and Tampadipa, and other great Empires and Countries, and of all the umbrella-wearing chiefs, the Supporter of Religion, the Sun-Descended Monarch, Arbiter of Life, and great righteous King, King of Kings and Possessor of boundless dominion and supreme wisdom—the following presents."

My presents were not of much account, but at leas' they were genuine, which was more than could be said for the Burmese monarch's return gifts. Among these was a ring of great size and seeming splendour. I looked upon myself as provided for for life: but my suspicious servant took the precaution of submitting it to a jeweller and having it priced. He returned with melancholy and disgust stamped on his swarthy but expressive countenance. The ring was worth but thirty shillings. In fact it was a "duffer." I set down the Lord of the Great White Elephant as a fraud. Indeed, the Great White Elephant was a fraud himself. I went to see the royal brute in the gilded pagoda which was his palace. I saw a lean, mangy, dun-coloured animal, with evil little red eyes, and dingy white patches on his head and trunk. And now the Great White Elephant, sold once to Barnum, is dead of white paint on the skin; Theebau is dethroned and a state prisoner; and his territory, to the great advantage of the people who were once his subjects, is incorporated into our ever-growing Indian Empire.

I have already told how the war correspondent learns to be a cook after a fashion, and, in truth, he finds it convenient to be a sort of jack-of-all-trades. Among other acquisitions, he has ample opportunity for picking up an elementary knowledge of rough surgery. Occasions in battles are frequent when no surgeon is near, and when the correspondent, having no fighting to do, is free to concern himself with aiding the wounded, and may have the happy chance to save human life. In the absence of professional appliances he may have to resort to curious impromptu expedients. During one of the expeditions in the winter Afghan campaign we were marching down the bed of a mountain-torrent, on each side of which rose precipitous crags. Suddenly the head of the column emerged from the gorge into a little open space. There came a ragged volley down upon us from a handful of Afghans perched high up among the rocks above. A private soldier marching by my side, fell across my path, shot through the thigh. Assisted by a young soldier I cut the cloth from the fallen man's leg, and found that he was bleeding very fast. No tourniquet was accessible, nor was any surgeon in the vicinity; so, closing with my thumbs both orifices of the wound, I directed my assistant to find two round stones and get out the surgical bandage which every soldier carries in the field. Just as I raised a thumb for him to introduce a stone, there came a second volley from the Afghans above. The young soldier hastily ran to cover, and I had no alternative, if I were not to allow the wounded man to bleed to death, but to remain pressing my thumbs on the orifices, kneeling out in the open under a dropping fire from the native gentlemen on the rocks above. After some minutes, a detachment, climbing the crags, gradually drove the enemy away; whereupon I was able to complete my rough operation and to get my patient comfortably on a stretcher. I was naturally proud that when the surgeons came to see to him an hour later, they found that my device had effectually arrested the bleeding, and that they did not think it necessary to interfere with my bandaging; nor, surely, was I less proud when the general in command did me the honour to mention me in his despatch, on account of the little service which I had the good fortune to render.

I had not reached South Africa when there occurred that ghastly misfortune, the massacre of Isandlwana. But I accompanied the first party that visited that Aceldama, and the spectacle which it presented I can never forget. A thousand corpses had been lying there in rain and sun for four long months. The dead lay as they had fallen, for, strange to relate, the vultures of Zululand, that will reduce a dead ox to a skeleton in a few hours, had apparently never touched the corpses of our ill-fated countrymen. In the precipitous ravine at the base of the slope stretching down from the crest on which stood the abandoned waggons, dead men lay thick—mere bones, with toughened discoloured skin like leather covering them and clinging tight to them, the flesh all wasted away. I forbear to describe the faces, with their blackened features, and beards blanched by rain and sun. The clothes, had lasted better than the poor bodies they covered, and helped to keep the skeletons together. All the way up the slope I traced, by the ghastly token of dead men, the fitful line of flight. It was like a long string with knots in it, the string formed of single corpses, the knots of clusters of dead, where, as it seemed, little groups must have gathered to make a hopeless, gallant stand, and so die.

Still following the trail of dead bodies through long rank grass and among stones, I approached the crest. Here the slaughtered dead lay very thick, so that the string became a broad belt. On the bare ground, on the crest itself, among the waggons, the dead were less thick; but on the slope beyond, on which from the crest we looked down, the scene

was the saddest, and more full of weird desolation than anything I had ever gazed upon. There was none of the stark,
blood-curdling horror of a recent battle-field ; no pools of yet
wet blood; no torn flesh still quivering. Nothing of all that
makes the scene of a yesterday's battle so repulsive shocked
the senses. A strange dead calm reigned in this solitude of
nature. Grain had grown luxuriantly round and under the
waggons, sprouting from the seed that had dropped from
the loads, fallen on soil fertilised by the life-blood of gallant
men. So long in places had grown the grass that it mercifully shrouded the dead, who for four long months had been
scandalously left unburied.

As one strayed aimlessly about, one stumbled in the
grass over skeletons that rattled to the touch. Here lay
a corpse with a bayonet jammed into the mouth up to the
socket, transfixing the head and mouth a foot into the ground.
There lay a form that seemed cosily curled in calm sleep,
turned almost on its face ; but seven assegai stabs had pierced
the back. It was the miserablest work wandering about the
desolate camp, amid the sour odour of stale death, and
gathering sad relics, letters from home, photographs, and
blood-stained books.

After many delays the day at length came when, as our
little army camped on the White Umvaloosi, there lay on
the bosom of the wide plain over against us the great circular
kraal of Ulundi, King Cetewayo's capital. After two days'
futile delay, on the third morning the force crossed the river
and moved across the plain, preserving in its march the
formation of a great square, until a suitable spot was reached
whereon to halt and accept the assault of the Zulu hordes
which were showing in dense black masses all around. This
point attained, the whole force then halted. Already there had
been ringing out around the moving square the rattle of
the musketry fire of Redvers Buller's horsemen, as they
faced and stung the ingathering impis that had suddenly
darkened the green face of the plain. A few yards beyond
the front stood the ruins of a mission station. The mouldering walls were ordered to be levelled, lest they should obstruct

the fire; and the sappers went to work with a will. But there lay within those walls a ghastly something that was not to be buried by the clay crumbling under the pick-axe —the horribly mutilated form of one of Buller's men, who had fallen in the reconnaissance of the day before. The mangled corpse was lifted out; half a dozen men with spades dug a shallow grave. The chaplain, who had donned his surplice, stood by the head of the grave and read the burial service, to which the shell fire of the artillery gave the stern responses, while the bullets whistled about the mourners.

The time had come. Buller's men, having done their work, galloped back into the shelter of the square till their time should come again. And lo! as they cleared the front, a living concentric wave of Zulus was disclosed. On the slope towards Ulundi the shells were crashing into the black masses that were rushing forward to the encounter. Into the hordes in front the Gatlings, with their measured volleys, were raining pitiless showers of death. Le Grice and Harness were firing steadily into the thickets of black forms showing on the left and rear. But those Zulus could die—ay, they could dare and die with a valour and devotion unsurpassed by the soldiery of any age or of any nationality. They went down in numbers; but numbers stood up and pressed swiftly and steadily on. The sharper din of our musketry fire filled the intervals between the hoarse roar of the cannon and the scream of the speeding shells. Still the Zulus would not stay the whirlwind of their converging attack. They fired and rushed on, halting to fire again, and then rushing on time after time. There were those who had feared lest the sudden confront with the fierce Zulu rush should try the nerves of our beardless lads; but the British soldier was true to his manly traditions when he found himself in the open and saw his enemy face to face in the daylight. For half an hour the square stood grim and purposeful, steadfastly pouring the sleet of death from every face. There was scarce any sound of human speech, save the quiet injunctions of the officers—"Fire low, men; get your aim, no wildness!" On the little rise in the centre the surgeons were plying their duties, regardless of the bullets that whistled about them. The Zulus could not get to close quarters simply because of the sheer weight of our fire. The canister tore through them like a harrow through weeds; the rockets ravaged their zigzag path through the masses. One rush came within a few yards, but it was the last effort of the heroic Zulus. Their noble ardour could not endure in the face of the appliances of civilised warfare. They began to waver. The time for the cavalry had at last come. Lord Chelmsford caught the moment. Drury Lowe was sitting on his charger, watching with ears and eyes intent for the word. It came at last tersely—"Off with you!" The infantrymen made a gap for the Lancers, and gave them, too, a cheer as they galloped out into the open—knees well into saddles, right hands with a firm grip of the lances down at the "engage." Drury Lowe collected his chestnut into a canter, and glancing over his shoulder gave the commands: "At a gallop; Front form troops!" and then "Front form line!" You may swear there was no dallying over these evolutions; just one pull to steady the cohesion, and then, with an eager quiver in the voice, "Now for it, my lads, charge!" The Zulus strove to gain the rough ground, but the Lancers were upon them and among them before they could clear the long grass of the plain. It did one good to see the glorious old "white arm" reassert once again its pristine prestige.

Lord Chelmsford, on the evening of the battle, announced that he did not intend to despatch a courier until the following morning with the intelligence of the victory, which was conclusive and virtually terminated the war. So I hardened my heart, and determined to go myself, and that at once. The distance to Landmanns Drift, where was the nearest telegraph office, was about one hundred miles; and the route lay through a hostile region, with no road save that made on the grass by our waggon wheels as the column had marched up. It was necessary to skirt the sites of recently burned Zulu kraals, the dwellers in which were likely to have resumed occupation. The dispersal of the Zulu army by the defeat of the morning made it all but certain that stragglers would be prowling in the bush through which lay the first part of my ride. Young Lysons offered to bet me even that I would not get through, and when I accepted, genially insisted that I should stake the money, since he did not expect to see me any more. It was somewhat gruesome work, that first stretch through the sullen gloom of the early night, as I groped my way through the rugged bush trying to keep the trail of the waggon wheels. I could see the dark figures of Zulus up against the blaze of the fires in the destroyed kraals to right and to left of my track, and their shouts came to me on the still night air. At length I altogether lost my way, and there was no resource but to halt until the moon should rise and show me my whereabouts. The longest twenty minutes I ever spent in my life was while sitting on my trembling horse in a little open glade of the bush, my hand on the butt of my revolver, waiting for the moon's rays to flash down into the hollow. At length they came; I discerned the right direction, and in half an hour more I was inside the reserve camp of Etonganeni imparting the tidings to a circle of eager listeners. The great danger was then past; it was a comparatively remote chance that I should meet with molestation during the rest of the journey, although Lieutenant Scott-Elliott and Corporal Cotter were cut up on the same track the same night. The exertion was prolonged and arduous, but the recompense was adequate. I had the good fortune to be thanked for the tidings I had brought by the General Commanding-in-Chief and by her Majesty's High Commissioner for British South Africa; and it was something for a correspondent to be proud of that it was his narrative of the combat and of the victory which Her Majesty's Ministers read to both Houses of Parliament, as the only intelligence which had been received up to date.

It may perhaps have occurred to some among those who may have done me the honour to read this chapter that the profession of war correspondent is a somewhat wearing one, calculated to make a man old before his time, and not to be pursued with any satisfaction or credit by any one who is not in the full heyday of physical and mental vigour. My personal experience is that ten years of toil, exposure, hardship, anxiety and brain-strain, such as the electric fashion of modern war correspondence exacts, suffice to impair the hardiest organisation. But given health and strength, it used to be an avocation of singular fascination. I do not know whether this attribute in its fulness remains with it under the limitations of freedom of action which are now in force.

II.

MOLTKE BEFORE METZ.

LORD WOLSELEY has characterised the German "Staff History of the Franco-German War" as a "weariness of the flesh." This is a hard saying, and, I respectfully submit, scarcely a just one. Necessarily minute in detail, the narrative of the "History" is always lucid, and there are few pages which are not illuminated by brilliant flashes of picturesque description that stir the blood like the sound of a trumpet. Apart from those "purple patches," in reading which one feels to hear the turmoil of the battle, the shouts of the combatants, the groans of the wounded, the scream of the shells, and the venomous whistle and sullen thud of the bullets, there are frequent stretches of disquisitional and elucidatory matter which are pregnant with sustained and almost majestic power and vigour, instinct with masterly thought and close reasoning, clothed in a style of singular simplicity, directness, and virile eloquence. Even if it were not an open secret that those passages— halting-grounds of instruction and reflection, studding the swinging march of minutely detailed action — came from the pen of the man who wielded the direction of the war, their intrinsic stamp of high, calm authority, disclosing in the writer the conceiver and the orderer, not less than the identity of the style with that of Moltke's "Russo-Turkish Campaign of 1828-29," would betray their authorship.

But if one may deprecate the strength of Lord Wolseley's

expression, Moltke himself is found to a considerable extent in accord with the English soldier-author. Proud as he was of the full adequateness of the "Staff History," he owned that "it is for the greater number of readers too detailed, and written too technically," and he recognised that "an abstract of it must be made some day." Of all men Moltke himself was plainly the man, not indeed to confine himself to an "abstract," but to write a concise history of the war, based chiefly on the authentic "Staff History" record, but infused also with his own unique knowledge of men and things, of springs of action and motives; revealing certain phases, in a word, of the inner history of the momentous period in which he was something more than merely one of the chief actors. His modesty, his dislike to personality even when not of an offensive kind, his detestation of gossip, were recognised characteristics; but he quite justly did not regard them as hindering him from writing the bright and amusing sketch of his personal experiences in the battle of Königgrätz, and the personally vindicatory denials of councils-of-war in 1866 and 1870–71 printed as appendices to his "Franco-German War" volume. Amidst the wealth of curious inner history of which this quiet, reticent old man was the repository, and which only now is gradually becoming divulged, there was, of course, much that could not then, or, indeed, ever be revealed; but beyond question there was much which, so far as principle and even policy were concerned, he needed not to reserve. And a book on the Great War, written not only for soldiers but for the nations, illuminated by the perspicuity and graceful strength of style that marked Moltke's previous works, enriched with such personal estimates of men and with such revelations of inner history as he could legitimately have made — would not that book have shared immortality with Xenophon's "Anabasis," with Cæsar's "Commentaries" on an earlier Gallic War, with Napier's "History of Wellington's Peninsular Campaigns"?

Such a book Moltke might have written, and could have written had he chosen. Whether he could have done so when, at the age of eighty-seven, he yielded to his nephew's entreaties, and began the work which was given to the world after the ending of a life so full of years and honours, is a question that cannot be conclusively answered. It is sufficient to say that he did not do this, nor attempt to do it. In the main, in the book he did write, he clung to his conception of an "abstract" of the "Staff History." While he followed that guide—virtually following himself as he was when his years had been fewer—he was on sure ground; and he followed it so closely that in three out of four of his pages there is the distinct echo of the "Staff History," the actual words of which, indeed, are adopted with great frequency. When he turned away from that lamp to his path, he did not uniformly maintain entire accuracy of statement. His style, though mostly retaining its directness and simplicity, is sometimes obscure; and its dryness and absence of relief betray a certain tiredness. His nephew holds that the work, "which," he says, "was undertaken in all simplicity of purpose as a popular history," is practically the expression of Moltke's personal opinions from his own standpoint as chief of the general staff. On this it may be remarked that the book he wrote in his extreme old age, entitled "History of the Franco-German War of 1870–71," exhibits no single element of a "popular history"; and that Moltke's statements are most open to question in the few passages in which he is transparently writing as the chief of staff.

How powerful is the glamour of Moltke's name was evinced in the all but unanimous gush of indiscriminate and uncritical eulogy with which this posthumous book was received. His prestige is so high that it is probable the work might be accepted both by writers and by students of war as absolutely accurate. It may not be considered as quite sacrilegious if one who was an eye-witness of the Franco-German War, who had the honour of some personal intercourse with Count Moltke in the course of that war, and who has studied that great personage in his various characters as organiser, strategist, writer, and man, should

E

venture to point out some errors in his "Franco-German War." It is not proposed to follow him beyond the first period of the campaign, which closed with the elimination of the French regular army from the theatre of actual war by the capitulation of Sedan.

Moltke states that on the 2nd of August, 1870, the German garrison evacuated Saarbrücken, "after a gallant defence and repeated counter-strokes." Gallant front, quaint, cheery, dashing Von Pestel did maintain, facing for fourteen days with his battalion of infantry and three squadrons of uhlans, the French masses gathered on the Spicherenberg over against the little open town at scarcely more than chassepôt-fire distance, and craftily displaying his handful so that companies seemed battalions and his battalion a brigade at the least. Gallant and prolonged defence Gneisenau and he did make when at length, under the eyes of their Emperor and his son, Frossard's three French divisions streamed down from their upland and swept across the valley on the 1,500 Rhinelanders calmly holding the little town. But there were no "counter-strokes" on the part of the German defenders, which would have been, indeed, as futile as foolish. For several hours two battalions of Prussians fended off three divisions of Frenchmen who vacillated in their enterprise, and then they withdrew leisurely and in order. The only semblance of a "counter-stroke" was made by one man, and that man a British officer—Wigram Battye of the "Guides," who died fighting in Afghanistan in the early campaign of 1879. Battye was with a Prussian company which was just withdrawing from an advanced position. A soldier was shot down by his side, whereupon Battye, rebelling vehemently against the retirement, snatched the dead man's needle-gun and pouch-belt, ran out into the open, dropped on one knee, and opened fire on Pouget's brigade. Pouget's brigade responded with alacrity, and presently Battye was bowled over by a chassepôt bullet in the ribs. A German professor and a brother-Briton ran out and brought him in, conveyed him to a village in the rear, plastered layer upon layer of stiff brown paper over the damaged ribs, and started him in a waggon to the Kreuznach hospital.

The battle of Spicheren was an unpremeditated fight, and like most contests of that character, was extremely confused, a real "soldiers' battle," in which generalship played but a subsidiary part. From the first, writes Moltke, an intermixture of battalions and companies set in, which increased with every repulse; and the confusion, he adds, was increased by the circumstance that three generals in succession nominally swayed the command. He might have said with truth that not three but five generals were successively in command on this afternoon of desperate strife. Kameke began the battle; Stülpnagel arrived and superseded him in virtue of seniority; later came Zastrow, who, as full general and corps-commander, superseded Stülpnagel in virtue of superior rank. Presently came Goeben and took command as being a senior general to Zastrow; and as the fighting was dying down, Steinmetz, who was an army commander and senior general, relieved Goeben and took over the command. Moltke, writing of the French possibilities on the day of Spicheren (August 6th), makes the statement that, since four French corps, the 3rd, 4th, 5th, and guard, were lying within a short day's march of Frossard's corps (the 2nd) on the Spicheren heights, the French Emperor, had he chosen, would have been fully able to collect five corps for a battle in the Cocheren region, five miles in Frossard's rear. But when he wrote this, he must have forgotten that in a previous page he had stated that the 5th corps (De Failly) had been assigned to the separate army which Marshal MacMahon commanded in Alsace; and it must have escaped his memory also, that on this very August 6th Lespart's Division of that corps was hurrying from Bitche towards Wörth, eager to participate in the battle raging there.

In his sketch of the battle of Vionville-Mars-la-Tour (16th August), Moltke states as follows, in regard to the 3rd German Army Corps: "It was not until after three p.m., after

E 2

it had been fighting almost single-handed for seven hours, that effective assistance was approaching." But the 3rd Corps did not come into action until after ten a.m.; and from ten a.m. until three p.m. is only five hours. The 5th and 6th Cavalry Divisions were on the battlefield considerably in advance of the arrival of the 3rd Corps. The horse-guns of the 5th Division were shelling Murat's camp near Vionville so early as half-past eight; and by nine Rauch's troopers of the 6th Division were falling fast under the fire of French infantry on the edge of the wood of Vionville. The two Divisions in conjunction had formed a wide semi-circle round the French flank and front, and, although yielding naturally to the pressure of heavy chassepôt fire, were in a measure "holding" Frossard's prompt infantry when the leading troops of the German 3rd Corps reached the field. Moltke entirely ignores this seasonable early work of the two Cavalry Divisions, which is described with full appreciation in the "Staff History." Throughout the hours specified both of them were continually under fire, and almost continuously in action, now supplying the place of infantry in constituting Alvensleben's second line, now engaged in independent fighting. When the crisis came, while as yet the day was young; when four French Army Corps were threatening to crush Alvensleben's depleted Divisions; when that commander stood committed up to the hilt—"no infantry, not a man in reserve"—all succour yet distant; there remained to him but one expedient which might avert the imminent defeat. That was the resort to a vigorous cavalry attack, "in which the troopers must charge home, and, if necessary, should and must sacrifice themselves." How Bredow's horsemen fulfilled the stern behest, and of what momentous service was their devotion unto death, the Fatherland will never forget. But while the gallant *reiters* of the two cavalry divisions were thus doing and dying, and when it is remembered that an infantry brigade of the 10th Corps had joined Alvensleben before noon, was it either true or just to claim for the 3rd Corps, whose constancy and devotion were superb, that it had been fighting until three o'clock "almost single-handed, and without any effective support?" How perfunctory is Moltke's sketch of this stupendous conflict, of which he was not a witness, may be estimated from the fact that he makes no reference whatsoever to the participation in the battle of portions of the 8th and 9th Corps, whose attitude and action mainly caused Bazaine to withhold troops from his front in order to reinforce his left and protect his communications with Metz, threatened by the troops referred to, which lost 1,200 of their strength.

Moltke makes some very remarkable statements in regard to the respective strengths of the armies which fought in the battle of St. Privat-Gravelotte. The French army which capitulated at Metz in October, he writes, numbered 173,000, "besides 20,000 sick who could not be removed; about 200,000 in all." And he builds on this foundation, which is in itself erroneous, the assertion that "consequently the enemy in the battle of 18th August had at disposal more than 180,000 men." He thus continues: "The exact strength of the eight* German Corps on that day amounted to 178,818. Thus, with the forces on either side of approximately equal strength, the French had been driven from a position of unsurpassed advantage." The terms used here can have but one meaning: that the French army was over 180,000 strong, and the German army exactly 178,818 strong. And that being so, the thousand or two of asserted French superiority counting for nothing, the two adversaries were, in a numerical sense, equally matched.

It was thus claimed, and that with all the prestige of Moltke's name in support, that the German strength in the battle of 18th August was not superior to that of the French. That the claim was untenable can be shown easily and convincingly. That Moltke greatly understated the German strength needs little further evidence than the following brief extract from the official "return, showing number of (German) troops employed in the battle of St. Privat-Gravelotte,"

* Moltke had inadvertently written "seven"; there were eight,—Guards, 2nd, 3rd, 7th, 8th, 9th, 10th, and 12th. The official state gives 178,818 as the collective strength of those eight corps

printed in the appendices to the second volume of the "Staff History."

TOTAL STRENGTH.

	Combatants, exclusive of officers and train.		
	Infantry and Pioneers.	Cavalry.	Horsed Guns.
First army	42,455	5,753	180
Second army	136,363	18,831	546
Total ...	178,818	24,584	726

Moltke, it will be seen, put forward the gross infantry strength of its eight corps, exclusive of officers, as the total strength of the German army on the field of battle. The addition of the cavalry, without reckoning officers, at once swells the total to 203,400. The Germans reckon their artillery by guns, not by gunners. While the latter are still hale and sound they do not show in the returns; but when killed or wounded they figure among the losses, an arrangement which seems anomalous. But as artillery is of no use without artillerymen, the men of that arm must obviously count in the actual strength of an army. In 1870 each German army corps before Metz had an artillery regiment 3,981 strong, so that the artillerymen of the eight corps on the field on the 18th of August would, at full strength, number 31,848. Making a very liberal deduction for previous casualties, there would remain 25,000, swelling the total army strength, exclusive of officers and train, to 228,400. Officers are not included in the figures of the above return; but they were unquestionably in the battle, and come within the count. Apart from artillery officers, who perhaps were included in their regiments, and not reckoning general and staff officers, the fifty-two infantry regiments and the 148 squadrons composing the infantry and cavalry forces of the army had about 4,000 officers on their establishments, of whom 400 may be written off for casualties. Adding, then, 3,600 officers to the previous count of 228,400, the German host "employed" in the battle of St. Privat-Gravelotte numbered, not as Moltke reckoned it for an obvious purpose, at a total of 178,818, but a total of 232,000 men; and, so far from the contending armies being of approximately equal strength, the Germans were stronger by at least 50,000 than were the French, even if Moltke's estimate of the numbers of the latter were correct.

But his estimate of the French strength was not correct—it could not, indeed, in the nature of things, have been correct. Apart from the incidental miscalculation that 173,000 + 20,000 make 200,000, Moltke erred in his statement that the 20,000 sick and wounded French soldiers found in Metz at the capitulation were in excess of the 173,000 officers and men recorded as having surrendered. The sick and wounded were included in the latter total, which comprehended every man, combatant and non-combatant, of the army and garrison of Metz at the date of the capitulation on the 29th of October. Moltke's train of argument that, since there were 173,000 French soldiers in Metz at that date, "consequently" 180,000 French soldiers confronted the German army in the battle of Gravelotte, it is impossible to follow. The number of French soldiers, effective and ineffective, in and about Metz and on the battlefield on the morning of Gravelotte, was, roughly, about 200,000. But deductions to the amount of 58,000 must be made as follows: wounded of previous battles, 20,000; mobiles constituting garrison of fortress and forts, 20,000; Laveaucoupet's regular division stiffening mobile garrisons, 5,000; departments, train, stragglers, etc., certainly over 8,000; sick, 5,000.

Giving effect to those deductions, the conclusion is, that about 142,000 French soldiers were "employed" in the battle, including the reserve consisting of the Imperial Guard which had three of its four brigades engaged. This reckoning accords with great closeness to the statement of the efficient strength of the Army of the Rhine given in to Marshal Bazaine four days after the battle of the 18th. The number of all ranks, according to the statement, was 137,728; adding to which the 7,800 killed and wounded in the battle, the French strength on the morning of the 18th works out at 145,528; the difference between that amount and the strength at the October capitulation consisting of garrison troops and casualties before and after Gravelotte. The statements by the French of their strength at Gravelotte range from 100,000 to 150,000 men effective, which latter estimate, made by a Frenchman whose figures were accepted as quasi-official in the "Staff History," had been the highest until Moltke overtopped it by 30,000. The official German statement is that the French "had an *available* force of from 125,000 to 150,000 men." Moltke did not claim any new information after authorising the statement quoted above; his swollen total was based on the capitulation figures, which were public property the day after the surrender. And a certain inconsistency reveals itself between that swollen total and the result of his statement that there were eight to ten men to every pace of the seven miles along which extended the front of the French position. At ten men to the pace there works out a total of 133,200 men—which contrasts somewhat abruptly with "more than 180,000."

In his preface to his uncle's posthumous book, Major von Moltke quotes an utterance of his great relative as "highly characteristic of Moltke's magnanimity." This is the utterance: "Whatever is published in a military history is always dressed for effect; yet it is a duty of piety and patriotism never to impair the prestige which identifies the glory of our Army with personages of lofty position." The *naïveté* is edifying with which the principle is in effect laid down, that truth must go to the wall in favour of patriotism. The supersession of truth by the other virtue is not precisely a novelty; but to Moltke belonged the frank avowal of the preference as a sacred duty, and to his nephew the characterisation of this avowal as magnanimity. Throughout his book Moltke was true to his principle except as regarded two leading actors in the great drama, of whom he himself was one and Prince Frederic Charles the other. The strange fact is that, as I believe can be clearly shown, the strictures in both instances are unmerited.

It never was any secret in the German Army that Moltke

disliked Prince Frederic Charles. There could be nothing in common between the composed, refined, accomplished and pious Moltke, fastidious, scholarly and reserved as he was; and the bluff, coarse, dictatorial, loose-lived and loose-mouthed Frederic Charles. They met as seldom as possible, and their relations were always confined to the strictest formality. To do the Red Prince justice, he always admired the military genius of Moltke; but Moltke, from his methodical and exacting standard and notwithstanding his cold, unemotional impartiality, had not a high opinion of Prince Frederic Charles as a commander. In reality, as but for a rare prejudice Moltke would have discerned, the two men were the complement of each other. Moltke directed the storm and swayed the whirlwind, although he habitually rode outside of its vortex. The Red Prince was the storm itself—the actual mighty rushing whirlwind—"a disciplined thunderbolt," as I once heard a fanciful trooper of the Zieten Hussars describe him. Perhaps his dislike to and non-appreciation of Frederic Charles was Moltke's weak point; and thence probably it was that he violated in the case of that Royal soldier his principle of upholding the prestige of "high-placed" warriors.

Moltke is nearing the end of his description of the battle of Vionville-Mars-la-Tour. He has just finished a sketch of the great cavalry fight, which he records was at its height at a quarter to seven in the evening. And he continues thus: "*Prince Frederic Charles had hastened to the battle-field. The day was near its ending, darkness was approaching, the battle was won.*" Does not the reader gather from the sentence in italics—the italics are mine—from the mentioned hour preceding that sentence, and from the words that follow it, that Prince Frederic Charles reached the field late—when it was falling dark, and when already the battle had been won? The absence of precision tends to mislead. For the Prince, as a fact, was late in reaching the field. The battle had begun two hours before noon; nearly five hours later Prince Frederic Charles was still in Pont-à-Mousson, quite fifteen miles from the scene of struggle. As is duly recorded in the " Staff History," the Prince reached the battle-field " about four o'clock."

It was barely that hour when he came galloping up the narrow hill-road from Gorze; the powerful bay he rode all foam and sweat, sobbing with the swift exertion up the steep ascent, yet pressed ruthlessly with the spur; staff and escort panting several horse-lengths in rear of the impetuous foremost horseman. On and up he sped, craning forward over the saddle-bow to save his horse, but the attitude seeming to suggest that he burned to project himself faster than the good horse could cover the ground. No wolfskin, but the red tunic of the Zieten Hussars, clad the compact torso, but the straining man's face wore the aspect one associates with that of the berserker. The turgid eyeballs had in them a sullen lurid gleam of blood-thirst. The fierce sun and the long hard gallop had flushed the face a deep red, and the veins of the throat were visibly swollen. Recalling through the years the memory of that visage with the lowering brow, the fierce eyes, and the strong-set jaw, one can understand how to this day the mothers in the Lorraine villages invoke the terror of " *Le Prince Rouge,*" as the Scottish peasants of old used the name of the Black Douglas, to awe their children wherewithal into panic-stricken silence. While as yet his road was through the forest, leaves and twigs cut by bullets showered down upon him. Just as he emerged in the open upland, a shell burst almost among his horse's feet. The iron-nerved man gave heed to neither bullet-fire nor bursting shell; no, nor even to the cheers that rose above the roar of battle from the throats of the Brandenburgers through whose masses he was riding, and whose chief he had been for many years. They expected no recognition, for they understood the nature of the man—knew that after his rough fashion he was the soldier's true friend, and also that he was wont to sway the issues of battle. He spurred onward to Flavigny away yonder in the front line; the bruit of his coming darted along the fagged ranks; and strangely soon came the recognition that a master-soldier had gripped hold of the command as in a vice.

In regard once again to Prince Frederic Charles, Moltke deviates from the principle which he expounded to his nephew, in relation to a critical incident which occurred later in the same evening. The long bloody struggle was in its final throes, and the Germans now stood on the ground held by the French in the morning. In those circumstances, writes Moltke :—

" It was clearly most unadvisable to challenge by renewed attacks an enemy who still greatly outnumbered the German forces; which, since no other reinforcements could be hoped for soon, could not but jeopardise the success so dearly bought. The troops were exhausted, most of their ammunition was spent, the horses had been under the saddle for fifteen hours without food. Some of the batteries could move only at a walk, and the nearest army corps which had crossed the Moselle, the 12th, was distant more than a day's march. Yet, notwithstanding, at about eight o'clock the Headquarter " [" Obercommando," an army euphemism for Prince Frederic Charles, who was no figure-head commander] " issued an order commanding a renewed and general attack upon the enemy's position."

The attack was but partially made owing to the darkness and the exhaustion of the troops, and it failed at most points, not without severe losses.

Than the aspersion conveyed in the quoted sentences, none more grave can well be imagined. The charge, in effect, is simply this, that in a reckless attempt which in the nature of things could not be other than futile, Prince Frederic Charles had wantonly squandered the lives of his devoted soldiers. That chief had much experience of command in the actual battle-field, and he closed his fighting career unvanquished in battle. In the Franco-German War he was in his mature soldierly prime, a veteran of war at the age of forty-two, as yet unimpaired by habits which subsequently deteriorated him. Experience had inured him swiftly yet coolly to penetrate the varying problems of the battle while it raged around him in its maddest chaotic turmoil—a less easy task than meets the retrospective military critic in the calm of his bureau. He had learned the stern lesson that gains can rarely be attained without incurring losses—the old cynical omelette-making, egg-breaking axiom; and this other lesson, too, that there are occasions when a commander must lay his account with severe inevitable losses while the chances of success are very precarious, yet which it behoves him to adventure. It was such an occasion which presented itself to Prince Frederic Charles on the evening of Mars-la-Tour. With a far-spent army of some 60,000 men, he was standing right in the path of a host more than double his own numbers. Of that host it was true that probably more than one-half was not less exhausted than were his own people; but it possessed powerful reserves comparatively fresh and unscathed, the possession of which might well encourage the French leader, with apparently so much at stake, to push a formidable night attack against a numerically inferior and worn-out adversary. Symptoms there already were, which seemed to portend such an effort. Bazaine in person, with fresh troops, was clearing his front towards the south-west, and thrusting the Germans thereabouts back into the woods. Moltke's statement is incorrect that the 12th Corps, twenty miles away, was Prince Frederic Charles' nearest reinforcement. One incentive to the operation which Moltke condemns was the Prince's knowledge that the 9th Corps was so near his right flank as to be able to make itself felt in the intended general movement. And this was actually so in the case of a brigade of that corps' Hessian Division, which came into action so early as half-past seven, and continued fighting until after ten. Part of its other division was indeed already in the field. Any argument of mine in justification of Prince Frederic Charles's motives can have no weight; and I prefer therefore to quote on this point the soldierly language of the "Staff History," compiled, it never must be forgotten, under the superintendence of Moltke himself:—

"As the firing became more vigorous after seven o'clock, and the reports gave reason to expect the arrival of the 9th Corps, Prince Frederic Charles considered the moment suitable for again making an attack in force. . . The staking of the last strength of man and horse, after hours upon hours of sanguinary fighting, was to show that the Prussians had both the ability and the firm will to triumph in the yet undecided struggle. The moral impression of such an advance, enhanced by the consternation to be expected from a sudden attack in the twilight, appeared to guarantee a favourable result."

No word of blame has Moltke for General Manstein, who, by his headstrong and reckless disobedience of orders, and his disregard of information brought him by his own scouts, dislocated the plan of the battle of Gravelotte, and gravely compromised the fortunes of the day ; no breath of reflection on General von Pape, who sacrificed thousands of brave men in a premature and impossible attack on St. Privat—too impatient to wait an hour for the development of the turning movement by the Saxons which would have averted most of the butchery. Both those officers were " personages of high position "—were of that " bestimmte Persönlichkeiten " order, to uphold whose prestige Moltke held it to be a sacred duty. Patriotism questionless shielded them from adverse comment ; yet it did not avail to withhold his censure on Prince Frederic and on himself. It was in respect of the participation of the 2nd Corps in the fighting during the latest phase of the battle of Gravelotte, that he considered himself to have incurred his unfavourable criticism upon himself, which he thus frankly expresses in his posthumous work on the Franco-German War :—

" It would have been more judicious on the part of the Chief of the General Staff, who was personally on the spot at the time, not to have permitted this movement at so late an hour. Such a body of troops, still completely intact, might have proved very precious next day, but on this evening could scarcely be expected to bring about a decisive reversal."

With all respect I make bold to aver that Moltke had no alternative but to permit—nay, to strenuously urge forward that advance of the 2nd Corps his sanction to which he disapproved many years later—if there was to be retrieved a situation which was dangerously compromised, and which imperatively called for a "reversal."

In the Gravelotte region of the vast battle-ground, the German right, consisting of the 7th and 8th Corps commanded by General Steinmetz, had been fighting fiercely and with varied fortune during the afternoon against the French soldiers of Frossard and Le Bœuf. As the day waned the cannonade abated its virulence and the musketry-fire fell almost silent. The French now lay supine in their shelter-trenches along the Point-du-Jour ridge crowning the bare glacis-like plateau which their fire had been sweeping; quiet in the buildings and behind the enclosures of the Moscou farm farther northward. The Rhinelanders and Westphalians huddled among their dead and wounded in the shallow folds of the plateau, in the bush fringing the deep and steep ravine of the Mance streamlet, in and behind the precincts of the battered St. Hubert auberge, and about the edge of the wood below Moscou. The lull lasted for an hour; the Germans believed that the Frenchmen over against them were exhausted, and that the strength of their resistance was broken. Away to the northward where Prince Frederic Charles held sway, the roar of battle was deepening in intensity; and this indication that the army of the Red Prince was entering on the decisive struggle was the signal for the order to the impatient Steinmetz, that he too should fall on and strain his uttermost to "end the business" in his specific sphere of action. In addition to his own two corps, the 2nd was placed at his disposal, to be used if it should be needed. The Pomeranians had travelled far and fast in their soldierly ardour to share in the battle. They panted for the fray, in spite of their fatigue after a long forced march ; but having regard to the seeming enfeeblement of the adversary, it was not expected that their services would be called for.

For once the French had hoodwinked their enemy. They were not exhausted, but were merely saving their ammunition and resting in the comparative safety of their shelter-trenches

and reverse slopes, while they watched for events. They
believed, it seemed, that they had virtually won the battle,
and were in full buoyancy and confidence. As the heads of
Steinmetz's columns came up out of the Mance ravine and
showed themselves on the lower verge of the plateau, the
French flung away the mask. Suddenly from their serried
lines shot furious blasts of chassepôt- and mitrailleuse-fire.
The thunder of their long-silent artillery burst forth in fullest
volume. The supports at all points came springing forward
to join their comrades of the front line. And then the
French infantry, for the moment relieved from the irksome
trammels of the defensive and restored to its congenial *métier*
of the attack, dashed forward with the grand old *élan*, and
swept the Germans backwards down the slope into the
Mance ravine. Under the stroke of that fierce impact, under
the hurricane of missiles that swept upon the troops assailed
by the French infantry, Steinmetz's army reeled to its base.
There was a period when it may be said without exaggeration
that the mass of that army was on the run. The old King
was carried backward in the press surging out from under the
rain of bullets and shells, expostulating with great fervour of
expression in his rearward career, with the component parts
of the all but universal *débâcle*. The Mance ravine was seething full of fugitives, struggling among themselves for cover
from the plunging shells which fell thick among them. The
quarries below Moscou were crowded with demoralised
soldiers. The garrison of St. Hubert remained there—in the
buildings and outlying enclosures it was safer than in the
bullet-swept open; the place was not assailed, and some
staunch troops out in the open clung to its lee. But the road
in front of St. Hubert leading from Point-du-Jour down into
the ravine, was a torrent of rushing, panting, panic-stricken
men. Down this torrent were actually swept some of the
brave Gnügge's field guns; I saw old Brigadier Rex thrown
down and overrun when striving energetically to stay the
rush.

The French infantry having repulsed their adversaries,
retired to their defensive positions, and the Germans began

to steady themselves in a measure. Reserves of the 7th Corps were sent forward, but made very little head; and it is not straining language to say that it was as a last resort that the 2nd Corps, no part of which had hitherto been engaged, was ordered up. The corps crossed the ravine by the great *chaussée* from Gravelotte. How important was regarded a fortunate issue to its exertions was vividly betrayed by the unparalleled anxiety to fire its ardour, and the exceptional solicitude for its most effective guidance. At the head of the corps rode down into the ravine old Steinmetz the army commander, and Franseky the corps commander; and with them rode none other than Moltke himself, accompanied by the staff officers of the royal headquarters. "Under the eyes of those officers of high rank," so it is written in the "Staff History," "the battalions hastened across the valley, drums beating and bugles sounding, previous to throwing themselves into the struggle amid the encouraging cheers of the commanding general." As the Pomeranians deployed on the edge of the plateau, the French fire struck them fair in the face; and they were struck, too, by a broad, rushing stream of fugitives from the front which, in the demure language of the "Staff History," "seemed to point to the advent of a fresh crisis in the engagement."

This last incident alone would appear to justify the utilisation of the 2nd Corps, which, although it made no serious impression on the French position, maintained a footing on the plateau during the night. But, when its employment is pronounced by the high officer who ordered it on that service to have been a surplusage and an error, a comment on this pronouncement may be made in the form of a couple of questions. Was not this the unique instance since Blücher's time of a Prussian army-commander—as Moltke virtually was—personally leading his troops into action? And on what other occasion throughout his career in his great position, did Moltke concern himself personally with the actual direction and encouragement of any specific movement on the battle-field?

The incidents narrated above are, in their broad features, recorded in the "Staff History," and some details which can be fully verified from other sources have been added, in part from personal knowledge as an eye-witness. Moltke's faculty of concentrated writing is strikingly shown in the following quotation, which embraces all he permits himself to say regarding the events adverted to:—

"Later, the still serviceable battalions of the 7th Corps were sent again across the Mance ravine, and were joined by battalions from the Bois de Vaux in the direction of Point-du-Jour and the quarries. Frossard's corps, thus attacked, was reinforced by the Garde Voltigeur Division, and all the French reserves moved up into the first line. The artillery came into action with redoubled activity, and an annihilating rifle-fire was poured on the advancing Germans. Then moved out to the attack the French soldiers in the shape of a powerful mass of tirailleurs, which drove the small leaderless bands of Germans lying on the plateau back to the skirts of the wood. Here, however, the outburst was arrested, and there still remained in the hand a fresh army corps in full strength."

Moltke's estimate of Bazaine as a commander was not high, and he distinctly recognised that he was influenced by political as well as military considerations; he, however, acquits Bazaine of the charge of having betrayed his country. There is in Moltke's last work one very curious and enigmatical sentence in regard to Bazaine. The period is shortly before the battle of Noisseville, 31st August, when Bazaine and his army had been enclosed in and about Metz for several days. This is the sentence—"Meanwhile Marshal Bazaine possibly might have recognised that he had deceived himself in regard to the release of his army by means of negotiation." Is it not the reasonable inference that thus early, much earlier than ever previously had been suspected, Bazaine had attempted to open negotiations with the Germans, and had been repulsed?

As a skilful, untiring, and far-seeing organiser of the

F

means which make for success in war, Moltke has never had an equal, and probably, in those respects, will never have a superior. The extraordinary success of the efforts on his part and that of his coadjutor von Roon, to perfect the national preparedness for war, produced the result that while those two lasted, Germany could find in no other European power an equal antagonist. Still less has any power produced a strategist who has given proof of ranking as Moltke's peer. Thus it is impossible to gauge the full measure of Moltke's potentialities. He may have had reserves of strategical genius which never were needed to be evoked. It is impossible to determine whether in the Franco-German War he put forth his full strength, or only so much of it as was proportionate to the requirements suggested by the known inferiority of the adversary.

One thing is certain, that never was fortune more kind to the director of any great war than she was to Moltke in 1870. In spite of the significant warning of Sadowa, it seemed almost that in its later years the Second Empire, as regarded its military position, had been deliberately "riding for a fall." With the melancholy exposure of its military decadence all the world is familiar. When Marshal Niel enjoined the defensive as the complement of the chassepôt, he throttled the traditional *élan* of the soldiers of France. Her army, deficient in everything save innate courage, lacked most of all competent leadership; and the assumption of the chief command by the Emperor Napoleon made the Germans a present of the issue before a shot was fired. The campaign begun, fortune continued to shower her favours on Moltke. It appeared as if the very stars in their courses fought for him. An essential feature of his plan was to push direct for the enemy's capital. Bazaine unwittingly helped him in this by bottling himself up in Metz, and MacMahon yielded him the fair-way by moving out of his path. Another element of Moltke's scheme was that the French should be driven from the spacious and fertile middle provinces into the barren and cramped precincts of the north. Bazaine did not lend himself directly to the accomplishment of this object of his adversary, but he disposed ·of himself otherwise in a manner equally satisfactory to Moltke. MacMahon obliged by going northward without being driven—at least by the Germans; his coercion was from Paris. Moltke, fully convinced of the paramount importance to the French that the army of Metz should make good its retreat on the Châlons force, concentrated every energy towards the prevention of that union. It happened that, as Moltke genially observes, Bazaine did not share the German chief's conviction, and indeed played into his adversary's hand by his preference for remaining in Metz instead of the prosecution of a retreat towards Châlons. Ready enough to fight—to do him justice—Bazaine was not earnest to march.

But Moltke's plan of campaign was based, beyond all other considerations, on the resolution at once to assail the enemy wherever found, and to keep the German forces so compact that the attack could always be made with the advantage of superior strength. Although the Germans had overwhelmingly superior numbers in the field, this latter aspiration was not uniformly fulfilled. Indeed, there is a certain pride in Moltke's assertion that the Germans fought —and won—four important battles with the numerical odds against them, Spicheren, Courcelles, Vionville-Mars-la-Tour, and Noisseville, not to mention his claim of equal strength on the French side at Gravelotte. The failure always to make good the wise postulate of his plan in regard to concentration, resulted inevitably from the free hand accorded to subordinate commanders to bring on an unexpected battle at their discretion or indiscretion. It is true that because of various more or less fortuitous circumstances, no actual defeat resulted from this licence; but the risks it involved were certainly in two instances disproportionate to the possible attainable advantages. Is it credible that, had not Frossard at Spicheren been trammelled by Imperial restrictions, his three divisions would not have smashed Kameke's two brigades as they clung to his skirts for hours before reinforcements arrived?

F 2

The German "Staff History" owns to the imminence of disaster at Courcelles; and but that the French were there tied to the defence, it is inconceivable that five French divisions should not have defeated five German brigades. What soldier who has realised the practical value of numbers in battle, will deny that had Bazaine with 150,000 regulars at his back, been in dead earnest to force through at Mars-la-Tour, he could have swept Alvensleben's 40,000 Prussians out of his path before support could have reached the latter? Moltke writes of Noisseville, that there 36,000 Prussians repulsed 137,000 Frenchmen. With such odds in their favour as four to one, the Servian militia, fighting in earnest, would crush the best troops in Europe. The French did not break out simply because Bazaine fought merely to save appearances. With superior forces and copious reserves the brusque and butcherly offensive is a tempting game; but its attractions wane when, as with the Germans at Gravelotte, it entails the slaughter of 20,000 men in inflicting on the enemy a loss of 8,000.

It remains that the Germans were the conquerors; and that they conquered in virtue chiefly of Moltke's strategical skill and infusion of energy into all ranks of the German army. It is a true saying that nothing succeeds like success, and its converse is not less true—that nothing fails like failure. But the spectator of the Franco-German War must have been purblind or warped who could dare to aver that the old spirit was dead in the army on which had once shone the sun of Austerlitz—that army which had stormed the Mamelon with a rush. No; the poor mis-commanded, bewildered, harassed, overmatched, out-numbered soldiers in the blue képis and red breeches, fought on with a loyal valour which ever commanded respect and admiration. The sad, noble story of unavailing devotion is to be told of the French regular army from the first battle to the ending at Sedan. With swelling heart and wet eyes I looked down on the final scene of that awful tragedy. The picture rises now before me of that terrible afternoon. The stern ring of German fire, ever encircling with stronger grip that plateau on which were huddled the Frenchmen as in the shambles; the storm of shell fire that tore lanes through the dense masses, bare to its pitiless blasts; the vehement yet impotent protests against the inevitable, in the shape of furious sorties. Now a headlong charge of Margueritte's cuirassiers thundering in glittering steel-clad splendour down the slope of Illy with an impetus that seemed resistless, till the fire of the German infantrymen smote the squadrons fair in the face, and heaped the sward with dead and dying. Now the frantic gallop to their fate of a regiment of light horsemen on their grey Arab stallions, up to the very muzzles of the needle-guns which the German linesmen held with steadiness so unwavering. Now a passionate outburst of red-trousered foot-soldiers, darting against a chance gap in the tightening environment, too surely to be crushed by the ruthless flanking fire. No semblance of order there, no token of leadership; simply a hell in the heart of which writhed an indiscriminate mass of brave men, with no thought in them but of fighting it out to the bitter end! I shudder as I write, at the recollection of the horrors of that ghastly field on the day after the battle. The ground was still slippery with blood, and in the hollows lay little puddles which made one faint. Napoleon's one wise act was his displaying the white flag on the afternoon of Sedan. But, in their passion to keep on fighting, with what fury the soldiers execrated him and his conduct!

III.

THE DARK DAYS OF SEDAN.

ONE day, no doubt, the inevitable historian will undertake
the task of writing a detailed account of the strange
events which occurred about Sedan during the first week of
September, 1870; but if in the endeavour he escapes falling
a victim to softening of the brain, he may be accounted
an exceptionally fortunate man. With certain salient facts,
it is true, no difficulties will present themselves. It is
unquestionable that a great battle was fought on the 1st,
resulting in the defeat and surrender of the French army;
that Marshal MacMahon, the French commander-in-chief,
was struck down wounded in the early morning of that
day; that on the same afternoon the white flag was hoisted
by order of the Emperor Napoleon, who sent out to the
German monarch a letter tendering the surrender of his
sword; that Napoleon on the early morning of the 2nd
came out from Sedan, and met and conferred with Bismarck at the weaver's cottage on the Donchery road; that,
subsequently, the capitulation of the French army having
been consummated, he had an interview with King Wilhelm
in the Château Bellevue; that on the following morning
he started on his journey to Cassel as a prisoner-of-war;
and that the French army of Sedan, more than 100,000
strong, was sent away into captivity in the German fort-
resses. Thus far, the historian's task will be simple enough;

it is the hopeless and bewildering discrepancies in regard
to details which will cause him to tear his hair, and bewail
himself of his folly in choosing the avocation of a writer
of history, instead of that of a frightener of crows.   In
those exciting Sedan days many people seem to have lost
their heads, and more the faculty of memory.   The hours
at which events occurred were either unnoted or so noted
as to be strangely discordant.   Even the customary precision of the German "Staff History" is for once in default;
and if it is vague, the vagueness of French generals and
of irresponsible persons at large may be imagined.

Marshal MacMahon was in the field by five a.m.   When
riding along the high ground above La Moncelle he was
severely wounded in the thigh by the fragment of a shell,
and he then nominated Ducrot as his successor in the
chief command.   It is impossible to fix the precise time at
which the marshal was wounded, or when Ducrot first learnt
of his promotion; but certainly before eight o'clock the
latter was exercising command and ordering a retreat on
Mézières, which, if it had been promptly carried out, might
have temporarily saved at least a portion of the French
army.   But presently Wimpfen produced his commission
from Palikao; and Ducrot, although for the moment indig-
nant at his supersession, was probably not sorry to be
relieved from a situation so complicated.   Wimpfen coun-
termanded the retreat on Mézières in favour of a hopeless
attempt to break out towards the east in the direction of
Carignan; and thenceforth there remained no hope for the
French.   The Emperor when riding out in the direction of
the hardest fighting, had met the wounded marshal being
brought in; one account says in the town, another on the
road beyond the gate.   No reference was thought worth
while to be made to Napoleon as to the command—
whether Ducrot or Wimpfen was to exercise it; the unfortunate Emperor mooned about the field for hours under fire,
but had no influence whatsoever on the conduct of the
battle; and he sent no reply to a letter from Wimpfen
begging his Imperial master "to place himself in the midst

of his troops who could be relied on to force a passage
through the German lines." When the Emperor returned
into Sedan is not to be ascertained; nor, except inferentially,
at what hour he first directed the white flag to be exhibited.
No person has avowed himself the executant of that order,
but the flag did not long fly; it was indignantly cut down
by General Faure, MacMahon's chief-of-staff, who did not
give himself the trouble to communicate with Napoleon
either before or after having taken this considerable liberty.
By one o'clock, the battle in effect was lost and won; what
followed was merely futile fighting and futile slaughter.

How anxious the Emperor continued to be for capitulation; how obstinate was Wimpfen that there should be no
negotiations and no capitulation, is shown, rather confusedly it is true, by the testimony of Lebrun and Ducrot.
"Why does this useless struggle still go on?" Napoleon
demanded of Lebrun, who, a little before three p.m., entered
his apartment in the sous-préfecture—"an hour ago and
more I bade the white flag be displayed in order to sue
for an armistice." Lebrun explained that certain additional
formalities were requisite—a letter must be signed by the
commander-in-chief and sent out by an officer with a
trumpeter and a flag of truce. That document Lebrun
prepared, and having procured officer, trumpeter, and flag of
truce, he went forth to where Wimpfen was gathering troops
for an attack on the Germans in Balan. As Lebrun approached
him, the angry Wimpfen shouted, "No capitulation! Drop
that rag! I mean to fight on!" and forthwith set out towards
Balan, carrying Lebrun along with him into the fight.

Ducrot had been fighting hard to the northward of
Sedan, about Illy and the edge of the Bois de Garenne;
straining every nerve to arrest, or at least to retard the
environing advance of the Germans. Recognising that his
efforts afforded no likelihood of success, he resolved soon
after three o'clock to pass southward through Sedan, and
join in an attempt to cut a way out towards Carignan and
Montmédy. Ducrot had no hope of success in such an
enterprise, but, nevertheless, was prepared to obey the order.

But, as he has written, he was alone ; he had not even a corporal's escort.   He sent word to Wimpfen by that commander's orderly, that he would enter Sedan and attempt to gather some troops in support of Wimpfen's effort. What Ducrot saw inside Sedan may be told nearly in his own words.

The state of the interior of Sedan he has characterised as indescribable. The streets, the open places, the gates, were blocked up by waggons, guns, and the *impedimenta* and *débris* of a routed army. Bands of soldiers without arms, without packs, were rushing about throwing themselves into the churches, or breaking into private houses. Many unfortunate men were trampled under foot. The few soldiers who still preserved a remnant of energy seemed to be expending it in accusations and curses. " We have been betrayed!" they cried—" we have been sold by traitors and cowards ! "   There was really nothing to be done with such men, and Ducrot repaired to the Emperor in the sous-préfecture.

Napoleon no longer preserved that cold and impenetrable countenance familiar to all the world. The absolute silence which reigned in the presence of the sovereign rendered the noise outside more awfully tumultuous. The air was on fire. Shells fell on roofs, and struck masses of masonry which crashed down upon the pavements. " I do not understand," said the bewildered Emperor—" why the enemy continues his fire. I have ordered the white flag to be hoisted. I hope to obtain an interview with the king of Prussia, and may. succeed in obtaining advantageous terms for the army." While the Emperor and Ducrot were conversing, the cannonade increased in violence from minute to minute. Conflagrations burst out. Women, children and wounded were destroyed. The sous-préfecture was struck ; shells exploded every minute in garden and courtyard.

" It is absolutely necessary to stop the firing !" exclaimed the Emperor. " Here, write this !" he commanded General Ducrot :—"' The flag of truce having been displayed, negotiations are about to be opened with the enemy. The firing must cease all along the line.' "   Then said the Emperor " Now sign it !"   " Oh no, sire," replied Ducrot, " I cannot sign: by what right could I sign? General Wimpfen is general-in-chief." "Yes," replied the Emperor, "but I don't know where General Wimpfen is to be found. Some one must sign!" "Let his chief-of-staff sign," suggested Ducrot, "or General Douay." "Yes," replied the Emperor, " let the chief-of-staff sign the order!"

The subsequent history of this order cannot be distinctly traced, nor whether, indeed, it ever got signed at all. It may have been enclosed in the missive from the Emperor which presently reached Wimpfen, and which that recalcitrant chief would not even open. It appeared that Wimpfen's troops had been gradually falling away from him; and he had ridden back to one of the gates of Sedan, on the double errand of procuring reinforcements and of trying to prevail on the Emperor to join him in his forlorn-hope attempt to break out. What then occurred may best be told in Wimpfen's own words:—

"Shortly before four o'clock," he wrote, "I reached the gate of Sedan. There, at last, there came to me M. Pierron of the Imperial Staff, who, instead of announcing the arrival of the sovereign which I was expecting with feverish impatience, handed me a letter from his Majesty, and he also informed me that the white flag was floating from the citadel of Sedan, and that I was charged with the duty of negotiating with the enemy. . . Not recognising the Emperor's right to order the hoisting of the flag, I replied to his messenger:—'I will not take cognisance of this letter: I refuse to negotiate!' In vain did M. Pierron insist. I took his Majesty's letter, and holding it in my hand without opening it I entered the town, calling on the soldiers to follow me into the fight. . . Having gathered about 2,000 men, at the head of this gallant handful I succeeded, about five o'clock, in penetrating as far as the church of Balan; but the reinforcements I hoped for did not arrive, and I then gave the order to retire on Sedan."

Wimpfen on his return to the fortress, forwarded his resignation to the Emperor, who then in vain attempted to persuade first Ducrot and then Douay to assume the command. Wimpfen finally was sent for, and in the presence of the Emperor a violent altercation occurred between him and Ducrot, in the course of which, it was believed, blows were actually exchanged. Ducrot, who was the more excited of the two, withdrew; and in the words of the Emperor, "General Wimpfen was brought to understand that, having commanded during the battle, his duty obliged him not to desert his post in circumstances so critical." Wimpfen would have been quite within his rights in persisting in resigning. The situation had been purely a military one, and he was commander-in-chief; yet the Emperor, who had no military position whatsoever, had overridden Wimpfen's powers while as yet that officer was in supreme command. Wimpfen showed patriotism and moral courage in taking on himself the invidious burden of conducting negotiations resulting from acts to which he had not been a party.

The scene may now be changed to the hill-top south of Frénois, from which the Prussian King and his *entourage* had been watching the course of events ever since the early morning. It would seem that the first white flag which Faure in his anger cut down, had not been noticed in the German army. As the afternoon drew on the French defeat was decisively apparent; yet, although the fierceness of the fighting waned, the now surrounded army remained heroically stubborn in its resistance to inevitable fate; and so its final death-throe had to be artistically quickened up. In the stern words of the German "Official History," "a powerful artillery fire directed against the enemy's last point of refuge appeared the most suitable method of convincing him of the hopelessness of his situation, and of inducing him to surrender. With intent to hasten the capitulation, and thus spare the German army further sacrifices, the King ordered the whole available artillery to concentrate its fire on Sedan." This command, so states the "Staff History," was issued at four p.m., and was promptly acted on. The consequent exacerbation of the cannonade was, no doubt that of which Ducrot tells, whilst he was in conversation with the Emperor in the sous-préfecture. Results of the reinforced and concentrated shell fire were soon manifested. Sedan seemed in flames. · The French return-fire, gallantly maintained for a short time, was by-and-by crushed into silence. The "Staff History" yields no more time-data; to me the hurricane of shell fire seemed to endure for quite half an hour. Under its cover a Bavarian force was preparing to storm the Torcy Gate. At this moment the white flag was definitively displayed on the citadel flagstaff, and the German fire at once ceased. At the solicitation of the French commandant of the suburb of Torcy, the Bavarian leader then refrained from assault and remained in position outside the gate. As the news of impending negotiations spread, hostility ceased everywhere save about Balan, where the contumacious Wimpfen was still battling impotently. Tidings of the situation at Torcy having reached him, and the white flag being visible, the King of Prussia directed Colonel Bronsart von Schellendorf of his staff to ride into Sedan under a flag of truce, and summon the French Commander-in-Chief to surrender his army and the fortress. The Prussian officer penetrated into the city and duly announced the nature of his mission; but to his surprise he was ushered into the presence of the Emperor Napoleon, of whose presence in Sedan the German head-quarters had been ignorant. In reply to Bronsart's application for a French officer of rank to be appointed to negotiate, the Emperor simply informed him that the French army was under the command of General Wimpfen. This answer he desired Bonsart to take back to the king; and to intimate further that he would shortly send out his aide-de-camp, General Count Reillé, with a letter from himself to his Majesty.

Personally I witnessed nothing of what was passing on the summit of the Frénois hill, being with the Prussian skirmishers on the plateau of Floing when the roar of the cannon fell suddenly still. But on the same evening a distinguished officer of the headquarter staff, who had been a witness of everything that occurred on the Frénois summit, dictated to me the following account :—

"Bronsart and his companion Winterfeldt came trotting up the hill, the time being a quarter past six. Bronsart spurred his horse into a gallop as he came near, and, flinging his arm behind him in the direction of Sedan, exclaimed in a loud voice: 'Der Kaiser ist da!' There was a loud outburst of cheering. But as Bronsart dismounted, Moltke, with a very serious face, strode towards him, and said something which gave Bronsart obvious chagrin—a rebuke, as I suppose, for his informality and lack of self-restraint in the immediate presence of the King. It was at a quarter to seven when, with a trooper in advance bearing on his lance the flag of truce and with an escort of Prussian cuirassiers, the French officer came up the hill at a walking pace. He halted and dismounted some horse-lengths short of where the King stood, out to the front of his retinue; then he advanced, doffing his képi as he came, and with a silent reverence handed to his Majesty the Emperor's letter. While the King, Bismarck, and Moltke conversed earnestly apart, the Crown Prince, with that gracious tact which is one of the finest traits of his character, entered into conversation with poor forlorn Reillé, standing out there among the stubbles. Presently Bismarck beckoned up from rearward a gentleman in civilian uniform, Count Hatzfeldt, I believe, of the Foreign Office, who withdrew after a short interview with the Chancellor, after having, I presume, received instructions for drafting the King's answer to the letter of the French Emperor. Presently there was a curious spectacle. The King, sitting on a chair, was using as his writing-desk the seat of another chair, which was being held in position by Major von Alten. The King, as we all knew later, was inditing his reply to Napoleon from Count Hatzfeldt's draft.* After expressing sympathy and intimating

* The following is the Emperor Napoleon's letter :—

"Sire, my Brother,—Not having been able to die in the midst of my troops, there is nothing left me but to render my sword into the hands of Your Majesty.

"I am, Your Majesty's good brother,   "Napoleon."

William's reply runs thus :—

"My Brother,—While regretting the circumstances in which we meet, I accept Your Majesty's sword, and request that you will appoint one of your officers, and furnish him with the necessary powers to treat for the capitulation of the army which has fought so valiantly under your command. I, for my part, have appointed General von Moltke to this duty.

"Your loving brother,   "Wilhelm."

his acceptance of the Emperor's sword, his Majesty desired that Napoleon should appoint an officer to conduct negotiations with General Moltke, whom he himself had delegated. Reillé rode back into Sedan with the King's reply. Soon after seven his Majesty and suite started on the drive back to Vendresse. Bismarck and Moltke rode into Donchery to take part in the conference for settling the terms of capitulation, and the Frénois hill was deserted."

The diary of Dr. Busch, Bismarck's secretary, who was with the headquarter staff, accords in essentials with the foregoing. Dr. Busch relates further that at a quarter past five a Bavarian officer came to the King with information that his general (Maillenger) was in Torcy, that the French desired to capitulate, and were ready to surrender unconditionally; and that this messenger took back orders that all proposals as to negotiations were to be sent direct to the royal headquarters. A little later an officer who had ridden out to ascertain something as to the German casualties, returned with the information that those were moderate.

"And the Emperor?" asked the King of him.

"Nobody knows!" announced the officer.

Thus far, if the hour-data are not very specific, there are no important discrepancies in the testimony of eye-witnesses. But they are conspicuous in the evidence of the two witnesses now to be cited. The late General Sheridan·of the United States army, a man of keen observation and unimpeachable veracity, trained by much experience to coolness in the midst of battle, was officially attached to the royal headquarters. He made notes on the spot which he told me he had implicitly followed when writing his memoirs, published immediately after his premature and lamented death in 1888. And the following is his testimony:—

"About three o'clock, the French being in a desperate and hopeless situation, the King ordered the firing to be stopped, and at once despatched one of his staff, Colonel von Bronsart, with the demand for a surrender. Just as this officer was starting I remarked to Bismarck that Napoleon himself would likely be one of the prizes; but the Count, incredulous, replied, 'Oh, no; the old fox is too cunning to be caught in such a trap. He has doubtless slipped off to Paris.' Between four and five o'clock Bronsart returned from his mission to Sedan, bringing word to the King that General Wimpfen, the commanding officer there, wished to know, in order that the further effusion of blood might be spared, upon what terms he might surrender. The colonel also brought the intelligence that the French Emperor was in the town."

The late Mr. Holt White, the correspondent of the *New York Tribune* and *Pall Mall Gazette*, was with Sheridan throughout the day. He wrote :—

"About five o'clock there was a suspension of fighting all along the line. Five minutes later we saw a French officer, escorted by two uhlans, coming at a hard trot up the steep bridle-path, one of the uhlans carrying a white duster on a faggot stick as a flag of truce. This officer, who came to ask for terms of surrender, was told that in a matter of such importance it was necessary to send an officer of high rank. About half-past six there was a sudden cry among members of the King's staff, 'Der Kaiser ist da!' and ten minutes later General Reillé rode up with a letter from Napoleon to his Majesty, who wrote a reply begging Napoleon to come out next morning to the royal headquarters at Vendresse."

Of course this is an error; but what of the French officer of whose mission Holt White reported? The Bavarian officer from Torcy to whom Busch refers might have been mistaken for a Frenchman, when as yet people were not very well up in uniforms, were it not for the flag of truce. The "white duster" was certainly no myth, for Holt White brought it to London, where many people saw it; and Sheridan told me he saw it given to White. Could this officer have brought out the paper drawn out by Lebrun, at which Faure would not look, but which some one other than the commander-in-chief might have signed, and which had got forwarded somehow? But if this were so, how comes it that no mention was ever made by French writers of its exodus, or by the German "Official History" of its reception?

As it fell dusk a strange uncanny silence and stillness

succeeded to the thunderous noise and turmoil of the day. The smoke of the long cannonade still hung low on the uplands of Floing and Illy, and around the sombre fortifications of Sedan. The whole horizon was lurid with the reflection of fires. All along the valley of the Meuse were the bivouacs of the German hosts. A hundred and fifty thousand Teuton soldiers lay in a wide circle around their beaten and shattered foe. On hill and in valley glowed in the darkness the flames of burning villages, the glare here and there reflecting itself on the face of the placid Meuse. What were the Germans doing on this their night of consummated triumph? Celebrating their victory in wassail and riot? No. There rose from every bivouac one unanimous chorus of song, but not the song of insolence or of ribaldry. The chaunt that filled with solemn harmony the wide valley was Luther's hymn, the glorious

"Nun danket alle Gott!"

the Old Hundredth of the German race. To listen to this vast martial choir singing this noble hymn on the field of hard-won victory was to understand, in some measure, under what inspiration that victory had been gained.

Late that same evening there was a great concourse of German officers in the little hotel in the Square of Donchery. The house had hours earlier been eaten out of everything except bread; but there was plenty of wine and champagne flowed freely. My companion and myself achieved great popularity by the free distribution of a quantity of sardines which were among the provisions stored in the well of our carriage. About eleven o'clock Bismarck, uniformed and booted to the thigh, strode into the *salle-à-manger*, hungry, and demanding supper. He made a formal statement to the assembled officers to the effect that the French Emperor had sent out to the King the surrender of his sword; and he read in a loud voice a copy of Napoleon's letter. Adding no comments, he led off a hearty cheer, and then gave the toasts of "the King" and the "Fatherland." But his supper tarried. An officer ventured into the kitchen with intent to ascertain what was being prepared , for the Chancellor. Alas, the unhappy hostess protested, with many *mon Dieus!* that the Germans might eat her if they chose and welcome, but that the only food in the place was half-a-dozen dubious eggs. From a ham among our stores we contributed sundry slices, and they, with the dubious eggs, were prepared for the Chancellor's supper. But even so great a man as he was not exempt from the practical realisation of the adage that there is many a slip between the cup and the lip. Between kitchen and dining-room the dish was cut out and carried off by a privateering uhlan officer; and it was not until after perquisition throughout the depleted little town that a beef-steak was found, on which Bismarck at last supped, washing it down with a bottle of Donchery champagne.

Thus fortified, the Chancellor about midnight joined Moltke, whom the King had designated to name terms for the capitulation of the French army. That was a strange conference which was held in the still watches of the night in the salon of a house just outside of Donchery. The greetings were curt. Wimpfen verified his powers, and presented to Moltke Generals Faure and Castelnau as his colleagues. Moltke, with a brusque wave of the hand, introduced Count Bismarck and General Blumenthal, and then seats were taken. On one side of the great central table sat the three Germans, Moltke in the centre with Bismarck on his right and Blumenthal on his left. On the opposite side of the table sat Wimpfen by himself; behind him, somewhat in shadow, Faure, Castelnau, and a few other French officers. A Prussian captain stood by the mantelpiece, ready to commit to paper the proceedings in shorthand; on the French side a vivid précis was taken by Captain of Cuirassiers d'Orcet. Moltke sat silent and impassive; and after an embarrassing pause, Wimpfen had at length to take the initiative by inquiring what were the conditions the Prussian King was prepared to accord.

"They are very simple," replied Moltke curtly. "The whole French army to surrender with arms and belongings: the officers to be permitted to retain their arms, but to be prisoners of war along with their men."

G

Wimpfen scouted those terms, and demanded for the French army that it should be allowed to withdraw with arms, equipment, and colours, on condition of not serving while the war should last. Moltke adhered inexorably to the conditions which he had specified, and was adamant to the pleading of the French general. Losing temper, the latter exclaimed—

"I cannot accept the terms you impose. I will appeal to the honour and heroism of my army, and will cut my way out or stand on my defence at Sedan!"

Moltke's reply was crushing.

"A sortie and the defensive," he grimly remarked, "are equally impossible. The mass of your infantry are de-moralised; we took to-day more than 20,000 unwounded prisoners, and your whole force is not now more than 80,000 strong. You cannot pierce our lines, for I have surrounding you 240,000 men with 500 guns in position to fire on Sedan and your camps around the place. You cannot maintain your defensive there, because you have not provisions for forty-eight hours and your ammunition is exhausted. If you desire, I will send one of your officers round our positions, who will satisfy you as to the accuracy of my statements."

At this point Bismarck and Wimpfen, somewhat to Moltke's discontent, entered into a political discussion, in the course of which the Chancellor spoke his mind very freely but in which Moltke took no share. Assured that there could be no mitigation of the terms, Wimpfen exclaimed—

"Then it is equally impossible for me to sign such a capitulation: we will renew the battle!"

Moltke's quiet, curt answer was—

"The armistice expires at 4 a.m. At that hour, to the moment, I shall reopen fire."

There was nothing more to be said. The Frenchmen called for their horses: meanwhile, not a word was spoken; in the language of the reporter, "Le silence était glacial." It was at length broken by Bismarck, who urged Wimpfen not to allow a moment of pique to break off the conference. Wimpfen represented that he alone could not undertake the responsibility of a decision, that it was necessary that he should consult his colleagues; that the final answer could not be forthcoming by 4 a.m., and that the prolongation of the armistice was indispensable. After a short colloquy between Bismarck and Moltke, the latter, with well-feigned reluctance, gave his consent that the truce should be extended until nine o'clock; whereupon Wimpfen quitted Donchery and rode back into Sedan. He went straight to the bedside of the Emperor, who, having been informed of the harshness of the German conditions, said—

"I shall start at five o'clock for the German headquarters, and shall entreat the King to grant more favourable conditions."

It was then about half-past three a.m.

Napoleon did his best to act up to his resolution. He was in his carriage at the hour he had named. Expecting that he would be permitted to return to Sedan, notwithstanding that he had formally constituted himself a prisoner of war, he bade no farewells. As he passed through the Torcy Gate a little before six o'clock, the Zouaves on duty there shouted "Vive l'Empereur!"—"the last adieu which fell upon his ears" from the voices of French soldiers. It was strange that the first greeting he received as he passed over the drawbridge, was a silent and respectful salutation from American officers. General Sheridan and his aide-de-camp Colonel Forsyth were conversing with the German subaltern on duty on the picket-line, when there came out an open carriage containing four officers, one of whom, in the uniform of a general and smoking a cigarette, the American officers recognised as the Emperor Napoleon. They followed the carriage, which proceeded towards Donchery at a leisurely pace. At the hamlet of Frénois, about a mile from Donchery, it halted for some time, Napoleon remaining seated in the vehicle, still smoking, and enduring with nonchalance the stare of a group of German soldiers near by, who were gazing on the fallen monarch with curious and eager interest.

G 2

Looking out from my bedroom window into the little
Place of Donchery at a quarter to six the same morning,
I observed a French officer, whom I afterwards knew to be
General Reillé, sitting on horseback in front of the house
which I knew to be Bismarck's quarters for the night.
Reillé presently rode slowly away. He was scarcely out of
sight, when Bismarck, in flat cap and undress uniform, his
long cuirassier boots stained and dusty, as if he had slept
in them, came outside, swung himself on to his big bay
horse and rode away in Reillé's track. I was close by him
as he forced his masterful way through the chaos that all
but blocked the Donchery street. There was no redness
about the deep-set eyes or weariness in the strong-lined
face ; it had been midnight when he drank his last glass
of champagne in the Hôtel de Commerce, and he and
Moltke had been wrestling with Wimpfen about the terms
of capitulation for some three hours longer : yet here he was
before the clock had chimed the hour of six, fresh, hearty,
steady of hand and clear of throat, as the ringing voice
proved in which he bade the throng of soldiery give him
space to pass. I followed him on foot at a little distance
as he crossed the bridge and rode at a walking pace towards Sedan, but fell behind when he started off at a
smart canter. I was not up in time for the actual meeting
between the Emperor and Bismarck ; Sheridan told me that
the latter came up at a canter, dismounted, letting his horse
go, and drawing near on foot, uncovered his head and
bowed low. The man to whom he spoke—the man with
the leaden-coloured face, the lines of which were drawn
and deepened as if by some spasm, the gaunt-eyed man
with the dishevelled moustache and the weary stoop
of the shoulders, was none other than Napoleon the
Third and last.

As I came up, Bismarck had remounted, and was now
following along the road towards Donchery a rather shabby
open carriage, on the right of the principal seat of
which I at once recognised the Emperor. He wore a blue
cloak with scarlet lining, which was thrown back disclosing

the decorations on his breast. There were three officers in the vehicle with the Emperor, and three more rode abreast of Bismarck behind the carriage. A few hundred yards had been traversed by the cortège in the direction of Donchery, when at Napoleon's instance the carriage was halted in front of a weaver's cottage on the left-hand side of the road. I saw him turn round in his seat and heard the request he made to Bismarck, that he should be allowed to wait in the cottage until he should have an interview with the King. Bismarck placed at his disposal his own quarters in Donchery; but the Emperor, who appeared to be suffering, reiterated his desire to wait in the roadside cottage. The cottage, two storeys high, its front painted a dusky yellow, is the nearest to Sedan of a block of three, standing some fifteen feet south of the highway and on a slightly higher elevation.

Up to this point on the morning of September 2nd, there is approximate accord among the authorities: but beyond it the discrepancies are considerable. Sheridan's account has the precedence, as he was earliest on the ground. His testimony was that the Emperor and Bismarck on alighting entered the cottage together, and that, reappearing in a quarter of an hour, they seated themselves in front of the cottage on chairs brought out by the weaver. There, for fully an hour, they were engaged in an animated conversation, if much gesticulation on the part of Bismarck was to be taken as an indication. At length, soon after eight o'clock, Bismarck arose, saluted the Emperor, and strode towards his horse. On the way he asked Sheridan if he had noticed how, when they first met, Napoleon had started; and Sheridan replying in the affirmative, Bismarck said—

"Well, it must have been due to my manner, not my words, for those were—'I salute your Majesty just as I would my own king."

Then, advising Sheridan to go to the adjacent Château Bellevue, as the next scene of interest, Bismarck himself, stated Sheridan, rode off towards Vendresse to communicate with his sovereign. On this point Sheridan was certainly in error: Bismarck merely went to his Donchery quarters to breakfast and get into full uniform.

Bismarck's account of the morning's occurrences was given by him to Busch a few days later; it is condensed as follows :—

He, Bismarck, met the Emperor near Frénois. Napoleon desired to speak with the King of Prussia, which Bismarck said was impossible, as the King was nine miles away. The Emperor then asked where meantime he could stay, and accepted Bismarck's offer of the latter's Donchery quarters. But he stopped the carriage opposite the weaver's cottage, and expressed his desire to remain there. Bismarck accompanied him to a small room on the upper floor of the cottage, a room with a single window, its sole furniture a deal table and two rush-bottomed chairs. The conversation lasted here for about three-quarters of an hour; at the end of which Bismarck rode away to dress, and, on his return in full uniform, conducted Napoleon to the Château Bellevue with a "guard of honour" of cuirassiers. There Bismarck presently had himself called out of the room to evade further conversation with the Emperor, who was told that he could not see the King until the capitulation was settled. Soon Moltke and Wimpfen came to terms, and then the sovereigns met. "When the Emperor came out from the interview, his eyes were full of tears." In his official report Bismarck specifically stated that his long interview with the Emperor, "which lasted nearly an hour," was held inside the weaver's cottage.

The following are the recollections of Madame Fournaise, the weaver's wife, a Frenchwoman, given soon after the close of the war, when, she maintained, the events were still fresh in her memory :—

The Emperor, said Madame Fournaise, disliking to pass through the crowds of German soldiers on the Donchery road, alighted and came up her narrow staircase. To reach the inner room he had to pass through her bedroom, where she had just risen. The furniture of the inner room consisted of two straw-bottomed chairs, a round table, and a press. Bismarck, "in a rough dress," presently joined the Emperor, and for a quarter of an hour, said Madame Fournaise, they talked in low tones, of which she, remaining in the outer room, caught occasionally a word. Then Bismarck rose and came clattering out. "Il avait une très mauvaise mine." She warned him of the break-neck stairs, but he "sprang down them like a man of twenty," mounted his horse and rode away towards Donchery. When she entered the room in which the Emperor was left, she found him seated at the little table with his face buried in his hands. "Can I do anything for your Majesty?" she asked. "Only to pull down the blinds," was Napoleon's reply, without lifting his head. He would not speak to General Lebrun, who came to him. In about half an hour Bismarck returned in full uniform; he preceded the Emperor down the stairs, facing towards him as to "usher him with a certain honour." On the threshold the Emperor gave her four twenty-franc gold pieces—he "put them into my own hand"; and he said plaintively, "This perhaps is the last hospitality which I shall receive in France." Bismarck, added Madame Fournaise, was looking hard at her, and recognised her as having served his supper in the Donchery hotel on the previous night. With a kindly word of farewell "which I shall never forget," the Emperor quitted the poor house in which he had suffered so much unhappiness, and entered the carriage which was to convey him to the Château Bellevue. Madame Fournaise's heart was better than her memory.

The following is what I personally saw, condensed from copious notes taken at the moment with watch in hand. Immediately on alighting, at ten minutes past seven, Napoleon, who was obviously suffering, hurried round to the back of the house, while Bismarck and Reillé went inside but almost immediately came out. Soon the Emperor returned, and he and Bismarck then entered together, ascending to the upper floor. At twenty minutes past seven they came out, Bismarck a few moments in advance.

Two chairs were brought out in front of the cottage by the
weaver living on the ground floor; the two then sat down
facing the road, the Emperor on the right; and the outdoor
conversation began which lasted nearly an hour. Bismarck
had covered himself in compliance with a gesture and a
bow from the Emperor. As they sat, the latter occasionally
smiled faintly and made a remark; but plainly Bismarck
was doing most of the talking, and that, too, energetically.
From my position I could just hear the rough murmur of
Bismarck's voice when he occasionally raised it; and then
he would strengthen the emphasis by the gesture of bringing a finger of the left hand down on the palm of the
right. The stubbly-bearded weaver living upstairs was
all the while overlooking the pair from a front window.
After they had parted, I asked this man what he had over-
heard. "Nothing," said he; "they spoke in German, of
which I know but a few words. When the monsieur in
the white cap first spoke to the Emperor, he addressed
him in French; then the Emperor said, 'Let us talk in
German.'"

Bismarck, happening to see my letter describing the
events of the morning, instructed Busch to contradict
certain of my statements. The assertion was persevered in
that "he had spent three-quarters of an hour at least
inside the cottage in the upstairs room; and was only a
very short time outside with the Emperor." He had never
struck finger into palm, which was not a trick of his; and
he did not speak German with the Emperor, although he
did so with the people of the house. In this connection
may be quoted the following extract from Sir W. H. Russell's
narrative of an account of the memorable morning given
to him by Bismarck:—"He [Napoleon] alighted, and I
proposed that we should go into a little cottage close by.
But the house. . . . was not clean, and so chairs were
brought outside, and we sat together talking."

After Bismarck's departure the Emperor, who was then
out-of-doors, spoke a few words with his officers, and then
for a time sauntered moodily and solitary up and down

the potato plot on the right of the cottage, his white-gloved hands clasped behind him, limping slightly as he walked, and smoking hard. Later he came and sat down among his officers, maintaining an almost entire silence while they spoke and gesticulated with great animation. Busch was among the spectators, and he has described the Emperor as " a little thick-set man, wearing jauntily a red cap with gold border, black paletot lined with red, red trousers, and white kid gloves. His whole appearance," to Dr. Busch's genial perception, "was a little unsoldierlike. The man looked too soft, too shabby, I may say, for the uniform he wore." At a quarter past nine there came from Donchery a detachment of Prussian cuirassiers, who briskly formed a cordon round the rear of the block of cottages. The stalwart lieutenant dismounted two troopers, and without a glance at the group of Frenchmen or a gesture of salute to the Emperor, marched them up to behind the Emperor's chair, halted them, uttered in a loud voice the command, " Draw swords !" and then gave the men their orders in an undertone. Napoleon started abruptly, glanced backwards with a gesture of surprise, and his face flushed—the first evidence of emotion I had observed him to manifest. At a quarter to ten Bismarck returned, now in full uniform, his burnished helmet flashing in the sun-rays. Moltke accompanied him, but while Bismarck strode forward to where the Emperor was now standing, Moltke remained among the group gathered on the road. Half-way to Vendresse Moltke had met the King, who approved of the proposed terms of capitulation, and intimated that he could not see the Emperor until they had been accepted by the French commander-in-chief.

Wiping his hot face, Bismarck strode up to the Emperor, and spoke with him for a few moments. Then he ordered up the carriage, which Napoleon entered, and the cortège, escorted by the cuirassier "guard of honour," moved off at a walk towards the Château Bellevue, which lies nearer Sedan than does the weaver's cottage. The charming residence, bowered in a grove, overlooks a bend of the

Meuse and the plain on which Sedan stands. The garden entrance was on the first floor, reached from without by a broad flight of steps. The Emperor occupied the principal salon in the central block, where he remained alone after Bismarck had left him, his officers remaining in the conservatories on either side. Napoleon seemed ill and broken as he slowly ascended the steps, with drooping head and dragging limbs.

It has been already stated that at the close of the nocturnal conference in Donchery, the armistice had been prolonged until nine a.m. The members of the council-of-war which Wimpfen had summoned for seven a.m., listened to that unfortunate chief, as with a voice broken by sobs he repeated the conditions stubbornly insisted on by Moltke. Two officers voted for continued resistance, but ultimately the council was unanimously in favour of acceptance of the conditions. Nevertheless, during hour after hour, Wimpfen procrastinated. Before riding away to meet the King coming from Vendresse, Moltke had sent into Sedan an officer with the blunt ultimatum that hostilities would without fail be renewed at ten o'clock unless by that hour negotiations should have been resumed. Wimpfen still hesitating to act, Captain Zingler remarked cheerfully that his instructions, in case of an unsatisfactory answer, were to give orders as he rode back that the German batteries, numbering some 450 field-guns and commanding the French army as if in a ring-fence, should open fire promptly at the hour specified. Under stress of an argument so stern as that, Wimpfen accompanied the Prussian captain to the Château Bellevue, in the panelled dining-room in the ground floor of which, about eleven o'clock, the articles of capitulation were signed by Moltke and the French commander. Then Wimpfen had a moment upstairs with his Imperial master, whom he informed with great emotion that " all was finished ! " " The Emperor," wrote Wimpfen, " with tears in his eyes approached me, pressed my hand, and embraced me. . . My sad and painful duty accomplished, I rode back to Sedan, ' la mort dans l'âme.' "

The Prussian monarch, with his son and their respective staffs, had been awaiting on the Frénois hill the tidings of the completion of the capitulation; and now the great cavalcade rode down into the grounds of the Château. As Wilhelm alighted, Napoleon came down the steps to meet him. What a greeting! The German, tall, upright, bluff, square-shouldered, with the flash of victory from the keen blue eyes under the helmet, and the glow of good fortune on the fresh old face; the Frenchman, bent with weary stoop of the shoulders, leaden-faced, his eye drooping, his lip quivering, bare-headed and dishevelled. As the two clasped hands silently, Napoleon's handkerchief was at his eyes, and the King's face was working with emotion. Then the "good brothers" mounted the steps and entered the château together. Their interview, which no man shared, lasted about twenty minutes; and then the Prussian King set off to ride through his victorious soldiers bivouacking on the battle-field. The Emperor remained in the Château Bellevue.

My companion and myself made haste to enter Sedan, now that the capitulation was completed. We got on to the glacis of the place without any difficulty, and found the soldiers lying on it to consist chiefly of Turcos and Zouaves, dirty fellows most of them, but certainly in better case to all appearance than the troops we subsequently saw inside Sedan. Everybody was friendly, and wine was pressed on us—the more warmly when it was discovered that we were Englishmen. One especially greasy and strong smelling Turco of a full Day-and-Martin colour, strove vehemently to kiss us, but we fled. Getting into Sedan itself was a difficult matter. The gates were closed, and were opened only to admit the wounded as they were brought in on waggons. By the advice of a friendly Turco who set us the example, we jumped into one of the waggons and passed in without hindrance. As rapidly as possible for the tumultuous press, we traversed several streets of the town. We saw where Marshal MacMahon lay wounded. The town was swarming with disbanded soldiers, every foot of space densely packed. Of the wounded some were in the churches, the houses, and the public buildings; many lay unheeded and jostled in the gateways and courtyards; the dead were everywhere—in the gutters, trampled on by the living, on the swampy margin of the moat, littering the narrow ways between the glacis and the ramparts, lying, some of them, on the steps of the churches. The sight was one never to be exorcised from the memory—a sight of misery, disorganisation, and general devilry assuredly unique in this generation—an eddying welter of ferocious or despondent humanity, trampling recklessly over the dead and the wounded, the men now yelling for the blood of their officers, now struggling in fierce contention for a morsel of bread.

The day was not yet far spent, and we betook ourselves to the section of the battle field on the plateau of Floing. The tract charged over by the Chasseurs d'Afrique was a scene of terrible carnage. The Arab stallions ridden by those troopers had died very hard; in many cases they had made graves with their struggles for their riders and themselves before they died. Higher up on the tableland there was fearful evidence of the power of shell-fire at short range. I counted half a dozen headless corpses within a space of two hundred yards—their heads had been blown away almost as clean as if they had been guillotined. Men disembowelled, trunks shattered into gory fragments, legs or arms blown away, were common but ghastly spectacles that turned one sick.

Late the same afternoon I saw the Emperor again. He had come out into the park of the Château to superintend the reorganisation of his train, which had quitted Sedan in the course of the day. He looked very wan and weary, but still maintained the old impassive aspect. The Imperial equipage in its magnificence, the numerous glittering and massive fourgons, the splendid teams of draught animals and the squadron of led horses, presented an extraordinary contrast to the plain simplicity of the King of Prussia's campaigning outfit. In gold and scarlet the coachmen and outriders of Napoleon glittered profusely. He of Prussia had his postillions in plain blue cloth, with oilcloth covers on their hats to keep the dust off the nap. The Emperor and his suite left the Château Bellevue on the morning of the 3rd, driving through Donchery and by Illy across the frontier to Bouillon in Belgium, on the way to Wilhelmshöhe.

Zola, in his vivid but often grotesquely erroneous *Débâcle*, has fallen into strange blundering on the subject of the Imperial equipage. He thus refers to it:—

"The Imperial baggage train—cause in its day of so much scandal—had been left behind at Sedan, where it rested in ignominious hiding behind the Sous-Préfet's lilac bushes. It puzzled the authorities somewhat to devise means of ridding themselves of what was to them a *bête noire* by getting it away from the city unseen by the famishing multitude, upon whom the sight of its flaunting splendour would have produced the same effect that a red rag does on a maddened bull. They waited until there came an unusually dark night, when horses, carriages and baggage waggons, with their silver stew-pans, plate, linen, and baskets of fine wines, all trooped out of Sedan in deepest mystery, and shaped their course for Belgium, noiselessly, without beat of drum, over the least frequented roads, like a thief stealing away in the night!"

This is utter nonsense. As I have stated, I saw the Imperial train in the park of the Château Bellevue on the afternoon of the 2nd September, the day after the battle. Apart from this personal testimony, the story told by Zola is transparently absurd. By the evening of September 3rd the capitulated French Army was disarmed and enclosed under guard on the peninsula of Iges. There remained then in Sedan only its normal, or less than normal population, far too crushed to attempt any irregularity. A German Governor of Sedan had been installed, German troops constituted the garrison of the place, and Sedan would not have dared to emit so much as a mild hiss if the Imperial train, assuming that it had remained in Sedan after Napoleon's departure, which it did not, had perambulated the city in face of the population all day long.

The Germans, having determined to utilise as a prison for the capitulated army the peninsula of Iges, surrounded by the Meuse on three sides, and on the fourth by the closely guarded line of the canal, had marched on to it during September 3rd the disarmed French troops to the number of at least 100,000. The Germans themselves were temporarily short of supplies, having outmarched their commissariat: and could spare little for their prisoners. But for the first day or two on the peninsula the captives fared better than the captors. Nobody can accomplish a savoury mess under difficulties like a Frenchman, or house himself when another man would have to put up with the heavens for his roof. Innumerable fires were blazing; on every fire there was a saucepan, and in the saucepan were potatoes and something else. Whence came the potatoes was plain enough—we could see the fellows digging them out with their bayonets: but about the "something else" all that one could tell was that it smelt nice. The men who were not cooking were rigging up their *tentes d'abris* and gathering bedding of boughs and leaves. They were the civillest, cheeriest, best-humoured set of fellows imaginable. We two, quite alone, and unable to contribute anything to the general good—for our flasks and tobacco pouches were but drops in the bucket—experienced no word but of the frankest courtesy and the heartiest cordiality, alike on the part of officers and men. After a long gossip with a group of captains, we strolled down to the river and accepted the invitation of a bivouac of Zouaves to join them at supper. The mess was better than good; it was superb. It consisted of potatoes, the mysterious savoury "something," and flesh of some kind or other. The sunburnt Zouaves treated us like princes, but evaded a direct reply to our question what was the flesh-ingredient of their mess. After we had bidden good-night to the merry rascals, we came on the carcass of a horse which had been killed by a shell, and there was missing a considerable section of a flank.

It was late before we quitted the peninsula, and when we were once outside and realised the difficulty of finding quarters, we were sorry that we had not stayed with the Zouaves. Donchery we knew to have been invaded by a whole army corps; Frénois was seething full of Bavarians; the gates of Sedan were closed for the night. Our vehicle was waiting for as at the canal, but the driver could suggest no night quarters. As we were discussing the probabilities of a bivouac we drove past the front of the Château Bellevue. All was in darkness. A happy if audacious thought struck my companion. " Let us sleep here ! " he cried with a veritable inspiration—" the place is empty." The gardener —now since the departure of the morning the sole inmate of the premises—seemed content enough to have for inmates a couple of quiet civilians, and he conducted us into the beautifully panelled dining-room, on the table in which the capitulation had been signed on the previous morning. Good quarters, it was true, we had, but no food ; for the Imperial party had exhausted the resources of the establishment, and the gardener assured us that he himself was extremely hungry. At the great oak table, sullen and hungry, I sat writing a letter to my newspaper, while my companion disconsolately gnawed a ham-bone, the miserable remnant of our store of provisions. It had but scant picking on it, and my companion, with a muttered objurgation, threw it angrily on the table. As the bone fell it upset my ink-bottle and spilt its contents. Revisiting the Château after the war, I was gravely shown a great ink-stain on the table, which, the guide solemnly informed me, was caused by the upsetting of the ink-bottle used at the signature of the capitulation of Sedan. Wimpfen, I was assured, had overturned it in the agitation of his shame and grief. The guide added that great sums had been offered for this table with the " historic " ink-stain, but that no money would induce the proprietor to part with it. Thus do delusions gradually crystallise into items of traditional history. The stain on the floor of Mary Stuart's room in Holyrood, caused, we are assured, by Rizzio's blood, is probably the result of a saucerful of beetroot vinegar upset by the janitor's baby centuries after Mary met her cruel fate.

To me was assigned the bedroom which had been occupied

on the previous night by the Emperor Napoleon. It was in the state in which he had left it. Sheets and a quilt were on the bed; but one of the window-hangings, with its semi-circular canopy, had been dragged down and used as an additional covering. The glass doors of a book-case stood open; and on the night-table at the bed-head lay open, face downwards, a volume which had been taken from the case. The reader of the night before had made a selection in which there was something ominous—the book was Bulwer Lytton's historical novel, " The Last of the Barons."

On the tenth anniversary of the great battle I revisited Sedan. Alike in city and on battlefield, there was scarcely a trace of the memorable contest. The bones of the fallen had been exhumed from the scattered graves and gathered into ossuaries, of which the largest is the great crypt under the joint memorial of the French and German dead of the desperate fighting about Bazielles—a gruesome place with an alley down the centre, on one side of which had been stacked the skulls and bones of the fallen French, on the other those of the slain Germans. The only pilgrimage then still some-what in vogue was to the weaver's cottage, which Madame Fournaise, now a widow, continued to inhabit. Her recollec-tions were still fresh of probably the most momentous day of her life; and she narrated them with not a little spirit and feeling. Good-hearted soul as was Madame Fournaise, she was, all the same, a woman of business, and had made the most of her opportunities. It was to Bismarck she sold—not at his own price—the table at which he had sat with the fallen Emperor. The purchasers of the two veritably original straw-bottomed chairs were the late Sir Beauchamp Walker, the English Military Commissioner with the German Crown Prince's army, and the late General Sheridan. For years, although by this time the pilgrims were not so plentiful, Madame Fournaise had done well for herself by showing the upper chamber in which the interview took place; and by selling, mostly, she said, to American travellers, relay after relay of straw-bottomed chairs which she frankly owned to have passed off as the originals.

" And what about the four twenty-franc pieces ?" I asked.
" No doubt you have sold them over and over again ?"

"Oh, my God, no!" she exclaimed. "Never—never! Did he not give them to her with his own hand? See! the original four are in that locked case with the glass top on the mantel yonder. Yes, I have had great offers for them. Over and over again I could have had 500 francs for the four pieces; but no money would tempt me to sell them!"

Ten years later it happened that I once again was in Sedan. On my way back from looking at the pathetic and graceful monument overhanging the bend of the Meuse, which France had recently raised to the memory of her dead, I halted in front of the historic cottage. I found it uninhabited and in dilapidation. The door was locked, and the key far away in the possession of the proprietor, a farmer of Carignan. There was no longer access to the upper room wherein sat Napoleon and Bismarck on that memorable morning of September 1870. In one of the adjacent cottages I found a crone who told me that Madame Fournaise had been dead for several years. She lies in the Donchery graveyard. Three of the twenty-franc pieces, it seemed, were coins of Louis XVIII. Of the four pieces she had cherished so long, she had directed that those three should be dedicated to the payment for her grave and to defray her funeral expenses; the fourth, a Napoleon, was to be buried with her—in the coffin of the poor woman who had given to the unfortunate Emperor Napoleon " the last hospitality which he received in France."

H

IV.

AMBUSH AGAINST AMBUSH.

"PLEASE you, Herr Major, Corporal Zimmermann has returned to the picket with Sly Patrol No. 2. He reports that in the gap of the hedge in front of the large field over against the park wall of the Schloss Launay, No. 1,420, soldier Claus Spreckels, of Captain Hammerstein's company, was killed by a shot fired from the little house by the gate. That makes the seventh man killed this week by the pig-dog who lurks there and never misses a chance!"

The speaker was Under-Officer Schulz, of the third battalion, infantry regiment No. 103, forming part of General von Montbe's division of the 12th (Royal Saxon) Army Corps, doing duty on the east side of Paris during the memorable siege in the winter of 1870–71.

Under-Officer Schulz would have made an excellent model for a painter anxious to limn a Cameronian or one of Cromwell's ironsides. Instead of Schulz, his name might have been Praise-the-Lord Barebones. Tall, gaunt, thin-flanked and square-shouldered, with high cheek-bones, lantern jaws, and narrow peaked forehead, Under-Officer Schulz, Saxon though he was, had nothing of the genial informality so characteristic of his countrymen. He had entered the apartment, taken three measured steps from the door with accurately pointed toes, had halted smartly, bringing his heels together with an audible click; and then he stood motionless, stiff, and severely erect while he made the above report to Major von Schönberg, the commander of the battalion.

"Pig-dog, indeed!" said the major savagely. "He takes every chance, as you say, and never gives one! Have the dead Spreckels buried according to form. That will do, Under-Officer Schulz!"

"At your order, Herr Major!" answered the under-officer,

with a salute; then he went right about in three motions as if he were a piece of mechanism, took three measured paces to the door, and disappeared.

The scene was a handsome but sorely dilapidated salon in a château on the outskirts of the village of Gagny, on the German fore-post line of the section of environment between Raincy and Ville Evrart right opposite to Mont Avron, over the lower summit of which showed grimly the sullen face and menacing embrasures of Fort Rosny. There were big guns then on Mont Avron, and yet bigger in Fort Rosny; and neither had been very tender to the fine suburban mansion which for the time was the headquarters of Major von Schönberg's battalion. There were shot-holes in the roof, the walls, and the parquet floor of the drawing-room which was now the common room of the officers, the furniture of which was in a curiously fragmentary condition. A shell had burst in the grand piano that stood in the bay-window looking towards Avron, and had wrought indescribable havoc among the keys, hammers, and strings. The place was rather a favourite target both from Avron and Rosny, and we may be said to have lived within constant fire. While, for instance, Schulz had been making his report, a shell had exploded on the roof of the château. It is needless to mention that this occurrence did not occasion in that automatic person so much as the twinkle of an eyelid.

Christmas, the time of peace and goodwill among men, was but three days off, and soldier Claus Spreckels, with the blood still oozing on to the doorstep on which the body had been deposited, lay waiting while his grave was being dug. His would be the most recent, but the region round about us was one great graveyard of recent dead. But seven weeks previously, on the swelling peninsula a little to the south of us formed by the loop of the Marne, had occurred the desperate struggle that ended, after several bloody days, in the defeat of Ducrot's great sortie—a struggle in which Schönberg's battalion had lost half its officers and one-third of its rank and file. On the day before but one it had been fighting hard for six hours to repel the sortie of a French force heading up the Marne Valley from Neuilly, between the Maison Blanche and Ville Evrart.

That had been a strange scene on the evening before, when, under cover of the dusk—no vehicle dared move hereabouts in broad daylight—one of the battalion carts had brought out to us from the field post-office in Le Vert Galant the Christmas "love-gifts" (Liebesgaben), packed by loving hands, that came to those fore-post regions of blood and death from the quiet homes in distant Saxon-land. It was a curious medley of souvenirs that streamed out as the tail-board of the cart was let down in front of the quarter-guard behind the house occupied by the major.

The German Feldpost was a more elastic institution than had ever been a king's messenger's service-bag in the good old unreformed days. I do believe that if his friends at home had chosen to send to a soldier in the field a bee-hive or a rabbit-hutch, there would have been no objection on the score of bulk. Out rolled cigar-boxes stitched up in canvas wrappers, long cocoon-like shapes every outline of which spelt "wurst," flabby packages which evidently consisted of underclothing, and little boxes that rattled as they dropped and, for certain, contained thalers. A pile of gifts was stacked against the wall, and a space in front was cleared in which stood, wooden and stiff even when off duty, Under-Officer Schulz, calling out the name as each packet was handed up to him by a corporal. It was rather a dreary, even, indeed, a solemn roll-call, deeply eloquent of the casualties which war had wrought in the ranks of the battalion.

"Schumann!" called out Under-Officer Schulz.

"Shot dead in battle!" was the curt response.

"Caspar!"

"Wounded!"

"Stolberg!"

"Dead."

"Bergmann!"

"In hospital."

"Schräder!"

"Weg."

Now the dictionary definition of the word “Weg” is “away,” “gone”; but on campaign it had a wide and rather vague significance. “Weg,” then, might mean indeed almost anything: prisoner, missing, unburied, deserted—only that one never heard of a German soldier deserting. The sum and substance of the word was, “Not here, and Lord knows where he is!”

When Schulz had done, there was still quite a heap of packets which the men to whom they were addressed would never claim. I had seen Spreckels tear open the box of cigars addressed to him, before I left the place of distribution. Now he was lying dead on the slab there, with a bullet-hole through his head; and from between the buttons of his tunic stuck out some half-dozen of the cigars that had come to him overnight from his mother in Kamenz.

The French outpost line opposite to that section of the German front occupied by the Saxon Regiment followed a road which skirted the lower slope of Mount Avron, crossed the little valley in front of the village of Villemomble which the French held, and then took up the line of the wall bounding the finely wooded park of the Château de Launay. Though here and there they approached more closely where the ground was broken, the opposing lines were for the most part distant from each other about eight hundred paces.

In most civilised wars it had been the humane custom that the outposts of two opposing armies in ordinary circumstances did not molest each other. In the Peninsular campaign this mutual forbearance was carried to curious lengths. In that excellent book, “The Subaltern,” the late Chaplain-General Gleig gives many instances of the “excellent understanding” which prevailed between the armies, and of their genuine cordiality one towards the other. At one time “the Subaltern” used to go a-fishing in a river which divided the lines, and he tells how “many a time I have waded half across the little river on the opposite bank of which the enemy's pickets were posted, whilst they came down in crowds only to watch my success, and to point out particular pools and eddies where they thought I could find the best sport. On such occasions the sole precaution I took was to dress myself in scarlet, and then I might approach within a few yards of their sentries without being molested."

Another instance which "the Subaltern" gives betokened so much too good an understanding between the outposts, as to cause Wellington to forbid all intercommunication whatsoever—a prohibition at which one can scarcely wonder when the story is told :—" A field-officer, going the rounds one night, found that the whole sergeant's picket-guard had disappeared. He was both alarmed and surprised at the occurrence ; but his alarm gave way to utter astonishment when, stretching forward to observe whether there was any movement in the enemy's lines, he peeped into a cottage from which a noise of revelry was proceeding, and beheld the party sitting in the most sociable manner with a similar party of French soldiers, and carousing jovially. As soon as the British officer presented himself, his own men rose, and, wishing their companions good-night, returned to their post with the greatest *sang froid.* It is, however, but justice to add that the sentries on both sides faithfully kept on their posts, and that on neither side was there any intention of desertion. In fact, it was a sort of custom, the French and British outposts visiting each other by turns."

Other times, other manners. In other respects than the observance of outpost etiquette, the French soldiers of 1870 were different from their ancestors of the Peninsular period. From the very beginning of the war, from the early days before Saarbrücken, before any battle had been fought, and therefore before defeat could have exacerbated the troops of the Second Empire, they had caught at every chance that offered of firing on the German outposts, sentries, and patrols. The first man I ever saw killed by a bullet was a poor fellow of the Hohenzollern Fusiliers—one of a " sly patrol " which I was accompanying one July morning through the copses lining the base of the Spicherenberg. The French soldiers on the outposts of the Paris defence-line often were not regulars, and when they were regulars, were recruits who, if they had ever heard of them, had no respect for the old civilised traditions. Every reverse made them the more venomous; and the Germans, who at first showed a great deal of forbearance, had, by the winter season, long ceased to refrain from reprisals. Accordingly, during the siege of Paris, there was a miserably great amount of simple cold-blooded murder perpetrated on the foreposts. No other term than murder expresses the killing of a lone sentry by a pot-shot at long range. It was like shooting a partridge sitting. Of this wretched work the French had the better, because of the longer range of their chassepôts. Their marksmen used to remain on the outposts and practise this deliberate homicide; when they had potted some half-dozen Prussians at 1,000 yards, they took rank as heroes, and were fêted by the citizens when they gave themselves a holiday from their trade of cheap death. One of those slaughter-men it was whom Under-Officer Schulz had taken the liberty of describing as a "pig-dog." He had located himself, apparently permanently, in a cottage which had probably been the gardener's residence, about a couple of furlongs in front of the approach-gate of the Château de Launay; and for days previous to that on which poor Spreckels came by his end, the Frenchman had occupied the period of daylight in taking deliberate aim at every Prussian soldier exposing himself within reach of the chassepôt. The Prussians had marksmen, and they had chassepôts too, by this time; but the fellow never gave them a chance. He shot out of a window, but he never showed himself, firing from the back of the room, and standing, no doubt, well out of the direct line of fire.

I fear I must own to the veteran's besetting sin of discursiveness. I apologise, and return to the departure of Under-Officer Schulz from the presence of Major Schönberg and his officers, after he had reported poor Spreckels as "expended."

"That scoundrel will decimate the battalion!" exclaimed the Major, as he took a long drink of the lager-beer, a little barrel of which had been among the Christmas love-gifts sent him by the Frau Majorinn. "And," he added, "how to mend matters beats me!"

Then impulsive Captain Kirchbach, the Hanoverian, spoke out. ' Let us rush the infernal hut, Major, and burn it down : that will destroy the fellow's cover. I volunteer to lead the arson-party. Why not to-night ? "

" It must not be as you propose, Kirchbach," said the Major mournfully. " You know the French fore-post line is close in rear of the cottage—I suspect it moves forward with nightfall ; and you know also that not half a rifle-shot to the rear there is a brigade of the red-legs in Villemomble. We'd risk them with as light a heart as Ollivier accepted the war, but you know my orders are absolute not to do anything that might bring on fighting now, while they are making the battery-emplacements for the siege-guns up there behind us in front of Maison Guyot."

" Ach, so ! " came from half a dozen lips, in that long, undulating intonation which is so characteristic of the Saxon speech.

" And yet," piped little Hammerstein, " it is a cursed pity that our good fellows should be murdered thus."

" Fortune of war ! " cried Helldorf the reckless, as he made for the herrings, sardellen, and schinken which a soldier-servant had just placed on a section of the shattered piano that did duty for a buffet ; " if you are to be bowled over, it may as well happen on a ' sly patrol ' as in the mêlée of Gravelotte. Spreckels' turn to-day ; mine, mayhap, to-morrow ! The Frenchman don't respect officers the least in the world. One of the seven he has already killed was, you will remember, our comrade Ensign von Ernsthausen."

" Permit me the word, Herr Major," spoken in a modest tone, were the bashful words that came from the mere lad in the light blue uniform who was standing by the door. The speaker was such a slight fellow, and had so young a face, that he did not seem full-grown. The moustache had not budded on his lip, but there was a fire in his eye and a quiet, modest resolution in the whole aspect of him, which gave the assurance that he was equal to a man's part. The brass scales on his shoulders showed him to be a cavalryman, the only representative of that arm present. His rank was that of

Ensign, and he commanded the little detachment of the Crown Prince's Reiter Regiment which was detailed with the infantry battalion in the forepost line to perform orderly duty.

" Well, baron, are you going to offer to cut the fellow out with your galloping sergeant's party ? " asked Schönberg, rather in a tone of banter—there was a little jealousy between the cavalry and infantry before Paris, as there mostly is during a long siege, because of the easy times the former have in comfortable quarters well to the rear. By the way, I have forgotten to mention that the name of the cavalry youngster was the Baron von und zu Steinfurst-Wallenstein. But if the young fellow had a swagger name, that was all of swagger there was about him ; though, mere lad as he was, the Iron Cross was at his button-hole, gained in a slashing charge on the evening of Beaumont.

" I think, Herr Major," said the baron quietly, " my fellows would snatch at the opportunity if you were to give it them. But, of course, from what you have just told Captain Kirchbach, that is out of the question. Yet if you will allow me— my sergeant can see to the duty for a day or two—I should like to try whether, with good fortune, I may not stop this fellow's devilry. They reckon me the best game-shot with the sporting-rifle in our part of the Saxon Switzerland, and I have got my favourite weapon with me here. One never knows when one may get a chance at something. What I want to do is to go and stalk this French devil. May I, Herr Major ? "

" Oh, you may try your luck, and welcome, baron, for me," replied the major. " Mind, unless you bring his head back with you, we shan't believe you've wiped him out."

It must be said that, besides the rather elephantine badinage of the worthy major, the young cavalryman was the butt of a good many jokes that evening. It was the brilliant Helldorf who christened him " David," and offered to go and help him search around for an eligible stone to put into his sling. But the little baron took the chaff with a modest serenity, ate a hearty dinner (I have said he was a Saxon), renounced both the Frau Majorinn's beer-barrel and the generous red wine which Kirchbach contributed to the joint-stock mess, and was in bed bright and early, after having first given his trusty rifle a thorough overhaul and filled a bandolier with Eley's best cartridges. Very early in the morning his batman brought him some breakfast. He dressed himself warmly, for the weather was very bitter, poured some schnapps into his pocket-flask, put some sandwiches into his haversack, and, rifle in hand, started out for the extreme front. He had the watchword and countersign, of course; but they would not avail to carry him outside the German cordon of advanced sentries, and that was just whither he meant to go. So at the *Repli* he had the officer on duty to go forward with him to the outlying picket—the *Feldwache;* the sergeant in command of which, at the officer's order, escorted him through the outer chain of sentries. It was on the railway embankment close to the long since burnt Gagny station that he left the sergeant and the final double-post; and after descending into the hollow beyond, began to climb the gradual slope on the crest of which, among the trees, stood the Château de Launay. It was not yet dawn, but the morning was not very dark and it was rather ticklish work. The ground was covered with deep snow the surface of which was frozen hard, and the crystallised surface threw up a faint sparkle even in the darkness, while it crackled crisply under every footfall. Clumps of evergreens were dotted over the slope, and if they had a danger of their own as possibly concealing French out-liers or patrols, they also gave the advantage of covering to some extent the young officer's advance. He had taken the bearings of the cottage to the watching of which he intended to devote himself, and instead of heading directly towards it, with the result that the hiding-place he designed to take up would be right in the French marksman's line of sight, he edged away somewhat to his own right, with intent to locate himself somewhere on the proper left front of the cottage. When about three hundred yards distant from it, he found him-self close to a dense clump of evergreen shrubbery—a bosquet forming the outer fringe of the pretty grounds, in the heart of which stood, and no doubt still stands, the villa then possessed by the late Dr. Nélaton, the famous surgeon of the Second Empire. This clump the baron penetrated, and lying down on the moss in the heart of it, whither the snow had not penetrated, he waited till dawn, and then gingerly twisted and broke the shrubs till he had a clear vista of aim on the cottage, now visible dimly through the frost-haze.

Its sharp-shooting occupant he judged to be cooking his breakfast, for smoke was lazily rising from the chimney of the cottage. Then the sun came out and chased away the haze, and the baron thought he caught a glimpse of the dull gleam of a rifle-barrel back in the room inside the wide orifice where in peace-time there had been a window-frame. His first impulse was to aim a little behind where he had seen the glint, and then fire ; but he restrained himself. In all likelihood, he reckoned as he steadied himself, not more than one chance would come to him, if even that much, so crafty, evidently, was the Frenchman. For that one hoped-for chance, then, it was for the baron to wait hour after hour with the patience of a red Indian—it might indeed be for days, for, to use Kirkpatrick's words, he was bound to " mak siccar." So he lay supine, gazing steadfastly at the white front of the cottage, up against which almost to the window-sill the whiter snow had drifted, making a bank sloping away from the wall, its frozen surface sparkling where the sunrays struck it.

The hours passed wearily but intently. Three times the flash of a shot and the little pillow-like cloud of white smoke had darted out from the window-space in the front of the cottage. For aught the baron could know, as he lay there in the slow torments of inability to accomplish his purpose, each shot meant the life gone from out a Saxon soldier. Would he risk a return shot? he asked himself each time, when next that cool, cruel devil up there pulled trigger. And each time the stern resolute answer he made to himself was, " No ! be calm ; everything comes to him who can wait."

The Frenchman fired a fourth time just as the sun was going down, but, as before, from out the gloom at the back of the room. When it became dark the lad, half frozen, stiffly rose and trudged his way back into the Saxon position. The sentries had been warned of his probable coming in, and did not interfere with him. He had rather a bad evening of it. During the day the marksman of the cottage had killed one sentry as he peered rather recklessly over the edge of the railway embankment, and had wounded another fellow when on " sly patrol " duty. The poor baron was ruthlessly chaffed. One officer supposed that he could not get his rifle to go off, another that he had gone to sleep and lost his opportunities ; a third gave it as his deliberate conviction that the baron had spent the day fraternising genially with " Bob the Nailer."

The mansion occupied by the headquarters of Major Schönberg's battalion had belonged to an English family, in whose library Hammerstein, who was himself half an Englishman, had found a history of the defence of Lucknow in the Indian Mutiny days, in which work was recorded the pestilential marksmanship of a native sharp-shooter, who from a turret opposite to the Bailey-Guard Gate used to take deadly pot-shots at members of the beleaguered garrison. The English soldiers, it seemed, had bestowed on this destructive individual the nickname of " Bob the Nailer "; and this appellation the Saxon officers had transferred to the objectionable Frenchman who did his shooting from the cottage in the foreground of the Château de Launay. Stern and serious business as is war, human nature is so constituted as to find a humorous side to the most ghastly transactions, but it must be owned that the complexion of the jokes is of the grimmest.

The little baron had an imperturbability beyond his years. The rough badinage of his comrades did not in the least disconcert him. He was modestly confident that if the Frenchman should but once give him the merest flicker of a chance, he could and would kill him ; and he had the conviction that, be the man ever so artful, this morsel of good-fortune was bound, sooner or later, to come to him. Next morning before daybreak he was back in his lurking-place among Dr. Nélaton's evergreens, lying prone there, his rifle ever at the shoulder, his gaze centred steadily on the aperture in the wall of the cottage.

On the second evening he sauntered into Major Schönberg's salon, his manner quiet, unassertive—almost timid,
indeed, as was his wont. A shout of derisive laughter greeted
his entrance.

"Back again empty-handed, O doughty younker?"
shouted Kirchbach.

The battalion surgeon in his silkiest manner—he was a
most sarcastic man, this quiet German Mr. Brown—asked
whether "Bob the Nailer" stood in need of his professional
services?

"Do you know, Herr Baron," said Captain von Zanthier
with a sneer, "that your adversary up yonder bowled over
another fellow of my company this afternoon?"

Then out spoke Major von Schönberg himself: from the
outset he had considered Steinfurst's offer as rather a piece of
impertinence.

"You have had two whole days, baron, for this experiment
of yours with the rifle that wrought such execution in the
Saxon Switzerland; to-morrow, if you please, you will return
to your regular duty with your cavalry detachment."

"Zu befehl, Herr Major!" replied Steinfurst, springing to
the attitude of rigid attention on receiving a formal order.
That acknowledged, he relaxed his muscles as much as a
German officer in his most unbending moments ever does, and
made a few quiet observations. "I should not," said he,
"have proposed going out again, major, in any case. Doctor,
I don't think 'Bob the Nailer,' as you call him, has the
slightest occasion to avail himself of your most valuable
offer. Captain Kirchbach, I have not come back empty-
handed; I brought with me my rifle—its barrel is fouled."

Then immediately arose the loud clamour of questioning.
"Have you really killed the fellow?" "Are you really
serious?" and so forth.

The little baron, in his quietest manner, demurely replied,
"Perhaps those gentlemen who are interested in this little
matter will take the trouble to-morrow morning to go out to
the front as far as the railway embankment, and from thence
survey the front of the Frenchman's cottage through their

field-glasses." And with that he bowed, said "Good-night !" and went away to his sleeping-quarters over the stables in which were the horses of his detachment.

Next morning was the morning of Christmas Day. In peaceful England, as throughout the German Fatherland—with peace indeed within its borders, but with sore or anxious hearts in palace and hovel, the church bells would presently be ringing out their chimes through the winter air. They were different sounds to which we listened that Christmas morning from the foreposts under the shadow of Mont Avron. From its blunt summit up yonder in the winter sunshine one of Colonel Stoffel's big guns at intervals gave fire, the great shell hurtling and screaming over our heads as it sped on its swift flight to wreak mischief in Clichy or Montfermeil on the upland behind us. Never for five minutes were the forepost lines wholly silent from that uncomfortable, venomous, inter-mittent crackle of musketry fire—so futile, so savage, so bitterly eloquent of inveterate man-to-man hatred. The Feld-pastor, a little later, would be essaying to deliver his message of "peace and good-will among men," mocked to his very face by those noisy tokens of strife and rancour; and for his poor consolation might bethink himself of the stern aphorism, "*À la guerre comme à la guerre.*" The war and its devilry meantime did not hinder us, as we met soon after sunrise for morning coffee in the *salon*, from wishing each other "A Merry Christmas"; and, coffee drunk and cigars lit, we started on the errand which the baron had so enigmatically suggested overnight. The major, devoured though he was by curiosity, did not think it compatible with his dignity to go; the baron himself did not put in an appearance. The ex-ploration party consisted of Kirchbach and his brother-in-law Hammerstein, Zanthier, Helldorf, Freiherr von Zehmen, three or four youngsters, and the Briton who had the run of the Maas Army forepost line from Sartrouville on the Seine north-west of Paris, round to Bonneuil and beyond to the Seine on the south-east.

When we reached the railway embankment we found the men of the picket peering over at the distant cottage, each man with his hand shading his eyes from the dazzle of the sun on the snow. Said the corporal of the picket to Captain Kirchbach :—

"There is something hanging out over the window-sill, Herr Hauptmann ; it looks like the upper part of a great-coat with the hood falling lower between the arms."

Hammerstein had his sight soonest adjusted. "By God ! it is a dead man !" he shouted on the instant.

Yes ; he was right. Hanging limply there from the lintel of the orifice that had been a window was the upper portion of the figure of a man, inverted and perfectly motionless. The broad shoulders showed out distinctly against the white of the wall, as did the black hair of the occiput ; the face of course was invisible, being towards the wall. The arms had dropped at full length, their extremities reaching down to the snow-bank piled up against the lower part of the cottage wall.

I was the only one of the party who carried a telescope. The binocular is handy, but its powers are limited. The telescope is a clumsier weapon, but once focussed and accurately aimed, it tells you twice as much as the best binocular. I had seen what I have just described through Hammerstein's binocular ; now I proceeded to train my telescope on to the spot, and with its assistance to go more into detail.

What I saw was this. The clenched hands had clutched into the snow. The long hair hung straight, discoloured—a dingy crimson. A rifle had slipped away from the figure's grasp, and I could see it some twenty feet away from the window, lying on the level after it had skidded down the frozen slope of snow. There was no mistake about the matter ; the baron had done his work thoroughly, and the sarcastic doctor's services were not in the least required.

It seems rather a ghastly sort of thing to recount ; but, as a matter of fact, the French marksman's extermination—the Irish equivalent, "removal," was an inapplicable term—was accepted by universal acclamation as Baron Steinfurst's Christmas-box to the battalion. A deputation formed up to him after Divine service, headed by Under-Officer Schulz, who, heels duly clinked together, the proper degree of motionless rigidity satisfactorily attained, opened his lantern-jaws, stammered vigorously, then got out: "In name of battalion, a thousand thanks—verdammte Französicher Schweinhund!" Whereupon he went right about with extraordinary abruptness, nor recovered his customary measured and angular gait until he had got away several paces from where the little baron stood blushing.

In as few words as might be, the modest lad told us the story as we stood around the piano buffet eating a scrappy luncheon. Till the afternoon of the second day of his watch he had resolutely held his fire, determined to wait till he could "mak siccar." During that day the Frenchman had fired several times, but had never given a glimpse of himself to the young marksman down among Dr. Nélaton's hollies and laurels. His last shot he fired just before dusk; this was the shot that killed the man of Zanthier's company, and the only occasion that day on which his fire took effect. He then, as ever, fired without exposing himself; but when the bullet had sped, he forgot himself for the first time during the two days. Anxious, no doubt, to ascertain whether he had done execution, he had moved forwards out of his safe retirement, and projected his head and shoulders over the window-sill, peering out to his own right front—the direction in which he had fired. All this he did with a jerk. He was in the act of retracting himself when the little baron took his snapshot at him. Steinfurst had not for nothing practised rabbit-shooting with the rifle. The Frenchman dropped on the instant, falling, as we had seen him, with head and shoulders outside the window. The baron had seen the momentary convulsive grasp, the tearing up of the snow with the hands, and then the sudden stillness which showed that the "pig-dog" would take no more German lives. Being within range of the French forepost line in rear of the cottage, he did not quit his position until the dusk was merging into darkness. That was all he had to say.

The dead marksman had no successor in the occupation of the cottage. Strangely enough, the French never ventured up to it, although there could have been little risk in doing so under cover of night; and the body hung there as it had fallen until early in January, when Colonel Stoffel, his big guns, and his troops were bombarded away from the summit of Mont Avron by the fire of the German "walruses," as we used to call the siege cannon, from Maison Guyot and elsewhere. Then the French outpost line was of course drawn in, and the region about Villemomble and the Château de Launay lapsed to the Saxons, who buried the dead sharpshooter under the window from which he had sped death so often while alive. He had regularly lived in the cottage, it seemed. It was found quite copiously victualled with bacon, tinned food, wine, and coffee; and the man had brought with him a small library of good solid reading, as well as writing materials. On the table in the back room there lay a halffinished letter which began, "Ma très chère femme," and which told in the most matter-of-fact manner of the results of his ball-practice. He sent his love to his children and begged them to pray for his continued success. He was not a soldier of the Line. He wore the coarse uniform of a private of the national guard, but his linen was fine and marked with a good name. In the left breast-pocket of his tunic was found the photograph of a handsome woman, with a little child at her knee and a baby in her arms.

No doubt the "verdammte Französicher Schweinhund" was a devoted patriot according to his lights, and regarded himself as fighting the good fight *pro aris et focis.* There are so many different ways of looking at a thing, you see. Schönberg's fellows gave me the relics of the dead man when next I visited them. The capitulation could not be very far off now, and I should be early in Paris.

Well, the capitulation came, and I was early into Paris. One of the first things I did after attending to my work was to deliver the relics at the address I had, leaving along with them a short note. The sharpshooter turned out to be one of our own profession. As did so many other gallant French soldiers of the pen, he had run to arms the moment danger threatened the sacred soil. He had escaped from the field of Sedan to form an item in the huge garrison of Paris, and

I

burning with zeal and devotion to duty, he had thrown himself into the unworthy business of pot-shooting. The poor wife thought him a veritable hero, and his work glorious and patriotic. His children had a cribbage-board, with the pegs of which they had proudly kept the tally of his homicides. I believe, before the Commune days came, that I had almost got to look at the matter from their point of view. I never knew sweeter children.

V.

PARIS IN PROSTRATION.

DURING the period from the surrender of Metz to the capitulation of Paris—in other words, from the beginning of November, 1870 until the end of January, 1871—I was attached to the headquarters of the Army of the Meuse, holding the northern and eastern sections of the investment of Paris. The chief of that army was the Crown Prince (now the King) of Saxony, who with his headquarter staff abode for the most part in the château of Margency, about ten miles due north of Paris, in the heart of the forest of Montmorency. At nine o'clock on the evening of January 28th, while the headquarter staff were assembled in the Crown Prince's drawing-room after dinner, an orderly brought in a telegram to the Prince. His Royal Highness, having read it, handed it to General von Schlotheim his chief-of-staff. That officer perused it in his deliberate way; then rising, he walked to the open door communicating between the billiard-room and the salon, and there read the telegram aloud. It was in the name of the German Emperor, and it announced that two hours earlier Count Bismarck and M. Jules Favre had set their hands to a convention in terms of which an armistice to last for twenty-one days was already in effect. It was not easy to settle down to cards or billiards after such news as that.

I 2

The terms of the armistice included the capitulation of the St. Denis forts, which had undergone a five days' bombardment by the heavy guns that the German engineers and artillerists had brought up and located in prepared battery-emplacements in commanding positions. On the morning of the 29th the Crown Prince and his staff rode towards St. Denis. There was a long halt at the half-way village, to await the return of the officer who had gone forward into the place to arrange with the commandant for the surrender of the forts. Reports came that Admiral de Ronciere, the officer commanding in St. Denis, was sulky and impracticable and that the aspect of the French troops was threatening. Meanwhile two infantry regiments and four field-batteries had pushed forward and occupied a low eminence midway between St. Denis and Enghien; and a staff of engineer officers with a detachment of pioneers and artillerymen had gone on into Fort de la Briche, to draw the charges from the mines and to take over the guns and magazines.

It was now afternoon, and although Major Welcke had not yet returned from the fortress, the Prince and his staff went forward. Near the enceinte Welcke was at length met, bringing the report that all the French troops had not yet evacuated St. Denis, and suggesting that as the civilian population, most part of which was armed, had rather a threatening aspect, a strong force of occupation should be sent on in advance. We rode forward with Fort de la Briche close on our right. It had suffered somewhat severely from the heavy German fire, but clearly no practicable breach had been effected. Fort du Nord, which was presently passed, had been more heavily dealt with. Great pieces of the earthwork had been torn away, and the wall of the scarp had been shattered and penetrated in places. A terrible fire had converged on the gate; one drawbridge had been demolished and the other could not be raised. Just inside the works there was a halt to permit the delegate from the French État Major to make some explanations. He came forward—a wan, sad-faced young officer of marine artillery, with a grave dignity in the pale face and in the weary, anxious eyes that commanded respect and commiseration. He was quite alone, and the solitary man looked forlorn yet full of a gallant mournful pride, as he rode up to the Crown Prince with a high-bred greeting that assuredly was not of republican France. His statement was that all the St. Denis troops had been withdrawn into Paris, that the mobiles, national guard, and sedentaries had been disarmed, and that the population had come to its senses.

The supporting force being close up, a German military band struck up the " Paris March "; and behind the music the Crown Prince and his staff rode up the main street over shattered barricades and undrawn mines. The whole town was a ruin. There was a strange, un-French silence: one marked the lowering brows and caught many a *" Sacré !"* muttered from between the teeth. That all the arms had not been given up was very apparent : and the chief-of-staff ordered to the front the Crown Prince's escort of Saxon Guard-Cuirassiers. As the splendid horsemen clattered forward at a sharp canter, the women and children and indeed many of the men, ran into the battered houses shrieking, " The Uhlans ! The Uhlans !" In the *Place* the Prince halted while there marched past him in solid ranks the brigade which had been detailed to garrison St. Denis, its band playing the " Paris March " and then " Ich bin ein Preusse." I could hear the French spectators gloomily owning one to another their admiration of the physique and soldierly bearing of the German troops. Strong patrols of occupation were at once marched into the forts, and a forepost line was established five hundred paces nearer Paris than the forts. The French commandant of Fort de l'Est reported that there had fallen in and on it during one day of the bombardment no fewer than 1,200 heavy shells.

When I rode into St. Denis in the forenoon of the 30th, I found that the town had in a measure recovered its tone since the German entry of the day before. Some business was already being transacted between the shop-keeping inhabitants and soldiers of the German garrison. I made in haste for the venerable cathedral, anxious to ascertain what amount of damage it had sustained. The Republicans who had painted *Liberté, Égalité, Fraternité* on its portals had not allowed their republicanism to render them negligent of the historic edifice and the monuments it contained: the exterior had been banked up high all round with sandbags which had stopped many shells. Only four shells had penetrated into the interior. The mediæval stained glass was almost entirely intact. One of the elaborately-carved crosses on the top of a buttress had been splintered off, and a coping-stone had been shattered; this, it appeared to me, summed up the damage done to the cathedral from the shell-fire of the enemy. The aspect of the interior was very strange. The tombs of the kings of France had all been protected by sandbags; the statues had been enclosed by wooden frames and sandbags built around the framework. Considering the weight and duration of the bombardment, the cathedral had escaped wonderfully well. The same could not be said of the utterly-demolished houses in its vicinity, nor of the new church of St. Denis, the steeple of which was wrecked, one side of it stove in, and its interior a chaos of mortar, stones, and smashed paraphernalia. The little Protestant chapel had suffered worse than any other religious edifice in St. Denis, and its poor pastor was to be seen trotting dolefully about, engaged in the task of picking up the fragments of his chapel from the open spaces in the vicinity.

It must have been verily the reign of the Prince of the Power of Darkness, that period of five days during which the bombardment of St. Denis lasted. The shells were continually crashing into the houses, and they were ploughing up the streets as with the deepest subsoil plough ever invented. There was no safety for any but in the cold and dark cellars; so heavy were the German projectiles that not always in the cellars was there found

safety. There were houses the garrets and cellars of which
had been battered into a shapeless mass of stone and
mortar. If you asked the loafing bystanders whether any
had been buried in the ruins, they moodily muttered " Qui
sait ? " shrugged their shoulders, and turned away. It
seemed to me that there must be not a few unfortunates
buried under those jagged rubbish heaps: but there was
nobody who had interest or energy to explore, and " Qui
sait ? " might have stood for the vague epitaph.

It happened that in St. Denis during the bombardment
there was a branch of the International Ambulance, the
devoted members of which took their lives in their hands
and bravely went out to do what good they might. They
dragged the maimed and ailing out of the shattered houses,
they collected the corpses from the streets and the ruins,
and they buried the dead with some semblance of decency.
They went round the town urging that the women and
children should go forth from the doomed town, and retire
into Paris. The women and children had huddled into
the semi-security of the cellars. The shells were crashing
into the streets, and avalanches of stone and brick were
continually crashing down upon the side-walks. The
women peeping forth shudderingly, declared that they would
rather die where they were than incur a more certain and
fearful death by sallying forth into that tempest of iron,
stone, and bricks. So they turned back to hunger and
cold in the dank caverns, and cuddling their children to
their bosoms utterly refused to budge. The Pastor Saglier
had gone to the commandant and asked for permission
to go out as a *parlementaire* and beg of the Germans to
grant but two hours' cessation of the bombardment, that
the women and children might have the opportunity to get
away without the risk of being struck down as they went.
The admiral refused, and the ruthless devilry went on.
Then the Pastor sent an appeal to the Paris journals,
begging all who owned vehicles to send them to St. Denis
for the removal of the women and children. The response
was weak: there appeared not a solitary representative of

those ambulances whose members took delight in flags and
gave themselves to the vanities of brass buttons and fantastic
uniforms. About half a dozen private vehicles did present
themselves, and the sick and wounded were removed into
factories on the plain between St. Denis and Paris. Then
children followed and women great with child, and then
the other women, till the factories on the plain became like
caravanseries. Meanwhile a detachment of this ambulance
was engaged in carrying under cover the wounded struck
down at the guns, toiling with a zeal and energy that
merited better support. For that species of service the bold
national guards did not offer themselves: their sphere of
duty was the wine-shop. There they drank till their
debauch made them reckless, and they sallied out into the
streets, as often as not only to give the ambulance more
trouble with their worthless carcases.

In the afternoon I accompanied two German officers in
a ride beyond the foreposts in the direction of the Paris
gate of La Chapelle. In the course of the day the restrictions on passing out of Paris had been materially
relaxed, and the Avenue de Paris was thronged with the
outward bound. It seemed to me that if they could get out I
could get in, and quitting my companions I rode towards
the gate. But as I went, it appeared advisable to make
sure that I had the important document with me which
vouched for me being a British subject, and, consequently,
a " benevolent neutral." Alas, not anticipating the occurrence of such an opportunity I had left my passport in
my Margency quarters, and there was no alternative but
to postpone the attempt to enter Paris until the following
day. Next morning, that of 31st January, I started out
better equipped. Calling *en route* on M. Saglier the good
pastor of St. Denis, he hospitably asked me to have lunch.
I accepted the invitation, he bade his servant " bring in
the meat," and I made an assault with vigour and per-
severance on the rather lean and ragged roast joint
which was placed before me, the good cleric looking on
benignantly the while. I asked no questions till the edge

was off my appetite, when I inquired of the minister what I was eating.

"Well," said he, "of course you are eating horse, and a very choice joint it is. I knew the animal very well while he was alive. He was young and plump and of a grey colour, which, it is well known, indicates tenderness."

The pastor had been eating horseflesh for four months; not because he was forced to do so, but because he had a numerous dependency of poor people to aid whom he chose to practise economy.

Taking leave of the good clergyman I rode towards Paris along the great *chaussée* to the gate of La Chapelle, which I found barred. After the group of which I was one had waited for half an hour, an officer appeared and shouted "To the gate of St. Ouen!" St. Ouen was the next gate to the northward, and we all therefore made to the right, I being mounted beating the others who were all on foot. This gate was open and a gendarme was examining passes. I rode on slowly, looking straight between my horse's ears; and somehow no person in authority took any heed of me. As I rode down the Boulevard Ornano, I came upon sundry groups of more or less drunk national guards. One of those, as I passed him raised the shout "*À bas le Prussien!*" for which I own he had some reason since I wore a Prussian cap and paletot. He further complimented me by calling me "cochon" and "assassin." Others took up the cry, and matters were getting serious. The clamour was spreading and men tried to clutch hold of my bridle. I judged boldness to be the wisest policy; so, facing about, I pushed up to the man who had first shouted, proclaimed myself a harmless Englishman, and reproached my denouncer for molesting an inoffensive and peaceable wayfarer. The demon of cowardly and venomous suspicion had not yet been developed. A fortnight or so later, I should have thought myself fortunate to get clear off after having been marched back to the guard-house, half a dozen roughs on each bridle-rein, half as many more at each leg, and made to exhibit my passport to the officer on duty. But hunger is a wonderful agent in tending to influence men to concern themselves with their own business, and in keeping truculence in a state of dormancy. I cannot say, even after I had got rid of the citizens who had assailed me with cries of " cochon," that I much admired the aspect of the Boulevard Magenta. It was densely crowded with soldiers, and some of them might be unpleasantly patriotic. But no; they were all too much busied with their own affairs, getting their pay and drinking it while they discussed events.

Halting to go into a shop to make an inquiry—I was not familiar with the geography of Paris—I called a soldier of the Line who was strolling on the pavement to hold my horse. On coming out I had a little talk with him. Yes, he had had enough of it! They had nearly killed him, those terrible Prussians, and he was very hungry. When would the gates open for the introduction of food? I put my hand into my pocket to find a tip for the poor fellow, when I discovered that I had only Prussian money. I asked him whether he could do anything with a ten-groschen piece. It was silver, and might have had the devil's pitchfork stamped upon it instead of the Prussian eagle, for all that the hungry linesman cared. Three weeks later it was not wise to carry, much less to show, German money.

" Paris is utterly cowed, fairly beaten," so said the first Englishman I met. I had not been long enough inside, either to agree with or to dissent from him. What I did see was that Paris was orderly and decent. The streets were crowded, almost wholly with men in uniform. Civilians were comparatively rare, and the few seen wore an aspect of dejection. Many shops were open, but a considerable proportion were closed. It seemed possible to purchase everything except edibles. There was assuredly no lack of intoxicants; yet with the exception of my friends in the Boulevard Ornano, I saw scarcely a tipsy man. The food shops had a very sparse show in their windows. There were confitures, jellies, preserves, etc.; but solid comestibles were conspicuous by their rarity and probably also by their price. In one shop I saw several large shapes of stuff that looked like lard. When I asked what it was, I was told that it was horse-fat. The bakers' shops were closed, and the gratings were down before those of the butchers'. Sad with an exceeding great sadness—that was my impression of Paris long before I reached the American Legation; self-respecting, too, in her prostration; not blatant; not disposed to collect in jabbering crowds. Each man went his way with chastened face and listless gait.

After visiting the American Legation, where undisguised amazement was expressed at my appearance, I made my way to the little Hôtel St. Honoré in the Faubourg of the same name, and close to the British Embassy. I had filled my wallet chiefly with newspapers, and had stowed away for an exigency only a few slices of ham. When I reached my quarters the women-servants of the house asked permission to take the meagre plateful out and exhibit it as a curiosity to their neighbours; and visitors, attracted by the news, came straggling in and begged to see the long unaccustomed viand. The worthy landlord of the house, himself a Briton, had for his boarder throughout the siege Dr. (now Surgeon-General) Charles Gordon, the British medical Commissioner in Paris; and he took pride in asserting that the doctor had lived as well as any man in Paris. When dinner came it bore out the boasts of our Boniface. Positively there was a fowl; pretty well, so it was said, the last fowl in Paris. Our host had been offered eighty francs for the bird while yet it had its feathers on, but had refused the tempting offer; and so we had him for dinner with my ham as an accompaniment—only I stood out of participation in the ham so that the rarity might go the further with the others. There are advantages in being a Scotsman, one of which this siege of Paris had developed in a curious way. There was some store of oatmeal in Paris. Porridge is a principal and palatable resultant from oatmeal, and some Scotsmen not only eat but enjoy porridge. Thus Dr. Gordon, a Strathdon man, had supped his wholesome and frugal bicker of porridge every morning, while men not born to the appreciation of that delicacy were giving themselves internal uneasiness by swallowing the stuff which in the later days of the siege still imposed on people under the conventional name of bread. Yet another national dainty was our host equal to, in the shape of a glass of such Scotch whisky as I had not tasted for months.

In a once famous, now dingy restaurant, I found at supper several of my journalistic comrades who had remained in Paris during the long siege. They were eating steaks of horseflesh, followed by ragout of dog; and the few scraps of bread on the table consisted of a sort of dingy paste of which about one half was sand. Horseflesh, as both they and I had learned, was very fair eating; only one requires to get a little accustomed to it before one can wholly relish it. It has a curious sweetish taste, and the fat is scarce and not quite satisfactory. The Parisians during the siege had become quite connoisseurs in horseflesh · and it was universally recognised, as Pastor Saglier of St. Denis had already apprised me, that the tenderest joints were furnished by a young grey animal, and that the toughest meat was that of a no longer young chestnut horse. I did not try the dog; anyone who is curious as to this viand can easily kill a dog and make the experiment for himself. Some people averred that dog went best with mushrooms; others praised it eaten cold in a pie.

There needed no acuteness to discern to what a poignancy of wretchedness Paris had been reduced, before she had brought herself to endure the humiliation of surrender. That night she was alone with her grief and her hunger; not until the morrow came the relief and consolation which the sympathy of Great Britain so promptly forwarded to the capital of the ally with whom had been undergone the hardships and won the successes of the Crimean war. Wan, starved citizens crept by on the unlit boulevards, before and since the parade ground of luxury and sleek affluence. No cafés invited the promenader with brilliant splendour of illumination and garish lavishness of decoration; for there

were few promenaders to be enticed, there was no fuel to
furnish gas, and there were no dainty viands wherewith to
trick out the plate-glass windows. The gaiety, the profusion,
and the sinfulness of the Paris which one had known in the
days of the Second Empire, had given place to quiet uncom-
plaining dejection, to utter depletion, to a decorum at once
beautiful, startling, and pathetic. The hotels were all
hospitals. The Red Cross flag floated from almost every
house, bandaged cripples limped along the pavements, and
almost the only wheel traffic consisted in the interminable
procession of funerals.

Very strange and touching was the ignorance in regard to
the outside world. " I have seen three English newspapers
since September," said Dr. Gordon. " Is Ireland quiet? Is
Mr. Gladstone still Prime Minister? Is the Princess Louise
married?" Such were samples of the questions I had to
answer. The ignorance as to the conditions of the German
besiegers was almost equally complete. The day after the
negotiations for the capitulation began, Paris had been
somehow assured that the investing army had not eaten for
three days, and that it was Paris which was granting terms
rather than the "Prussians." I was continually asked
whether the latter had not been half-starved all through.
What had they done for quarters? Whether they did not
tremble in their boots at the mere name of the franc-tireurs?
Whether they were not half-devoured by vermin? Whether
the Prussian King still resided in Versailles?—the questioners
had not heard of his having been proclaimed German
Emperor ; and so on.

The great and beautiful feature of Paris under siege had
been the absence of crime. No murders, no robberies, but a
virtue in which there was really something pathetic. I had
intended to walk about the city most of the night so as to
make the most of my necessarily limited time. But before
ten o'clock my promenade had become almost a solitary one.
By nine the dim lights were extinguished in the kiosks, and
the petroleum was waning in the sparse street lamps. By
ten o'clock the world of Paris was left to darkness and to me ;

and so I went to bed. I woke up once in the night, and the dead silence made me for the moment imagine myself back in rural Margency.

It seemed that the pinch for food was more severe than ever, pending the result of the negotiations for its supply. From one who had paid the prices himself and had the precise figures down in black and white, I had the following list:—Two francs for a small shrivelled cabbage; one franc for a leek; forty-five francs for a medium-sized fowl; forty-five francs for a so-called rabbit—most probably a cat; twenty-five francs for a pigeon; twenty-two francs for a 2lb. chub; fourteen francs per lb. for stickleback; two francs per lb. for potatoes; forty francs per lb. for butter; twenty-five francs per lb. for cheese—very scarce. Meat other than horseflesh was absolutely not to be procured. I was assured that if I were to offer £50 down in bright shining gold for a veritable beef-steak, I should have no claimant for the money! The last cow that had changed hands had been bought for an ambulance, and fetched £80. The few beasts still left could not be bought. The bread was abominably bad; something between putty and chopped straw bound together with farina starch and a little flour. But its badness was not the worst thing about it—the difficulty was to get it at all. Gentle and simple had to wait their turn in the queue in the bitter cold outside the shops of the butchers and the bakers. On the following morning, as I rode eastwards through Paris to gain the train which would carry me into a country whence it was possible to despatch telegrams, I saw great throngs outside both, chiefly women, waiting in silent shivering in the cold.

VI.

THE CRUSHING OF THE COMMUNE.

Left London for Paris 19th May, 1871—Hindrance at St. Denis—Advice of
Crown Prince of Saxony—The " Cocotte Train "—Entered Paris, Sunday,
21st—The good lady of the kiosk—The War Ministry of the Commune
—" No, I have Children ! "—Dombrowski in the Château de la Muette—
Nonchalance in Shell Fire—The Scared Commandant — Dombrowski
marches—Fighting inside the Enceinte—Entry of Versaillists—Morning
of 22nd — Versaillist Plan of Campaign — Hard Fighting throughout
Week—Embrasure-making—The Target of a Firing Party—Quit Paris
Wednesday, 24th—Bringing Tidings to London—Return to Paris, 26th
— The Dead-hole in Père-Lachaise — MacMahon's Announcement on
28th : " I am absolute Master of Paris."

THE Franco-German War was over. I had witnessed the
great Kaiser's parade on the Longchamps racecourse on
the 1st of March, 1871 ; and the same afternoon had accompanied the German troops who marched down the Champs
Elysées into the Place de la Concorde and the wrecked gardens
of the Tuileries. A week later I had ridden behind the old
Emperor and the Crown Prince of Saxony as the former
reviewed the " Maas Armee " which the latter commanded,
drawn up on the plateau between Champigny and Brie,
among the grave mounds beneath which lay the Germans
and the Frenchmen who had fallen in the stubborn fighting
of Ducrot's great sortie on the east side of Paris. Then my
field work was done ; and I had hurried home to London to
begin the task which I had set myself of writing a book
describing what I had seen of the great conflict.

I was toiling ten hours a day at this undertaking when the
Commune broke out. Promptly the manager of the *Daily
News* dashed upon me in a swift hansom, and urged me with
all his force to start for Paris that same night. I declined ;
I was under contract to my publishers and I burned to see
my first book in print. For two months that peremptory
manager gave me innumerable bad quarters of an hour, for

he was not being served to his liking by the persons whom, in my default, he had commissioned to "do" the Commune for him. At length, on the afternoon of May 19th I finished the last revise of my book, and the same evening—to the great relief of my managerial friend, for a desperate crisis in Paris was clearly imminent—I left London by the Continental Mail.

In those troubled times the train service of the Northern of France railway was greatly dislocated, and it was nearly mid-day of the 20th when we halted in the St. Denis station. I foreboded no difficulty, since the halt at St. Denis was normal for ticket-collecting purposes; and I was chatting with a German officer of my acquaintance who commanded the detachment of the Kaiser Alexander Prussian Guard regiment in occupation of the St. Denis station. The collector serenely took up my ticket. There followed him to the carriage door two French gendarmes, who, with all the official consequentiality of their species, demanded to be informed of my nationality. I enlightened them on that point, and turned to continue the conversation with von Bergmann. But it seemed that the gendarmes were not done with me. They peremptorily ordered me to alight. I requested an explanation, and was told that no more foreigners were now permitted to enter Paris, as the fighting force of the Commune was understood to be directed chiefly by desperadoes not of French nationality. "But," said I, "I am a newspaper correspondent, not a fighting man." "*N'importe*," replied the senior gendarme, "you look, too, not unlike a military man. Anyhow, you must alight!"

"What does this mean, Bergmann?" I asked, when I had obeyed. "Surely you can do something for me, in charge as you and your fellows are of the station?" "No, my dear fellow," replied the Prussian officer: "we are here only to maintain order. Two days ago these swallow-tailed gentlemen came from Versailles, and our orders are not to interfere with them." The train went on, leaving me behind; then the senior gendarme came up to me and told me that I should have to return to Calais by the next outgoing train. A thought struck me, and I pleaded hard to be allowed to take instead a local train to Enghien-les-Bains, a few miles off near the forest of Montmorency, where von Bergmann told me was still residing the Crown Prince of Saxony to whose staff I had been attached during the siege of Paris. Bergmann added his persuasions to my solicitations and finally the gendarme thus far mitigated my sentence.

The Crown Prince was at luncheon when I reached the château in which he had his quarters. He roared with laughter when I told him how the French gendarme had served me. "Those people at Versailles," his Royal Highness explained, "have been leaving the mouth of the trap open all these weeks, and pretty nearly all the turbulent blackguards of Europe have walked into the snare. Now the Versaillists believe that all the blackguards are inside ; and since they are just about to begin business, they have stopped both ingress and egress. Still," he continued, musingly, "I am surprised that they did not let you in !" The Prince had something of a sardonic humour, and he made his point ; I, for my part, made him my bow in acknowledgment of his compliment. Presently the Prince remarked : "Mr. Forbes, when you were with us in the winter we used to think you rather a *rusé* and ingenious man ; but I fear that now, since you are no longer with us, you have become dull. Have you never heard the proverb that there are more ways of killing a pig than by cutting its throat ? There is a railway to Paris, my friend ; and there is also a *chaussée* to Paris. On the railway there are these French gendarmes ; on the *chaussée* there is only a picket of your friends of the Kaiser Alexander regiment, who have no orders to stop anyone. Now, you join us at luncheon ; then we shall have coffee and you will smoke one of those long corkscrew cigars which you may remember ; and in the evening you will take the 'cocotte train' here in Enghien. If the gendarmes at the St. Denis station haul you out a second time, make them a polite bow and walk into Paris by the *chaussée ;* or, for that matter, you can take the 'bus from St. Denis."

It was already dusk when I boarded the "cocotte train" ;

J

and I ensconced myself between two young ladies of gay and affable manners, who promised so to conceal me with their ample skirts when we should reach St. Denis that the gendarmes would be unable to unearth me. The train was full of the frail sisterhood of Paris, who were wont to pay afternoon visits to the German officers of the still-environing army and who were now returning to town. Fairly hidden as the ladies and I considered myself, the lynx-eyed gendarme detected me and I again had to alight. A commissary of police in the station courteously offered me quarters for the night, but assured me that my entrance into Paris was impossible. I declined his offer and went out into the street, where I found the German soldiers enforcing the old curfew laws. "Everybody must be indoors by nine o'clock," said the grizzled sergeant, "else I take them prisoners, and they are kept for the night and fined five francs in the morning." He did not interfere with me because I spoke German to him ; and I found a hay-loft where I slept. The charge for sitting for the night in a room in St. Denis was ten francs: beds were luxuries unattainable by casual strangers.

On the morning of the 21st I left St. Denis by road, and walked straight into Paris without hindrance. The national guards of La Chapelle were turning out for service as I passed through that suburb, and there seemed nothing to find fault with either in their appearance or their conduct. Certainly no reluctance was manifest on the part of the citizen-soldiers, but indeed the reverse. Paris I found very sombre, but perfectly quiet and orderly. It was the Sabbath morn, but no church-bells filled the air with their music. It was with a far different and more discordant sound that the air throbbed on this bright spring morning—the distant roar of the Versaillist batteries on the west and south-west of the enceinte. "That is Issy which gives !" quietly remarked to me the old lady in the kiosk at the corner of the Place de l'Opéra, as she sold me a rag dated the 22nd and printed on the 20th. I asked her how she could distinguish the sound of the Issy cannon from those in the batteries of the Bois de Boulogne. "Remember," she replied, " I have been listening now for many days to that delectable bicker, and have become a *connaisseuse.* The Issy gun-fire comes the sharper and clearer, as you may hear, because the fort stands high and nothing intervenes. The reports from the cannon in the Bois get broken up, for one thing, by the tree-trunks ; and then the sound has to climb over the enceinte, the railway viaduct, and the hill of Passy." She spoke as calmly as if she had been talking of the weather ; and it seemed to me, indeed, that all the few people who were about shared the good woman's nonchalance. Certainly there seemed nowhere any indication of apprehension or expectation that the Versaillist hand was to be on the Communist throat before the going down of that Sabbath sun.

I had a horse in Paris, which I had left there since the days of the armistice. It was the same noble steed on which I had ridden in through the gate of St. Ouen, the " first outsider " into Paris after the capitulation, on which occasion the hungry Bellevillites had gazed upon the plump beast with greedy eyes. My earliest quest now was for this animal. I found it, but there was an armed sentry on the stable. The Commune had requisitioned the horse, and the stable-keeper had resisted the requisition on the ground that it belonged to a foreigner. The matter had been temporarily compromised by the posting of a sentry over the animal until the authorities should have maturely weighed the grave question. The sentry declined to depart when I civilly entreated him, nor would he allow me to take out the horse ; so in the mean-time I had to leave the matter as it stood. From the stable I went to the War Ministry of the Commune, on the south side of the river. The utter absence of red-tape and bureau-cracy there, was quite a shock to the mental system of the Briton. I remember having been pervaded by the same sensation when, years later, I went to see the late General Sherman in the Washington War Department. Ascending a staircase—in Paris, not in Washington—I entered a great room full of sergeants and private soldiers bustling to and fro. Unheeded I passed into an inner room, where I found the man whom I wanted writing among a number of other men in uniform and a constantly changing throng of comers and goers. "Can I see the Chief-of-Staff?" I asked. "Of course you can—come with me!" We went into a third room, a fine apartment with furniture in the style of the First Empire: officers swarmed here from commandants to lieutenants. Privates came in and had a word, and went away. Amid the bustle there was a certain order, and also, seemingly, a certain thoroughness. Without delay I was presented to an officer, who, I was told, was the *sous-chef* of the Staff. I told him that I desired to witness the military operations in the capacity of a correspondent. With a bow he turned to a staff-lieutenant and bade him write the order. The lieutenant set to work at once. He asked me whether I wanted an order for the exterior as well as for the interior operations, and said "*bon*" approvingly when I told him that I wanted an order which would allow me to go anywhere and see everything. The *sous-chef* signed it with the signature "Lefebre Toncier;" told me if ever I needed any favour or information to come to him; and made me a civil bow. I think I may reckon that this was the last permit issued to a correspondent and signed by Communist authority.

General Dombrowski was the last of the many generalissimos of the Commune; he had held the command for about a day and a half. His headquarters, I was told, were away out to the west in the Château de la Muette, a little way inside the enceinte and close to the railway-station of Passy on the ceinture line. I went to the cab-stand in the Place de la Concorde and bade the first cabman drive me to the château. "No, monsieur; I have children!" was the reply. I got a less timid *cocher* who agreed to drive me to the beginning of the Grande Rue de Passy. As we passed the Pont de Jéna the Communist battery on the Trocadéro began to give fire. Mont Valérien replied. Shell after shell from that fortress fell on the grassy slope on which I had seen the German soldiers, on their entry into Paris on March 1st, lie down and drink their fill of its beauties. One shell felled a lamp-post on the steps close by, and burst upon the pavement. My driver struck, and very nearly carried me back with him in his hurry to be out of what he evidently considered an unpleasant neighbourhood. There was nothing for me but to alight, and to go on foot up the Grande Rue. Here there was hardly any resident population, but a large colony of shell holes. National guards, sailors, and franc-tireurs had quartered themselves in the abandoned houses, and lounged idly on the sidewalks in comparative shelter. There were nowhere any symptoms of uneasiness, although the shells were dropping into the vicinity with great freedom. At the further end of the street I turned to the right through a large gateway into a short avenue bordered by fine trees, at the end of which I entered the Château de la Muette. Dombrowski gave me a most hearty and cordial greeting, and at once offered me permission to attach myself to his staff permanently, if I could accept the position as it disclosed itself. "We are in a deplorably comic situation here," said he, with a smile and a shrug, "for the fire is both hot and continuous!"

Dombrowski was a neat, dapper little fellow of some five feet four, dressed in a plain dark uniform with very little gold lace. His face was shrewd—acuteness itself; he looked as keen as a file, and there was a fine frank honest manner with him, and a genial heartiness in the grip of his hand. He was the sort of man you take to instinctively, and yet there were ugly stories about him. He wore a slight moustache, and a rather long chin-tuft which he was given to caressing as he talked. He spoke not much English but was very fluent in German. His staff consisted of eight or ten officers, chiefly plain young fellows who seemed thoroughly up to their work, and with whom, not to be too pointed, soap and water seemed not so plentiful as was their consummate coolness. Dombrowski ate, read, and talked all at once, while one could hardly hear his voice for the din of the cannonade and the yell of the shells. He showed great anxiety to know whether I could tell him anything as to the likelihood of German intervention, and it struck me that he would be very glad to see such a solution of the strange problem. We had got to the salad when a battalion commandant, powder-grimed and flushed, rushed into the dining-room and exclaimed in great agitation that the Versaillist troops were streaming inside the enceinte at the gate of Billancourt, which his command had been holding. The cannonade from Issy had been so fierce that his men had all got under shelter; and when the Versaillists came suddenly on and his men had to expose themselves and deliver musketry fire, the shells, he said, fell so thick and deadly that they bolted, and then the Versaillists had carried the porte and now held it. His men had gone back in a panic. He had beaten them— yes—"*Sacré nom,*" etc.—with the flat of his sword until his arm ached, but he had not been successful in arresting the panic and his battalion had now definitively forsaken the enceinte. The Versaillists were massing in large numbers to strengthen the force that had already carried the gate of Billancourt. Dombrowski waited quietly until the gasping commandant had exhausted himself, then handed him a glass of wine with a smile; turned with a serene nod to his salad and went on eating it composedly and reflectively. At length he raised his head, and ordered in a strong voice—

"Send to the Ministry of Marine for a battery of seven-pounders; call out the cavalry, the *tirailleurs* [of some place or other; I did not catch where], and send forward such and such battalions of national guards. Let them be ready by seven o'clock. I shall attack with them, and lead the attack myself."

The Ministry of Marine, I may observe, had been turned into an arsenal. It was a curious sign of the time that the officer to whom Dombrowski dictated this order, like himself, a Pole, did not know where to find the Ministry of Marine. Directions having been given to him as to its locality, the lieutenant then suggested that he might not be able to obtain a whole battery.

"Bring what you can then," exclaimed Dombrowski; "two, three, four guns—as many as you can, and see that the tumbrils are in order. Go and obey!"

"Go and obey!" was the formula of this peremptory, dictatorial, and yet genial little man. He had a splendid commanding voice and one might have judged him accustomed to dictation, for he would break off to converse and take up the thread again, as if he had been the chief clerk of a department.

While Dombrowski was eating his prunes after his salad —like most Poles, he seemed a miscellaneous feeder—there came bustling in a fussy commandant with a grievance. His grievance was thus expressed: "General, I have been complained against because I have too large a staff, and have been ordered to bring the return to you." Dombrowski silently took from him the return and read it. Then he broke out in passion. "A commandant!" he exclaimed, "and with a staff of ten officers! What!" Here he rose and swept his arm round the table with a gesture of indignation. "Look, citizen commandant! Here am I, the general, and behold my staff, nine hard-working men; and you, a commandant, have ten loafers! I allow you one secretary; go and obey!" and the discomfited commandant cleared out.

The shell fire was increasing. Dombrowski told me that the Château de la Muette belonged to a friend of M. Thiers, and that, therefore, although it was known to be his—Dombrowski's—headquarters, there were orders that it should be somewhat spared. All I have to say is, that if there were indeed any efforts made to spare the château the Versaillist gunners were shocking bad shots. While we sat one shell came through the wall bounding the avenue; another struck the corner of the house so hard that I thought it was through the wall. Dombrowski's nerves were strong, and he had trained his staff to perfection. When this shell burst he was speaking to me. I started. I don't think his voice vibrated a single chord. The officers sitting round the table noticed the explosion no more than if it had been a snapping-bonbon at a ball supper. A soldier-waiter was filling my cup with coffee. The spout of the coffee-pot was on the edge of the cup.

There was no jar; the man's nerves were like iron. There was certainly good, quiet, firm undemonstrative stuff here, whatever there might have been elsewhere. Dombrowski's adjutant took me upstairs to the roof where there was an observatory. The staircase and upper rooms had been very freely knocked about by the shell fire, notwithstanding the friendship of M. Thiers for the owner of the château. The observatory, which was constructed of thick planking, was nevertheless riddled with chassepôt bullets; and when I showed myself incautiously on the leads I drew fire with an alacrity so surprising, that I was not in the slightest degree ashamed to make a precipitate retreat.

The park of the Château de la Muette sloped down to the enceinte in front of Passy. One could scarcely see the enceinte for the foliage. Beyond the enceinte was a belt of clearing, then came the dense greenery of the Bois de Boulogne, and behind this green fringe was the bed of the great lake. From this fringe of wood great isolated puffs of smoke were darting out. Those were from single cannon. I saw no massed battery. But there were clearly at intervals single cannon in small emplacements at distances from the enceinte of from 400 to 500 paces. From the edge of the fringe also, behind little trenches at the throats of the drives, smaller puffs spurted from the chassepôts of Versaillist marksmen trying to pick off the Communists on the enceinte and on the advanced horn-works in front of the gates of Passy and Auteuil. Just above the gate of Passy the Communists had a battery on the enceinte which was firing steadily and with good effect. The gate of Passy was not much injured and might have been stormed by a resolute forlorn hope, were it not for the earthen outwork thrown up during the Prussian siege. The gate of Auteuil and the enceinte for some distance on each side were utterly ruined. This Dombrowski did not attempt to deny. But he pointed out that the advanced earthwork was held—and strongly held; not an obstacle, perhaps, it seemed to me, to thwart men bent on gaining an object or losing their lives, but quite sufficient to all appearance, to keep the cautious Versaillists from exposing themselves in the open on the way to it. Farther south, by the gate of Billancourt and round to the Seine, the enceinte was no great things to boast of. Certainly no man needed wings to get inside thereabouts. In proof of this, since I had joined him, Dombrowski, as I have related, had received tidings that the Versaillists had carried that gate.

There was a good deal more of risk than amusement in remaining in the observatory; and I descended presently to the ground floor. Dombrowski was standing sword in hand, dictating three orders at the same time. He stopped to ask me what I thought of the prospect I had looked down upon from the roof. I could not conscientiously express the opinion that it was reassuring from the Communist point of view. "I am just dictating an order," said Dombrowski, "which will inform Paris that I am abandoning the enceinte from the Porte d'Auteuil to the river. If you are a military man you must recognise the fact, that our loss of Fort Issy has made virtually untenable that section of the continuous line of fortification of which I speak. Its province was to co-operate with, not to resist, Fort Issy. For several days past I have foreseen the necessity of which I am now informing Paris, and I have prepared a second line of defence, of which the railway viaduct defines the contour and which I have made as strong as the enceinte and more easily tenable. Yes; the Versaillists are in possession of that gate you heard the flurried commandant talk of. They may have it and welcome; the possession of it will not help them very much. But all the same I don't mean to let them keep their hold of it without giving them some trouble; and so I am going to make an attack on them to-night. As like as not they will fall back from their occupancy of to-day, and then they will have their work to do over again to-morrow. But I am not going to fight with serious intent to retrieve this condemned section of enceinte, as the order which I have been dictating for publication will show; but merely, as I may say, for fighting's sake. There is plenty of fight still in our fellows, especially when I am leading them."

I could not for the life of me make up my mind then, nor have I done so to this day, whether Dombrowski's cheerful words were mere *blague* or whether the little man was really in dead earnest. With a promise from him that he would not start on his enterprise without me, I went into a side room to write a few lines for my newspaper. I had finished and was instructing the soldier messenger whom Dombrowski's adjutant was good enough to place at my disposal, where to deliver the packet containing my message, when an urgent summons came to me to join the general. The little man I found on the outside of a very lofty charger, which was dancing about the lawn on its hind legs. For me, alas! there was no mount, big or little; my horse was in the stable behind the Rue Faubourg St. Honoré with that relentless sentry standing over him. Messenger after messenger had come hurrying in from the Point du Jour quarter entreating for immediate succour, as the holders of the positions thereabouts were being hard pushed. The cannonade and fusillade from the Seine all the way to the Neuilly gate and probably beyond, continued to increase in warmth as we hastened down the Rue Mozart. The Versaillist batteries were in full roar; and it was not possible, even if some guns still remained undismounted on the enceinte, to respond effectively to their steady and continuous fire of weighty metal. Some reinforcements were waiting for Dombrowski on the Quai d'Auteuil, partly sheltered by the houses of the landward side of the quay from the fire which was lacerating the whole vicinity. The tidings which greeted the little general were unpleasant when he rode into the Institution de Ste. Périne, which was temporarily occupied as a kind of local headquarters. It was the Commandant of the 93rd national guard battalion who had come to the Château de la Muette in the afternoon to tell Dombrowski how his men had been driven from the gate of Billancourt. From what I could hurriedly gather there had subsequently been a kind of rally. National guards had lined the battered parapet of the enceinte between the gates of Billancourt and Point du Jour, and farther northward to and beyond the St. Cloud gate. For some time they had clung to the positions with considerable tenacity under a terrible fire, but then had been forced back with serious loss, mainly by the close and steady shooting of the Versaillist artillery from the breaching batteries about Boulogne and those in the more distant Brimborion. The St. Cloud gate as well as that of the Point du Jour, had followed the Billancourt gate into the hands of Versaillist troops who having occupied the enceinte in force and the adjacent houses inside the enceinte, had pushed strong detachments forward to make reconnaissances up the Rues Marois and Billancourt, one of which bodies at least had penetrated as far as the railway viaduct but had been driven back.

Dombrowski smiled as this news was communicated to him ; and I thought of his " second line of defence," and of his assurance that " the situation was not compromised." By this time it was nearly nine o'clock, and it seemed to me that the Versaillists must have got cannon upon or inside the enceinte, the fire came so hot about the Institution de Ste. Périne. Dombrowski and his staff were very active and daring, and his troops seemed in good heart enough. There was some cheering on the order to advance, and the troops, consisting chiefly of francs-tireurs and men wearing a zouave dress so far as I could discern through the gloom, moved out from behind the railway embankment into the Rue de la Municipalité—that was its name then, but I believe it is now called the Rue Michel. A couple of guns—only field guns, I believe—opened fire on the Ceinture railway to the left of the Rue de la Municipalité, and under their cover Dombrowski's infantrymen now debouched with a short-lived rush. Almost immediately after, however, utter disorganisation ensued, the result of a hot and close rifle fire which seemingly came chiefly from over a wall which I was told enclosed the Cimetière des Pauvres. The Communists broke right and left. One forlorn hope I dimly saw spring forward and go at the corner of the cemetery wall in the angle formed by a little cross-street, under the passionate leadership of a young staff-officer whom I had noticed in the Château de la Muette at dinner time. There was a few moments' brisk cross-fire; then the Communist spurt died away and the fugitives came running back, but without their gallant leader. Some affirmed that Dombrowski himself took part in this rash, futile attempt; but the locality was too warm for me to be able to speak definitely on this point. Meanwhile there seemed to be almost hand-to-hand fighting going on all along the exterior of the railway embankment. I could hear the incessant whistle and patter of the bullets and the yells and curses of the Communists, not a few of whom evidently owed the courage they displayed to alcoholic influence. Every now and then there came a short rush, then a volley which arrested the rush, and then a stampede back into cover. Soon after ten it was obvious that the fight was nearly out of the Communists. Dombrowski I had long since lost sight of. One officer told me that he had been killed close to the grave-yard wall; another, that his horse had been shot under him and that the speaker had last seen the daring little fellow fighting with his sword against a Versaillist marine who was lunging at him with the bayonet. After the Commune was stamped out, accusations of treachery to the cause he was professing to serve were made against Dombrowski. All I can say is that so far as I saw of him, he bore himself as a true man and a gallant soldier, and, seeing that before the Commune ended he had lost his life in the struggle, it seems the reverse of likely, as was averred, that he had sold himself to the Versaillists. He came of a fighting race. An ancestor of his was one of the gallant Polish leaders under the first Napoleon.

Then came a sudden and apparently general panic and I was glad to make good my retreat behind " the second line of defence," which was not easily recognisable as a line of defence at all, and concerning which I suspected that Dombrowski had been gasconading. Once behind the railway, the Communist troops held their ground for some time with a show of stiffness. Occasional outbursts of firing indicated desultory attacks

made by detached parties of Versaillists; but those flashes of
strife gradually died away and about eleven o'clock the quietness had become so marked, that I thought the work was over
for the night and that Dombrowski's anticipations had been
at least partly realised. The pause was deceptive. The
Versaillists must have been simply holding their hands for
the time, to make the blow the heavier when it should fall.
No doubt they had their combinations to mature in other
directions—no doubt they were pouring in force into the
area between the enceinte and the Ceinture railway. They
were comparatively quiet for their own purposes while they
were doing this—lining the enceinte and packing the
thoroughfares with troops and artillery. We could hear in the
distance behind us the *générale* being beaten in the streets of
Paris. A staff-officer who spoke English as if it were his
mother tongue, came to me and told me how he mistrusted
the pause, and expressed his fear that the supreme hour had
come at last. It must have been near midnight when a
strong fire of cannon and musketry opened from the enceinte.
At the same time there came on the wind the sound of heavy
firing from the northward. I heard someone shout "We are
surrounded! The Versaillists are pouring in by the gates of
Auteuil, Passy, and La Muette!" This was enough. A wild
panic set in. The cry rose of "Sauve qui peut!" mingled
with yet more ominous shouts of "Nous sommes trahis!"
Arms were thrown down, accoutrements were stripped off, and
everyone bolted at the top of his speed, many officers taking
part in the *débâcle.* I came on one party—a little detachment
of franc-tireurs—standing fast behind the projection of a
house, and calling out that all the chiefs had run away and
had left their men. Whether this was the case as regarded
the higher commands I could not tell. I do not believe that
Dombrowski was the man to run, nor any of his staff. But
certainly none of them was to be seen. There was the cry,
too, that there was a Versaillist inrush from the south. And
so men surged, and struggled, and blasphemed confusedly up
the quay of Passy in wild confusion, shot and shell chasing them
as they fled. In the extremity of panic mingled with rage,

men blazed off their pieces indiscriminately and struck at one another with the clubbed butts. Upon the battalions coming up in support there surged the rushing tide of fugitives, thus imparting their panic to the newcomers and carrying them away with them in the torrent.

There was an interval of distracted turmoil during which in the darkness and in my comparative ignorance of that part of Paris, I had no idea for a time whither I was being carried in the throng of fugitives. The road was wide, and I was able to discern that it was bounded on the right by the Seine ; it was by after-reference to the map that I found the thoroughfare we had been following was the Quay of Passy. After a while I struck out of the press up a silent way to the left, and for a time wandered about in utter ignorance of my whereabouts. I could hardly tell how it came about that in the first flicker of the dawn I found myself on the Trocadéro. There was a dense fog which circumscribed narrowly my sphere of vision, and I knew only that I was standing on sward in an utter solitude. A few steps brought me into the rear of a battery facing westward, from which all the guns had been carried away except one which had been dismounted, evidently by a hostile shell, and it now lay among the shattered fragments of its carriage. Close by, no doubt killed by the explosion of the shell which had wrecked the gun, were two or three dead Communist gunners. As it became lighter and the fog was slowly dispersing, the slopes of the Trocadéro disclosed themselves on my left, and I realised that I must be standing in the Trocadéro battery of which I had heard Dombrowski speak on the previous afternoon. Looking westward along the Avenue de l'Empereur— now the Avenue Henri Martin—I saw a battery of artillery advancing up it at a walk, with detachments of sailors abreast of it on each sidewalk. I had not to ask myself whether these troops advancing with a deliberation so equable, could belong to the beaten and panic-stricken levies of the Commune. No! that could not be. They were, for sure, Versaillist troops coming on to take possession of the Trocadéro position. Indeed, had there been no other evidence, their method of announcing themselves by half a dozen chassepôt bullets fired at the lone man standing by the battery, would have been conclusive. I took the hint to quit, and started off abruptly in the direction of the Champs Elysées. I came out on the beautiful avenue by the Rue des Chaillots about midway between the Arch of Triumph and the Rond Point. And lo! round the noble pile which commemorates French valour there stood in close order several battalions of soldiers in red breeches. Thus far then, at all events, had penetrated the Versaillist invasion of Paris in the young hours of the 22nd. The French regulars were packed in the Place de l'Étoile as densely as had been the Bavarians on the day of the German entry some three months earlier. No cannon fire was directed on the Versaillist masses from the great Communist battery on the Place de la Concorde end of the gardens of the Tuileries; but men in national guard uniform were showing themselves about it and now and then sending a rifle-bullet into the ranks of the Versaillists by the Arch. The latter, for their part, seemed to be taking things very deliberately, and to be making quite sure of their ground before advancing farther. They had a field-battery in action a little way below the Arch, which swept the Champs Elysées very thoroughly. I saw several shells explode about the Place de la Concorde, and was very glad when I had run the gauntlet safely and had reached the further side of the great avenue. I was making towards the Parc Monceau when a person I met told me that Versaillist troops marching from the Arch along the Avenue de la Reine Hortense (now the Avenue Hoche) had come upon Communists throwing up a battery, and had saved them the trouble of completing it by taking it from them at the point of the bayonet. Here I very nearly got shut in, for as we talked there was a shout, and looking westward I saw that a strong force of Versaillists with artillery at its head, was marching along the Avenue Friedland towards the Boulevard Haussmann. I was just in time to dodge across its front, and tracking the force by side-streets I found that it pressed on steadily, firing now and then but not heavily, until it reached the open space at the upper end of the Boulevard Haussmann, in front of the Pépinière Barracks. This was a singularly commanding position, and thus early one could fathom the tactics of the Versaillists Occupying in strong force and with a numerous artillery certain central points from each of which radiated several straight thoroughfares in different directions, their design clearly was to cut Paris up into sections, isolating the sections one from another by sweeping with cannon-fire the bounding streets. From this position at the Pépinière, for example, they had complete command of the Boulevard Haussmann down to the foot of it at the intersection of the Rue Taitbout, and of the Boulevard Malesherbes down to the Madeleine, thus securing access to the Grand Boulevards and to the Rue Royale, by descending which could be taken in reverse the Communist battery at its foot facing the Place de la Concorde. Desirous of seeing what might be occurring in other parts of the city, I made my way by devious paths in the direction of the Palais Royal. Shells seemed to be bursting all over Paris. They were time-fuse shells, and I could see many of them explode in white puffs high in air. Several fell on and about the Bourse while I was passing it, and the boulevards and their vicinity were silent and deserted save for small detachments of national guards hurrying backwards and forwards. It was difficult to tell whether the Communists meant to stand or fall back; but certainly everywhere barricades were being hastily thrown up. All those I evaded until I reached the Place du Palais Royal. Here two barricades were being constructed, one across the throat of the Rue St. Honoré, the other across the Rue de Rivoli between the Louvre and the hotel of the same name. For the latter material was chiefly furnished by a great number of mattresses of Sommier-Tucker manufacture which were being hurriedly pitched out of the windows of the warehouse; and also by mattresses from the barracks of the Place du Carrousel. The Rue St. Honoré barricade was being formed of furniture, omnibuses and cabs; and in the construction of it I was compelled to assist. I had been placidly standing in front of the Palais Royal, when a soldier approached me and ordered me to lend a hand to the work. I declined, and turned to walk away; whereupon the soldier brought his bayonet down to the charge in unpleasantly close proximity to my person. This was an argument which in the circumstances I could not resist, and I accompanied him to where a red-sashed member of the Committee of the Commune was strutting to and fro superintending the operations. To him I addressed strong remonstrances, explaining that I was a neutral and exhibiting the pass I had received from the War Department the day before. He bluntly refused to recognise this document, and offered me the alternatives of being shot or going to work. I was fain to accept the latter. Even if you have to do a thing by compulsion, it is pleasant to try to do it in a satisfactory manner; and observing that an embrasure had been omitted in the construction of the barricade notwithstanding that there was a gun in its rear, I devoted my energies to remedying this defect. The Committeeman was good enough to express such approbation of the amendment I had made, that when the embrasure was finished he very civilly allowed me to go away. Looking up the Rue de Rivoli I noticed that the Communists had erected a great battery at its junction with the Place de la Concorde, armed with cannon which were in action, firing apparently up the Champs Elysées. Leaving the vicinity of the Palais Royal I went in the direction of the new Opera House. On reaching the boulevard I discovered that the Versaillists must have gained the Madeleine between which and their position at the Pépinière no obstacle intervened; for they had thrown up across the Boulevard de la Madeleine a barricade of trees and casks. The Communists, on their side, had a barricade composed chiefly of provision-waggons across the boulevard, at the head of the Rue de la Paix. For the moment no firing was going on; and as it was getting towards noon I determined to try to reach my hotel in the Cité d'Antin and there obtain some breakfast.

Leaving the boulevard by the Rue Taitbout, I found my

K

progress hampered by a crowd of people as I approached the foot of the Boulevard Haussmann. By strenuous pushing and shoving I got to the front of this throng, to witness a curious spectacle. There was a crowd behind me. Opposite to me, on the further side of the Boulevard Haussmann, another crowd faced me. Between the two crowds was the broad boulevard, actually alive with the rifle-bullets sped by the Versaillists from their position about a thousand yards higher up. On the iron shutters of the shops across the foot of the boulevard—shops in the Rue Taitbout—the bullets were pattering like hailstones, some dropping back flattened, others penetrating. This obstacle of rifle-fire it was which had given rise to the massing of the crowds on each side. Nor were the wayfarers thus given pause without obvious cause, for in the space separating the one crowd from the other lay several dead and wounded who had dared and had suffered. My hunger overcame my prudence, and I ran across without damage save to a coat-tail through which a bullet had passed making a hole in my tobacco-pouch. A lad who followed me was not so fortunate; he got across indeed, but with a bullet-wound in his thigh.

Having ordered breakfast at my hotel in the Cité d'Antin, a recessed space close to the foot of the Rue Lafayette, I ran out to the junction of that street with the Boulevard Haussmann, just in time to witness a fierce fight for the barricade across the latter about the intersection of the Rue Tronchet. The Communists stood their ground resolutely although falling fast under the overwhelming fire, until a battalion of Versaillist marines made a rush and carried the barricade. It was with all the old French *élan* that the marines leaped upon and over the obstacle, and lunged with their sword-bayonets at the few defenders who would not give ground. Those who had not waited for the end fell back towards me, dodging behind lamp-posts and in doorways, and firing wildly as they retreated. They were pursued by a brisk fusillade from the captured barricade, which was fatal to a large proportion of them. Two lads standing near me were shot down. A bullet struck the lamp-post which constituted my shelter, and fell flattened on the asphalt. A woman ran out from the corner of the Rue Chaussée d'Antin, picked up the bullet, and walked coolly back clapping her hands with glee.

After eating and having written for a couple of hours, I determined to make for the Northern Railway terminus and attempt to get a letter to my paper sent out. One saw strange things on the way. What, for instance, was this curious fetish-like ceremony going on in the Rue Lafayette at the corner of the Rue Laffitte? There were a waggon, a mounted spahi black as night, and an officer with his sword drawn. A crowd stood around, and in the centre of the strange scene was a blazing fire of papers. Were they burning the ledgers of the adjacent bank, or the title-deeds of the surrounding property? No. The papers of a Communist battalion it was which were thus being hurriedly destroyed, no doubt that they should not bear witness against its members. The little episode was a significant indication of the beginning of the end. Nor were other tokens wanting, for English passports were being anxiously sought for. At the terminus the unpleasant report was current that the Prussians were shunting at St. Denis all the trains leaving Paris, and were preventing everybody from passing their lines. There was but one chance. I suborned a railway employé of acute aspect to get out of Paris by walking through the railway tunnel, and, should he reach St. Denis, to give my letter to a person there whom I could trust to forward it. My emissary put the missive cheerfully in his boot and departed, having promised to come to my hotel at 8 p.m. and report his success or failure. I never saw him or heard of him any more.

On my way back from the Gare du Nord I met with an experience which came near being tragical. Hearing firing in the direction of the Church of Notre Dame de Lorette, I left the Rue Lafayette for the Rue Châteaudun. When I reached the open space in the centre of which stands the beautiful church, I found myself inside an extraordinary triangle of barricades. There was a barricade across the end of the Rue St. Lazare, another across the end of the Rue Lorette, and a third

K 2

between the church and the front of the Place looking into the Rue Châteaudun. The peculiarity of the dispositions consisted in this—that each of these barricades could either be enfiladed or taken in reverse by fire directed on any or all of the others, so that the defenders were exposing themselves to fire on flanks and rear as well as from front. I took up a protected position in the church porch to watch the outcome of this curious state of things. But the officer in command happening to notice me, approached and ordered me to pick up the musket of a man who had just been bowled over, and to take a hand in the defence of the position. I refused, urging that I was a foreigner and a neutral. He would by no means accept the excuse, swearing angrily that he too was a foreigner yet was fain to fight, and giving me the choice of the cheerful alternatives of forthwith complying or being incontinently shot. I did not believe him, and, indeed, laughed at him. Thereupon he shouted for four of his men to come and place me up against the wall of the church, and then act as a firing party. They had duly posted me and were proceeding to carry out the programme to its inconvenient ending, when suddenly a rush of Versaillist troops came upon and over the Rue St. Lazare barricade. Thereupon the defenders precipitately evacuated the triangle, the firing-party accompanying their comrades. I remained, not caring for the society I should have to accompany if I fled; but I presently came to regard my fastidiousness as folly, for several shots from Versaillist rifles came too near to be pleasant. One bullet went through my hat; and in a twinkling I was in Versaillist grips and instantly charged with being a Communard. The people in the red breeches set about sticking me up against the church wall again, when fortunately I saw a superior officer and appealed to him. I was bidden to hold up my hands. They were not particularly clean, but there were no gunpowder stains on the thumbs and forefingers. Those stains were, it seemed, the brand marking the militant Communard, and my freedom from them just pulled me through. It was a "close call"; but then a miss is as good as a mile.

Late in the afternoon the drift of the retreating Communists seemed to be in the direction of Montmartre, whence their guns were firing over the city on the Versaillist artillery now in great measure massed on the Trocadéro. The Versaillists, for their part, were also moving deliberately in the Montmartre direction, and before dusk they had reached the Place de l'Europe at the back of the St. Lazare terminus. From this point on the north they held with their advanced forces a definite line down the Rue Tronchet to the Madeleine. They were maintaining their fire along the Boulevard Haussmann, and from their battery at the Madeleine they had shattered the Communist barricade on the Boulevard des Capucines at the head of the Rue de la Paix. The Communists were undoubtedly in part demoralised; yet they were working hard everywhere in the construction of barricades.

About eight p.m. the firing had died out almost everywhere, and for an interval there was an all but dead calm. What a strange people were those Parisians! It was a lovely evening, and the scenes in the narrow streets of the Rue Lafayette reminded me of the aspect of the "down-town" residential streets of New York on a summer Sunday evening. Men and women were placidly sitting by their street doors, gossiping easily about the events and rumours of the day. The children played around the barricades; their mothers scarcely looked up at the far-away sound of the *générale*, or when the distant report of the bursting of a shell came on the soft night wind. Yet on that light wind was borne the smell of fresh blood, and corpses were littering the pavements not three hundred yards away.

Shortlived was the halcyon interval of quietude in Paris during the late evening of Monday, May 22nd. Before midnight, as I lay in my clothes on a sofa in the Hôtel de la Chaussée d'Antin, I could not sleep for the bursting of the shells on the adjacent Boulevard Haussmann. In the intervals of the shell-fire was audible the steady grunt of the mitrailleuses, and I could distinctly hear the pattering of the bullets as they rained on and ricocheted off the asphalt of the boulevard. There came in gusts throughout the night the noise of a more distant fire, the whereabouts of which it was impossible to locate.

The dismal din, so perplexing and bewildering, continued at intervals all through the night; and daybreak of the 23rd brought no cessation of the noise. Turning out in the chilly dawn, and from the hazardous corner of the Rue de la Chaussée d'Antin looking cautiously up the Boulevard Haussmann, I saw before me a weird spectacle of desolation and slaughter. Corpses strewed the broad roadway and lay huddled in the recesses of doorways. Some of the bodies were partially shrouded by the foliage of the branches of trees which had been torn off by the storm of shot and shell. Lamp-posts, kiosks, and tree-stems were shattered or upset in all directions. The Versaillists, at least hereabouts, had certainly not advanced during the night: indeed it seemed that they had in a measure drawn back, and that the Communists were now holding positions which the day before they had abandoned. The big battery of the former in front of the Pépinière Barracks at the head of the Boulevard Haussmann, a position beyond which the Versaillists had attained to on the previous day, was still, so far as that boulevard was concerned, the apparent limit of their occupation in force, although they held as an advanced post the slight barricade which they had taken the day before across the boulevard and about half-way down it, at the intersection of the Rue Tronchet. Over this outpost the battery at the Pépinière was steadily sending the fire of cannon and mitrailleuses towards the eastern end of the boulevard, where a few national guards still prowled about behind casual cover, firing a shot now and then into the intermediate barricade. Communist sergeants were running about the side-streets and the Rue Lafayette, ordering the inmates of houses to close their windows but to open their shutters—this, no doubt, as a precaution against Versaillist sympathisers firing down on the insurgents from the house-fronts. It was to be noticed that there had been no attempt anywhere on the part of the Communists to occupy the houses and fire from them on the advancing Versaillists. They had been content to utilise the shelter of barricades and such cover as the streets casually afforded. The Versaillists, on the other hand, were reported to be freely occupying the houses and to be firing down from the windows. This I did not yet know of my own knowledge; but I did know that they were for the most part extremely cautious in exposing themselves; and that, except in isolated instances, they had shown little enterprise and had done scarcely anything in the way of hand-to-hand fighting.

About six o'clock I went for a walk—not an unmixed pleasure just at the moment, nor to be indulged in without considerable circumspection. Getting into the Boulevard des Capucines I found it still held by strong bodies of national guards, a large proportion of whom were very drunk notwithstanding the early hour, while all were quite at their ease and in lively spirits. The cross-barricade between the head of the Rue de la Paix and the corner of the Place de l'Opéra, which had been shattered the day before by artillery fire from the Versaillist position at the Madeleine, had been restored, strengthened, and armed with cannon and mitrailleuses. Nay, more: I was assured by Communist officers that the night-firing one had heard had mainly been directed by them from this barricade, and that it had compelled the Versaillist withdrawal from the Madeleine position. There was a certain confirmation of this in the fact that the Grand Boulevards were now quite unharassed by Versaillist fire, save for occasional vagrant obuses which appeared to come from the Trocadéro direction. I did myself the honour to partake of morning coffee with an hospitable but particularly tipsy squad of national guardsmen. They had been fighting, they said between their yawns, through the greater part of the night; and they owned, without any great concern, that there had been not a few casualties among them during the hours of darkness. Their women—I do not imagine that many of those were linked to their men by the bond of marriage— had come to them in the early dawn bringing food and the spirits which had caused the intoxication that obviously affected, more or less, quite three-fourths of the detachment with the members of which I was casually and temporarily consorting. It was rather a chilly morning for the time of year; and fires were alight and blazing cheerfully. Over the fires the good ladies of the detachment were making coffee and handing it round among their men, who insisted on lacing the beverage with brandy, and pressing on the ladies the rough-and-ready and somewhat rudimentary *mazagran*. It was a comforting drink enough; and I had no hesitation, but the reverse, in hobnobbing with the male and female Communists of the boulevards.

Leaving my boon companions, I then struck southwards, down towards the Palais Royal, to ascertain how it had fared during the night with the Rue St. Honoré and the Rue de Rivoli. Several of the cross-streets had suffered considerably from the shell-fire which was still slowly dropping; but the barricades at the Place du Palais Royal were intact, armed, and garrisoned; and the great barricade across the Rue de Rivoli at its junction with the Place de la Concorde was still strongly held by the insurgents, sure evidence that the Versaillists were not yet in possession of the Place. The Rue St. Honoré, along which I walked westwards, was crossed by frequent barricades strongly manned by detachments of drunken but resolute men. The strongest barricade was at the junction of the Rue St. Honoré with the Rue Royale. Just here I witnessed one of the strangest imaginable cross-question and crooked-answer spectacles. The Versaillists held in force the Rue du Faubourg St. Honoré west of the Rue Royale. They were thus in rear of the great Communist battery facing the Place de la Concorde at the foot of the Rue Royale, yet could not take it in reverse because of the cross-fire from the battery which stood across the head of the Rue St. Honoré. And they were further blocked by the Versaillist fire from the front of the Corps Législatif across the Seine on the further side of the Place de la Concorde, directed against the Communist battery at the foot of the Rue Royale, and sweeping that thoroughfare in its rear. The following diagram will make the curious

situation more clear : it was a deadlock the forcing of which
neither side seemed inclined to attempt. The situation as
things stood was passively in favour of the Communists :—

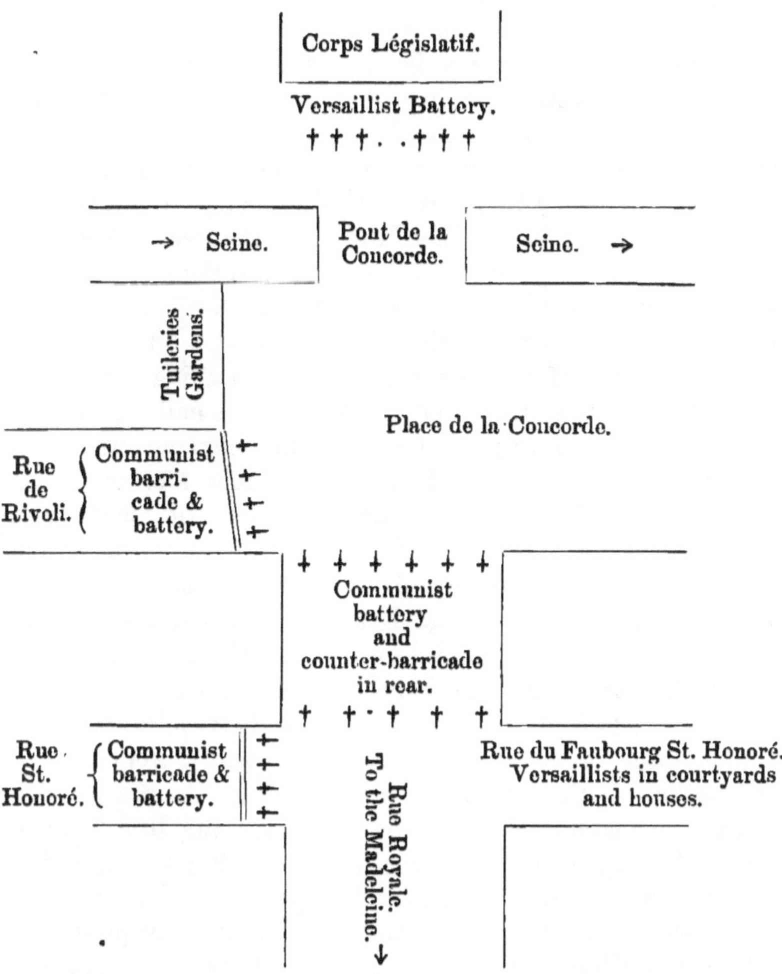

To all seeming there were now no Versaillists about the
Madeleine, whither on the previous day they had reached in
force and where apparently they had made good their foothold. Clearly their policy was to take no risks, and to
economise as much as possible in the matter of their own
skins. A direct offensive effort along the wide bare boulevard

would certainly have cost them dear; and, fresh as the red-breeches were from their German captivity, their spirit was probably not quite an assured thing. It became presently plain, however, that the policy of the Versaillist leaders overnight had been *reculer pour mieux sauter.*

Returning towards my hotel, I recognised how the Versaillist troops were engaging in the development of a great turning movement by their left. Yesterday they had reached the St. Lazare terminus, apparently on their way to Montmartre. Now they had sure grip of the Place and Church of the Trinité at the head of the Rue de la Chaussée d'Antin, and were working eastwards by the narrower streets in preference to traversing the wider Boulevard Haussmann. Between ten and eleven o'clock we in the hotel heard the din of a fierce fire at the back of the Cité d'Antin; and running out into the Rue Laffitte I discerned that the Versaillists had regained the Place de Notre Dame de Lorette—the mantrap triangle in which I had got involved on the previous afternoon; and were now fighting their way along the Rue de Châteaudun, which opens into the Rue Lafayette considerably eastwards of the Cité d'Antin. Meanwhile a heavy Versaillist fire was being maintained down the Boulevard Haussmann, so that my hotel seemed to be in imminent danger of being surrounded. Regaining the front of it and going into the Rue Lafayette, I looked up eastwards to the barricade across it at the junction of the Rue de Châteaudun and prolonged across the issue of the latter street; and I could see its Communist defenders firing vehemently along the Rue Châteaudun. At length, after a strong resistance, they broke, and the Versaillists gained the commanding position. I watched the red-breeches climbing over the barricade as they poured out of the Rue Châteaudun and established themselves in possession of the barricade across the Rue Lafayette. Now (at 1 p.m.) they were firing westwards down the latter street into the lower end of the Boulevard Haussmann, while other Versaillist troops were pressing down that wide boulevard, firing heavily, and covered by shell-fire describing a parabola over their heads and falling in front of them. Thus the

scanty Communist detachments still hanging about the foot
of the Boulevard Haussmann—not, it was true, numerically
strong, but singularly obstinate—were taken simultaneously
in front and rear, and indeed in flank as well; for rifle-fire
was reaching and striking them down the Rue de la Chaussée
d'Antin from the Church of the Trinité. Parenthetically I
may observe that, standing in the lee of a projection at the
foot of the Rue Lafayette, I was hemmed in between three
separate fires. There was not a civilian out of doors anywhere within sight: even the women who had been so fond
of shell-fragments were under cover now. Communard after
Communard, finding the Boulevard Haussmann considerably
too hot to hold him, was sneaking away out of the devilry,
availing himself of the protection afforded by the Opera
House.

Yet the Versaillists still hung back. At half-past two they
had not got so far down the Boulevard Haussmann as to
be abreast of the Opera House, from the arms of the Apollo
on the summit of which the red flag still floated. The
Versaillists simply would not expose themselves. About five-
and-twenty obstinate Communists, coming out from the
cross streets, were blocking the advance of the Versaillist
column with an intermittent fire. Ten minutes of the *pas
de charge* would have given the regulars the boulevard from
end to end; but they would not make the effort, and instead
were bursting their way from house to house and taking pot-
shots from the windows. This style of cover-fighting on
their part, of course left the boulevard free for artillery and
mitrailleuse fire, and certainly neither was spared. The Versaillist shells and bullets were passing my corner in one continuous shriek and whistle; the crash of falling stucco and
the clash of broken glass were incessant. So scanty were the
defenders that scarcely any execution was done by all this ex-
penditure of ammunition, but it probably tried the nerves of
the few Communists left to fight it out to the bitter end. Yet
their efforts were truly heroic. Just as all seemed over they got
a cannon from somewhere up to the head of the Rue Halévy,
and brought it into action against the Versaillist position at

the Church of the Trinité. All was weird and curious chaos. It was only of one episode that I could be the witness; but the din that filled the air told vaguely of other strenuous combats that were being fought elsewhere. Above the smoke of the villainous gunpowder the summer sun was shining brightly, and in spite of the powder-stench and the smell of blood, the air was balmy. It was such a day as made one long to be lying on the grass under a hawthorn-tree in blossom watching the lambs at play, and made one loathe this cowering in a corner, dodging shot and shell in a most undignified manner and without any matches wherewith to light one's pipe.

For another hour or more my neighbours the Communists, who had been reinforced, gave pause to the Versaillist effort to descend the Boulevard Haussmann, and were holding their own against the Versaillist fire from the Place of the Trinité and from the barricade on the rise of the Rue Lafayette. The house at the left-hand corner of the Rue de la Chaussée d'Antin and the Rue Lafayette—the house whose projecting gable had been my precarious shelter so long—had caught fire, to my disquietude and discomfort; but before the fire should seriously trouble me the impending crisis seemed likely to be at last over. Furious and more furious waxed the firing all around. About the Opera House it was exceptionally fierce. I had glimpses of fighting at close quarters in the open space before its rear front, and I could discern men shuffling along behind the low parapet of its roof. They carried packs, but I could not see the colour of their breeches and therefore was not wholly certain that they were Versaillists. A woman had joined me in my post behind the gable—a woman who seemed to have a charmed life. Over and over again she walked out into the fire, looked deliberately about her, and came back to recount to me with excited volubility the particulars of what she had seen. She was convinced that the soldiers on the roof of the Opera House were Versaillists; yet, as I pointed out to her, the *drapeau rouge* still waved above the statue on the summit of the lofty edifice. The people of the hotel in our rear clearly shared her belief. Gathered timidly in the porch they were shouting "Bravo!" and clapping their hands, because they hoped and believed that the Versaillists were winning.

The woman was right; they were Versaillist linesmen whom we saw on the parapet of the Opera House. There was a cheer; the people of the hotel ran out into the fire, waving handkerchiefs and clapping their hands. The tricolor was waving now above the hither portico of the Opera House. The red flag floated still on the further elevation. " A ladder! a ladder to reach it!" was the excited cry from the group behind me; but for the moment no ladder was available. As we waited impatiently there darted down the side-walk of the boulevard to the corner of the Rue Halévy a little grig of a fellow in red breeches—one of the old French linesman breed. He was all alone, and he seemed to enjoy the loneliness as he took up his post behind a tree, and fired his first shot at a Communard dodging about the intersection of the Rue Tait-bout. When is a Frenchman not dramatic? He fired with an air, he reloaded with an air, he fired again with a flourish, and was acclaimed with cheering and hand-clapping from the "gallery" behind me to which the little fellow was playing. Then he beckoned us back dramatically, for his next shot was to be sped up the Rue Lafayette at a little knot of Communists who from a fragment of shelter at the intersection of the Rue Laffitte were taking him for their target. Then he faced about and waved his comrades on with exaggerated gestures which recalled those one sees in a blood-and-thunder melo-drama, the Communist bullets all the while cutting the bark and branches of the tree which was his cover. Ah! he was down! Well, he had enjoyed his brief flash of recklessness. The woman by my side and I ran across and carried him in. We might have spared ourselves the trouble and risk: he was dead, with a bullet through his head.

This little distraction had engrossed us for only a few minutes; the moment it ended thus tragically, all our atten-tion went back to the scene on the roof of the Opera House. A ladder had at length been got up, and a Versaillist soldier was now mounting the statue of Apollo on the front elevation of the building, overhanging the Place de l'Opéra. He tore down the *drapeau rouge* and substituted the tricolor just as the head of a great column of Versaillist troops came streaming out of the Rue de la Chaussée d'Antin across the Boulevard Haussmann, and down the wide streets towards the Grand Boulevards. The excitment was hysterical. The inhabitants rushed out of the houses with bottles of wine, from their windows money was showered down into the street, the women fell on the necks of the sweating dusty men in red breeches and hugged them with frantic shouts of *"Vive la ligne!"* The soldiers fraternised heartily, drank and pressed forwards. Their discipline was most creditable. When their officers called them away from the conviviality and the embraces, the men at once obeyed and re-formed companies promptly at the double. Now that the Versaillist wave had swept over us for good, we were again people of law and order, and thenceforward abjured any relations some of us smug citizens might have temporarily had with those atrocious miscreants of Communists who were now getting so decisively beaten. Everybody displayed raptures of joy, and Communistic cards of fellowship were being surreptitiously torn up in all directions. It was now no longer "citoyen" under pain of being held a suspect; the undemocratic "monsieur" revived with amusing rapidity.

The Versaillist troops—horse, foot, and artillery—pouring in steady continuous streams down the Rue de la Chaussée d'Antin and the Rue Halévy, debouched into the great boulevard at the Place de l'Opéra, taking in flank and rear the insurgents holding positions thereabouts, and getting presently a firm grip of the Boulevard des Capucines westwards almost to the Madeleine. This was done not without hard fighting and considerable loss, for the Communists fought like wild cats and clung obstinately to every spot affording a semblance of cover. Even when the success described had been attained the situation was still curiously involved. The Versaillists, moving down the Rue de la Paix, were threatening the Place Vendôme but avoiding close quarters. The Communists, for their part, threatened as they thus were with being cut off,

nevertheless still held obstinately their artillery barricades at
the foot of the Rue Royale and at the western end of the Rue
St. Honoré. The rear face of the former had been fortified and
armed; and so, although the Versaillist artillery hammered at
its proper front from the Corps Législatif, its rearward guns
were abler to interfere with the Versaillist efforts to make good
a hold on the much-battered Madeleine.

I was exceedingly anxious to get some intelligence sent
out, for nothing had been transmitted from the hermetically
sealed capital for three days; and in order to ascertain whether
there was any prospect of the despatch of a bag to Versailles
from the Embassy in the Rue du Faubourg St. Honoré, I
started up the now comparatively quiet Boulevard Haussmann, and by tacks and zigzags got into the Rue d'Aguesseau,
which debouches into the Faubourg nearly opposite to the
British Embassy. Shells were bursting very freely in the
neighbourhood, but my affair was urgent, and from the corner
of the Rue d'Aguesseau I stepped out into the Rue du Faubourg St. Honoré, intending to dart across to the Embassy
gates. I drew back hastily as a shell-splinter whizzed past me
close enough to blow my beard aside. The street was simply
a great tube for shells; nothing could live in it. Hoping
that the firing might soon abate, I waited in an entry for
an hour. Around about me were several ambulances, as the
field hospitals had come to be called in the recent war. Into
one close by I saw, during a quarter of an hour, one wounded
man carried every minute: I timed the stretchers by my
watch. In others into which I looked the courtyards were
full of mattresses and groaning men. A good many corpses,
those chiefly of national guards, lay in the streets, behind the
barricades and in the gutters.

It fell dusk as I waited, the fire rather increasing in
intensity than abating, and I would spare no more time. As
I returned towards my hotel I had to cross the line of Versaillist artillery still pouring southwards from the Church of the
Trinité, and thence down the Rue Halévy towards the quarter
where the noise indicated that hot firing was still proceeding.
The gunners received a wild ovation from the inhabitants of

the Chaussée d'Antin. Where, I wondered, had the good folk secreted the tricolor flag during all those days of Communist domiciliary visits? It hung now in the still air from every window, the shouts of " *Vive la ligne !*" stirring it occasionally with a lazy throb. Stray bullets whistled everywhere—the women in their crazy courage had come to call them sparrows. And as the night closed in, there came from the Rue St. Honoré, from the Place Vendôme, and from the vicinity of the Palais Royal and the Hôtel de Ville, the noise of heavy, steady firing of cannon, mitrailleuse, and musketry, accentuated occasionally by explosions which made the solid earth tremble.

After a night of horror which seemed interminable, there broke at length the morning of Wednesday, May 24th. When the sun rose, what a spectacle flouted his beams ! The flames from the palace of the Tuileries, kindled by damnable petroleum, insulted the soft light of the morning, and cast lurid rays on the grimy recreant Frenchmen who skulked from their dastardly incendiarism to pot at their countrymen from behind their barricades. How the palace blazed ! The flames revelled in the historic rooms, made embers of the rich furniture, burst out the plate-glass windows, brought down the fantastic roof. It was in the Prince Imperial's wing, facing the gardens of the Tuileries, where the demon of fire first had his fiercest sway. By eight o'clock the whole of this wing was nearly burnt out. When I reached the end of the Rue Dauphin the red belches of flame were shooting out from the corner facing the private garden and the Rue de Rivoli. It was the Pavillon Marsan, containing the apartments occupied by the King of Prussia and his suite during the visit to Paris in the year of the great Exposition. A furious jet of flame was pouring out of the window at which Bismarck used to sit and smoke and look out on Paris and the Parisians. There was a sudden crash. Was it an explosion or a fall of flooring that caused the great burst of fat black smoke and red sparks right in one's face ? Who could tell what hell-devices might lurk within that blazing pile ? It were well, surely, to keep at a respectful distance from it ! And so I went eastwards to the Place du Palais Royal, which was still unsafe by reason

of shot and shell from the neighbourhood of the Hôtel de
Ville. Opposite was the great archway by which the troops
of Napoleon had been wont to enter into the Place du
Carrousel. Was the fire there yet? Just so far and no
more. Could the archway be broken down, the Louvre, with
its artistic and historic riches, might still be saved. But
there was none to act or to direct. The Versaillist soldiers
were lounging supine along the streets, intent—and who
could blame the weary powder-grimed men?—on bread and
wine. So the flames leaped on from window to window, from
chimney to chimney. They were beyond the archway now :
the Pavillon de la Bibliothèque was kindling—the connecting
link between the Tuileries and the Louvre, built by the late
Emperor to contain his private library. Unless an effort to
stay the progress of the flames should be made, the Louvre
and its inestimable contents were surely doomed. Indeed,
the Louvre might be said to be on fire already, for the
Pavillon de la Bibliothèque was counted a part of it. And on
fire, too, were the Palais Royal, and the Hôtel de Ville where
the rump of the Commune were cowering amidst their
arson ; and the Ministry of Finance and many another public
and private building. No wonder that Courbet, *soi-disant*
Minister of Fine Arts, should have been sending far and wide
among friends native and foreign, in quest of a refuge wherein
to hide his head !

I turned, sad and sick, from the spectacle of wanton
destruction, to be saddened and sickened yet further by
another spectacle. Versaillist soldiers, hanging about the
foot of the Rue St Honoré, were enjoying the cheap amusement of Communist-hunting. The lower-class Parisians of
civil life seemed to me caitiff and yet cruel to the last drop
of their thin, sour, *petit bleu* blood. But yesterday they had
been shouting " Vive la Commune ! " and submitted to be
under the heel of the said Commune. To-day they rubbed
their hands with livid currish joy to have it in their power to
denounce a Communard and to reveal his hiding-place.
Very ardent in this pseudo-patriotic duty were the dear
creatures of women. They knew the rat-holes into which the

L

poor devils had squeezed themselves, and they guided the Versaillist soldiers to the spot with a fiendish glee. *Voilà* the braves of France, returned to such a triumph from an inglorious captivity! They have found him, then, the miserable! Yes, they have dragged him from out one of the purlieus which Haussmann had not time to sweep away, and a posse of them hem him round as they march him into the Rue St. Honoré. A tall, pale, hatless man, with something not ignoble in his bearing. His lower lip is trembling, but his brow is firm, and the eye of him has some pride, and, indeed, scorn in it. "A veritable Communard?" I ask of my neighbour in the throng. "Questionable," is the reply; "I think he is a milk-seller to whom the woman who has denounced him owes a score." They yell, the crowd—my neighbour as loud as any—"Shoot him! shoot him!"—the demon-women of course the most clamorous. An arm goes up into the air; there are on it the stripes of a *sous-officier* and there is a stick in the fist at the end of the arm. The stick descends on the bare head of the pale prisoner. Ha! the infection has caught; men club their rifles and bring them down on that head, or smash them into splinters in their lust for murder. He is down; he is up again; he is down again—the thuds of the gun-stocks sounding on him just as when men beat a carpet with sticks. A momentary impulse prompts one to push into the *mêlée;* but it is foolish and it is useless. They are firing into the flaccid carcass now; thronging around it as it lies prone, like blow-flies on a piece of meat. Faugh! his brains are out and oozing into the gutter, whither the carrion is presently heaved bodily, to be trodden on and mangled presently by the feet of the multitude and the wheels of the gun-carriages. But, after all, womanhood was not quite dead in that band of bedlamites who had clamoured for the dead man's blood. There was one matron in hysterics who did not seem more than half drunk. Another with wan, scared face drew out of the press a child-bedlamite presumably her offspring, and, one might hope, went home ashamed and shuddering. But surely for the time all manhood was dead in the soldiery of France to do

such a deed as this. An officer—one with a bull-throat and
the eyes of Algiers—stood by and looked on at the sport,
smoking a cigar. A sharer in the crime surely he was if
there was such a thing as discipline in the French ranks; if
there was not he might have been pitied but for his smile
of cynical approval.

The Commune was in desperate case; but it was dying
hard, with dripping fangs bared and every blood claw pro-
truded. It held no ground now west of the Boulevard
Sevastopol from the river north to the Porte St. Denis. The
Place Vendôme had been carried at two in the morning.
After a desperate struggle the last man of its Communist
garrison had been bayonetted on the great barricade at the
junction of the Rue Royale with the Place de la Concorde,
and the Versaillist masses could now gather undisturbed
about the Madeleine. But how about the wild-cat leaders of
the Commune still in possession of the Hôtel de Ville, on which
the Versaillist batteries were now concentrating a fire heavy
enough to be reckoned a bombardment? Their backs were
to the wall, and they were fighting now, not for life—about
that, to do them justice, they were reckless enough—but that
they might work as much evil as might be possible before
their hour should come. The Versaillists did not dare to
make a quick ending by rushing straight on the barricades
surrounding the open space about the Hôtel de Ville; they
were timid about explosions. But they were mining, sapping, burrowing, circumventing, breaking through party walls,
and advancing from backyard to backyard; and it was a
question of only a few hours when they should pierce the
cordon. Meanwhile the holders of the Hôtel de Ville were
pouring out death and destruction over Paris with indiscriminate malignity and fury. Now it was a bouquet of shells on
the Champs Elysées; now a heavy obus crashing upon the
already battered Boulevard Haussmann; now a great shell
hurtling in the direction of the Avenue de la Reine Hortense.
Cut off by this time from La Chapelle and the Gare du Nord,
the reds still clung to a barricade in the Rue Lafayette near
the Square Montholon. For its defenders the way of retreat

L 2

was open towards Belleville. Canny folk, those Versaillists ! The Prussians, no doubt, would have let them into Belleville from the rear, as they had already let them into La Chapelle. But Belleville, whether in front or from rear, scarcely offered a joyous prospect. It seemed to me that for days to come there might be fighting about that rugged and turbulent region, and that there, probably, the Commune would find its last ditch. As for the people in the Hôtel de Ville, they, in the expressive old phrase, were between the devil and the deep sea. One enemy with arms in his hands, was outside ; another fire—and fire kindled by themselves—was inside. Would they roast, or would they accept death at the bayonet-point ? was the question I asked myself, as I left the soldiers stacking the corpses on the flower-beds of the garden of the Tour St. Jacques and tried in vain to see something of the Hôtel de Ville from the Pont Neuf. Its face towards the river was hidden by a great blanket of smoke, through the opacity of which shot occasional flashes of red flame.   .

Farther westward the merry game of the morning was in full swing. Denouncement by wholesale had become the fashion, and denouncement and apprehension were duly followed by braining. It was a relief to quit the truculent cowards, and the bloody gutters, and the yelling women, and the Algerian-eyed officers. I strolled away into the Place Vendôme, of which there was current a story that it had been held for hours by twenty-five Communist men and one woman, against all that the Versaillists found it in their hearts to do. A considerable force had been massed in the Place : sentries were in charge of the ruins of the famous column. In the gutter before the Hôtel Bristol lay a corpse buffeted and besmirched—the corpse, I was told, of the Communist captain of the adjacent barricade, who had held it to the bitter end and had then shot himself. The Versaillist braves had made assurance doubly sure by shooting over and over again into the clay that was once a man. And in the Place there lay another corpse, that of the Hecate who fought on the Rue de la Paix barricade with a persistence and fury of which many spoke. They might have shot her—

yes! when a woman takes to war she forfeits her immunities —but in memory of their mothers they might at least have drawn her scanty rags over the bare limbs that now outraged decency, and refrained from abominable bayonet-thrusts.

And now here was the Rue Royale, burning right royally from end to end. Alas for the lovers of a draught of good British beer in this parching lime-kiln, the English beer-house at the corner of the Rue du Faubourg St. Honoré was a heap of blazing ruins. Indeed, from that corner up to the Place de la Madeleine, there was scarcely a house on either side of the noble street that was not on fire. And the fire had been down the Rue St. Honoré and up the Faubourg, and was working its swift hot will along the Rue Boissy d'Anglas. It was hard to breathe in an atmosphere mainly of petroleum smoke. There was a sun, but its heat was dominated by the heat of the conflagrations; its rays were obscured by the lurid blue-black smoke that was rising with an unctuous fatness everywhere into the air, filling the eyes with acrid water, getting into the throat with a rank semi-asphyxiation, poisoning the sense of ordinary smell, and turning one's gorge with the abomination of it. All up the Rue du Faubourg St. Honoré the gutters were full of blood; there was a barricade at every intersection; the house-fronts were scarred by shell-fire; and corpses lay about promiscuously. As I reached the gate leading into the forecourt of the British Embassy, the sight of a figure leaning against one of the pillars gave me a great shock. Why I should have been thus affected it is necessary to explain.

Neither my colleagues nor myself had been able to get a scrap sent out of Paris since Monday morning; and it was now noon of Wednesday. It was not for pleasure or excitement that we were standing by the Commune's bloody death-bed; we were on duty. I was wretched. Here I was, on tenterhooks; witnessing, indeed, a momentous and memorable struggle; but the spectacle only useful professionally in order that I might with all speed transfer the pictures which had formed themselves on my mental retina to the columns of my newspaper, and thus make the world an early sharer with me in a knowledge of events on the phases and issue of which the world was hanging. This aim, this burning aspiration, must ever absorb the zealous correspondent, to the exclusion of any other consideration whatsoever. It is for the accomplishment of this purpose that he lives: I do not know that he ought to continue to do so if he fails—certainly not if he fails because of a miscarriage for which he himself is responsible. On the Tuesday night I could endure the blockade no longer. Somebody must get out, if he should descend the face of the enceinte by a rope. It was arranged that at sunrise on the Wednesday morning the attempt should be made by a colleague whose cool courage events had well tested, who had a good horse, knew Paris thoroughly, and had a large acquaintance among officers of the Versaillist army. He took charge of one copy of the scrappy letters which I had written in duplicate in the intervals of watching the fighting; we shook hands, wishing each other a good deliverance; and at noon of Wednesday I was congratulating myself on the all but certainty that our letters were already somewhere about Amiens on the way to London.

This cheerful conviction was abruptly dissipated by the sight which caught my eye as I entered the Embassy court-yard. My unfortunate colleague was leaning against one of the pillars of the gate, deadly sick, his complexion positively green, his nerves utterly shattered. He had tried to get out— I doubt not, boldly and energetically; but he had failed. He had been fired upon and maltreated, he had been denounced as a Prussian spy, and had escaped death by the skin of his teeth. Poor fellow! He had been spattered with the blood and brains of denounced men who had not escaped. He had given up and had taken post where I found him, as the likeliest point at which to meet me and tell me of his failure.

Of course, as the consequence of that misfortune, it devolved upon me to make the attempt. I pondered a few moments, and then went into the chancellary of the Embassy, where I found Mr., afterwards Sir Edward Malet. Malet, who was then Second Secretary, had remained in Paris to represent Great Britain when Lord Lyons and the rest of the Embassy *personnel* had migrated to Versailles at the beginning of the Commune. He may be said to have been sitting among ruins, for the smash of the big house had been severe. In the garden walls were great gaps through which the Versaillists had worked their strategic progress round the barricades, respecting much the wholeness of their skins. I had met Malet in the early days of the recent war, when he came out from Paris to Meaux with communications for Bismarck. I told him I meant to attempt getting out, and asked him whether I could take anything to Versailles for him.

"My dear fellow," said Malet, "it's not the least use your trying to get out. I sent two messengers off this morning; both have come back; both had been fired on. We must wait a day or two until things settle."

"I am going to try to-day, and immediately," was my answer. "You can help me and at the same time further your own objects. Put your despatches for Versailles into a big official envelope, seal it with the red seal, address it to 'Her Majesty the Queen of England,' and entrust me with the packet. No harm can come of it, anyhow."

After a little excogitation Malet complied; and, pocketing the envelope, I went to the stable where my little horse was standing at livery. The Communist sentry had relieved himself, and the embargo was off; but the poor beast, having been half-starved and long deprived of exercise, was in a state of great debility. However, I jogged gently along, meeting with no molestation until, on the Quay of Passy, I essayed a little trot, for time was of value. Presently the poor animal staggered and then fell on its side, pinning me down by the leg. I sickened, partly with pain, for I thought my leg was broken; more, however, in the foreboding of failure to accomplish my purpose if this hurt had indeed befallen me. A line battalion of Versaillist troops was passing; and half-a-dozen soldiers were instantly around me. Some dragged the horse up on to his legs; others raised me and carried me into a wayside cabaret. A glass of wine revived me; my leg was not broken, only the ankle dislocated. I ordered and paid for half-a-dozen bottles of wine; my military friends carried me out and lifted me into the saddle; and I went on at a walk, thankful that I came so well out of the little disaster.

I encountered and surmounted sundry subsequent difficulties and dangers; but the crucial obstacle was still before me—at the Point du Jour Gate, whither I was making on my way to Versailles. Walking up and down on the pavement in front of the guard-house were a colonel and a major of the Line.

"No, it is impossible!" said the colonel. "Very sorry, but our orders are imperative. You must apply for a permit to Marshal MacMahon, whose quarters are at the École Militaire." I urged, I entreated, I produced my envelope; but all to no purpose. At length the colonel went away. The major remained, and was so good as to accept a cigar. On his breast was the British Crimean medal and on that hint I spoke yet again, dwelling on the old comradeship of the French and English soldiers during the days of fighting and hardship before Sevastopol. That medal he wore was the Queen of England's souvenir: could he delay a courier carrying to her important despatches? The old warrior looked cautiously around; we were alone. He spoke no word, but silently, with his thumb over his shoulder pointed down the tunnel under the enceinte, at the further end of which was the open country. When I had passed the sentry at the exit I drew a long breath of relief and pottered on to Sèvres, at which place I left my horse and took carriage for Versailles, where my old war-time courier was residing in the despatch-service of the *Daily News* resident correspondent.

As I drove up the broad avenue between Viroflay and Versailles I overtook a very miserable and dejected company. In file after file of six abreast tramped a convoy of Communist prisoners, numbering over two thousand souls. Patiently and with some consciousness of pride they marched, linked tightly arm to arm. Among them were many women, some of them

fierce barricade Hecates, others mere girls, soft and timid—
here, seemingly, because a parent was here also. All were
bareheaded and foul with dust, many powder-stained as well;
and the burning sun beat down on the frowsy column. Not
the sun only beat down, but also the flats of sabres wielded by
the dashing Chasseurs d'Afrique who were the ruthless escort
of those unfortunates. Their own recent experiences might
have taught them humanity towards their captives. No
sabre-blades had descended on their pates during that long
weary march from Sedan to their German captivity; they
were then the prisoners of humane soldiers. But they were
prisoners now no longer as they capered on their wiry barb
stallions, and in their pride of cheap success belaboured un-
mercifully the miserables of the Commune. For any over-
wearied creatures who fell out or dropped there was short
shrift: my driving-horse had been shying at the corpses on
the road all the way from Sèvres. At the head of the sombre
column were three or four hundred lashed together with ropes
—all powder-stained those—and among them not a few
men in red breeches—deserters taken red-handed. I rather
wondered what they did in this gang; they might as well
have died fighting on the barricades as survive to be made
targets of a day or two later with their backs against a wall.

To hand Malet's despatches to the First Secretary of the
Embassy, Mr. Sackville West, and to eat a morsel, did not
detain me in Versailles beyond half an hour; and then I was
off again on wheels by the circuitous route through Rueil and
Malmaison, and over the pontoon bridge above Argenteuil to
St. Denis and the railway. As I drove along the green
margin of the placid Seine, the spectacle which the capital
presented can never fade from my memory. On its white
houses the sun still shone; he did not withhold his beams
in spite of the deeds they illumined. But up through the sun-
beams struggled and surged ghastly swart waves and folds
and pillars of dense smoke. Ha! there was a sharp crack,
and then came a dull thud on the air. No gun-fire that, but
some great explosion which must have rocked a district
almost to its base. Then there rose with a jet-like spurt,

a convolvulus-shaped column of white smoke, such as men describe when Vesuvius bursts into eruption; then it broke up into fleecy waves and eddied away towards the horizon all round, as the ripple of a stone into a pool spreads to the water's edge. The crowds of German soldiers who sat by the Seine steadily watching were startled into a burst of excitement. The excitement well might have been world-wide. " Paris the beautiful" was now Paris the ghastly, Paris the battered, Paris the blood-drenched. And this in the present century—ay, but four-and-twenty years ago—Europe professing civilisation, France boasting of culture and refinement, Frenchmen braining one another with the butt-ends of their rifles, and Paris blazing to the skies ! There needed but a Nero to fiddle.

Travelling to England, and writing hard all the way in train and boat, I reached London on the early morning of Thursday, May 25th, and was back in Paris the following day. All was then virtually over. The hostages in La Roquette had been shot, and the Hôtel de Ville had fallen on the afternoon of the day I had left. When I returned the Communists were at their last gasp in the Château d'Eau, the Buttes de Chaumont, and Père-Lachaise. On the afternoon of the 28th, after just one week of fighting, Marshal MacMahon announced, " I am absolute master of Paris." On the following morning I visited Père-Lachaise, where the very last shots had been fired. Bivouac fires had been fed with the souvenirs of pious sorrow, and the trappings of woe had been torn down to be used as bedclothes. But there had been no great amount of fighting in the cemetery itself. An infallible token of close and heavy firing are the dents of many bullets, and of those there were comparatively few in Père-Lachaise. Shells, however, had fallen freely, and the results were occasionally very ghastly. But the ghastliest sight in Père-Lachaise was in the south-eastern corner, where, close to the boundary wall, there had been a natural hollow. The hollow was now filled up by dead. One could measure the dead by the rood. There they lay, tier above tier, each successive tier powdered over with a coating of chloride of lime—two hundred of them patent to the eye, besides those underneath hidden by the earth covering layer after layer. Among the dead were many women. There, thrown up in the sunlight, was a well-rounded arm with a ring on one of the fingers ; there, again, was a bust shapely in death. And yonder were faces which to look upon made one shudder —faces distorted out of humanity with ferocity and agony combined. The ghastly effect of the dusty white powder on the dulled eyes, the gnashed teeth, and the jagged beards, cannot be described. How died those men and women ? Were they carted hither and laid out in this dead-hole of Père-Lachaise ? Not so : the hole had been replenished from close by. Just yonder was where they were posted up against that section of pock-pitted wall—there was no difficulty in reading the open book—and were shot to death as they stood or crouched. Let us turn our backs on the awful and melancholy scene, and pray that never again may the civilised world witness such a week of horrors as Paris underwent in those sunshiny summer days of May, 1871 !

VII.

OUR PARISH MURDERER.

SINCE the days of my youth—now, alas! very remote—I have lost touch in a great measure of the quiet northern region in which I was born and reared. Many things, which in my young days were regarded in that once simple and primitive community as surprising novelties, have, no doubt, long since passed into the category of things of course, or even in their turn have fallen obsolete. But forty-five years ago our parish, primitive as it was, possessed an unique if sinister distinction. Among its inhabitants there lived, and moved, and had his being, a completely authenticated and, indeed, self-acknowledged murderer. His long-planned and deliberate crime had been perpetrated in our midst. I myself saw the stain of blood on the sand of the roadside just in front of the wayside smithy; there had been an actual witness of the act, who was ready and, indeed, eager with damning testimony; the doer of the deed never wagged his tongue in defence of his guilt, and when it pleased him to do so confessed his blood-guiltiness with perfect frankness. Yet when, a few years after the grim transaction, I went out into the world from my native valley, this local murderer of ours was living there in complete immunity, earning his bread in rural labour among his fellow men, unshunned by them as a pariah, and held in all respects save for occasional lapses into unconvivial inebriety, a not discreditable member of the sequestered and primitive community.

I never made a boast of it, because I did not consider the *trouvaille* as anything to be greatly proud of; but, as a matter of fact it was I who found him. I did so on the morning after one of the half-yearly " feeing " markets in Rottenslough, a village about six miles from our valley. Our parish post-office was about a mile from the manse, and it was one of the pleasant duties which my father the minister devolved on me, to ride the old pony there every morning and bring back the manse letter-bag. Doing so on the morning after this Rottenslough market day, in the deep wayside ditch near the cross-roads I found an upturned old gig in an advanced state of smash. Broken and battered though it was, I knew it at a glance as the rattletrap appertaining to Sandy Grant, the drunken farmer of Bodenfinnoch. The horse apparently had kicked himself free, and since he was nowhere to be seen, had probably gone home to his stable. Sandy himself, with a strange man by his side, was slumbering sweetly in the clover of the field beyond the ditch. In answer to my hail, he sat up, rubbing his eyes and yawning with great vigour. "Whaur am I?" was his ingenuous question. Informed on this point, and his attention directed to the fragmentary condition of his vehicle, he swore with extreme fervour, and protested that the " wyte " of his mischance was wholly due to his still slumbering companion, who, it appeared, had on the previous evening " made him blin' fou' " in one of the booths on the market stance. This companion he incontinently proceeded to kick with great emphasis, a process which ultimately succeeded in arousing the strange man, whom Sandy swore he " didna ken frae Adam."

Sandy's tempter and boon companion, as he rose to his feet and stared around him, was a person of singular aspect. Hair and beard—and he had a good deal of both—were coalblack, and his strong-lined face—as I supposed naturally swarthy—was tanned so deeply that the skin might have been leather. His eyes were small, black, and keen. He was of fair stature, and carried his head well ; but, although his shoulders were square as one looked at him in front, they were so rounded at the back that it almost seemed as if he had a hump. When he moved he lifted his feet in a curious dragging fashion, as if they or his boots were too heavy for him to move in the ordinary way. Years after when visiting the Cascade Prison at Hobart in Tasmania, I saw the convict lunatics remaining from the transportation times, whose backs had been humped by countless lashes and whose ankles had been clogged for years with heavy irons at Norfolk Island and Port Arthur; and there came back to me then the vivid memory of this strange casual incomer into our valley, as I first saw him on this morning slouching in the clover-field by the cross-roads of Blackhillock.

Hospitable Sandy Grant took this chance companion of his home to breakfast. A few days later I saw the " foreigner," as some of the neighbours had begun to call him, driving one of Bodenfinnoch's carts from the moss with a load of peat. It appeared that he had taken service temporarily with Sandy as odd, or, as it used to be called among us, "orra" man, quietly remarking that he did not particularly care where he lived so long as he was able to earn an honest living. And he had thought proper to give some account of himself. His name, it appeared, was David Morgan; he was, he said, a Welshman by birth; he had been a slate-quarrier at Bethesda, near Bangor, and later had been navvying on a railway in the north of France. It seemed that he had come north in quest of a brother who had come bridge-building somewhere into Aberdeenshire, but that the search had come to nothing. His money was done; he was tired of tramping; he liked oatmeal—the simple fare of our valley; and so, now he was there, he was content to stop.

I think he was for some six months "orra" man at Bodenfinnoch. Then he struck out into independence, constructed for himself a hovel of turf on the muirland of Knockans, and undertook piecework as a ditcher and drainer. When that work was slack he was in the habit of working on the neighbouring farm of Coldhome, the tenant of which was an old man named Macdonald, who had for housekeeper a middle-aged woman whom we knew as Mrs. Trevallack. Life went on so quietly in this sequestered parish of ours that the history of this woman, as it was known among us, was quite a world's wonder in a small way. She was a south country woman, who, it seemed, had been married to a Cornish man named Trevallack, a private soldier of our local Highland regiment. Trevallack had died on service in India, and (so the story went) she had been fallen in love with by a man named Macdonald, who was a sergeant in the regiment and was the son of the old farmer of Coldhome. He could not marry her, because the married strength of the regiment was full and there were many applicants in front of him. So he sent her home to the care of his father, who was a widower; promising that in a few years when the regiment in its turn should come home, he would buy his discharge, marry her, and settle down on the farm. But war after war—in Afghanistan, in Gwalior, in the Punjaub—had detained the regiment in India. The Scottish sergeant had been for several years its regimental sergeant-major; and, if he had desired, while fighting and promotion were the order of the day he could not have bought his discharge. While the regiment remained in India, Mrs. Trevallack had been living among us now for nearly twelve years, waiting patiently for the happy time of which she steadfastly professed her assurance, tending the old farmer faithfully, managing, as far as a woman might, the details of the work of the sour upland farm, and bearing a good repute in the parish as a worthy and courageous woman. It was reported now that her long expectancy was soon to have a happy ending. The term for which Macdonald had enlisted was rapidly drawing to a close; and, in the joy of her heart Mrs. Trevallack made no secret of the knowledge which had come to her, that the gallant soldier for whom she had waited so patiently all those long years would reach home in the course of a few weeks.

That time soon passed. One cold November evening my father was driving home from a meeting of Presbytery, and I was his companion in the old gig which he had bought when he married my mother. As we came round a sharp turn in the road the mare shied violently at the blaze of light streaming across the road from the windows and open door of Wullie Watt's smithy. On the open space outside was visible in the glow of light a group of men and women from the neighbouring cottages. They were silent, as is the wont of Scottish country folk in the actual presence of calamity; but the white blaze from the forge illuminated the horror that possessed every face. From inside the smithy the sound was heard of sobs and moans, broken intermittently by heart-piercing wails. "The minister!" "The minister!" came in low tones from the group as the light fell on my father's face. Old Geordie Riach of the Rashes, the elder of the district, came forward, doffing his broad bonnet and so baring his grand old head, and said in a hoarse whisper: "It's murder, your Reverence—rank bluidy murder, dune here barely ten minutes syne; an' the murdered man—ye kirstened him yersel', sir—gane tae his account i' the twinklin' o' an e'e. For God's sake, sir, tak' tent"—the minister was alighting—"tak' tent, sir, or ye'll step intae the puddle o' his life's bluid!"

I followed my father and his venerable elder into the smithy. Right in the blaze from the forge, on a couple of sacks which had been hurriedly spread, lay the stark, motionless form of a tall, powerfully-built man, the strongly-marked face livid in the pallor of the white light. At a glance my father recognised the dead man, whom in childhood he had baptised, in youth had prepared for his first communion, in early manhood had bidden God-speed when he left the parish to take the Queen's shilling and join the old corps in whose ranks had served many of the good old stock to which he belonged. The head of the dead soldier lay in the lap of Mrs. Trevallack, whose tears were raining down on the fast-setting face; whose moans and wails it was that we had heard while yet outside on the road . and that we still listened to as we looked down upon her and her dead.

"Who hath done this?" asked my father in his solemn tones of quiet authority.

The woman looked up, dashed the tears from her streaming eyes, and between her bursting sobs replied in her south country Scots:—

"I met Macdonald at the cross-roads whaur the coach passes. We traivelt thegither through the moss an' ower the muir. Juist as we gaed by the smiddy here Dauvit Morgan, the foreign ditcher, dairted oot frae the gable end an' gae Macdonald ae strong stab in the breist wi' a lang knife. Oh, sir, but I saw the cruel flash o't i' the munelight as he drove it hame! He left it stickin'. See, sir, it's in my man's heart still! An' syne, withoot a word, the murderin' villain sprang the hedge on the far side o' the road, an' got clean awa'!"

Before midnight the rural policeman made his appearance, and remained in charge of the body until, in the small hours of the morning, arrived from Rottenslough Neil Robertson, the superintendent of police for the county. He authorised the removal of the dead man to his father's house, whither came, before the short winter day was done, the Procurator Fiscal from the county town; and this functionary of justice promptly set about the "taking of precognitions"—the Scottish legal expression for the preliminary examination of persons whose evidence might be found relevant. The only witness to the actual deed was the woman Trevallack, who positively testified to David Morgan as the murderer. She knew him well, since from time to time he worked on old Macdonald's farm; and when he did so, he took his meals in the farmhouse and was served by herself. She further testified that Morgan was actually in the kitchen of Coldhome when she set out to meet the returning sergeant-major, and that he was the only person to whom she mentioned the errand on which she was leaving home. Asked whether she was aware of any reason that could have actuated Morgan to take the life of the sergeant-major, she deposed that she had sometimes thought Morgan had, in her own words, "ta'en a notion" of herself, but owned that this was merely an impression on her part. Outside of Mrs. Trevallack's direct testimony, the circumstantial evidence collected by the Procurator Fiscal against Morgan was not in itself of great strength. Wullie Watt the blacksmith deposed that "the foreigner," as Morgan was commonly called, had been in the smithy in the course of the "forenicht," but had left quite half an hour before Mrs. Trevallack's scream of horror was heard out in the road. But every rural smithy in the north of Scotland was in those days the evening gossiping-place of the countryside; and the blacksmith testified that "the foreigner" was among the habitual frequenters of the place. Several people on the

M

evening of the murder had met Morgan, apparently on his way home to his hovel on the muir, and had exchanged with him a word of greeting in the by-passing. None had observed in him anything "by ordnar," and none could approximately specify the time of meeting him.

Morgan had been apprehended in the early morning after the night of the murder, and had been straightway carried to the county jail. The police had found him sleeping calmly in his hovel; and when awakened he had evinced no sign of perturbation. A smart young local solicitor volunteered to undertake his defence; and, under his advice the prisoner declined the offer made to him by the Procurator Fiscal that he should, in Scottish legal phraseology, "emit a declaration" —in other words, make a statement on his own behalf. He lay in the county jail for some months, and then was removed to Aberdeen to stand his trial there before the Circuit Court, which corresponds to the English Assizes. The bloody tragedy in our quiet sequestered valley had thrilled the whole north country; and within the memory of man the old Court House of the good city of Bon Accord had never been so crowded as on the morning when David Morgan was brought into the dock between two prison-warders to stand his trial for the wilful murder of ex-Sergeant-Major John Macdonald.

A judge of the stern old school was on the bench. The prosecution by the Crown was conducted by the Senior Advocate Depute, the best criminal lawyer of his day in Scotland. The prisoner had no means wherewith to secure the services of an advocate of high standing at the Scottish bar; but his solicitor had retained for the defence a young advocate, Mr. Daner, whom he knew to be a man of great ability and who later rose to high eminence in his profession. My father had come into town to be present at a trial in which folk of his own parish were deeply concerned; and young as I was, I had a seat by his side in the body of the court.

Of the details of the initial legal proceedings I have not

retained any close recollection, nor of the quaint old-world phraseology which I remember to have found bewildering; but I do remember wondering why the prisoner was uniformly spoken of as the "panel." In my recollection the indictment was read, after which the Counsel for the Crown briefly and temperately opened the case for the prosecution and promptly proceeded to call his witnesses. Those taken first, and I thought this strange, were people who gave merely circumstantial evidence—the old blacksmith and the men who had met Morgan on his way home. Then Margaret Trevallack was placed in the witness-box. She wore mourning, her once comely face was now deeply worn, but her bearing was firm and composed. The evidence she gave in answer to the questions of the Crown Counsel was in effect the same as that which had been embodied in the precognitions taken by the Procurator Fiscal. She swore positively to Morgan as the murderer of Macdonald. She had distinctly seen his face, and it was simply impossible that she could have been mistaken. Her evidence was given with a quiet force of conviction which justly created a powerful impression on the crowded court.

Then Mr. Daner rose to cross-examine the woman who confronted him so impassively.

"You say you are a widow, Mrs. Trevallack?" he began.

"Ay, sir," was the quiet answer.

"Who and what was your husband?"

"Willam Trevallack, a private in the Abernethy Highlanders."

"Where and when did you lose him?"

"He died of cholera at Kurnaul in India, twal' year ago last January."

"Have you any paper to prove your marriage and your husband's death?"

"No, sir. A box in which I keepit my papers was stolen frae me on the voyage hame frae India."

"Of what country was your husband?"

"A Cornishman, he tellt me; frae the south-west o' England—a miner tae trade."

"That will do, Mrs. Trevallack," said Mr. Daner suavely, as he resumed his seat. The woman had perceptibly paled under his quiet and brief cross-examination, and I noticed her upper lip tremble more than once; but she maintained her calm, sad composure, and left the witness-box with a respectful curtsey to the judge.

The Advocate Depute stated that Mrs. Trevallack's evidence completed the case for the Crown, and Mr. Daner rose to address the Court for the defence. He spoke as unemotionally as if he had been arguing in a dry commercial suit, and his quiet measured manner seemed to send a chill through the audience. In half-a-dozen sentences he brushed aside as futile and feeble the circumstantial evidence adduced on the part of the prosecution. "Practically," said he, "in this case the Crown has cited but a single witness. I will not pause to argue whether a conviction could legally or justly follow on the evidence of a single witness who confessedly caught a mere glimpse of the face of the murderer of Macdonald, whoever he may be. I simply proceed to destroy the case for the Crown by informing the jury that the testimony which has just been uttered by Margaret Trevallack is wholly inadmissible, and must be expurgated from the record. And this, my lord and gentlemen of the jury, because the said Margaret Trevallack is no widow, as she perjured herself by swearing in your hearing that she is; and further, and of far more importance, because"—here Mr. Daner paused for a moment in the midst of a silence so dead that a pin-fall could have been heard; then he quietly resumed: "because the said Margaret Trevallack is the wife of the panel; and it is a principle of our law that a wife cannot give evidence against her husband."

The scene was indescribable. The silence in which the young advocate had been speaking was broken, as he ended, by an universal gasp of utter astonishment. The judge himself evinced a most unwonted excitement; the audience simply seethed in a paroxysm of surprise. Three men only remained unmoved: the prisoner, his counsel, and his solicitor. Mrs. Trevallack had fainted dead away and was being carried out of court by the people about her. The "crier" called for "Silence!" at the judge's command, and Mr. Daner quietly resumed :—

"It only remains that I prove the truth of the statement which I have made to the satisfaction of your lordship and of the jury. I produce a certificate of the marriage of Margaret Alison of Maybole, Ayrshire, spinster; and William Trevallack of Camborne, Cornwall, private in the Abernethy Regiment of Royal Highlanders, celebrated at Cawnpore, India, and duly dated and authenticated. I produce a certified copy obtained from the Adjutant-General's office, of the sentence of a general court-martial held at Kurnaul in the Upper Province of Bengal on January 9, 1836, upon No. 4,130 Private William Trevallack of the Abernethy Regiment of Royal Highlanders, convicted for assaulting and beating on parade his superior officer Sergeant John Macdonald of the same regiment, and sentenced to be discharged from the service and transported to Botany Bay for ten years. I produce original of warrant issued by the Superintendent of Convicts at Port Jackson, New South Wales, dated January 9, 1846, certifying that William Trevallack late of the Abernethy Highlanders had duly served his allotted sentence of ten years' transportation and was now a free man, at liberty to leave the colony for whatever destination he might choose. And finally I call John Parry, late warder in Paramatta Prison near Port Jackson, to swear to the identity of the panel, who for reasons of his own with which we have no concern has chosen to call himself David Morgan, with the ex-convict William Trevallack, of whom he had charge when Trevallack worked in his chain-gang, engaged in road-making in the Blue Mountains of New South Wales in the years 1844-45. Call John Parry!"

John Parry, a tall, grizzle-bearded veteran, entered the box and curtly identified the prisoner. Cross-examined for the Crown, he read from his note-book the particulars of sundry marks, scars, and mutilations on the prisoner's person which an examination would reveal. Two surgeons from the audience volunteered to make the examination, furnished with a copy of the ex-warder's particulars. Returning into court with the prisoner after a short absence, they testified on oath that they had found on his body all the evidences of identification which Parry had specified. Mr. Daner then claimed that he had completely proved every link in the chain of identification of the panel as the husband of the woman who in the witness-box had falsely sworn that he was dead and that she was his widow. He added that since the direct evidence inculpating him as the murderer of Macdonald had failed and was of no avail for the cause charged and proven, and since the circumstantial evidence was clearly of no account, his client was entitled to a finding of "Not guilty" at the hands of the jury.

The judge, however, demurred to this demand. In his judgment the persons concerned with conducting the defence of the prisoner, knowing what they knew, had not done their best by their client. Whether they had in a measure sacrificed him to an anxiety for a sensational *dénouement* or not, he would not pretend to say. The witness Margaret Trevallack should have been challenged as soon as she entered the witness-box, and the reason which rendered her evidence inadmissible should have been at once brought forward as the justification of the challenge. Instead of this, she had been allowed to give her evidence, and that evidence must have impressed the jury, as he confessed it had impressed himself. Legally, it was true that it was not good evidence, but nevertheless the serious tenor of it remained with him, and, he doubted not, with the jury also. In the exercise of his discretion he would direct the jury to bring in a finding of "Not proven."

The verdict of "Not proven," which the Scottish law permits, is in the nature of a compromise—when the person on his trial has not succeeded in proving his innocence of the offence laid to his charge, and when, nevertheless, the evidence does not warrant the finding of "Guilty." The jury after an absence from court for a few minutes, returned with the verdict the fitness of which had been impressed upon them by the judge.

Mrs. Trevallack never returned to our glen, and I never heard what became of her. Her husband came back among us to his bothy on the muir. A week later, on a Saturday evening, he presented himself at Wullie Watt's smithy. The rustic congregation around the forge rather drew away from him, and old Wullie frankly told him that he was not welcome there. Trevallack, or Morgan, as he was still mostly called, replied that he had no intention or desire to intrude; but that now that he had undergone his trial—I think the old Scots legal expression is "tholed his assize"—and could not be tried again, he would fain be permitted to tell his story to the folk who had come to know him as a good comrade and harmless fellow, and whose goodwill, come what might, he was loth to lose. The vote of the smithy-parliament was in favour of his being allowed to deliver himself, and the manse grieve, who was among the auditors, brought me the gist of the strange tale.

Trevallack, it seemed, while the regiment was quartered in Kurnaul, had reason to suspect Sergeant Macdonald of paying undue attention to his wife, had words with him, and finally gave him a thrashing. For this assault on a superior officer the sergeant dared not in the circumstances report him; but, in his spite against him subjected him to a course of tyranny which ultimately became intolerable, till at length in an ungovernable fury of despair, Trevallack struck down the sergeant on regimental parade in face of the commanding officer. He was fortunate to have escaped the death-sentence, although at the time, he said, he would have preferred being shot, and so ending the misery of his life; for he was certain Macdonald had deliberately ruined him because of his passion for the private soldier's wife. As he sailed down the Bay of Bengal to his ten years of living death in New South Wales, he swore unto himself an oath that if he lived to regain his freedom, he would never rest until he had slain the man who had doubly wrecked his life. The long years passed; and his pass of emancipation was in his pocket as he stood on the shore of Port Jackson and looked seaward between Sydney Heads. He worked his passage to Calcutta and painfully and slowly travelling up country, found indeed the old regiment at Umballa, but no Sergeant Macdonald was now serving in it. He had been promoted to sergeant-major, the old soldiers told the tramp, whom, after his ten years of hardship and harsh discipline in the Australian chain-gang, they did not recognise; but who knew them yet refrained from revealing himself. Macdonald had some time previously been detached on some special staff-duty, whither Trevallack could not discover. The orderly-room clerk could not enlighten him; but from that functionary he ascertained the name of the Highland parish of which Macdonald was a native, and also the date at which would expire the term of service for which he had enlisted. Then he learned from an old married woman of the regiment— who knew him not, although he and his wife had lived in Kurnaul next room to her, and who wondered why this stranger tramp wanted the information—that after Private Trevallack was transported eleven years gone, Sergeant Macdonald had sent that poor fellow's wife to Scotland to live in his father's house until such time as the regiment should go home, and he then be able to buy his discharge. As for Trevallack, everybody held him as good as dead when he was carried down country in irons to be shipped to Australia.

In Macdonald's native parish, then, Trevallack had con-cluded, was the place where he could be most surely marked down; and thither by slow degrees and devious ways he betook himself, changing his name and his place of origin. No more than had his old comrades did the woman who really was his wife recognise in the bowed and clumsy Welsh stranger her Cornish husband of the long bygone time in Kurnaul. Unconsciously the wretched woman set him on the track of his enemy whom she loved. It was he, and none other, who had struck Macdonald to the heart out yonder in the road, as the man who had ruined his life neared him with an arm round the waist of the woman of whom the ex-sergeant had robbed the victim of his tyrannic malevolence; nor did he repent the deed. He had resolved to avow it in the dock and go to the gallows with a light heart, now that he had taken his revenge. But the young solicitor who had come to him in the county gaol represented to him that, having regard to the long cruel provocation and suffering he had endured, what he had done was, in the title of an old book, "Killing no Murder," and that it behoved him to make a fight for life. They all knew what had been the result. He would very fain be allowed to stay among them, since he had no friends elsewhere; he would not obtrude himself so long as they would just pass him the "Good day." But if they shunned him for the blood on his hands, he would go away out into the hard world.

There was an interval of silence. Then Wullie Watt, baring his old head, said solemnly, "What saith the Book, 'Vengeance is Mine; I will repay, saith the Lord.' Ye've been a sinfu' man, an' a bluidthirsty man, William Trevallack; but ye've been sair tried and sair vranged; and here is my haun'!"

VIII.

I AM well aware that in giving the above heading to this chapter I am exposing myself to scorn, obloquy, and contumely. Throughout life I have consistently tried to be a man of truth ; but I am mournfully conscious that this attribute will now be strenuously denied me. "To speak of a pretty Bulgarian woman," I hear Mr. Frederick Boyle assert in his mild yet direct manner, "is to enunciate a contradiction in terms." Mr. Beatty-Kingston, a judge of the sex, will probably formulate the axiom that "it is not in the nature of things that there can be a pretty Bulgarian woman." I am with both those gentlemen to a modified extent; physical repulsiveness is the rule as regards the female Bulgarian : but there never was a rule without at least one exception. So far as my experience goes, Maritza of Tirnova was the unique exception. Some people may say that since she was simply not so grim as were her fellow-countrywomen, I over-estimate her attractions in describing her as "pretty;" but this I do not conceive to be case. For I have a constitutional dislike to a pretty woman, although my impartiality compels me to acknowlege her beauty. I have never known a pretty woman who was not impertinently conscious of her charms, and who did not conduct herself as if she herself had some meritorious share in the construction of herself as a thing of beauty, instead of being, as a matter of fact, wholly unconsidered and unconsulted in that operation. That this illogical self-consciousness extends beyond the sphere of sophisticated and artificial society, was exemplified somewhat vividly in the case of the fair Maritza of Tirnova. She was a finished coquette, and no spoiled beauty of the season could be saucier. When I met her

I was—well, not to say old: the proper expression, perhaps, would be—in my mature prime, with a distinct sprinkling of grey in my hyacinthine locks. I ventured to make a few flattering remarks to this flower of a primitive semi-civilisation. She laughed, made a *mou*, and cheerfully suggested that I should go and make love to her mother, a portly matron of an advanced age; she herself meanwhile renewing her flirtation with Villiers, who at that stage of his career was still young and beautiful. I dispassionately cite this little episode to vindicate my impartiality, notwithstanding the young woman's melancholy lack of appreciation of my merits, in ascribing to her the epithet of the " pretty Maritza."

It was not to make the acquaintance of the young lady in question that we had penetrated into the bowels of the ugly and squalid Bulgaria—that game, even to the more youthful Villiers, would have been scarcely worth the candle. The fact was that we were with the Russian army which crossed the Danube in the end of June, 1877. We had been with gallant old Yolchine's stout soldiers of the Volhynia and Minsk regiments when in the sullen darkness of the early morning of the 27th, they had crossed the Danube in the pontoon boats and had fallen upon the Turkish detachment at the Tekir-Dere. A few days later the pontoon bridge was completed, and there crossed into Bulgaria the column, 18,000 strong of all arms, at the head of which Gourko was to penetrate into the Balkans and take in reverse the Turkish garrison in the Passes. Gourko pushed on ahead of his infantry with his two cavalry brigades, one of dragoons commanded by Prince Eugene of Leuchtenberg, and one of hussars commanded by the late Duke (Nicholas) of Leuchtenberg, both near relatives of the Czar. The first three days' march was over a bare, rolling country studded with villages and farms; on the morning of the 4th of July we were at the mouth of the Zavada gorge in the trough of which flows the Jantra, skirted by the road which leads up to the irregular precipice-fringed mass of rock on which Tirnova is built.

Turkish troops were reported still in possession of the town, but Gourko drove them away with insignificant loss and we entered the same afternoon. Tirnova is perched on a veritable eyrie, the rock summit having just space for a cramped market-place and a tortuous narrow street, flanked by tall, quaint-fronted wooden houses with projecting balconies and a continuous arcade over the side-walks. MacGahan had been in Tirnova in the previous summer during his "atrocities" investigations, and had then been the guest of Maritza and her mother, to whose domicile we were all now heartily welcomed. Ascending to the first floor—there was a shop on the street level—we found ourselves in a spacious lofty room, with a divan along all the four sides; the floor was covered with fine old Eastern rugs and in one corner was the shrine or *ikon* with a lamp burning in front of it.

We were well fed, our meal being served on a round table about a foot high, around which we lay or squatted on the rugs; Maritza sang to us and played on an instrument whose name I did not know, making eyes at Villiers all the time, and taking occasion to wound my *amour propre* in the manner already alluded to—a snub which afforded infinite amusement to MacGahan, who was a genial cynic in his easy-going way.

Next morning Gourko's hussar brigade came prancing through the town, bands playing, colours flying, swords at the "carry," Prince Eugene curvetting at the head of his command, and every officer and every trooper making the most of himself in the eyes of the "good brothers" who were being rescued from Turkish tyranny. From the Maritza balcony we were all looking down on the martial scene, Maritza in raptures over the brave Russian soldiers, kissing her hand to the officers whom she had already distinguished from the troopers, and babbling "Welcome, brothers!" in her pretty lisping accent. Villiers, quite out of it, was salving his wounds by assiduous sketching, and MacGahan was exchanging greetings with his many friends in the brigade. Suddenly MacGahan gave a great shout of astonishment, bolted down into the street, and was presently seen to be dragging a hussar officer off his horse by main force. This feat accomplished, the pair were visibly hugging each other with great warmth. A word to the colonel, a direction to a trooper to look after the officer's horse; and then MacGahan led his friend upstairs into the *salon* of the Maritza mansion and introduced the latter to us all.

The hussar officer was certainly one of the handsomest men I have ever seen—tall, square-shouldered, clean-flanked, with a small well-poised head, regular features, laughing blue eyes, and a smile of singular winsomeness. Closer inspection revealed lines which told of dissipation and a wild reckless life, but somehow those tell-tale tokens gave the man a certain added attractiveness. It appeared that MacGahan and this Russian officer, whose name was Andreiovich, had been close comrades in the Khivan campaign of 1873. His career had been a strange one—or, rather, it would have been so in any other service than the Russian. Of a noble family, he had begun his military life in the Guards. Three years of St. Petersburg dissipation saw him "stone-broke" and, as the custom is in respect of Guard officers who have "expended" themselves, he was sent to serve in the army of Asia. For some misconduct he had been reduced to the ranks, but had retrieved his position by an act of signal valour in the Khivan campaign; and later he had been permitted to return to Europe and take service in the hussar regiment in which he now commanded a troop.

Seated side by side on the divan MacGahan and the officer affectionately recalled many reminiscences of their Khivan intimacy; but I noticed that the subject by no means wholly engrossed the sprightly Russian. Maritza sat by her musical instrument, occasionally playing a note, and ignoring the dashing soldier with a profound intensity that was clearly over-acted. His eyes, on the contrary, were continually wandering in the direction of the artless young coquette; and when MacGahan left him to pay a visit to

General Gourko, the captain opened the trenches with a gay *insouciance* to which Maritza could not help but respond. There was every indication in the earlier stages of the affair that the gallant captain regarded himself as irresistible, and assumed that his success would be of the *veni, vidi, vici* kind. Maritza, it is true, had little knowledge of the world, but nature had bestowed on her a gift that was a full equivalent. She parried the thrusts of the captain with a demure ingenuousness that irritated him while inspiring him with additional ardour; she affected not to understand the meaning of his impassioned protestations; and on the third day drove him all but frantic by informing him in the most innocent manner, that a captain of the Leuchtenberg dragoons who was to remain in Tirnova while Gourko's expedition crossed the Balkans, had been billeted on her mother. The same evening the dragoon captain took up his quarters; and, if appearances went for anything, promptly fell in love with Maritza. As the latest arrival he rather scored off poor Andreiovich, who was none the happier that he had to leave next morning the field of love for quite another field. But he did not depart utterly disconsolate; Maritza was kind to him as he took his farewell on the staircase; and I came to the belief that the little coquette really did care for the handsome hussar.

Meanwhile the wooden but enamoured dragoon captain did not have things all his own way. Gourko's people marched away on the morning of the 12th; on the afternoon of the same day there arrived in Tirnova the Grand Duke Nicholas the commander-in-chief of the army, with a great staff of princes and nobles. His reception in the ancient capital was full of character and enthusiasm. At Zavada, across the mouth of the gorge leading up to the town, a picturesque arch had been constructed with branches of trees under which as they passed, the soldiers uncovered without orders to the great delight of the Bulgarians. During the four hundred years of the Turkish supremacy no Christian bell had chimed throughout all the land, but the old bells had been hidden away until the day of emancipation should come; and now from the two high-perched monasteries overhanging the gorge came the blithe carillon to the sound of which the venerable priests came down to meet the brother of the Czar with banners and pictures and with a large old Bible in the now obsolete Sclavonic which the soldiers kissed as they passed. At the chief entrance of the town the Grand Duke was met by robed priests chanting prayers, and by great crowds of townsfolk. After a short service in the quaint old Byzantine church he passed through the streets preceded by a crowd of girls singing. Flowers and wreaths rained down upon him from the windows — Maritza extremely active in this department—and the town rang with joy and excitement.

The Grand Duke was quartered in the Konak, which had been somewhat hurriedly evacuated by the Turkish Governor a few days previously; but for a large proportion of his Highness's staff billets had to be found in the houses of the inhabitants. They were delighted to show hospitality to the Russian officers. Maritza's mother received a young gentleman of distinction—if my recollection serves me right—none other than the Prince Alexander of Battenberg whom the world later knew as Prince Alexander of Bulgaria, and who was more recently known under the title of Count Hartenau. Maritza would not have been true to herself if she had not done her level best to fascinate this young pseudo-Serenity, but his Highness was not found to be more than civilly susceptible. What might have happened if the stay in Tirnova of the headquarter staff had been prolonged, it is impossible to guess. Maritza might have become for a time the foremost Bulgarian of her sex, since subsequent events proved that the Prince did not regard rank in a wife as indispensable. But he was at the mercy of Maritza only for a few days; and when he went away with his chief she had only the dragoon captain to operate upon. This officer was not so impetuous as his hussar rival; he knew how to dissemble his love, and Maritza by no means had it all her own way with him.

Piqued by the dragoon's strategic reserve Maritza exerted all her blandishments, and the captain thawed by degrees until at length he melted altogether. It was then Maritza's turn to hold off, the more so that she really cared nothing for the dragoon officer and merely was amusing herself *pour passer le temps.* Early in August Andreiovich returned to Tirnova, after sharing in Gourko's wonderful and adventurous raid to the southward of the Balkans. I had ridden out to Nikup to meet the returning squadrons which MacGahan had accompanied, and to hear the detailed account of their adventures. We spent the night in that village gossiping with the returned wanderers. Andreiovich had won the St. George's Cross. He had ascended the Schipka from the south, had been in the fire treacherously given by the Turks after they had displayed the white flag, and on the following day had seen the headless Russian corpses strewn over the slope before the abandoned Russian camp, and the Russian heads which in wanton devilry the Turks had severed from the bodies and piled, in a symmetrical heap with the faces outward. He had ridden with his squadron southward from Eski Zagra, crossed the Maritza River at Güterbü, and destroyed a section of the Adrianople and Philippopolis Railway; and when Sulieman Pasha suddenly surrounded Prince Leuchtenberg in Eski Zagra, he had gained distinction by his cool daring in the cavalry charge which cut through the Turks' environment of that town, and enabled the Russian horsemen to relieve the pressure on Gourko's right wing. He had shared the miseries of the retreat through the Dalboka and Hankioi Passes, during which the wounded died like flies from jolting and exposure and hale men succumbed from fatigue and sunstroke.

It was not he, the reader may be sure, who told us all those exploits of the young hussar; indeed, during the recital he evinced considerable impatience, and on the first available opportunity he asked me to take a stroll with him in the twilight. He wanted to know all about Maritza, and what were the relations between her and Sablanoff—that I should have mentioned earlier, was the name of the dragoon captain. I was strictly non-committal; Andreiovich became huffed, and we parted. I rejoined the other officers and saw no more of him that night.

Next morning early I rode towards Tirnova, and a mile outside came on Andreiovich sitting on horseback under a tree, evidently waiting for me. A glance at his face showed me that he was in a state of excitement. He came at me as if he intended to ride me down, roaring: "That pig! That what you call low cad!" I refused to speak to him until he moderated his tone, and he became quieter. "When I left you last evening," said he, "I rode into Tirnova, gave up my horse, and went straight to Maritza's house. I entered without warning, and lo! Maritza and Sablanoff sat together on the divan, abominably close, my friend, and I believe his arm was round her waist! The interloping dog knew well my prior intentions, and it was mean beyond conception on his part to take advantage of a brother officer when absent on service in the field. I told him so with great fervour and directness, and then I called him a *cochon*, pulled his nose, and cut him across the shoulders with my riding-whip. Of course he must fight, and, to do him justice as a Russian officer, I do not for a moment suppose that he can have any wish to evade fighting."

Now the regulations of the Russian military service prohibit duelling by officers, but it is nevertheless winked at so long as the *casus belli* is not of a disreputable character; only under no conditions are officers allowed to act as seconds. Andreiovich requisitioned my services in this capacity, and I reluctantly consented to act on his behalf; a German ex-officer who was corresponding for a Berlin paper, agreed to be the second of the dragoon captain. The latter, in his cool, sententious way, was extremely bloodthirsty. He demanded that the duel should be fought with revolvers, the firing to be maintained until results occurred or the weapons be emptied. The hussar, who as the challenged had the choice of weapons, fell in warmly with the views of his

N

antagonist in the matter of weapons, and was resolute that the duel should be *à outrance.* The German ex-officer turned out a vicarious fire-eater; and my task, that of modifying the ferocity of the combat, was no easy one. At length, by arguing that it beseemed cavalry officers to fight with the weapon of that service to which they belonged, I succeeded in bringing it about that the duel should be fought with sabres, and hoped that the worst that would happen would be a flesh wound or two. The meeting took place in a wood close to Tirnova one morning soon after daybreak. Andreiovich pushed the attack from the first, Sablanoff, who was the cooler man and the better swordsman, standing on the defensive. But it happened that once the latter missed his guard, and the nimble hussar promptly giving point ran his sabre through the dragoon's left shoulder so forcibly that a foot of the weapon came out behind.

Mischief would have come of it had we carried Sablanoff to the military hospital; and we had no alternative but to bring him to his billet in the Maison Maritza and have him seen to there by the surgeon of his regiment, who might be trusted to report him ill of some other malady than a sabre-thrust. Maritza had known nothing of the duel before its occurrence; and when she had to be told of it as the wounded man was being brought into the house, she showed truer and deeper feeling than I had given her credit for possessing. Coquette though she was the girl had a heart, and was honestly shocked that she should have been the cause of the shedding of blood. Her repentance was most genuine. She nursed the wounded Sablanoff with unremitting care. When Andreiovich came to see her the day after the duel, and reproached her—not very severely—for having caused it, she owned her fault with many tears, entreated his forgiveness, confessed that all her heart belonged to him, and definitely plighted her troth to the handsome hussar. He would fain have perpetrated matrimony then and there, so ardent were his emotions; but Maritza, although in love, had not wholly taken leave of her senses, and prevailed on him to wait until the war was over.

Such renown had Andreiovich earned in the Gourko expedition that on his return to Tirnova, stout old General Radetsky the commander of the 8th Army Corps, appointed him to his staff in the capacity of aide-de-camp. During the quiet days in Tirnova the duties of that billet were very light, and the hussar was free to spend most of his time in the society of his pretty Maritza. But this halcyon interval of love-making was to be of short duration. About the middle of August there came tidings to Radetsky that Sulieman's Turkish army some 50,000 strong, was threatening the Balkan passes from the south. General Darozinski with but some 5,000 men was holding the Schipka; to strengthen him Radetsky ordered a regiment from Selvi, commanded by the Colonel Stolietoff who a year later was the head of the Russian Mission to Cabul which caused the Afghan war of 1878–79. Radetsky himself, thinking the Elena Pass in greatest danger hurried thither with a brigade; but presently learned it was the Schipka against which the Turks were concentrating, and therefore made for that position with all the speed he could compass. No man was ever nearer being too late than was he when he climbed the Schipka on the afternoon of August 23rd. For three long days 40,000 Turks with a powerful artillery had been continually assailing the gallant handful commanded by Darozinski and Stolietoff. As the sun was sinking, the Turks had so wound round both the Russian flanks that the Moslem soldiery were on the point of joining hands in the Russian rear.

A reinforcement opportunely arrived, consisting of a battalion of riflemen brought up on Cossack horses by Radetsky himself, who, having saved the day and the position, was now marching up the road with his staff at his back, and running the triple gauntlet of the Turkish fire to join the two commanders on the peak close to the battery of the first position. But one member of the general's staff was not following him. In front of the sombre green line of riflemen down the glen I marked a figure in blue uniform, and when the detachment returned from its successful dash,

N 2

there came marching on its flank that extremely reckless
warrior, Captain Andreiovich.   He said the general had
given him permission to take part in the lively affair, but—
well, I shall not pursue the subject.

Of the following day, the 24th of August, I never think
without a shudder. The Russian position was on a long
serpentine ridge along the top of which ran the road,
spreading out somewhat toward the summit where was the
earthwork known as Fort St. Nicholas. On each side of
this ridge there was a deep depression, beyond which, both
right and left of the central ridge, stretched a parallel
elevation held by the Turks, whose fire commanded and
swept the whole length of the Russian position. There was
no spot on the central ridge which was not exposed to fire.
At the bandaging place men already wounded were killed;
the surgeons were shot in the midst of their ministrations
to the wounded.   The cooks were struck down as they
tended the soup-kettles far to the rear. General Darozinski
was killed while resting on what was thought the shelter
of a reverse slope. General Petroceni was slain away back
among the reserves.   General Dragomiroff was wounded
when on the glacis of St. Nicholas, and among those who
took part in carrying that gallant officer to the hut which
did duty as a field hospital, only two (of whom I was one)
escaped injury from bullet fire.   The Turks made attack
after attack with extraordinary dash and resolution; but the
Russian resistance was stubborn, and as the day began to
wane Radetsky believed that the time had come for him to
take the offensive. The Tirailleurs and the Brianski regiment were thrust down into the deep wooded hollow intervening between the Russian ridge and the steep slope
leading up to the "Woody Mountain" on which the Turks
had a battery and redoubt. For hours the struggle swayed
to and fro down there among the trees. There is something exceptionally gruesome about a fight in a wood. You
can see nought save an occasional glimpse of dark colour
among the foliage, and the white clouds of smoke rising
above it like soap-bubbles. Hoarse shouts and shrill cries come

back on the wind from out the mysterious inferno. Wounded men come staggering out from among the swarthy trunks, and collapse in a heap or crawl backwards to the ambulance men.

To help the riflemen and Brianskis, the two battalions of the Jitomer regiment were summoned from their shelter in the ditch of St. Nicholas Fort, and went away to the right almost along the sky line. Covered by artillery fire they made good progress for a while, but then came to a standstill. The battalions had left two companies behind to act as supports. Radetsky took one company his chief-of-staff another, and led them on to the fight. His staff accompanied the brave old chief. I shook hands with Andreiovich, as with a smile in his eye and a cigarette between his lips he lingered one moment to give me a message in case he should not come back.

And he did not come back. I watched him till the handful of reinforcements entered the wood, and then I could see nothing more. But the Jitomers did not succeed, although they lost enormously in the stubbornly-made attempt. They came back a good deal broken up, with heavy loss of officers, and nobody could tell when or how Andreiovich had gone down. For my own part I do not hesitate to admit that I fervently hoped my poor friend had been shot dead; for the warfare in which the Russians were engaged had a feature of savagery which marked the perpetrators as unworthy to rank among civilised nations. The Turks invariably slaughtered their wounded antagonists found by them on the field, and the butchery was freely accompanied by aggravations of barbarity and torture such as cannot be described. In common with all Russian officers, Andreiovich carried a dagger with which to take his own life in case of being wounded and left without a chance of removal by the Russian Krankenträger.

Radetsky, although he had not entirely made good the position, had so prospered that when leaving him in the evening I ventured to express my belief that he need not fear dislodgment. "With God's help," said the old warrior, "I shall hold on here till I am ordered away."

Early next morning I was in the Imperial head-quarters at Gorni Studen, where, as the bearer of the latest intelligence, I was called on to report the same to the Tzar. Thence I hurried to the telegraph office at Bucharest, and, my telegram despatched, immediately began my return journey towards the Schipka.

On my way down therefrom I had made a short détour into Tirnova on the melancholy errand of breaking to poor Maritza the sad tidings regarding her betrothed. Minutes were of importance to me, and I had left the poor girl in a dead faint in her mother's arms. On my return I found no Maritza in the Tirnova house. Her mother told me sadly that on the morning after my night visit she had started for the Schipka, refusing the companionship of the mother, because of the certain absence of such comfort as the old lady was accustomed to.

Returning to the Schipka on the fifth day after having quitted it, I found Radetsky drinking tea, seated in a bower of leaves perched on the summit of the peak. "Here I am," said he, "as I told you I should be ; and there are no bullets flying now. Berdek, the Woody Mountain, and the Bald Mountain are now clear of Turks ; they have got their belly-ful of fighting, and are now licking their wounds down below in the valley villages."

You could still get shot on the outlying spurs if you wanted to very badly, for occasional Turks did continue to prowl; but the chief was substantially correct. It would have been pleasanter if he had employed burial parties a little more freely, but Radetsky was not a fastidious person. In the stone hut on the ridge which had been the field hospital, I found poor Maritza tending two soldiers so severely wounded that they could not be moved. She had in her possession her lover's uniform all torn and soiled with blood and clay. The sorry fragments had been found in a little hollow somewhat wide of the line of the charge, and there lay beside them a naked corpse whose state was such after three days' exposure to sun and weather, that no identification was possible. Maritza steadily refused to believe that the body was that of

Andreiovich, but she was alone in her conviction ; and indeed the name of Captain Michael Andreiovich of the 9th Hussars had been included among the " killed " in the supplement to General Radetsky's despatch.

I tried in vain to persuade Maritza to return with me to her mother. Her pretext for refusal was her duty to the two poor broken fellows whom she was nursing ; but it was not difficult to perceive she still hoped against hope that her lover might yet turn up. The Gabrova woman who was sharing the nursing duty promised faithfully that as soon as the two wounded men were dead—they were beyond recovery—she herself would accompany Maritza down to Tirnova and would not leave her till she was in her mother's arms. So I bade a sad farewell to the poor wan-faced girl, so changed from the still recent days of coquetry ; and departed to another section of the theatre of war, where amid the carnage of Plevna I did not lose the memory of the tragedy now associated in my mind with the once gay Maritza.

It was in the Podo Mogosoi of Bucharest in the following February that, to my unutterable surprise, I met Maritza arm-in-arm with Andreiovich, he in civilian dress and walking very lame with the support of a stick.

" Yes," said Maritza, all her archness restored, " this fellow one morning last month coolly sauntered into our house, sup-ported on crutch and staff and with one leg supported by a strap round his neck, condescended to kiss me, and then sat down and demanded vodki. Since then, I may inform you, I have amused myself by marrying him. I've told you all that is important; he must give himself the trouble of recounting the details." We went into Brofft's restaurant, and Andreiovich told his strange story :—

" During our attack on the Woody Mountain a Turk and I were at close quarters, when a bullet shattered my leg and I rolled into a hollow carrying along with me the Turk whom I killed with my dagger. Averting faintness by resorting to my flask, I first bandaged my leg; and hoping to escape the fate which so many of our poor wounded fellows incur, I tore off my uniform, stripped the dead Turk, and contrived to work

myself into his garments.   All night I lay there uninterfered
with, but suffering great agony.   Early on the following morning
there passed close to me, going to the front, a tall man in the
dress of a Turkish officer.   I was about to risk it and call to
him, when he tripped over a root and as he recovered himself
I distinctly heard him say 'Damn.'   That satisfied me he was
an Englishman, and I addressed him in your language.   He
was most kind.   His name was Campbell, and he commanded
a battalion in Sulieman's army.*   He got a stretcher on which
I was placed, Campbell's Turks, who carried me, believing that
I was a wounded countryman.   Campbell accompanied me
down into Schipka village and handed me over to the care of
the British surgeons of the Red Crescent organisation.   Drs.
Leslie, Hume, and Sandwith treated me with the greatest skill
and assiduity, but months passed and I was still on my back.
Sulieman marched westward about the New Year, leaving
Vessil Pasha at and about the Schipka with some 40,000 men.
You must have heard how Radetsky, Mirsky, and Skobeleff
came wallowing through the ten-feet deep snow on the Schipka
in January, and how Skobeleff after a desperate struggle for
the possession of the Shenova redoubts, received the surrender
of Vessil and his whole army.   That evening I ceased to be a
wounded Turk and became a lame Russian—good for no more
soldiering, worse luck.   When the track got beaten over the
pass, I found a Turkish pony on which I rode into Gabrova
and thence down the valley to Tirnova.   Maritza didn't in the
least expect to see me any more ; but I will say this for her,
that although that dragoon fellow was still wistfully promenad-
ing Tirnova, she never gave him the slightest encouragement.
One fine morning she went to church with me and came
out Madame Andreiovich ; and now we are on our way to
Russia, when I shall have to make things unpleasant for my
father if he does not behave handsomely to us."

And so now there is not any more a " pretty Maritza " in
Tirnova.

* He was a man of exceptional daring, who, having seen much service in
many countries, was killed in the attack on Sekukuni's Mountain in South
Africa, when in command of the Swazi contingent.

IX.

THE DEATH OF THE PRINCE IMPERIAL.

IT was in Zululand, on the evening of June 1, 1879. A little
group of us were at dinner in the tent of General Marshall,
who commanded the cavalry brigade in the British army
which was marching on Ulundi, King Cetewayo's royal
kraal. The sun was just going down when Colonel Harrison,
the quartermaster-general, put his head inside the tent door,
and called aloud in a strange voice, "Good God! the Prince
Imperial is killed!" Harrison, though stolid, sometimes
jested, and for the moment this announcement was not taken
seriously. Lord Downe, Marshall's aide-de-camp, threw a crust
of bread at his head, and Herbert Stewart, then Marshall's
brigade-major, afterwards killed during the desert march in the
Soudan, laughed aloud.

But, sitting near the door, I discerned in the faint light of
the dying day the horror in Harrison's face, and sprang to my
feet instinctively. The news was only too fatally true; and
when the dismal, broken story of the survivors of the party
had been told, throughout the force there was a thrill of
sorrow for the poor gallant lad, a burning sense of shame
that he should have been so miserably left to his fate, and a
deep sympathy for the forlorn widow in England on whom
fortune seemed to rejoice in heaping disaster on disaster,
bereavement on bereavement.

I knew the Prince well. On the first two occasions I saw
him it was through a binocular from a considerable distance.
On August 2, 1870, the day on which the boy of fourteen in
the words of his father "received his baptism of fire," I was
watching from the drill-ground above Saarbrücken in company with the last remaining Prussian soldiers, the oncoming
swarm-attack of Battaille's tirailleurs firing as they hurried
across the plain. The tirailleurs had passed a little knoll

which rose in the plain about midway between the Spicheren hill and where I stood, and presently it was crowned by two horsemen followed by a great staff. The glass told me that without a doubt the senior of the foremost horsemen was the Emperor Napoleon, and that the younger, shorter and slighter —a mere boy he looked—was the Prince Imperial, whom we knew to be with his father in the field.

A fortnight later, in the early morning of the 15th, the day before Mars-la-Tour when the German army was as yet only east and south of Metz, I accompanied a German horse-battery which, galloping up to within five hundred paces of the château of Longueville around which was a French camp of some size, opened fire on château and camp. After a few shells had been fired great confusion was observed about the château and in the camp, and I distinctly discerned the Emperor and his son emerge from the building, mount, and gallop away, followed by suite and escort.

Years later in Zululand, when the day's work was done for both of us and the twilight was falling on the rolling veldt, the Prince was wont occasionally to gossip with me about those early days of the great war which we had witnessed from opposite sides, and he told me his experiences of the morning just mentioned. A crash awoke him with a start and he was sitting up in bed, bewildered, when his father entered with the exclamation " Up, Louis ! up and dress ! The German shells are crashing through the roofs." As the Prince looked out of the window while he was hurriedly dressing, he saw a shell fall and burst in a group of officers seated in the garden at breakfast, and when the smoke lifted three of them lay dead. That the story of his nerves having been shattered by the bullet-fire at Saar-brücken was untrue, was proved by an episode he related to me of that same morning an hour later. On the steep ascent of the *chaussée* up to Châtel the imperial party was wedged in the heart of a complete block of troops, waggons, and guns. A long delay seemed inevitable. But the lad had noticed a wayside gate whence a track led up through the vineyard. He followed it to the crest and marked its trend ; then, riding back, he called aloud " This way, papa !" The Prince's side-track turned the block, and presently the party were in the new quarters in the house which is now the post-office of Gravelotte.

That excellent American publication "Johnson's Universal Cyclopædia," errs for once in stating that after the downfall of the empire the Prince "escaped with his mother to England." He never saw his mother after leaving Paris for the seat of war until she came to him in Hastings after the revolution in Paris. When the shadows were darkening on MacMahon's ill-fated march, the Emperor sent his son away from the front; and the story of the vicissitudes and dangers the lad encountered before reaching England after Sedan would make of itself a long chapter.

When his parents settled at Chislehurst, the Prince, then in his fifteenth year, entered the Royal Academy at Woolwich to receive a scientific military education. He had not undergone the usual preparation, and he might have joined without the preliminary examination; but never then nor throughout the course would he accept any indulgence, and his "preliminary" was satisfactory in spite of his want of familiarity with the language. In the United States West Point affords the same instruction to all cadets alike, those who are most successful passing into the scientific branches; but in England the cadets for the Line are educated at Sandhurst, and the severer tuition of Woolwich is restricted to candidates for the engineer and artillery branches. The Prince took his chance with his comrades both at work and play. His mathematical instructor has stated that he had considerable powers, evincing an undoubtedly clear insight into the principles of the higher mathematics; but he added that he often failed to bring out specifically his knowledge at examinations, owing to his imperfect grasp of the necessary formulæ and working details. Indeed, details wearied him, then and later. In Zululand he more than once told me that he "hated desk work;" and M. Deleage, his countryman and friend who accompanied the Zululand expedition, wrote that on the day before his death after he had left the staff office tent, "Lieutenant Carey found the Prince's work done

with so much haste and inattention that he had to sit up all
night correcting it." In spite of this defect in steady concentration at the end of his Woolwich course he passed
seventh in a class of thirty-five, and had he gone into the
English service he would have been entitled to choose between the engineers and artillery. He would have stood
higher but that, curiously enough, he comparatively failed in
French. He was an easy first in equitation. During his
Woolwich career he won the love and respect of his comrades : his instructors spoke warmly of his modesty, conscien-
tiousness, and uprightness, and pronounced him truthful and
honourable in a high degree.

After leaving Woolwich he lived mostly with his widowed
mother at Chislehurst, but travelled on the Continent
occasionally, and mixed a good deal in London society where
from time to time I met him. After he attained manhood it
was understood that a marriage was projected between him
and the Princess Beatrice, the youngest of the Queen's
daughters, who is now the wife of Prince Henry of Battenberg.
The attainment of his majority was made a great occasion by
the Imperialist adherents, as a test of their adherence to a
cause which they refused to consider lost. More than 10,000
Frenchmen of all ranks and classes congregated on Chislehurst
Common that day. The tricolour waved along the route to
the little Roman Catholic chapel on the outskirts of the quiet
Kentish village ; as the members of the Imperial family
passed from Camden Place to the religious service every head
was uncovered ; and shouts of " Vive l'Empereur !" rose from
the ardent partisans, numbers of whom had already paid
homage to the remains of their dead Emperor lying in
the marble sarcophagus in front of the high altar of the
chapel. Later in the day the large company of French
people assembled in the park of Camden Place, in rear of the
deputations from the different provinces of France, each
deputation headed by a leader bearing the provincial banner.
The Prince with his mother by his side stood forward ;
behind them the princes, nobles, and statesmen of the late
empire, and many Imperialist ladies of rank. When the Duc

de Padoue had finished reading a long address expressive of attachment and devotion, the young Prince spoke to his supporters with great dignity, earnestness, and modesty. I heard the final sentences of his speech, the manly tone of which I can never forget. "If the time should ever arrive when my countrymen shall honour me with a majority of the suffrages of the nation, I shall be ready to accept with proud respect the decision of France. If for the eighth time the people pronounce in favour of the name of Napoleon, I am prepared to accept the responsibility imposed upon me by the vote of the nation." Once again, and only once, I heard the Prince speak in public. It was at the annual dinner of an institution known as the "Newspaper Press Fund." Lord Salisbury, one of the most brilliant speakers of our time, was in the chair. Cardinal Manning, the silver-tongued; Lord Wolseley, good speaker and brilliant commander; and Henry M. Stanley, fresh from "darkest Africa," were among the orators. But, quite apart from his position, the short address made by the Prince Imperial was unanimously regarded as the speech of the evening.

In features, with his long, oval face, black hair and eyes—attributes of neither of his parents, and his lean, shapely head, the Prince was a Spaniard of the Spaniards. One recognised in him no single characteristic of the Frenchman; he was a veritable hidalgo, with all the pride, the melancholy, the self-restraint yet ardour to shine, the courage trenching on an ostentatious recklessness, and indeed the childishness in trifles which marked that now all but extinct type. Whether there was in his veins a drop of the Bonapartist blood (remembering the suspicions of King Louis of Holland with regard to Hortense) is a problem now probably insoluble. Certainly neither he nor his father had any physical feature in common with the undoubted members of the race. The Montijos, although the house in its latest developments had somewhat lost caste and had a bourgeois strain on the distaff side, were ancestrally of the bluest blood of Spain; and it has always been my idea that the Prince Imperial illustrated the theory of atavism by throwing back to the Guzmans, the Corderas or the Baros, all grand old Spanish families whose blood was in his veins. How strong was his self-restraint even in youth, an anecdote told in Miss Barlee's interesting book* of his Woolwich days may evidence. Hearing one day that a Frenchman was visiting the academy, he sent to say that he should be glad to see his countryman. The person, who as it happened was a bitter anti-Imperialist, was presented, and the Prince asked him from what part of France he came. The fellow, looking the youth straight in the face with a sarcastic smile, uttered the one word "Sedan," and grinningly waited for the effect of his brutality. The Prince flushed, and his eye kindled; then he conquered himself, and, quietly remarking, "That is a very pretty part of France," closed the interview with a bow.

I never saw dignity and self-control more finely manifested in union than when the lad, not yet seventeen, wearing a black cloak over which was the broad red ribbon of the Legion of Honour, followed his father's coffin as chief mourner along the path lined by many thousand French sympathisers; and his demeanour was truly royal when later on that trying day the masses of French artisans hailed him with shouts of "Vive Napoleon IV.!" He stopped the personal acclaim by saying: "My friends, I thank you; but your Emperor is dead. Let us join in the cry of 'Vive la France!'"—baring at the same time his head and leading off the cheering. His craving for effect curiously displayed itself during a parade in Scotland of a number of Clydesdale stallions, at which were present the Prince of Wales and a number of noblemen and gentlemen. One horse, which was plunging violently, was described as never having allowed a rider to remain on its back. At the word the Prince Imperial vaulted on to the bare back of the animal, mastered its efforts to dislodge him, and rode the conquered stallion round the arena amid loud applause.

The forced inaction of his life irked him intensely. His good sense and true patriotism induced him steadily to

* "Life of the Prince Imperial," compiled by Helen Barlee. Griffith and Farran, London.

decline the urgency of young and ardent Imperialists, that he should disturb the peace of France either by intrigue or by more active efforts to restore the dynasty. It stung him to the quick that the scurrilous part of the French press taunted him with the quietness of his life, which it chose to attribute to cowardice and lack of enterprise. In Zululand he told me of a circumstance which I have nowhere seen mentioned, that a year before he had applied to the French Government for permission to join the French troops fighting in Tonquin; that MacMahon, who was then President, was in his favour; but that the Ministry refused the request. The English war of 1879 in Zululand was his opportunity. His constant belief was that ten years would be the term of his exile. "Dix ans de patience, et après!" he used to mutter in his day-dreams. The ten years were nearly up. And what prestige would not accrue to him if he should have the good fortune to distinguish himself in the field, which he was resolved to do at any cost! The disaster of Isandlwana to retrieve which troops were being hurried out, and the heroic defence of Rorke's Drift, were lost opportunities at which he chafed. He felt that he was forfeiting chances which, taken advantage of, might have aided his progress to the Imperial throne. Determined to lose no more chances, he went to the British Commander-in-Chief and begged to be permitted to go on service to South Africa.

His attitude and yearnings were quite intelligible, and were in no sense blameworthy. He desired to further the means towards a specific and obvious end, if England only would give him the helping hand. But this ultimate aim of his being so evident, it was singularly improper and ill-judged on the part of the English authorities to give well-grounded umbrage to the friendly power across the Channel, by forwarding an enterprise the purpose of which was to help toward changing Republican France into Imperial France, and to contribute toward the elevation of this young man to the throne which his father had lost. The Commander-in-Chief had his scruples, for he is a man of some discretion; but they were overruled. And it was from Windsor, bidden

God-speed by the Sovereign, that the Prince departed to embark. France sullenly watched his career in South Africa. Had it ended differently the mood would have become intensified. If it be asked why for the last sixteen years France has never for an hour worn a semblance of cordial accord with the insular power its neighbour, the answer is, that this attitude of chronic umbrage has one of its sources in the intrigue which sent the Prince Imperial to Zululand.

At the news of Isandlwana I had hurried from the Khyber Pass to South Africa, and the Prince had already joined the army when first I met him in May, 1879 at Sir Evelyn Wood's camp of Kambula, which he was visiting with Lord Chelmsford and the headquarters' staff. The Duke of Cambridge had specially confided him to his lordship's care. But poor Lord Chelmsford's nerve had been sore shaken by the tragedy of Isandlwana, after which he had begged to be relieved. Like Martha, he was careful and troubled about many things; his will-power was limp and fickle and the Prince was to him in the nature of a white elephant. The latter, for his part, was ardent for opportunities of adventurous enterprise, while the harassed Chelmsford had been bidden to dry-nurse him assiduously. The military arrangements were lax and the Prince had been able to share in several somewhat hazardous reconnaissances, in the course of which he had displayed a rash bravery which disquieted the responsible leaders. After one of these scouting expeditions in which he actually had come to close quarters with a party of Zulus, and it was asserted had whetted his sword, he was said to have remarked naïvely:—"Such skirmishes suit my taste exactly, yet I should be au désespoir did I think I should be killed in one. In a great battle, if Providence so willed it, all well and good; but in a petty reconnaissance of this kind—ah! that would never do."

His penultimate reconnaissance was with a detachment of Frontier Light Horse under the command of Colonel Buller, V.C., now Sir Redvers Buller, Adjutant-General of the British Army. The Zulus gathered and a fight seemed impending, to the Prince's great joy; but they dispersed. A few, however, were seen skulking at a distance, and against them he rode at full gallop in a state of great excitement. He had to be supported, which occasioned inconvenience; during the night, which was bitterly cold and during which the Prince's excitement continued, he tramped up and down constantly, singing at intervals " Malbrook s'en va-t-en-guerre" not wholly to the contentment of the phlegmatic Britons around him. Colonel Buller reported his inconvenient recklessness, protested against accepting responsibility for him when his military duties called for all his attention, and suggested that he should be employed in camp on staff duty instead of being permitted to risk himself on reconnaissance service. Thereupon Lord Chelmsford detailed him to desk-work in the quartermaster - general's department, and gave Colonel Harrison a written order that the Prince should not quit the camp without the express permission of his lordship. The Prince, made aware of this order, obeyed, for he had a high sense of discipline; but he did not conceal his dislike to the drudgery of plan-making in a tent. He was fond of and expert in sketching in the field.

The orders issued to the little army in the Koppie Allein camp on the 31st of May for the morrow were, that the infantry should march direct to a camping-ground on the Itelezi hill about eight miles forward, the cavalry to scout several miles farther and then to fall back to the Itelezi camp. Early on the morning of June 1st the Prince, dead tired of routine desk-work, begged Colonel Harrison to allow him to make a sketching expedition with an escort, beyond the ground to be covered by the cavalry. The matter was under discussion—Harrison reluctant to consent, when Lieutenant Carey, a staff officer of the department, suggested that he should accompany the Prince, and proposed that the expedition should extend into the Ityotyozi valley, where the next camp beyond the Itelezi was to be and a sketch of which he (Carey) had two days previously left unfinished. Harrison then made no further

o

objection, consenting the more readily because the whole terrain in advance had been thoroughly scouted over recently.   He instructed Carey to requisition a mounted escort of six white men and six Basutos, and he subsequently maintained that he had entrusted the command of the escort to Carey.   This Carey denied, repudiating all responsibility in regard to the direction of the escort since the Prince in his rank of honorary captain, was his superior officer, and holding that his function as regarded the latter was simply that of friendly adviser.   I was afterwards told that before leaving camp the Prince wrote a letter—the last he ever wrote—to his mother, and that hearing I was about to ride back to the post-office at Landmann's Drift, he left the message for me with his best regards, that he should be greatly obliged by my carrying down his letter.   As it happened, I did not quit the camp until I did so as the bearer to the telegraph-wire of the tidings of the Prince's death.

I was with Herbert Stewart, the cavalry brigade-major, when Carey came to him with Harrison's warrant for an escort.   Carey did not mention, nor did the document state, that the escort was for the Prince Imperial.   Stewart ordered out six men of Beddington's Horse—a curiously mixed handful of diverse nationalities—and he told Carey that he would send Captain Shepstone an order for the Basuto detail of the escort; but that time would be saved if Carey himself on his way back to headquarters would hand Shepstone the order and give his own instructions. Carey chose the latter alternative and departed.   An hour later, while I was still with Stewart, the six Basutos paraded in front of his tent.   Either Carey or Shepstone had blundered in the instructions given them, that was clear; but nothing could now be done but to order the Basutos to hurry forward and try to overtake the other instalment of the escort.   Meanwhile the Prince had been impatient; and he, Carey, and the white section of the escort had gone on.   Carey made no demur to the scant escort, since nothing was to be apprehended and since he himself had been recently chaffed for being addicted to requisitioning inordinately large escorts. Harrison later met the party some miles out, and sanctioned its going forward notwithstanding that the Basutos had not joined, which indeed they never succeeded in doing. The party then consisted of the Prince, Carey, a sergeant, a corporal, four troopers, and a black native guide—nine persons in all.

When Harrison had announced the tidings of the tragedy, I went to my tent and sent for each of the four surviving troopers in succession. They were all bad witnesses, and I could not help suspecting that they were in collusion to keep something back. All agreed, however, that Lieutenant Carey headed the panic-flight; and next day it transpired that, when a mile away from the scene and still galloping wildly, he was casually met by Sir Evelyn Wood and Colonel Buller, to whom he exclaimed: "Fly! Fly! The Zulus are after me and the Prince Imperial is killed!" The evidence I took on the night of the disaster, and that afterwards given before the court of inquiry and the court-martial on Carey, may now be briefly summarised.

The site of the intended camp having been planned out by the Prince and Carey, the party ascended an adjacent hill and spent an hour there in sketching the contours of the surrounding country. No Zulus were visible in the wide expanse surveyed from the hill-top. At its base, on a small plain at the junction of the rivers Tambakala and Ityotyozi, was the small Zulu kraal of Etuki, the few huts of which, according to the Zulu custom, stood in a rough circle which was surrounded on three sides at a little distance by a tall growth of "mealies" (Indian corn) and the high grass known as "Kaffir corn." The party descended to this kraal, off-saddled, fed the horses, made coffee, ate food, and then reclined, resting against the wall of a hut in full sense of assured safety. Some dogs skulking about the empty kraal and the fresh ashes on the hearths might have warned them, but they did not heed the suggestion thus afforded. About

o 2

three o'clock Corporal Grubbe, who understood the Basuto language, reported the statement of the guide that he had seen a Zulu entering the mealie-field in their front. Carey proposed immediately saddling-up. The Prince desired ten minutes' longer rest, and Carey did not expostulate. Then the horses were brought up and saddled. Carey stated that at this moment he saw black forms moving behind the screen of tall grain, and informed the Prince. Throughout the day the latter had acted in command of the escort, and he now in soldierly fashion gave the successive orders, " Prepare to mount!" "Mount!" Next moment, according to the evidence, a volley of twenty or thirty bullets—one witness said forty bullets—were fired into the party.

Let me be done with Carey for good and all. He had mounted on the inner, the safe, side of the hut, and immediately galloped off. On the night of the event he expressed the opinion that the Prince had been shot dead at the kraal, but owned that the first actual evidence of misfortune of which he became cognisant was the Prince's riderless horse galloping past him. The men were either less active or less precipitate than was the officer. One of their number fell at the kraal, another on the grassy level some 150 yards wide, between the kraal and a shallow "donga" or gully across which ran the path towards the distant camp. As to the Prince· the testimony was fairly unanimous. . Sergeant Cochrane stated that he never actually mounted, but had foot in stirrup when at the Zulu volley his horse, a spirited grey sixteen hands high and always difficult to mount, started off, presently broke away, and later was caught by the survivors. Then the Prince tried to escape on foot, and was last seen by Cochrane running into the donga, from which he never emerged. Another trooper testified that he saw the Prince try to mount, but that, not succeeding, he ran by his horse's side for some little distance making effort after effort to mount, till he either stumbled or fell in a scrambling way and seemed to be trodden on by his horse. But the most detailed evidence was given by trooper Lecocq, a Channel-Islander. He stated that after their volley the

Zulus bounded out of cover, shouting " Usuta ! " (" Cowards ! ")
The Prince was unable to mount his impatient horse, scared
as it was by the fire. One by one the troopers galloped by
the Prince who, as he ran alongside his now maddened horse,
was endeavouring in vain to mount. As Lecocq passed lying
on his stomach across the saddle, not yet having got his seat,
he called to the Prince, " Dépêchez-vous, s'il vous plait,
Monseigneur ! " The Prince made no reply and was left alone
to his fate. His horse strained after that of Lecocq, who
then saw the doomed Prince holding his stirrup-leather with
one hand, grasping reins and pommel with the other, and
trying to remount on the run. No doubt he made one
desperate effort, trusting to the strength of his grasp on the
band of leather crossing the pommel from holster to holster.
That band tore under the strain. I inspected it next day and
found it no leather at all, but paper-faced—so that the Prince's
fate really was attributable to shoddy saddlery. Lecocq saw
the Prince fall backwards, and his horse tread on him and
then gallop away. According to him the Prince regained his
feet and ran at full speed towards the donga on the track of
the retreating party. When for the last time the Jerseyman
turned round in the saddle, he saw the Prince still running,
pursued only a few yards behind by some twelve or fourteen
Zulus with assegais in hand which they were throwing at him.
None save the slayers saw the tragedy enacted in the donga.

Early next morning the cavalry brigade marched out to
recover the body, for there was no hope that anything save
the body was to be recovered. As the scene was neared,
some of us rode forward in advance. In the middle of the
little plain was found a body, savagely mutilated ; it was not
that of the Prince, but of one of the slain troopers. We found
the dead Prince in the donga, a few paces on one side of the
path. He was lying on his back, naked save for one sock ;
a spur bent out of shape was close to him. His head was so
bent to the right that the cheek touched the sward. His
hacked arms were lightly crossed over his lacerated chest, and
his face, the features of which were in no wise distorted but
wore a faint smile that slightly parted the lips, was marred by

the destruction of the right eye from an assegai-stab. The surgeons agreed that this wound, which penetrated the brain, was the first and the fatal hurt and that the subsequent wounds were inflicted on a dead body. Of those there were many, in throat, in chest, in side, and on arms, apart from the nick in the abdomen which is the Zulu fetish-custom, invariably practised on slain enemies as a protection against being haunted by their ghosts. His wounds bled afresh as we moved him. Neither on him nor on any of the three other slain of the party was found any bullet-wound ; all had been killed by assegai-stabs. Round the poor Prince's neck his slayers had left a little gold chain on which were strung a locket set with a miniature of his mother, and a reliquary containing a fragment of the true Cross which was given by Pope Leo III. to Charlemagne when he crowned that great Prince Emperor of the West, and which dynasty after dynasty of French monarchs had since worn as a talisman. Very sad and solemn was the scene as we stood around, silent all and with bared heads, looking down on the untimely dead. The Prince's two servants were weeping bitterly and there was a lump in many a throat. An officer, his bosom friend at Woolwich, detached the necklet and placed it in an envelope with several locks of the Prince's short dark hair for transmission to his mother, who a year later made so sad a pilgrimage to the spot where we now stood over her dead son. Then the body, wrapped in a cloak, was placed on the lanceshafts of the cavalrymen, and on this extemporised bier the officers of the brigade bore it up the ascent to the ambulancewaggon which was in waiting. The same afternoon a solemn funeral service was performed in the Itelezi camp, and later in the evening the body, escorted by a detachment of cavalry, began its pilgrimage to England, in which exile, in the chapel at Farnborough, where the widowed wife and childless mother now resides, the remains of husband and son now rest side by side in their marble sarcophagi. The sword worn in South Africa by the Prince, the veritable sword worn by the first Napoleon from Arcola to Waterloo—in reference to which the Prince had been heard to say, " I must earn a better right to it than that which my name alone can give me"—had been carried off by his Zulu slayers, but was restored by Cetewayo when Lord Chelmsford's army was closing in upon Ulundi.

To be slain by savages in an obscure corner of a remote continent was a miserable end, truly, for him who once was the Son of France!

X.

WAR CORRESPONDENCE AS A FINE ART.

Early War Correspondence—Mr. G. L. Gruneisen, Wm. Howard Russell, Col.
C. B. Brackenbury and Captain Henry Hozier—Hilary Skinner—George
A. Henty and Frederick Boyle—Henry M. Stanley's Earliest Triumph—
Murder of Mr. Bowlby in China—Absence of Enterprise in Beginning of
Franco-German War—Holt White's Promptitude After Sedan—The
Mysterious Müller—Personal Experiences in 1870-71—The Triumphal
Entry into Berlin—Co-operative Correspondence in the Russo-Turkish
War; MacGahan, Millet, Jackson and Grant.

IT is the foible of the veteran to be the *laudator temporis
acti*. I must speak in the past tense of the craft of
which I have been a humble follower. Not, however, because
I am unable any more to pursue it—although, as it happens,
that is the case; but because its conditions are being so
altered that it may be said, I fear, to have ceased to be the
fine art into which zeal, energy and contrivance elevated it
for a brief term. It is now an avocation at once simplified
and controlled by precise and restraining limitations. In all
future European wars, by an international arrangement the
hand of the censor will lie heavy on the war-correspondent.
He will be a mere transmitter by strictly defined channels
of carefully revised intelligence liable to be altered, falsified,
cancelled, or detained at the discretion of the official set in
authority over him. I am far from objecting to the changed
conditions, in the capacity of a citizen of a nation which may
have the wisdom to prefer victories to news. The point I desire
to emphasise is simply this, that the new order of things has
taken war correspondence out of the category of the fine arts.

It was by slow degrees that it had temporarily attained
that position. In a sense Julius Cæsar was a war-correspondent; only he did not send his "Commentaries"
piecemeal from the "theatre of war," but indited them at his
leisure in the subsequent peace time. The old "Swedish
Intelligencer" of the Gustavus Adolphus period was genuine
war correspondence; published indeed tardily compared with

the alacrity of our news of to-day, but nevertheless fresh from the scene of action, full of distinctiveness, quaint and racy beyond compare. The first modern war-correspondent professionally commissioned and paid by a newspaper was Mr. G. L. Gruneisen, a well-known literary man not very long dead, who was sent to Spain by the *Morning Post* with the Spanish Legion consisting of 10,000 men raised in Great Britain to fight for the Queen of Spain, which Sir de Lacy Evans commanded in the Peninsula from 1835 to the end of 1837. But this new departure was not followed up, and no English newspaper was represented in the ill-fated Afghan campaigns of 1838-42, or in the great battles of the first and second Punjaub wars. When at the outset of the Crimean war in the early summer of 1854 William Howard Russell presented himself to old Sir George Brown in the roadstead of Malta, announcing himself as the correspondent of the *Times* and tendering an authorisation from the War Minister, the apparition was regarded by the worthy General not so much in the light of a revolution as of an unprecedented and astounding phenomenon. But Russell's credentials could not be ignored; and all the world knows how he became " the pen of the war," and how his vigorous exposure of abuses, neglect, and mismanagement contributed mainly to the rescue from absolute extermination of the British Army wintering in misery on the Sebastopol plateau. Other papers followed the lead given them by the *Times*, and the artist-correspondent made his appearance also in the person of Mr. William Simpson, now a veteran, but still in the active service of the illustrated paper with which he has been worthily identified for more than forty years.

Russell represented the *Times* in the war in Denmark of 1864, when that poor gallant kingdom suffered so severely at the hands of the twin bullies, Prussia and Austria; and he was again in the field two years later when the bullies, having fallen out over their Danish spoils, turned their weapons on each other in the "Seven Weeks' War" of 1866. By this time war correspondence, if not yet a profession, was becoming a necessity for all our important newspapers. Russell and his colleague the late Colonel C. B. Brackenbury were for the *Times* with the Austrian Army; the great English journal was admirably represented with the Prussians by Captain Henry Hozier, whose book on that campaign is to this day a standard authority. Mr. William Black, then scarcely known to fame as a novelist, wrote war-letters for the now defunct *Morning Star;* and the late Mr. Hilary Skinner was the brilliant and versatile representative of the *Daily News.* Quite a little army of war-correspondents accompanied the Abyssinian expedition of 1867. Of those who then marched with Napier two are still alive and available for service to-day—George A. Henty, the voluminous author of books dear to boys; and Frederick Boyle, who, besides being a war-correspondent, is a novelist and has been a traveller even unto the ends of the earth. But the journalistic honours of the expedition rested with Henry M. Stanley, then an unconsidered youngster from the great republic across the Atlantic, but born alert and enterprising, and destined to attain to a pinnacle of fame as the greatest explorer of our time. Stanley rode to the coast with the earliest tidings of the fall of Magdala; and it was his message which communicated the tidings of that event both to Europe and America. I ought to have mentioned that Russell described for the *Times* many of the battles and shared most of the dangers of the Indian Mutiny in 1857-58 as a received member of Lord Clyde's headquarters staff; and that Mr. Bowlby, a barrister and a *Times* correspondent with the British forces in the war with China of 1860, having been taken prisoner by the Chinese, was murdered by them with the cruellest barbarity, being thus the first war-correspondent of an Old World newspaper to meet a violent death in the line of duty.

The war journalists who, previous to the Franco-German war of 1870 made for themselves name and fame, achieved their successes by the vivid force of their descriptions, by their fearless truthfulness, by their staunchness under hardships and disease. I can recall no instance in the Old World, with the single exception of Stanley's *coup*, in which a war correspondent before 1870 succeeded in outstripping all competition in

forwarding the intelligence of an important event. The
electric telegraph had been but sparingly utilised in the
Austro-Prussian war; in the Franco-German war it was to
revolutionise the methods of war correspondence. But the
conservative spirit of the Old World was singularly illustrated
in the tardiness—the apparent reluctance, indeed—with
which the revolutionising agency was accepted. In the great
contest of the American civil war the wires had been resorted
to with a fulness, an alacrity, and an ingenuity which should
have been pregnant with suggestion to the war journalism of
Europe. But this was not so. The outbreak of the war of
1870 was accompanied by no stirring of the dry bones. At
Saarbrücken on the French frontier, the point for which
instinct had led me to make on the declaration of war, there
was an immediate concentration of momentary interest
scarcely surpassed later anywhere else; yet to no one of the
correspondents gathered there, whether veteran or recruit,
had come the inspiration of telegraphing letters in full—a
practice now so universally resorted to in war time that letters
sent by post are an obsolete tradition. For the moment press
telegrams from Saarbrücken were prohibited, and we
supinely accepted the situation and resorted to the post; no
man recognising or, at all events, acting on the recognition,
that from the nearest telegraph-office in the Duchy of
Luxembourg attainable by a few hours' railway journey, the
despatch of messages was quite unrestricted. Enterprise thus
far was dead, or rather had never been born. The stark
struggle of the Spicheren fought out within two miles of the
frontier, was described in letters sent by the slow and
circuitous mail-train. The descriptions of the important
battles of Wörth and Borny were transmitted in the same
unenterprising fashion.

The world's history has no record of more desperate fighting than that which raged the live-long summer day on the
plateau of Mars-la-Tour. The accounts of that bloody battle
went to England by field-post and mail-train; yet the
Saarbrücken telegraph-office, from which the embargo had
been taken off, was within an easy five hours' ride from the

field. The battle of Gravelotte fought on the next day but one, did at length get itself described after a fashion over the wires; but it was no Englishman who accomplished this cheap pioneer achievement. The credit thereof accrues to an alert American journalist named Hands, who, I believe, was a representative of the *New York Tribune.* Whether, when the long strife was sullenly dying away in the darkness the spirit suddenly moved this quiet little man or whether he had prearranged the undertaking, I do not know; nor do I know whether he carried, or whether he sent, his message to the Saarbrücken telegraph office. But this is certain that it reached there in time to be printed in New York on the morning but one after the battle. British correspondents were on the field in some strength; American journalism was represented by such deacons of the craft as Moncure D. Conway and Murat Halstead; but nevertheless it remained for obscure little Hands to make the *coup.* It was, indeed, no great achievement intrinsically, looked back on in the light of later developments; yet Hands' half-column telegram has the right to stand monumentally as the first successful attempt in the Old World to describe a battle over the telegraph wires.

Sedan was marked by efforts of journalistic enterprise, crude, it is true, but at least indicative of budding energy. Again it was the *New York Tribune* which took "first spear," only the wielder of the weapon this time was a Briton. Holt White, a man whose abilities should have given him a better fate than a premature death in an Australian hospital, was with the Germans on the day so unfortunate for France. He stood by Sheridan when Napoleon's letter of surrender was handed by General Reillé to old King Wilhelm. The napkin which had been Reillé's flag of truce was given to him as a souvenir. And then with dauntless courage he walked right across the battlefield through the still glowing embers of the bitter strife, reached the frontier, made for the nearest railway station and got to Brussels on the following morning. He could not telegraph from Brussels. His own story was that when he tendered his message the people in the Brussels telegraph-office refused to transmit it, scouting him as either a lunatic or a "bear" bent on creating a panic on the bourses; but I have also heard that he had not the cash with him to pay for a long message. Anyhow, he came on to London, getting there the day but one after the battle, in time for a short synopsis of his narrative to be printed in the *Pall Mall Gazette*. It appeared next morning in the *New York Tribune*.

Dr. Russell of the *Times* and the late Mr. Hilary Skinner of the *Daily News*, were attached to the staff of the Crown Prince and were billeted together in a village near Sedan. The following story regarding them was current at the time, and is, I believe, substantially true. After the battle they wrote steadily all night long, seated at the same table. In the morning—perhaps the next morning save one—each elaborately and ostentatiously sent a big budget to the field-post. Presently Skinner in his bird-like, airy manner ordered his horse, carefully explaining to Russell that he intended riding over the battlefield. "Happy thought!" cried the crafty Russell; "my letter is off my mind and I will go, too." So on the two rode through the dead and wounded till they reached the Belgian frontier, when Skinner with his fluttering jauntiness chirruped, "Well, Russell, good-bye for an hour or two. I'll just ride on into Bouillon and get a morsel of luncheon there." "Faith," observed Russell, with all imaginable innocence, "I'm hungry, too. I don't mind if I go with you!" So they rode, and they lunched, and they remounted; and then they started, but not by the way they had come; indeed, in the contrary direction. Then it was that they looked each other straight in the face, and burst into a simultaneous roar of laughter. Each from the first had meant going through to England. They went on together.

Personally in those days, however enterprising were my aspirations, I had no means to make the most trivial attempt to realise them. I represented then a newspaper which had sent me into the field not lavishly equipped with financial resources. I was not mounted; I had no relations with any staff; I tramped with the fighting men knapsack on my

back. I saw then more, perhaps, of the realities of actual
hard fighting than I ever did later; but to what purpose?
All that I could do was to drop my missives into the field-post
waggon, to a belated and precarious fate. I, too, had gone
across the frontier to Bouillon, tramping the distance on foot;
and I was broiling a piece of meat at a fire which I had
kindled in the dry bed of the rivulet under the hotel window
at which Russell and Skinner were lunching. I should not
have thought of taking the liberty to accost them—they were
of the *élite* of the profession: I was among the outsiders.

But presently better things befell me. The *Daily News*
took me on its strength, and sent me to the siege of Metz
with plenty of money, and the most unrestricted injunctions
to be enterprising laid upon me by Mr. (now Sir John)
Robinson, the far-sighted and clear-headed chief of that
journal. But I come of a race whose untutored impulse is to
bewail the catastrophe in which " bang goes saxpence," and I
had been stunted by the conservatism of my earlier newspaper.
I lacked courage to be lavish no matter how tempting the
opening, and I look back on my niggardly sacrifice of opportunities with sincere self-contempt. Thus I was the only
civilian spectator of the stubborn fight of Mézières-les-Metz
on the afternoon of October 7th, 1870, a combat which was the
immediate antecedent of Bazaine's surrender; but I could not
bring myself to let loose about it over the telegraph-wires to a
greater length than half a column. A greater opportunity
still I let slip when Metz capitulated. It was a rare chance—
probably such another may never offer itself to the war
journalist. So far as I knew, there was no competitor nearer
than the frontier. I was quick to enter the beleaguered city;
from an American gentleman who had been inside the place
throughout the siege I gathered a great mass of information;
I saw the French army and garrison march out and surrender;
I saw Bazaine drive away to Corny; I visited the hospitals,
talked with military and civilian Frenchmen, and wrote all
night in a room in the Hôtel de l'Europe in the grand old
city by the Moselle. Of course I should have hurried by road
or rail over the forty-five miles to Saarbrücken, there written

for my very life, and sent sheet by sheet to the telegraph office as each was finished. *Mea culpa!* and it was no palliation of my shortcoming in alacrity that, dull as I was, I was ahead of my comrades.

But there was a real live man among us, although scarcely of us—a man whose trade was not war correspondence, yet who did a piece of work in that department which was a veritable example of fine art. The capitulation of Metz was consummated on October 28th. The morning but one after this event all England was startled by a telegram which was published in the *Daily News*. This memorable despatch, printed verbatim from the telegraphic slips, was over two columns long and it described with minute detail, with admirable vigour, with effective if restrained picturesqueness, the incidents and events of the colossal surrender. On the day after its appearance in the *Daily News* the *Times* quoted the message in full, with the introductory complimentary comment that it envied its contemporary "so admirable a correspondent." The credit of having been that "admirable correspondent" was long ascribed to me, and notwithstanding constant repudiation on my part—for no honest man can endure to enjoy credit which is not justly his—I believe myself still generally regarded as the author of this yet unforgotten telegram. I sincerely wish that this had been so; but the truth is that I was then among the unemancipated. I had done my best according to my lights, and blindly thought that I had done fairly well. A few days after the capitulation I was breakfasting in a Metz hotel, when a *Daily News* containing the telegram I have been telling of was handed to me. The sense of self-abasement as I read it turned me physically sick. I had been smugly believing in myself; and lo! here was the crushing evidence how completely and mysteriously a better man, whoever he might be, had beaten me. It was a stern lesson; I all but succumbed under it; but took heart of grace and swore to profit by the wholesome teaching. It was not until some time later that I came to know who the man was that had thus at a stroke revolutionised war correspondence in the Old World—for this in effect was what, all unwittingly, this casual outsider had done. A young surgeon or hospital-dresser, a German-American named Müller, was professionally attached to one of the ambulances or field-hospitals of the German Army which had been beleaguering Metz. On his way from America to the seat of war he had accepted in London some kind of commission to do any journalistic work that might come in his way, not incompatible with the professional duties which he intended to undertake. Probably, as a volunteer, he had more time at his disposal than if he had been a surgeon of the regular service.

Anyhow, this Müller saw the capitulation, looked on at the taking over of the Porte Serpenoise by the German troops, witnessed the march out of Bazaine's dejected cohorts, penetrated into the city, and was in the vortex of the confusion and anarchy temporarily reigning there. Müller and I may have rubbed shoulders in the Place d'Armes. Then, having "taken in" the whole situation, he set about utilising the advantage he had gained in the most effective, daring, and purposeful manner. He rode out of Metz away northward along the Moselle valley, through a region infested with franc-tireurs, through villages bitterly hostile to the Germans, past the venomous cannon of Thionville—he rode, I say, the long forty miles north to the Luxembourg frontier, and crossing it reached a village called Esch, a place so petty that it is marked on few maps and is named in no gazetteer. How he got his long telegram expedited from that place I know not—nobody has ever known—but there is no doubt that he did so somehow; and then, strange to tell, he vanished utterly; *absit, evasit, erupit.* He was advertised for and searched for, but in vain. The man who had made what I do not hesitate to pronounce the greatest journalistic *coup* of our time on this side of the Atlantic, effaced himself utterly thenceforward. No laurels twined themselves round his name, which to all save a few is now for the first time revealed. I do not even know that he was aware he had earned any laurels. I have never seen the man, much and often as I and others have tried to do so. In a word, of Müller it may be said, *stat nominis umbra.*

But this brilliant Müller-flash stirred in us all a new

conception of our reason for existing. We had previously, of course, been aware that it was our duty to see all that we could see, know all that we could know—always with self-respect; but we had not adequately realised that the accomplishment of this to its fullest was merely a means to an end. At a casual glance it might seem that the chief qualification requisite in the modern war correspondent is that he should be a brilliant writer, able so to describe a battle that the reader may glow with the enthusiasm of the victory, and weep for the anguish of the groaning wounded. The capacity to do this is questionless a useful faculty enough; but it is not everything—nay, it is not even among the leading qualifications. For the world of to-day lives so fast, and is so voracious for what has come to be called the "earliest intelligence," that the man whose main gift is that he can paint pictures with his pen is beaten and pushed aside by the swift, alert man of action, who can get his budget of dry, concise, comprehensive facts into print twenty-four hours in advance of the most graphic description that ever stirred the blood. In modern war correspondence the race is emphatically to the swift, the battle to the strong. The best organiser of the means for expediting his intelligence, he it is who is the most successful man—not your deliberate manufacturer of telling phrases, your piler-up of coruscating adjectives.

Müller, it is true, opened our eyes to a new comprehension of our most urgent duty; yet the scales did not wholly fall away from them until long after they were opened. It is strange now to look back on the supineness throughout the Franco-German War in what I may call craft, and on the feebleness of the practical recognition of opportunity. It cannot be said that there is anything of fine art in the dropping of a letter into a slit in the side of a field-post waggon; yet that method of despatch was the usual resort. Occasionally, when anything important occurred, Mr. Russell would send his courier to Sedan, where the *Times* had located a forwarding agent; but the journey from Versailles to Sedan was tedious and the train service very irregular. He, and I think also Skinner of the *Daily News*, were allowed, on

P

special application for each message, to send short messages to England over the wires; I had the same privilege at the headquarters of the army which the Crown Prince of Saxony commanded; and Bismarck allowed Mr. Beatty-Kingston, the accomplished correspondent of the *Daily Telegraph*, to telegraph at length the conditions of the capitulation of Paris. But such devices and so sparse facilities were simply tantalising alike to the correspondent and his public, yet there was, as a general thing, no alternative between them and the routine crudeness of the field-post.

In a measure, it is true, I had been so fortunate as to discern where lay the better way and to utilise it. From the beginning of November, 1870 until the fall of Paris in the end of January 1871, my sphere of duty was in the northern and eastern sections of the German environment of Paris; and the celerity with which my correspondence reached its destination and appeared in print created not a little surprise and speculation as to my methods. A respected rival on the same ground was so stung by this superior celerity that, in the conviction that it must be due to exceptional telegraphic facilities accorded to me, he made an official complaint of the undue favouritism which he believed I enjoyed. He was assured that there was no such favouritism, and remained bewildered and dissatisfied until the end. The Crown Prince of Saxony's Chief-of-Staff told me of this complaint, and desired that I should explain to him the method by which I accomplished the exceptional rapidity of transmission which he as a newspaper reader had observed. I revealed to him the extremely simple secret, under pledge that he should respect the confidence, since I did not devise methods for the behoof of competitors. Some little time afterwards I chanced to be dining at the headquarters of Prince George of Saxony to which my rival was attached, when one of Prince George's staff-officers accused me of post-dating my letters and thereby giving them a fictitious appearance of freshness. I asked him, if his charge were true, how it happened that my letters recorded events occurring on the dates they bore; and I offered to make a bet with him that if he should there and then inform me of some specific item of information, that item would appear in the *Daily News* of the following morning but one. He accepted the bet, mentioned a particular movement of troops, and then left the room. I guessed the errand on which he had withdrawn, and to verify my suspicion presented myself at the military telegraph office on the way to my sleeping-quarters. "No! no! Herr Forbes!" said the soldier-operator with a grin—"I have orders to accept no message from you." I feigned disappointment and departed. Next morning my friend of the staff assailed me with fine Saxon persiflage, and demanded that I should pay the bet which I must know I had lost. I did not comply with this requisition, and in a few days was in a position to send him a copy of the *Daily News* of the stipulated date containing his piece of information, and to point out that he owed me five thalers.

The secret was so simple that I am ashamed to explain it, yet with one exception I had it all to myself for months. When before Metz I had done my telegraphing from Saar-brücken, depositing a sum of money in the hands of the telegraph-master there, and forwarding messages for England to him from the front against this deposit. Before leaving the frontier region for the vicinity of Paris, I learned that a train starting in the small hours of the morning from a point in rear of the German cordon on the east of Paris, reached Saarbrücken in about fifteen hours. The telegraph-master there would receive a letter by this train soon enough to wire its contents to England in time for publication in the paper in London of the following morning. I put a consider-able sum into his hands to meet the charge of messages forwarded to him by me; and I arranged with a local banker to keep my credit with the Saarbrücken telegraph-master always up to a certain figure. Every evening a field-post waggon started from the Crown Prince of Saxony's headquarters on the north side of Paris, picked up mails at the military post-offices along its route, and reached the railway terminus at Lagny in time to connect with the early morning mail train to the frontier. At whatever point of my section of the environment I might find myself a military post-office served by this post-waggon was within reasonable distance; and my letter addressed to the Saarbrücken telegraph-master went jogging towards the frontier once every twenty-four hours, with a fair certainty of its contents being in print in England within twenty-four hours or thereabouts, from the time when it was posted. There certainly was nothing very subtle or complex in this expedient, yet the only other correspondent before Paris to whom it suggested itself was my colleague Mr. Skinner, who posted telegrams from Versailles to his wife at Carlsruhe, whence she transmitted them to London; but I believe that he lost a mail because of the greater distance of Versailles from the railway at Lagny. It was by the simplest method that I won my bet with the Saxon staff-officer. As I walked towards my quarters I scribbled his item on a leaf torn from my note-book, put it into an envelope already addressed, and as I passed the post-office quietly dropped the missive into the slot. My visit to the telegraph-office was merely a bluff.

There was perhaps a scintilla of innocent and simple strategy in the device which stood me in such good stead in the winter of 1870-71; but there certainly was nothing in it that could by any stretch of language be called fine art. And there was merely some forethought and pre-organisation in the circumstances attending my entrance into Paris immediately after the capitulation, and my rush eastward into Baden to telegraph a detailed account of the condition in which I had found the great city after its long investment. I was fortunate in getting in early; I made the best use of my time during the eighteen hours I was inside; and I was fortunate in getting out, which I did before any competitor had entered. My scheme was all laid. I had to ride some fifteen miles from the Porte de Vincennes on the east side of Paris, to catch the day-train leaving Lagny for the frontier at 1 p.m. Had all gone well with me I should have accomplished this without hurrying.

But after I had cleared Paris and when I believed that there were now no more difficulties in front of me, I was detained in the Bois de Vincennes by a cordon of Würtemberger hussars whose orders were to turn back all and sundry, and who would not so much as look at the great-headquarters pass which I tendered. Such an accident as this seems of little consequence, yet it may spell ruin to the correspondent's combinations. After a while, however, an officer whom I knew delivered me, and the Würtemberger obstacle was overcome. As I rode on I found that I should have made more allowance for the condition of the roads, long neglected as they had been and scored across at frequent intervals by the trenches, first of the defenders and then of the besiegers. To reach Lagny in time I had to ride my poor horse almost to death; in leaping trenches he had torn off shoe after shoe, and he was quite exhausted when I galloped up to the station just in time to put him in charge of a German cavalry soldier, and to jump into the train.

It was two o'clock on the following morning when I reached Carlsruhe, which place I had chosen as my objective point because I happened to know that the telegraph office there was open all night. I had some difficulty with the female telegraphist, who only knew her own language, and who had never seen so long a telegram as the one I presented to her for transmission. She sent for the telegraph-master who was in no good humour at being roused from bed and whose first question when he arrived yawning, was how much so long a message would cost and where was the money to frank it. In reply I emptied the belt in which round my waist I carried my portable financial resources, and, making a heap on the counter told him to wire against that pile. Then there was trouble with the female operator, who required to be helped over the stiles of awkward English words in Mr. Labouchere's not very plain handwriting. She, however, had finished by 7 a.m., and the telegraph-master and myself settled our accounts. I had just time for a hurried breakfast before getting into the return train for Paris at 8 a.m., and I was back in Paris some forty hours after I had left it—one of the earliest in of my fraternity on this my second entrance. Walking into the Hôtel Chatham, I found there two journalists who had just arrived from Versailles. I was the victim of their badinage. They had got into Paris before me from their point of view, and they crowed over this their achievement with no little self-complacency. A few days later I saw one of them reading a *Daily News* containing the telegram which I had sent from Carlsruhe. He did not seem to be disposed to be facetious any more.

There certainly was a stroke of fine art in the well-planned and successful arrangements made by the *Times* in order to have the earliest detailed account of the entry into Paris of the German troops on March 1st, 1871. William Howard Russell witnessed the grand review by the German Emperor on the Longchamps racecourse, of the representative contingents detailed for the temporary occupation of a portion of the French capital; and he accompanied the head of the in-marching column until it reached the Place de la Concorde. Then, after some obstruction, he joined his colleague Mr. Kelly, who had been assigned to watch the demeanour of Paris under the humiliation of a hostile occupation; and about 4 p.m. the pair left the Gare du Nord in a special train bound for Calais. On the journey Russell dictated to Kelly the account of what he had witnessed, and he remained at Calais while Kelly, crossing the Channel in a special steamer which was in waiting, reached London by special train in time to have Russell's and his own narratives in the *Times* of March 2nd. The *Daily News* had no interest with the " Northern of France " directorate for a special train, and I had to do the best I could without any adventitious advantages. I remember reading a statement in an American paper of the period, to the effect that I journeyed surreptitiously by the Russell-Kelly special in the disguise of its fireman, but I need not say that this was a playful invention. Elsewhere in this volume I have said something of my personal experiences on this eventful day, and will not here expatiate on the subject. A knot of Frenchmen followed me when I passed the German cordon, and then promptly raised the cry of "Spy!" I was attacked, knocked down, most of my clothes were torn off me, a sabot split my lip open, and men danced on me and kicked at me while I was being dragged along the gutter, until I was rescued by a picket of national guards. As soon as I was free and had fulfilled a grateful duty towards one who had helped me to my freedom, I hurried to the place where I had engaged that a dog-cart should be in waiting with a fast and stout horse. It was neither a safe nor pleasant drive through Paris to the St. Ouen gate. But once outside I could shake up the horse and he made good time to Margency, the Crown Prince of Saxony's headquarters, whence I was allowed to despatch a telegram to London of some length. That accomplished, I drove back to St. Denis in time to catch the regular afternoon train for Calais. Writing throughout the journey in train and boat—I was the only passenger by the latter—I reached London early next morning, brought out a second edition of the *Daily News* which was selling in the streets by 8 a.m., and then lay down on the floor of the editor's room, and went to sleep with the "London Directory" for a pillow. I started back to Paris the same evening.

I had an opportunity for getting in a little bit of fine work on the occasion of the triumphal entry into Berlin of the home-returned conquerors, with Kaiser Wilhelm and his generals at their head. That event occurred on Friday, June 16th, 1871. I left for Berlin a week earlier. Two days after leaving England the following telegram from me reached the manager of the *Daily News:* "Despatch youngster from office, with passport good for France, to report to me at Berlin 14th inst." A young gentleman duly presented himself on the specified date. I fear that my young friend never forgave me for having, during the next two days permitted him less liberty than he not unnaturally desired. In point of fact I confined him to his bedroom, not even allowing him to go to the *table d'hôte*. The *Einzug*, in all its pomp and fervid national feeling, was over about 6 p.m. After writing and despatching a two-column telegram, I dined and then sat down to write a full narrative of what I had seen on this memorable day. About six next morning I wrote the last words of a letter six columns long; then I went round to the Dorotheen Strasse, and roused my two colleagues from their sleep to hand me their contributions. Returning to my own quarters I ordered breakfast for my prisoner, and while he was eating made up my packet. Then I instructed him—by this time it was nearly seven o'clock—to start forthwith for the Potsdamer Railway Station, take a second-class ticket for Brussels, get early into his compartment and keep out of sight until the train should start at eight. On reaching Brussels, he was to buy another ticket for London *via* Calais by the train leaving Brussels soon after his arrival there. Following this route he would reach London at 6 p.m. on Sunday, when he was to go immediately to the office and deliver his despatches.

All went well. From a corner in the station I saw the correspondents of the other London newspapers consign their letters to the post-office van attached to the outgoing train, caught a glimpse of my emissary as the train rolled out of the station, and then went to breakfast in a contented spirit. The confidence was justified. On the Monday morning the *Daily News* had a page and a half descriptive of the entry; no other newspaper had a line.

The accomplishment of this priority was simply the result of the forethought which becomes a second nature in a man concentrated on the duty he has in hand. On the voyage from Dover to Ostend I remembered that during the recent disturbed condition of France, and because of the diminished passenger traffic to and from the Continent generally, the Sunday day-boats from Ostend to Dover had been suspended. It occurred to me to ask the captain if they had been put on again. "No," he answered; "they are to begin running again at the beginning of next month."

It was then clear to me that the mails leaving Berlin on Saturday morning—the Berlin Festival was fixed for Friday the 16th—would lie in Ostend till late on Sunday night, when the night-boat would carry them to Dover; but that thus they could not reach London until 7 a.m. on Monday, too late for publication on that day. I knew that Sunday day-boats were already running from Calais to Dover, but that the German mails were not sent by that route. A passenger, however, could utilise it—thence my telegram for a young gentleman from the *Daily News* office. My instruction that he should carry a French passport was because I knew that the war-time enforcement of passports at the French frontier had not yet been abolished. It had occurred to no other competitor to make a study of this little problem.

During the campaigns in Spain and Servia there were few opportunities for artistic performances in the transmission of intelligence, nor did the amount of public interest make expensive organisation worth while. But the men engaged in those campaigns were steadily concentrating their energies on the elaboration of improved devices for the swift forwarding of news, and the old crude methods were drifting into limbo. The Russo-Turkish war formed a new era in war correspondence. The journalism of both worlds made up its mind to put forth its full strength when in the spring of 1877 the Russian hosts destined for the invasion of Turkey were slowly massing in the squalid villages of Bessarabia. There had been a thorough awakening as to the advantages of copious telegraphy in war correspondence, and it was now for the first time thoroughly realised that strategic organisation for the rapid transmission of intelligence was a thing sedulously to study. Some of the ideas were no doubt ridiculous. I remember a young correspondent coming to me for advice in a state of profound bewilderment. He had received instructions from the manager of his newspaper to the effect that he was to keep himself aloof from both combatants, to flit impartially about the space intervening between them, and to use for telegraphic purposes the offices behind the Turkish front or those in the Russian rear, according to convenience or proximity. In other words, he was to place himself in the precise position where he could not possibly know anything, with the reasonable certainty of being hanged if he escaped being shot!

In the earlier months of this war there was a reciprocal alliance between the *Daily News* and the *New York Herald*. The representatives in the field of the former journal were the late Mr. J. A. MacGahan—the most brilliant correspondent I have ever known—and myself. The *Herald* sent Mr. Frank D. Millet who later has achieved deserved distinction as a painter, and that able journalist and genial comrade Mr. John P. Jackson. When the alliance terminated in the September of the war, I was fortunate enough to obtain Millet's services for the *Daily News*. The organisation of our methods of action and the disposition of our forces, were matters deliberated on and settled in friendly conclave. The correspondence campaign was regarded *à priori* from a strictly strategical point of view. Bucharest was the obvious base of operations, as the nearest telegraphic point to the theatre of war. But insuperable difficulties would beset the correspondent hurrying back from the field himself, and rushing into the Bucharest telegraph-office with his matter partly in his head, partly in his note-book; or in forwarding by a courier a hastily written despatch for the wires. For one thing, ready cash in hard money would have to be paid over the counter of the telegraph office, and gold is the most inconvenient and most dangerous thing a correspondent can carry about with him in the field. For another, the operators knew no language but their own, transmitting mechanically letter by letter; and therefore messages had to be written in plain round school-hand. I telegraphed for a young gentleman who had previously served me well in Servia as base-manager to act in Bucharest in the same capacity. He engaged for our uses a spacious suite of apartments consisting of an office, manager's private room, and a couple of bedrooms to accommodate weary correspondents coming in from the field. Two capable copyists were engaged to write out in easily legible characters

messages for the wires brought or sent in by correspondents.
The injunctions to the base-manager were that one of these
transcribers was to be on the premises day and night; and
that he himself was to have constantly in his possession for
telegraphic purposes a sum of at least £500. His duties were
to make as amenable as possible the Russian censor of telegraphic messages who from the beginning had been established in the Bucharest telegraph-office; for which purpose,
and for gaining and maintaining the goodwill and alert
service of officials and operators by presents of boxes of
cigars, opera tickets, etc., he was authorised to disburse secret
service money with due discretion. Further, it was his duty
to gather and transmit what trustworthy news he could pick
up in Bucharest; and in pursuit of this object he was to
present himself frequently at the bureaux of the members of
the Roumanian Cabinet, call on their wives, and attend their
receptions. He also had to be *bien vu* by the foreign Ministers
to the Roumanian Court, especially the British and Russian
representatives.

We four quite amicably arranged the section of front to be
covered by each, and there was never any clashing or poaching.
Millet was a good deal out of things in the early days, down
in the Dobrudcha with old General Zimmermann; but later,
after the fall of Plevna, he had a splendid innings with Gourko
in and beyond the Balkans. Nothing in the whole range of
war correspondence is more brilliant.as war correspondence or
more instructive in a professional sense, than Millet's work
during this period; and so thorough was his organisation for
the transmission of his letters that Gourko was glad to forward
his despatches and the Russian officers their private correspondence, by his courier service. MacGahan was lame all
through the war; but lameness had no effect in hindering a
man of his temperament from going everywhere and seeing
everything. As for myself, until struck down by Danubian
fever, after the September attack on Plevna, I worked very
hard and was singularly fortunate. General Ignatieff was
very kind in giving me hints as to impending events. Apart
from this, I had a curious intuition of a coming battle; I

seemed to feel it in my bones, and I almost invariably backed my presentiment with good results. It happened that I was the only English correspondent at the Russian crossing of the Danube, the capture of Biela, the combat of Pyrgos, the battle of Plevna of July 30th, and the desperate struggle on the Schipka Pass, which lasted from the 22nd to the 24th August. Frederic Villiers, the *Graphic* artist, was my companion on all these occasions.

It may easily be imagined that the expenses of a correspondence service conducted on a footing so thorough, were very great; I can only hope that the results justified the cost. Each of us had a waggon and a pair of draught-horses, several saddle-horses, a couple of servants, and couriers at discretion. The purely telegraphic charges were enormous, for almost everything was telegraphed. The scale, if I remember correctly, was about eighteenpence a word, and I myself sent several messages of more than 8,000 words each. But there was no stinting; it seemed as if a thing could not cost too much that was well done. Let me cite an example. In the early days we were nervous about the Bucharest censor, and on the suggestion of the ingenious Jackson it was determined to establish a pony-express service across the Carpathians to Kronstadt in the Austrian province of Transylvania, for the despatch thence of telegraph messages which the censor in Bucharest might decline to pass. That service accordingly was promptly organised. The ground covered was about eighty miles. The stages were ten miles long. Eight horses were bought, and eight men were engaged to attend to them. When I reached Bucharest on August 2nd with the tidings of the Russian defeat before Plevna of July 30th, the base-manager assured me that the censor would not dare to permit transmission of a message so adverse to the defeated Russians. Thereupon I utilised this Carpathian express service, and sent my account of the disaster from the Hungarian town. When my narrative reached them from England, the Russian authorities at headquarters in the field were so satisfied with its tenor notwithstanding its uncompromising frankness, that they ordered it to be printed in every newspaper in Russia.

It was apparent that thenceforth the censor could not obstruct messages to the *Daily News;* so I directed that the pony express should be . disestablished. It had lasted for about nine weeks, it was used once, it cost abominably, and the decision was that it had paid for its keep.

Let me give an instance of the methods by which intelligence was expedited from the front. I started from the Danube for the Schipka Pass with four horses and three men. At the end of about every thirty miles I dropped a man and horse, with firm orders to the former to be continually on the alert. With a hired pony I rode up from Gabrova to the Schipka, spent some thirty hours amidst the carnage on the pass, and at night I started on the return journey. This I was able, by utilising horse after horse, to perform at a continuous rapid pace ; and thus, as I was informed on reaching the imperial head-quarters at Gorni Studen, I had travelled so fast as to outstrip the official couriers. The young officer who was afterwards Prince Alexander of Bulgaria was so good as to send me in his carriage from Gorni Studen down to the Danube, and on the following morning I was telegraphing hard in Bucharest.

We acted habitually on certain fundamental axioms. Each man of the four had, as I have said, his individual specific sphere of action, which altered with the course of events, but to which, whatever and wherever it might be, he habitually restricted himself. But the restriction had a certain elasticity. The motto of all was in effect that of the Red Prince—" March on the cannon-thunder." When that sound was heard, or when one of us chanced on reasonably good intelligence as to the probable locality of impending fighting, then it behoved that man to disregard all restriction to a specific region, and to ride with all speed for the scene of actual strife. For it was possible that his colleague within whose allotted sphere the clash of arms was resounding might be hindered from reaching the fray. Tidings of it might not have come to him ; he might be intent on impending fighting nearer at hand to him, or, indeed, engaged in watching its actual outbreak and progress ; he might be down with sunstroke or Bulgarian fever ;

all his horses might be lame—in fine, any one of many contingencies might hinder his presence. And if it should happen that two colleagues found themselves spectators together of the same fight, what harm was there? None; but rather it was well, since by dividing between them the field of strife the course of the battle would be discerned more closely and described more minutely. During the five days' fighting before Plevna in the September of the war, three of us—MacGahan, Jackson, and I—watched that great struggle, and if Millet could have been withdrawn in time from the Dobrudcha he would have found ample scope as well for his keen insight and brilliant faculty of description. As it was we did have a fourth colleague before Plevna, in young Salusbury, who was on duty with the Roumanians. Here, as in the wider field, each man had his allotted place. MacGahan was with his constant ally the gallant Skobeleff, on the extreme left; and because Skobeleff was the fiercest fighter of the Russian chiefs, the opportunities for thrilling narrative possessed by the correspondent attached to him were incomparable, and were incomparably utilised. I had the central section along the Radischevo ridge; and Jackson placidly surveyed the scene of slaughter over against him about the Grivitza redoubt, regardless of the shells which occasionally fell about the hayrick outside of which he sat and wrote by day, and in the hollowed-out interior of which he spent his nights. Always once and often twice a day, couriers were despatched to Bucharest from Jackson's hayrick, where his cheery and quaint fellow-countryman, Grant of the *Times*, habitually kept him company, and whither MacGahan or his messenger, and myself from time to time, converged with written matter to be despatched across the Danube to the Bucharest telegraph-office.

Not less imperative on the war correspondent than the axiom that bids him "ride on the cannon-thunder," is the necessity that when he has learned or seen something of interest and value, he shall forthwith carry or send it to the wires without delaying for further information or the issue of renewed strife. "Sufficient for the day is the fighting thereof," should be his watchword, if he can

discern aught decisive in the day's fighting. If he has
couriers with him or can find trustworthy messengers, it is,
of course, his duty to remain watching the ultimate issue;
but if he has no such service, there is no more trying
problem for the correspondent than to decide whether or
not the day's work has been so conclusive one way or the
other as to justify him in going away with the information
he possesses. Never did I find the solution of this problem
more difficult than on the evening of the long day's fighting of August 24th in the Schipka Pass. I had the
impression that Radetsky could hold his own, and I knew
that reinforcements· were on the way to him; but meanwhile, as I rode away, the Turks were renewing the combat.
I was in MacGahan's country, and, knowing his instinct for
a battle, I had been looking out for him all day. On the
morning of the 25th he arrived in the Schipka, having
ridden hard on the fighting the moment he had heard of
the outbreak. There was severe fighting all that day, and
the Russians had the worst of it. That evening MacGahan
in his turn had to consider his position, and his problem
was more complicated than had been mine; for the day's
work had resulted in rendering the Russian position very
precarious. But a few days later Loftcha was to be assailed, and it behoved him to witness that undertaking.
So he in turn quitted the Schipka on the evening of the
25th, hurried to Bucharest with the result of that day's
work for the telegraph wire, and, by all but incredible
exertion for a sound man, not to speak of a lame one, he
was back in the vicinity of Plevna in time to witness
Osman Pasha's furious sortie on the morning of the 31st.

Another illustration may not be inapposite of the paramount duty of the war correspondent to transmit important
information without delay, to the abandonment or post-
ponement of all other considerations. MacGahan had
accompanied the raid across the Balkans made by Gourko
almost immediately after the passage of the Danube by
the Russians. I had been on the Lom with the army of
the Tzarewitch, whence I had to return to Bucharest with

despatches for the wire. On my return journey I passed near Biela the hamlet of Pavlo, in a garden of which the imperial camp was pitched. It occurred to me to look in on General Ignatieff, and ask whether he had any news for me. "News, Mr. Forbes?" exclaimed Ignatieff, "to be sure I have; here is a despatch just arrived from General Gourko, giving all details about his crossing of the Balkans, and his march up the Tundja valley towards Kezanlik!" Ignatieff translated the whole despatch, which I took down from his lips; then thanked him, took leave, mounted my horse, and rode hard back over the forty miles between Pavlo and the Danube bridge. For I knew that what Ignatieff had given me was absolutely the earliest and the sole intelligence of Gourko's doings; and until this intelligence was on its way to England my intention to rejoin the Tzarewitch had to stand over. At Sistova I found a trustworthy messenger to Bucharest, and on the following morning I rode a second time to Pavlo. Again Ignatieff waved triumphantly a despatch from Gourko, describing hard and successful marching and fighting beyond the Balkans; again his translation of that despatch was scribbled down in my note-book; again I hurried back to Sistova; and again sent a courier with the interesting and valuable message. Precisely the same routine occurred on the following day; and I owned to a certain modified satisfaction when the fourth day was barren of a despatch. For during the four days I had ridden 280 miles in a heat as fierce as that of India, over tracks from which the dust rose so dense as to obscure the sun. But then the information given to me by Ignatieff was the only tidings of Gourko, on whose enterprise the interest of Europe was concentrated; for it was not until several days later that anything came from the correspondents who accompanied the expedition.

XI

THE FUTURE OF THE WOUNDED IN WAR.

"Amenities of Warfare" a Contradiction in Terms—"Yanks" and "Johnnies"—
"Amenities" in the Russo-Turkish War—Napoleon after Austerlitz—The
Geneva Convention—English and German arrangements for Wounded—
"Vae Vulneratis!" in future Wars—New Weapons and New Explosives
—Endurance of Wounded on Battle-field—Examples in Peninsular War
—The Millennium.

WHAT are genially termed "the amenities of warfare" are quite pretty, but, in the nature of things, they are also quite artificial; and as a matter of hard fact they are in principle nothing other than a contradiction in terms. What of chivalry has lasted into modern times resolves itself into a kind of Quixotic notion that rose-water and bloodshed are compatible one with the other. Occasionally a man arises among us frank enough, bold enough—many people may say brutal enough—who dares to brush aside the sophistical upper layer of conventional amenities, and to go straight down to the bed-rock of the subject. "The main thing in true strategy," said General Sheridan once, in his most trenchant manner, "is simply this: first deal as hard blows at the enemy's soldiers as possible, and then cause so much suffering to the inhabitants of a country that they will long for peace and press their Government to make it. Nothing should be left to the people but eyes to lament the war." The Russian General Gourko is another great soldier who has expressed himself to the same effect, and who, indeed, evidenced the courage of his opinions in an extremely practical manner.

Nevertheless, the "amenities of war" have held their own more or less among civilised nations ever since standing armies came into existence. Frederick the Great had to ignore them in great measure during the Seven Years' War, because of the hordes of Pandours—Carlyle's "Tolpacheries and kindred doggeries"—which hung venomously

Q

on the fringes of his armies. But every reader of military history will remember Fontenoy and the ceremonious little episode between Lord Charles Hay of the English Guards, and the Count d'Auteroche of the Gardes Françaises. The "amenities" fell into abeyance during the ferocious wars of the French Revolution, but revived genially in Wellington's Peninsular campaigns, during which the mutual understanding of non-molestation between the outposts of the opposing armies was carried to curious lengths. In the American Civil War there was little, if any, personal rancour between the soldiers of the respective regular armies. The "Yanks" and the "Johnnies" on outpost duties were for the most part quite fraternal, and there were constant friendly barterings in tobacco, coffee, and whisky. In the Franco-German campaign in 1870, however, war once more in a great measure went back to grim first principles. During the sieges of Paris and Metz an immense amount of simple cold-blooded murder was perpetrated on the fore-posts, of which the French had the best because of the longer range of their chassepôts. In the Russo-Turkish War of 1877-78 the "amenities" on the part of the Turks took the simple form of mutilating the Russian wounded before killing them, while the Muscovites confined themselves to refusing quarter and refraining from burying dead Turks.

The abstract theory of the "amenities" is nothing other than preposterous. You strain every effort to reduce your adversary to impotence. He falls wounded, whereupon should he come into your hands, you promptly devote all your exertions to saving his life and restoring him to health and vigour, in order that he may go home and swell the ranks of your enemy. This, no doubt, is humanity, but it is supremely illogical. Marbot recounts in his Memoirs perhaps the most thorough *reductio ad absurdum* of the "amenities." In the battle of Austerlitz, a body of beaten Russians about five thousand strong strove to escape across the ice on the Satschan Lake. Napoleon ordered his artillery to fire on the ice, which was shattered, and men and horses slowly settled down into the depths, only a few escaping by means of poles and ropes thrust out from shore by the French. Next morning Napoleon riding round the positions, saw a wounded Russian officer clinging to an ice-floe a hundred yards out, and entreating help. The Emperor became intensely interested in the succour of the man. After many failures Marbot and another officer stripped and swam out, gradually brought the ice-floe towards the shore, and laid the Russian at Napoleon's feet. The Emperor evinced more delight at this rescue than he had manifested when assured of the victory of Austerlitz. He had no compunction as to the fate of the unfortunates whom his artillery practice of the day before had sent to their deaths. *À la guerre, comme à la guerre!*

It has been the wounded in war who up till now have owed the most to its amenities. Prisoners of war have not fared so well; it makes one shudder to recall the horrors of Andersonville, or the deadly tramp across the snow-covered Wallachian plain of the Turkish army which had held Plevna so long and so valiantly. But in civilised countries, since Lützen onward, the commander of a routed army, or, as after Talavera, of an army that has conquered but whose subsequent retreat circumstances have compelled, has not hesitated to leave his wounded to the good offices of his adversary; and seldom indeed has the onerous duty not been humanely fulfilled. After Coruña and after Talavera the French took medical charge of the wounded left to their care by the British; after Salamanca, Vittoria, Orthez and Waterloo the British hospitals were full of French wounded. In any of the German field and base hospitals in 1870, in every alternate bed might have been found a wounded *piou-piou*, sharing in every respect alike with his friends the enemies on both sides of him. In recent wars—the Crimean War was a melancholy exception—vast strides have been made in the methods of dealing with the wounded on the actual battlefield, as well as in the hospitals to which the more severely wounded are now so promptly relegated. Of the voluntary aid which the peoples of neutral states, as well as those of the combatant powers, have contributed and are ready to contribute again

Q 2

in the disinterested service of humanity, some details may
subsequently be given. In one case in which no foreign aid
was tendered when, I may add, it ought in brotherliness to
have been tendered, a nation proved itself fully capable of
performing unaided its duty to its wounded in the most
zealous and efficient manner. The Sanitary Commission of
the United States was among the noblest works in the world's
record of devotion. Well might its historian write of it as
"the true glory of our age and our country, one of the most
striking monuments of its civilisation." The Geneva convention has worked ardently if not always quite practically or
consistently, in the cause of humanity, although there is
certainly point in Mr. Niemann's sententious remark that
"in order fully to carry out the ideas of the Geneva
Convention, it would be necessary to cease to make war."

In principle the existing arrangements for medical assistance in the field and for the removal of the wounded
therefrom, are in great measure identical in most European
armies. The English system may be briefly summarised. In
the field there is a medical officer with each unit—regiment
of cavalry, battalion of infantry, body of artillery, etc. He
has at his disposition the trained regimental stretcher-bearers
of his particular unit, two per company or troop. To each
brigade are attached specifically one bearer company and one
field hospital; to each division an additional field hospital.
For an army corps the medical establishment consists of ten
field hospitals and six bearer companies, exclusive of the
regimental aid; and, in addition to this, a certain number of
officers of the medical staff are utilised for staff purposes.
The entire service is under the command of a surgeon-major-
general, subject to the authority of the general commanding.
There are three stages for the wounded man between where
he falls and the field hospital, where he either temporarily
remains if his case is not serious, or whence he is sent
back to the base hospital if he has been severely wounded.
The first stage is from the fighting-line to the collecting-
station. Where he has fallen he receives medical aid from
one or other of two sources, whichever may the sooner

reach him: the surgeon of his own particular unit accompanied by that officer's orderly from the regiment carrying the field-companion, water-bottle, and surgical haversack; or a surgeon belonging to the bearer company with a private similarly equipped. At this stage the surgeon, whether of the unit or of the bearer company as the case may be, affords the wounded man merely temporary aid and does not undertake any serious surgical operation. The patient is placed on a stretcher, which may belong to the bearers of the unit or to one of the eight stretcher squads of the bearer company; and he is carried back to the collecting-station, which, while if possible under shelter, is as near as may be to the fighting-line consistently with safety. The collecting-station is in charge of a sergeant equipped with field-companion and water-bottle, and a small reserve of bandages and first dressings to replenish the surgical haversacks of the stretcher-bearers. From the collecting-station to the dressing-station farther rearward, and if possible out of fire, a certain specified number of ambulances ply, loaded with their complement of wounded men, each vehicle under the care of a corporal or private of the bearer company. These two stages, from the fighting-line to the collecting-station and from the collecting-station to the dressing-station, constitute the "first line of assistance."

At the dressing-station, located if possible in a building— if not, in a tent and in proximity to a good supply of water— the medical officer in command is on duty assisted by another medical officer, a sergeant-major, and sundry other non-commissioned officers and men, acting as compounders, cooks, etc. Here the wounded receive more detailed attention than could previously have been paid to them. Beef-tea and stimulants are supplied when needed; minor, and in case of emergency, even capital operations are performed. As the wounded are dressed they are placed in the ambulances plying between the dressing-station and the field hospital, which stage is known as the "second line of assistance." The collecting and dressing stations may have to be advanced or retired according to the ebb or flow of the battle; but the general principle holds good that the two shall never be far apart, so as to shorten the journeys in the first line and thus bring the wounded within reach of surgical aid as speedily as possible. In the Egyptian campaign of 1882 a quarter of an hour was held to be the extreme length of time for the wounded man to lie on the field before receiving assistance; but then there were but a few hundreds of men to be dealt with, in contradistinction to the thousands of wounded which a great battle necessarily produces.

The following table may be of interest as marking the difference in detail between the German and the English appliances and methods for dealing with the wounded. The unit of comparison is in each case that of an army corps numbering 30,000 combatants:—

	Medical Officers.		Regimental Stretcher-Bearers per 1,000 Men.	Total for Army Corps.	Medical Officers.	Non-commissioned Officers and Men.	Stretchers.	Ambulance Waggons.	"Beds."	Remarks.
	Per 1,000 Men.	Total for Army Corps.								
GERMAN.										
Regimental aid · · ·	2	60	16	480	—	—	120	—	—	* Including 240 for transport duty.
Three bearer companies	—	—	—	—	21	717	124	24	—	
Twelve field hospitals ·	—	—	—	—	60	564	—	—	2,400	
Totals · · ·	2	60	16	480	81	1,281*	244	24	2,400	† Excluding 500 for transport duty.
ENGLISH.										‡ Only 48 of these actually in use on battle - field, remainder are in the ambulance waggons.
Regimental aid · · ·	1·4	41	16	480	—	—	226	—	—	
Six bearer companies ·	—	—	—	—	18	306	168‡	60	—	
Ten field hospitals ·	—	—	—	—	40	400	80	—	1,000	
Totals · · ·	1·4	41	16	480	58	766†	474	60	1,000	

1,281 less 249 = 1,032.
766 plus 506 = 1,272.

Thus the German corps has one-third more regimental medical officers per thousand men than the English. It has twice as many beds in field-hospitals, but fewer ambulance-waggons by one half. Taking the means of carriage from fighting-line to dressing-station, the English corps has 274 stretchers and carriage for 360 wounded per ambulance-waggon, making 634 in all. With the average distance of dressing-station from fighting-line taken at 1,500 yards, the number of journeys to and fro that could be estimated for would not exceed five, or 1,500 wounded moved by carriage. Taking 50 per cent. of the wounded as requiring carriage from the field, this would give 3,000 wounded that would arrive at the dressing-stations for transfer to the rear, or 10 per cent. of the whole force.

This much of detail has been gone into in regard to the present system of dealing with the wounded in battle with the motive of accentuating the contrast between that system with its promptitude of succour, and the harsher conditions which must inevitably be endured by the wounded of future warfare. One day about three years ago, I happened to be listening in the theatre of the Royal United Service Institution, to a lecture which was being delivered by Mr. John Furley, one of our oldest and most devoted volunteer Red Cross men on many a stricken field. He talked of a new pattern of stretcher with telescopic handles and drew fine distinctions between the patterns of ambulances of infinitesimal shades of differences; apparently in the full conviction that the wounded of the future would fare as do the wounded of the present. Called upon to speak, I ventured to observe that if in the next great war Mr. Furley should be in the field, about the second evening after the battle he would probably find a wounded brigadier-general competing eagerly for a share of a country dung-cart for his conveyance to the field-hospital. I regard this as no strained illustration of the state of things that will exist in the future after a great battle, in consequence of the immense number of wounded which the altered conditions of military armaments and of fighting will bring about. The Philistine audience, which included sundry brigadier-generals, gibed at me; but when later I happened to go into the matter more closely with intent to write this chapter, I found myself in accord with all the best authorities. " Vae vulneratis !" will be the cruel watchword of future wars. The late Dr. Billroth, the greatest of Austrian surgeons, who made the Franco-German War on the Prussian side, held that " we must come to the conclusion that in future it will be no longer possible to remove the wounded from the field during the battle by means of bearers, since every man of them would be shot down, as bearers would be more exposed than men in the fighting-line; and the most that can be aimed at is that the wounded man of the future shall be attended to within twenty-four hours." Bardeleben, the surgeon-general of the Prussian Army, has said : " Some urge an increase of bearers ; but we must not forget that bearers have to go into the fire-line and expose themselves to the bullets. If we go on increasing their number, shall we not also be simply increasing the number of the wounded? The number of men provided for the transfer of the wounded now exceeds 1,000 for each army corps. It is no true humanity that in order to effect an uncertain amount of saving of human life a number of lives of other men should be sacrificed. The whole system of carrying away the wounded on litters during the battle must be abandoned, for it is altogether impracticable." There are many other testimonies to the same effect. In the Franco-German and Russo-Turkish wars I had already personally recognised and had written in that sense in my war correspondence, that the losses among the bearers and surgeons were so great that the service already "approached impracticability." And I added with a prescience which stands justified to-day, that " in the warfare of the future the service as now existing will be found utterly impracticable, since with the improved man-killing appliances certain to be brought into action, the first battle would bodily wipe out the bearer organisation carried on under fire."

It is virtually impossible that anyone can have accurately pictured to himself the scene in its fulness which the next great battle will present to a bewildered and shuddering world. We know the elements that shall constitute its horrors; but we know them only, as it were, academically.

Men have yet to be thrilled to the heart by the weirdness of wholesale death inflicted by missiles poured from weapons the whereabouts of which cannot be discerned because of the absence of powder-smoke. Nay, if Dr. Weiss's recently-invented explosive, of which great things have been predicted, is to be brought into use in the German army, there may no longer be any powder—the "villainous saltpetre" superseded by the more devilish "fatty substance of a brownish colour." The soldier of the next war must steel his heart to encounter the deadly danger incident to the explosions of shells filled with dynamite, melinite, ballistite, or some other form of high explosive, in the midst of dense masses of men. The recent campaign in Matabeleland has informed us with a grim triumph of the sweeping slaughter the Maxim gun can inflict with its mechanical stream of bullets. Quick-firing field-guns are on the eve of superseding the type of cannon in use in the horse and field batteries of to-day. All these instruments are on *terra firma*—if that be of any account. But, if there is anything in Edison's and Maxim's claims to have invented a flying-machine for military purposes which can be so steered as to carry and drop with accuracy five hundred pounds of explosive material at a given point, or to shed on an army a shower of dynamite, then death incalculable may rain down as from the very heavens themselves.

Most of the European powers have equipped their armies with one or other form of the new small-bore rifle, and those which have not completed their re-armament are making haste to do so. The only type of new weapon the results of the fire from which have been actually tested on the battle-field, is the Männlicher, which was used to a considerable extent in the Chilian civil war of 1891. As is generally known, the 8-millimetre projectile which the Männlicher throws is much lighter and of much flatter trajectory than any of the old larger bullets. Owing to its higher velocity and pointed shape its power of perforation is extraordinary. In the matter-of-fact language of Bardeleben, " Owing to the immense velocity of the Männlicher bullet and its small surface of contact, it meets with little resistance in striking,

causes little commotion of the neighbouring parts, has no time
to stretch the various tissues it encounters, and merely
punches out a hole, carrying the contused elements before it
clean out of the wound without seriously damaging the
surrounding wall of track." The now obsolete bullets fired
from great distances and striking a bone, frequently glanced
off or rebounded. This will occur no longer; the new long-
range projectile, if it strikes at all, has sufficient force to pass
through, cutting any vessels or organs it may meet in its
path. It is, therefore, all the more deadly. Whereas the
accepted estimate of casualties in modern warfare has been
in the ratio of about four men wounded to one killed, the
percentage in the Chilian fighting is authentically given as
four killed to one wounded. This ghastly proportion will
probably not maintain itself in future battles on a larger scale;
but there can be no doubt that the fighting of the future will
be deadlier than that of the past. Yet the properties of the
new bullet are not entirely lethal, although it will slay its
thousands and its tens of thousands. Its characteristic of
absence of contusion, which contusion from the old bullet
frequently stayed the bleeding of injured vessels, must result
in more frequent deaths from hæmorrhage, more especially in
the inevitable lack in the future of prompt surgical intervention. But the wounds it causes, if they do not produce
immediate death or speedy dissolution from hæmorrhage, are
expected to be more amenable to treatment than those which
were occasioned by the old bullet.

It is remarkable that the more modern battles of Europe,
in which great numbers of men have been engaged—battles
in which were used rifled cannon and small arms—have
afforded greatly less percentages of casualties than those of
earlier battles in which smooth-bore cannon and muskets
were the sole weapons of fire. At Borodino in 1812, there
fought 250,000 French and Russians with a result of 80,000
killed and wounded. At Salamanca in the same year, when
90,000 English and French were engaged, the casualties
amounted to 30,800. In each case the proportion of
casualties to forces engaged was one-third, and the proportion

was the same in the battle of Eylau in 1807. In the battles of Magenta and Solferino in the Franco-Italian war of 1859 when the French armament was in great part rifled, the proportion of killed and wounded to the total forces engaged was but one-eleventh. At Königgrätz in 1866, the proportion was one-ninth. In the two days' fighting before Metz in August, 1870—the battles of Mars-la-Tour on the 16th, and the battle of Gravelotte on the 18th—there were in all on the ground about 450,000 Germans and Frenchmen. The casualties of the two days amounted to 65,500, affording a proportion to the total strength of one-seventh. These figures work out that the old Brown Bess and the smooth-bore guns inflicted proportionately more injury to life and limb than occurred in the battles later in the century with all the appliances of improved armaments. But the largest army placed on a battle-field on any one occasion by any European Power within the present century—the Prussian army which fought at Königgrätz—did not amount to more than 260,000 fighting men. To-day, the war-strength available for the field of the German Empire is close on 2,500,000 men; that of France, 2,715,000; that of Russia, 2,450,000; that of Austria, 1,600,000. When the first great battle of the next great war comes to be fought, a million of combatants will be in the field. On the percentage of 1870, and putting aside altogether the effects of the recent developments in man-hurting, the casualties will exceed 140,000. According to the existing ratios, of this number 35,000 would be slain, 70,000 would be comparatively slightly wounded, and 35,000 would be severely wounded. In the absence of actual experience the Chilian statistics could not be relied upon, at all events, in full. It follows that if the wounded of the next great battle are to be dealt with as the present arrangements prescribe, apart from the gleaning of the bearers during the battle, surgical assistance will have to be provided for 105,000 wounded, and hospital accommodation for 70,000, namely, the 35,000 severely wounded, and one-half of the 70,000 comparatively slightly wounded.

To cope adequately with this vast aggregate of human

suffering—with this gigantic example of "man's inhumanity to man"—is obviously impossible; it confessedly cannot and will not be attempted. The primary object of war is manifestly not to succour wounded men; but to engage in battles, to beat the adversary, to win victories. The battles of the future may or may not be less prolonged than those of recent campaigns. We cannot prognosticate. The battle of Gravelotte lasted from noon until 10 p.m.; the battle of Mars-la-Tour right round the clock, from 9 a.m. to 9 p.m. It is certain, because of the vast strengths engaged, that the battles of the future will cover much more ground than heretofore, and it is probable that the fighting will be more stationary. Let me briefly adumbrate the possibilities—indeed I may say the probabilities—of the results of a great battle in the next great war, which is sure to be " short, sharp, and decisive." The fighting has been prolonged and bloody, with the result that one side is definitely beaten, evacuates its positions, and retreats more or less precipitately, leaving on the ground its wounded, none of whom could be cared for while the conflict lasted. The successful commander's ground is littered with his own wounded; he has them on his hands in thousands, and he has also on his hands the thousands of the wounded of the vanquished force which has gone away. The conqueror of the future, if he accepts the old-time conventional burden of his adversary's wounded, will become its victim. He will not accept the incubus. Is it to be imagined that the victor in such circumstances will think twice even about his own wounded, let alone the wounded of the other side ? No. He is in the field, not to be a hospital nurse, but to follow up his advantage by hammering on the enemy who has departed leaving his own wounded behind—and who may come back again to-morrow to strike him while clogged to the knees in the live and dead *débris* of yesterday's battle. The victor will hasten away to overtake or hang on the skirts of the vanquished army, leaving the wounded of both sides to be dealt with as may be possible by such surgeons as he can afford, in view of future contingencies, to leave behind, and to the ministrations of cosmopolitan amateur philanthropists of the Red Cross and kindred organizations. For there will be no more military bearer companies; in the hunger for fighting men the 1,000 bearers per army corps of the present will have been incorporated into a strong brigade with arms in their hands and a place in the fighting line. On the line of communication of the future, reserve ammunition trains are to precede the military ambulances which up to now have headed the columns of vehicles. The German instructions in the present regulations for medical services are, that when a battle is engaged in all available vehicles of whatever kind, empty regimental provision and meat waggons, empty supply-column waggons, country carts and waggons requisitioned, ambulances of medical establishments in rear, and the like, are to be brought up for the transport of the wounded in order to "satisfy requirements as far as possible." But the inevitable delays are obvious, and in view of further fighting in the immediate future the whole available vehicles could not be devoted to the service of the wounded in the recent battle. The order is specific that the Red Cross *personnel* and ambulances are henceforth never to be allowed to do duty in the first line, namely, on the field of battle, and that their activity must be confined exclusively to the period after the battle; that is, to the *étape* transport of the wounded to the base hospitals.

I have tried to foreshadow what I believe will be the plight of the wounded of the next great war. The prospect seems very disheartening; for the described dealing with poor mangled fellow-men is not of a progressive but of a reactionary character, and reaction is repulsive to our age. Yet there may be some features of the prospect tending to mitigate its gloom. I venture to think, for instance, that the enforced remaining of the wounded on the field until the battle is over, and indeed for hours afterwards, notwithstanding the suffering such delays must in many cases entail, will not for the most part produce consequences so calamitous as may be not unnaturally apprehended by those who "sit at home at ease." I am of opinion—and I venture to believe that I have bandaged and attended to more wounded under fire than any man in Europe who is not a professional military surgeon—that the severely wounded soldier under the existing system of prompt removal to the dressing-station, does not uniformly benefit by the hustling and physical disturbance his removal necessarily entails while he is suffering from the first shock of being severely wounded. It is true that he may bleed to death if no ministration has been afforded him where he lies; but that risk apart, if the bleeding shall have been stanched or shall have stanched itself, I conceive that he may lie without serious detriment, often perhaps with actual advantage, even for so long a period as twenty-four hours if the weather is not bitter. All men conversant with war know instances of extraordinary tenacity of life in wounded men who had received no attention. Segur's well-known story of the man wounded at Borodino having been found alive by the army returning from Moscow has been discredited. But my comrade and myself found on the fifth day after the battle of Sedan, a wounded Frenchman walking about in a sequestered part of the battle-field, not indeed with sprightliness but without evidencing great debility; yet his lower jaw had been shot away, a wound which precluded him from eating solid food. I found also on the third day after the battle of November 30, 1870, on the east of Paris, in weather so bitter that sentries were actually frozen to death on their posts, a nest of three wounded Frenchmen lying in a hollow, not starved to death, not frozen to death, but pretty hungry and quite alive. I may even dare go so far as to hold that, at all events, in the British service in small wars, the soldier is coddled nowadays to the extent of being really deteriorated by over-tenderness of treatment. He has an anæsthetic administered when the top joint of his little finger is being taken off; he has hypodermic injections when he has a twitch of pain; he is treated with champagne, with all sorts of delicate extras, and everything that can make a man reluctant to own to convalescence. In the old days of the Peninsular war men had natures of more pith and did not seem to die in much greater proportion than nowadays, although they were entire strangers to all this demoralising excess of dry-nursing. Take for instance Major George Napier, one of the Napier brothers who were always being wounded. Shot down in the breach of Ciudad Rodrigo, he was made a football of for about a quarter of an hour while the column passed over him as he lay. He was picked up with his arm shattered; Lord March bound his sash about it and bade him go and find the amputating-place. He discovered that locality after an hour's search, and then sat down at the end of a queue of men to wait for his turn, which came two hours later. Then there was a dispute between the surgeons on a point of etiquette. Napier had asked his own regimental surgeon to do the business, but a superior staff-surgeon successfully asserted his right to perform the operation of amputation. It took twenty-five minutes, the staff-surgeon's instruments being blunted by much use. The stump was bandaged and Napier bidden go and find quarters. He walked about on this quest most of the evening, finding at last a house in which a number of other wounded officers had gathered, and he remained there sitting by the fireside with his stump taking its chance for a considerable time longer, until the death of the gallant General Crawfurd gave him a bed vacancy. During that same night there arrived a soldier of his regiment who had been searching for his officer for hours. Napier said to the man: " I am very glad to see you ; but, John, you are wounded yourself—your arm is in a sling." " Arrah, be Jasus, your honour," answered honest John Dunn, "sure its nothing to shpake about—only me arrum cut off below the elbow, just before I shtarted to look for your honour ! "

To conclude, stern experience of future warfare will one day, please God, force home upon the nations the decision, whether their wounded and necessarily untended warriors in their thousands and their tens of thousands are to lie bleeding on the battle-fields while the strife is raging above them, or whether the peoples of the civilised world shall take the accomplishment of the blessed millennium into their own hands, and bring it about, in the words of the old Scottish paraphrase, that

> " No longer hosts encountering hosts
> Shall crowds of slain deplore;
> They'll hang the trumpet in the hall,
> And study war no more!"

XII.

IT was not a very enlivening spot, lying as it did on the
bleak lower shoulder of a lumpy hill, just where the heather
merged into the coarse tufty grass that marked the margin
of cultivation; yet it bore tokens of having been at some
time or other a fair-sized homestead. There were the remains
of the rough turf dyke which had once surrounded a cabbage-
garden, inside which the grass was shorter and greener,
while here and there a neglected tuft of southernwood or
a gooseberry-bush raised its ragged head, like the unkempt
poll of some homeless street Arab. In a corner overhung
by a graceful but decaying weeping-willow, was a little plot
which manifestly had once been a flower-garden. The tortuous paths were still faintly defined by the straggling
edgings of box, with many a gap and many a withered stem;
and through the luxuriant wilderness of chickweed, groundsel
and tansies there peered forth an occasional cowslip and
polyanthus, or a heart's-ease in its forlornness belying its
name. There was a gap in the turf wall just under the
willow-tree; and passing out by it I entered what had once
been a trimly-kept back-yard. The well was there with its
rough stone coping mouldering and displaced. At one time
there had been a not unambitious attempt to imitate an
inlaid pavement with variegated pebbles laid down in a
fantastic pattern, but the round stones had in places been
displaced from their bed, and in other places a layer of
mould coated them, out of which the rank strong grass
grew with a wild luxuriance. A pile of stone mingled with
and matted together by turfs, or as they are called in
Scotland, "divots," marked the site of the dwelling-house.
Only a fragment of one gable still kept its upright position,
from the centre of which, about half way up, projected the

iron support for the crook a few links of which still dangled
as in mockery over the empty and green-moulded hearth-
stone. The whole scene wore an aspect of the forlornest
desolation; no trace of human life was visible. The spring
wind soughed through the quivering leaves of the willow,
and played fitfully with a few scraps of paper which apparently could find rest nowhere—not a friendly crevice to
drop into and moulder into pulp; but seemed condemned
to be tossed to and fro on the wind eternally, as if they
were the symbol of some sinful human soul to which rest
and peace were denied. One of those fragments I caught
after quite a lively chase. It appeared to have been the
fly-leaf of a pocket-bible, and on it were written the two
names—

" ISABEL CROMBIE
JOHN FARQUHARSON "

and the legend underneath—

"Hereby plight constancy one to the other."

"Ah!" said my friend and companion the old minister
when I showed him the writing on the scrap I had picked
up, "that is the keynote to a long and sad tale. My heart
is always heavy when I come up out of the valley among
these memorials of a once happy family. A parish minister
sees some joy and much more sorrow in the course of what
the busy world may consider an uneventful life; but the
story of these ruins is the saddest within my experience."

I pressed the white-haired old man to tell me the tale,
and at length he yielded reluctantly to my importunity.
We seated ourselves on a fragment of the turf garden wall,
and the old minister, after a short silence occupied in the
consumption of huge pinches of snuff, which perhaps
accounted for a certain moisture of the eyes and a somewhat
profuse use of his pocket handkerchief, began his story :—

"I was returning one winter's evening from holding a
catechising in a remote district of my parish, which lies at
the back of the hill yonder. My pony had fallen lame,

and I turned off the hill road to the house the ruins of which are now before us, to find quarters for her for the night. When I entered the kitchen, the cold ingle of which you see below that still standing gable, a very pleasant domestic scene met my eye. The gudeman was sitting in the chimney-corner reading aloud in a quaint and effective manner one of the hill-stories of the Ettrick Shepherd. James Crombie, or 'Honest James,' the name he was known by far and wide, was one of my most respected elders. He was a man somewhat of the old Cameronian type, with strongly-marked harsh features, a kindly grey eye, and a great pile of bald head covered by the 'braid bonnet' of the Scottish peasantry. The gudewife sat by the table opposite to her 'man,' listening to his reading with interest, and knitting a pair of 'furr and rigg' stockings for his sturdy shins. At the foot of the table sat their daughter Isabel, or 'Bell' as was her familiar name, a good and good-looking girl as there was in the parish. By her side sat a strapping young fellow, John Farquharson by name, the son of a neighbouring farmer, who was serving his father as ploughman and who had very good expectation of soon having his name in the lease along with him. It was easy enough to discern that there was a quiet courting match going on between the young people; and as the gudewife wore a complacent smile and as James certainly did not frown—I set down the matter in my mind as settled, and jocularly asked John when he should be coming down to the manse to arrange about the banns. He, of course, looked much as if he had been detected in stealing the pulpit Bible, and Bell gave me a half shy, half roguish glance out of the corner of her blue eye, which I accepted as a tacit pledge that I was to perform the ceremony at a convenient season. After sitting for a while with the family group the gudeman begged me to conduct the evening worship, and this over I set out for the manse accompanied by John Farquharson, because, as he said, 'the road was gey an' kittle, an' your reverence micht lair in some o' the bog-holes.'

R 2

"Time wore on. It was getting near to midsummer, the season of the annual sacrament of the Communion. The spring had been a very bad one and last year's crops had threshed out wretchedly. A pestilence called the 'quarter-ill' had smitten many of the cattle, and in particular, James Crombie's byres had been almost emptied. His face had become perceptibly thinned and more haggard, and I used to meet him stalking moodily along with his hands under his coat tails and his head sunk on his breast. The young laird had come home from college—a handsome, wild young scapegrace of whom some ugly stories were already afloat. John Farquharson's face was no longer blithe as it had been wont to be. On the few occasions I met him in those bad days he seemed sullen and moody, and I feared that something had intervened to prevent the course of true love from running smooth between him and Bell. As for her, she too was altered. She had not come at all to the last catechising, and I had observed her in church dressed in a style which did not become her station.

"The Sacrament Sunday had come, and James Crombie, moody and careworn, was in his place with his brother elders. The preliminary sermon had been preached, the sacred elements were on the white cloth which covered the table running along the whole space of the centre of the church; and I ascended the pulpit to perform the awe-inspiring and terrible duty of 'fencing the tables.' Perhaps you do not know the strict meaning of the phrase and the duty. It is this. With the Saviour's body and blood in a symbolical form before the minister and the intending communicants, it is the momentous task of the former to warn away from that table, as he would from the very mouth of hell itself, all who would partake thereof with the stain of unrepented sin on their guilty souls. It is his dreadful duty to lift up his stern voice, and, in the name of the Most High, solemnly to warn the 'fornicators, idolaters, adulterers, effeminate, thieves, covetous, drunkards, revilers, extortionists, those full of envy, murder, deceit, malignity, backbiters, haters of God, despiteful, proud, boasters, inventors of evil things, disobedient to parents, without understanding, covenant-breakers, implacable, unmerciful'— to warn all such, I say, in the name of the Master that if they come to that table in their sins, they commit 'the sin against the Holy Ghost' and incur the fate of the apostate Iscariot.

"This duty, as I have said, is a dread one; but it is not for the conscientious minister to shrink from it in all its awful significance. I was finishing the solemn sentences wherewith I had fenced the table, when there was a sudden stir in the body of the church before me. I saw my favourite elder, James Crombie, spring to his feet and bareheaded rush frantically out of the church, his long grey locks streaming behind him as he fled. It was only with an extraordinary effort that I controlled my emotion and was able to proceed; and when I saw the sensation which the occurrence caused throughout the congregation— heightened when James's wife rose from her seat in the gallery, and with white face and tottering steps followed her husband—I wavered whether it would not be advisable to postpone the ordinance altogether. But I judged it better not, and table after table was served and the after- noon sermons had begun in church and in churchyard, ere I ventured to commune with myself over the extraordinary occurrences of the forenoon. I tried to connect it in some curious rambling fashion with the absence of the daughter, Isabel, from her place in church; but, failing in this, the moment the benediction had been pronounced I deputed a brother minister to fill my place at the manse dinner- table, and wended my way up the shoulder of the hill to James Crombie's house. A neighbour opened the door for me, and silently led the way into the kitchen. There, in her accustomed seat, sat the gudewife; but, oh, how changed from the last time I had seen her there! She sat silent and motionless, as if she had been smitten by a stroke; nor was she to be roused from the deadly numbness into which she had been struck. There were no tidings of James, but the neighbour-woman pointed silently to an open letter which lay on the table. I took it up and read it. It ran as follows, commencing with the stereotyped epistolary phraseology of the Scottish peasantry—

'Sunday Morning.

'DEAR MOTHER,—I write these few lines to let you know that I have gone away with young Mr. Harry, who has promised to marry me when we get to parts abroad. Dear father and mother, do not fret, for I will come home soon, and be the leddy down at the big house. Tell John Farquharson that he will get a better wife than your dutiful daughter till death,

'ISABEL CROMBIE.'

"My heart turned sick, and after an ineffectual effort to rouse the old woman from her lethargy of woe, I left the grief-smitten farmhouse. On my way home I met John Farquharson coming towards me with rapid strides, and a wild, dangerous light in his eye. He had heard a rumour, and he was hurrying to learn whether it were truth or falsehood. I stopped the poor fellow and strove, while I did not withhold from him the sad truth, to soften its terrible significance; but so soon as he was told that the report was but too true, he broke away with a bitter curse and a wild laugh, and ran madly across the moor as if flying from himself. There were sore hearts that night in the manse as well as up on the hillside.

"Next morning came tidings of James Crombie himself. Bonnetless as he was he had walked straight from the kirk door to the gate of the jail in the county town, and had set to battering at the door as if trying to break it in. The warder looked through the wicket and, knowing James, asked in surprise at the wildness of his aspect, what he wanted.

"'I want in,' was the answer, 'an' I maun be in! Gin ye dinna lat me in, by God, I'll loup aff the pier head, an' my death will be on your head!'

"'Is the man mad?' was the warder's reply; 'troth, there's mony want oot frae here, but few want in! I tell ye, gae awa', man!'

"'Lat me in, I say!' begged the elder—'pit me in a cell, or I'll ding out my brains on the lintel o' the yett. I tell ye I have guilt on my sowl an' I maun dree the law for it!'

"The astonished official knew not what to make of a demand so crazy, and he determined to free himself from responsibility by bringing James under the cognisance of the Procurator Fiscal, who lived in the next street. For his part James was nothing loth to accompany the warder, his whole being seemingly centred in a feverish craving to be inside a felon's cell at the earliest moment. Before the Fiscal he abruptly owned to his crime. Impelled, he said, by inability to meet the impending instalment of his rent, he had forged the name of a neighbour to the bill which he had handed to the factor in discharge of the rent due by him. Yes, 'honest James' was honest no longer—he was a confessed forger and felon. He had fallen, indeed, but he could not sear his conscience; and when my awful message in the fencing of the tables had sounded in his guilty ears, the burden of his secret sin had proved greater than he could bear.

"The Procurator Fiscal of course took his 'deposition,' and equally as a matter of course committed him to prison on the charge of forgery on his own confession. It was my task to tell the tale to his wife, and I would rather not trust myself to describe the effects on her of blow after blow. The morning after my interview with her she was at the prison door, and before the week was out there was a sale of the belongings at the steading among the ruins of which we are seated. James's debts were paid, and the poor gudewife moved into the town into a humble lodging to be near her husband on the day of trial.

"That day was not long of coming. The Lords of Circuit arrived, and on the following morning the court was duly constituted. Whereas, according to my belief, were this case to have occurred in England, the factor, a private individual, would have been the prosecutor and might have withdrawn the charge had he thought proper, the law is different here in Scotland. The moment that the Procurator Fiscal, who is a Crown official and the Public Prosecutor, has heard of the case, from that moment it is beyond the pale of private inveteracy, or mercy, as the case may be; and if in the exercise of his judgment he reports that the charge is one on which there is a reasonable probability of obtaining a conviction, no influence in the land can withhold it from the impartial arbitrament of the law. So, notwithstanding that the factor's claim had been satisfied and that he was ready to give evidence as to character on behalf of the prisoner, an example which the man whose name had been forged desired to imitate, James Crombie stood before the Circuit Judges to answer to the charge, with a Crown counsel as prosecutor. As he stood in the dock with downcast eyes and worn face I noticed that the sparse grey hairs had turned to snow-white, and that the once stout, upright figure had become wasted and bent.

"'How say you, James Crombie—are you guilty or not guilty?'

"His head sank still lower on his breast as the answer, although little louder than a whisper, sounded over the hushed court; 'Guilty, my lord, before my God, and before my fellow-men!'

"'The daumed feel!' I heard the Fiscal's clerk mutter angrily; 'an' me drew the process loose eneuch tae drive a coach an' sax through't, tae give honest James a chance!'

"'Have you any counsel?' asked the Court.

"'None, my lord, except a guilty conscience.'

"A whispered consultation ensued between the Fiscal and the Crown counsel, and the latter, rising, requested that the Court should proceed to take proofs of substantiation of the charge, negativing the prisoner's confession and plea of 'guilty,' and that it would be pleased to appoint one of the counsel present to conduct the defence of the prisoner at·the bar.

"A brisk young advocate who had been glancing over the papers, sprang up and volunteered his services which the Court accepted on behalf of the prisoner; and the first witness, the factor, was called. He had not, however, entered the witness-box when the dapper young advocate was on his legs.

" ' My lord,' said he, ' I rise to save the time of the Court and of my learned brother who appears on behalf of the Crown. I beg to call your lordship's attention to the irrelevancy of the libel. It contains no specification of the date or approximate date of the uttering of the document alleged to be forged.'

" The Fiscal's clerk seemed inclined to give vent to a hurrah; the Judge looked at the Crown counsel, who looked at the Fiscal, who smiled at his clerk and then shook his head. And then the Crown counsel rose and announced that ' he deserted the diet against James Crombie,' or, in other words, that he abandoned the charge. The bar of the panel (or, as you would call it, the dock) was raised, and the dazed, half unconscious man was let free and was taken possession of by his faithful wife.

" Next Sunday James Crombie was in the kirk in his usual seat. After public worship the kirk-session met according to wont, and James came and stood by the door of the pew which he had so often entered of right as a respected elder of the congregation. The elders and myself judged that in the circumstances he might be permitted to resign *simpliciter*, and so denude himself of the office which he was no longer worthy to hold. But no; James insisted on drinking the bitter cup to its dregs. ' I have been latten off ac punishment,' said he, ' oh, ye that I ance cud call brethren, but I maun dree this weird tae the verra end.' He was immovable. So next Sabbath day a Presbytery meeting was convened in the kirk down yonder, and James Crombie was formally deposed from the office of the eldership in the face of the congregation. With his fine bare head bent meekly downwards he went out from our midst, his faithful wife guiding his footsteps. Next week the couple sailed for America. The ship was lost on the coast of Ireland, and not a soul was saved."

It was with difficulty that the old minister reached what I took to be the conclusion of his melancholy story. He rose from the turf seat, and walked with hasty steps down the slope through the rough grass, and among the whin bushes. I followed him at a short interval, unwilling to interrupt his meditations, and we went on in this order till we came within a little distance of the graveyard wall. Here the minister halted and faced about. Waiting until I came up, he abruptly burst again into speech:—

"It was several years after this," he said, "that a woman came to the manse and told me that I was wanted up at the steading on the shoulder of the hill. Crombie's farm had been incorporated into a neighbouring one, and the buildings the ruins of which we have just left, remained unoccupied and were gradually becoming dilapidated. With some curiosity I went up the hill, and crossing the threshold from which the door-posts had rotted away, I entered the once-familiar kitchen. At first there seemed no sign of life in the place, but a low moaning drew me towards the chimney corner. There, all along on the earthen floor, in a huddled mass of draggled, tawdry finery lay a female form face downwards. I stooped, raised the passive head, and turned it to the light. For a little time I gazed on the lineaments, worn, wild, yet beautiful as they were, without recognition; then, as the eyes opened, the awful conviction dawned on me that in this poor wreck, this waif and stray of shattered and blighted womanhood, I was looking upon none other than Isabel Crombie. She recognised me, too, seemingly, after a little while, for she began in a low broken tone to repeat scraps of the Shorter Catechism and the texts of Scripture on which I had been wont to question her in the Sabbath school and on my season visitations. Then her mood suddenly changed, and, sitting up with wild, distorted face and arms thrown frantically about, she burst into a torrent of raving oaths and blasphemy such as curdled the blood in my veins. This outburst of horrible language lasted for a few minutes, and then the mood changed again, and she began to rock herself to and fro as if she were dandling an infant, crooning at the same time a low lullaby song. Finally she sank in a state of syncope, and then I sent the woman who had fetched me for a couple of neighbours, and we had her carried to the nearest house. There she lay some days, evidently dying fast. Hers was the sad old story, so old in the history of womanhood that I need not name it to you. It was a curious coincidence that while she was lying there fading out of the world, a letter came to me from a chaplain of the Scutari Hospital intimating that Private John Farquharson of the Scots Greys, had died in that hospital on a day stated, of desperate wounds received in the heavy cavalry charge at Balaclava. We spared the poor wretch this last drop of the cup she had poured herself out. Halt! or you will tread on her grave."

XIII.

MY SERVANTS ON CAMPAIGN.

ANDREAS.

THERE is an undoubted fascination in the picturesque and adventurous life of the war correspondent. One must, of course, have a distinct bent for the avocation, and if he is to succeed he must possess certain salient attributes. He must expose himself to rather greater risks than fall to the lot of the average fighting man, without enjoying any of the happiness of retaliation which stirs the blood of the latter; the correspondent must sit quietly on his horse in the fire, and while watching every turn in the battle, must wear an aspect suggesting that he rather enjoyed the storm of missiles than otherwise. When the fighting is over the soldier, if not killed, can generally eat and sleep; ere the echoes of it are silent the correspondent of energy—and if he has not energy he is not worth his salt—must already be galloping his hardest towards the nearest telegraph wire, which, as like as not, is a hundred miles distant. He must "get there" by hook or by crook, in a minimum of time; and as soon as his message is on the wires he must be hurrying back to the army, else he may chance to miss the great battle of the war.

The career, no doubt, has some incidental drawbacks. General Sherman threatened to hang all the correspondents found in his camp after a certain day, and General Sherman was the kind of man to fulfil any threat he made. But the casual obstructions, half irritating, half comic, to which he may be subjected, do not bother the war correspondent of the Old World nearly as much as do the foreign languages which, if he is not a good linguist, hamper him every hour of every day. He really should possess the gift of tongues. But how few in the nature of things can approximate to this polyglot versatility. I own myself to be a poor linguist, and have many and many a time suffered for my dulness of what the Scots call "up-take." It is true I know a little French and German, and could express my wants, with the aid of pantomine, in Russian, Roumanian, Bulgarian, Servian, Spanish, Turkish, Hindostanee, Pushtoo, and Burmese, every word of which smatterings I have long since forgotten. But the truth is that the poorest peoples in the world in acquiring foreign languages are the English and French; the readiest are the Russians and Americans. It was after a fashion a liberal education to listen to the fluency in some half-dozen languages of poor MacGahan, the "Ohio boy" who graduated from the plough to be perhaps the most brilliant war correspondent of modern times. His compatriot and colleague, Frank Millet, seemed to pick up a language by the mere accident of finding himself on the soil where it was spoken. In the first three days after crossing the Danube into Bulgaria, Millet went about with book in hand gathering in the names of things at which he pointed, and jotting down each acquisition in the book. On the fourth day he could swear in Bulgarian, copiously, fervently, and with a measure of intelligibility. Within a week he had conquered, roughly, the uncouth tongue. As he voyaged lately down the Danube from source to mouth, charmingly describing the scenic panorama of the great river for the pages of *Harper's*, the readers of these sketches cannot have failed to notice how Millet talked to German, Hungarian, Servian, Bulgarian, Roumanian, and Turk, each in his own tongue, those languages having been acquired by him during the few months of the Russo-Turkish War.

By this time the reader may be wondering where "Andreas" comes in. Perhaps I have been over long in getting to my specific subject; but I will not be discursive any more. It was at the table d'hôte in the Serbische Krone Hotel in Belgrade, where I first set eyes on Andreas. In the year 1876 Servia had thought proper to throw off the yoke of her Turkish suzerain, and to attempt to assert her independence by force of arms. But for a very irregularly paid tribute she was virtually independent already, and probably in all Servia there were not two hundred Turks. But she ambitiously desired to have the name as well as the actuality of being independent; the Russians helped her with arms, officers, and volunteer soldiers; and when I reached Belgrade in May of the year named, there had already been fighting in which the Servians had by no means got the worst. No word of the Servian tongue had I; and it was the reverse of pleasant for a war correspondent in such a plight to learn that outside of Belgrade nobody, or at least hardly anybody, knew a word of any other language than his native Servian. As I ate I was attended by an assiduous waiter whose alertness and anxiety to please were very conspicuous. He was smart with quite un-Oriental smartness; he whisked about the tables with deftness; he spoke to me in German, to the Russian officers over against me in what I assumed was Russian, to the Servians dining behind me in what I took to be Servian. I liked the look of the man; there was intelligence in his aspect. One could not call him handsome, but there was character in the keen black eye, the high features, and the pronounced chin fringed on each side by bushy black whiskers.

I had brought no servant with me; the average British servant is worse than useless in a foreign country, and the dubiously-polyglot courier is a snare and a deception on campaign. I had my eye on Andreas for a couple of days, during which he was of immense service to me. He seemed to know and stand well with everyone in Belgrade. It was he, indeed, who presented me in the restaurant to the Prime Minister and the Minister for War, who got together for me my field necessaries, who helped me to buy my horses, and who narrated to me the progress of the campaign so far as it had gone. On the third day I had him in my room and asked whether he would like to come with me into the field as my servant. He accepted the offer with effusion; we struck hands on the compact; he tendered me credentials which I ascertained to be extremely satisfactory; and then he gave me a little sketch of himself. It was somewhat mixed, as indeed was his origin. Primarily he was a Servian, but· his maternal grandmother had been a Bosniak, an earlier ancestress had been in a Turkish harem, there was a strain in his blood of the Hungarian zinganee—the gipsy of Eastern Europe, and one could not look at his profile without a suspicion that there was a Jewish element in his pedigree. " A pure mongrel," was what a gentleman of the British Agency termed Andreas, and this self-contradictory epithet was scarcely out of place.

Andreas turned out well. He was as hardy as a hill-goat, careless how and when he ate, or where he slept, which, indeed, was mostly in the open. It seemed to me that he had cousins all over Servia, chiefly of the female persuasion, and I am morally certain that the Turkish strain in his blood had in Andreas its natural development in a species of *fin-de-siècle* polygamy. Sherman's prize "bummer" was not in it with Andreas as a forager. At first, indeed, I suspected him of actual plundering, so copiously did he bring in supplies, and so little had I to pay for them; but I was not long in discovering that all kinds of produce were dirt cheap in Servia, and that as I could myself buy a lamb for a shilling, it was not surprising that Andreas, to the manner born, could easily obtain one for half the money. He was an excellent horse-master, and the stern vigour with which he chastised the occasional neglect of the cousin whom he had brought into my service as groom, was borne in upon me by the frequent howls which were audible from the rear of my tent. There was not a road in all Servia with whose every winding Andreas was not conversant, and this "extensive and peculiar" knowledge of his was often of great service to me. He was a light-weight and an excellent rider; I have sent him off to Belgrade with a telegram at dusk, and he was back again within less than twenty hours, after a gallop of quite a hundred miles.

No exertion fatigued him; I never saw the man out of

humour.   There was but one matter in regard to which I ever had to chide him, and in that I had perforce to let him have his · own way, because I do not believe that he could restrain himself.   He had served the term in the army which is, or was then, obligatory on all Servians; and on the road or in camp he was rather more of a " peace-at-any-price " man than ever was the late Mr. John Bright himself.   When the first fight occurred Andreas claimed to be allowed to witness it along with me.   I demurred; he might get hit; and if anything should happen to him what should I do for a servant?   At length I gave him the firm order to remain in camp; and started myself with the groom behind me on my second horse.   The fighting occurred eight miles from camp; and in the course of it, leaving the groom in the rear, I had accompanied the Russian General Dochtouroff into a most unpleasantly hot place, where a storm of Turkish shells was falling in the effort to hinder the withdrawal of a disabled Servian battery.   I happened to glance over my shoulder, and lo! Andreas on foot was at my horse's tail, obviously in a state of ecstatic enjoyment of the situation. I peremptorily ordered him back, and he departed sullenly, calmly strolling along the Turkish line of fire.   Just then, it seemed, Tchernaieff, the Servian commander-in-chief, had ordered up a detachment of infantry to take in flank the Turkish guns.   From where we stood I could discern the Servian soldiers hurrying forward close under the fringe of a wood near the line of retirement along which Andreas was sulking.   Andreas saw them too, and re-treated no step farther, but cut across to them snatching up a gun as he ran; and the last I saw of him was while he was waving on the militiamen with his billycock, and loosing off an occasional bullet, while he emitted yells of defiance against the Turks which might well have struck terror into their very marrow.   Andreas came into camp at night very streaky with powder stains, minus the lobe of one ear, uneasy as he caught my eye, yet with a certain elateness of mien.   I sacked him that night, and he said he didn't care and that he was not ashamed of himself. Next morning as I was rising, he rushed into the tent, knelt down, clasped my knees, and bedewed my ankles with his tears. Of course I reinstated him; I couldn't do without him and I think he knew it.

But I had yielded too easily. Andreas had established a precedent. He insisted in a quiet, positive manner on accompanying me to every subsequent battle; and I had to consent, always taking his pledge that he would obey the injunctions I might lay upon him. And, as a matter of course, he punctually and invariably violated that pledge when the crisis of the fighting was drawing to a head, and just when this "peace-at-any-price" man could not control the blood-thirst that was parching him.

One never knows how events are to fall out. It happened that this resolution on the part of Andreas to accompany me into the fights once assuredly saved my life. It was on the day of Djunis, the last battle fought by the Servians. In the early part of the day there was a good deal of scattered woodland fighting in front of the entrenched line, which they abandoned when the Turks came on in earnest. Andreas and I were among the trees trying to find a position from which something was to be seen, when all of a sudden I, who was in advance, plumped right into the centre of a small scouting party of Turks. They tore me out of the saddle, and I had given myself up for lost—for the Turks took no prisoners, their cheerful practice being to slaughter first and then abominably to mutilate—when suddenly Andreas dashed in among my captors, shouting aloud in a language which I took to be Turkish, since he bellowed "Effendi" as he pointed to me. He had thrown away his billycock and substituted a fez, which he afterwards told me he always carried in case of accidents, and in one hand he waved a dingy piece of parchment with a seal dangling from it, which I assumed was some obsolete firman. The result was truly amazing and the scene had some real humour in it. With profound salaams the Turks unhanded me, helped me to mount, and as I rode off at a tangent with Andreas at my horse's head, called after me what sounded like friendly farewells. When we were back among the Russians—I don't remember seeing much of the Servians later on that day—Andreas explained that he had passed himself off for the Turkish dragoman of a British correspondent whom the Padishah delighted to honour, and that after expressing a burning desire to defile the graves of their collective female ancestry, he had assured my captors that they might count themselves as dead men if they did not immediately release me. To his ready-witted conduct I undoubtedly owe the ability to write now this record of a man of curiously complicated nature.

When the campaign ended with the Servian defeat at Djunis, Andreas went back to his head-waitership at the Serbische Krone in Belgrade. Before leaving that capital I had the honour of being present at his nuptials, a ceremony the amenity of which was somewhat disturbed by the violent incursion into the sacred edifice of sundry ladies, all claiming to have prior claims on the bridegroom of the hour. They were, however, placated, and subsequently joined the marriage feast in the great arbour behind the Krone. Andreas faithfully promised to come to me to the ends of the earth on receipt of a telegram, if I should require his services and he were alive.

Next spring the Russo-Turkish war broke out, and I hurried eastward in time to see the first Cossack cross the Pruth. I had telegraphed to Andreas from England to meet me at Bazias, on the Danube below Belgrade. Bazias is the place where the railway used to end and where we took steamer for the Lower Danube. Andreas was duly on hand, ready and serviceable as of old, a little fatter and a trifle more consequential than when we had last parted. He was, if possible, rather more at home in Bucharest than he had been in Belgrade, and recommended me to Brofft's Hotel, in comparison with which the charges of the Savoy on the Thames Embankment or the Waldorf in New York are infinitesimal. He bought my waggon and team for me; he found riding-horses when they were said to be unprocurable; he constructed a most ingenious tent of which the waggon was, so to speak, the roof-tree; he laid in stores, arranged for relays of couriers, and furnished me with a coachman in the person of a Roumanian Jew, who, he one day owned, was a distant connection, and whose leading attribute was that he could survive more sleep than any other human being I have ever known. We took the field auspiciously, Mr. Frederic Villiers, the war artist of the London *Graphic*, being my campaigning comrade. Thus early I discerned a slight rift in the lute. Andreas did not like Villiers, which showed his bad taste or rather, perhaps, the concentratedness of his capacity of affection; and I fear Villiers did not much like Andreas, whom he thought too familiar. This was true, and it was my fault; but it really was with difficulty that I could bring myself to treat Andreas as a servant. He was more, to my estimation, in the nature of the confidential major-domo, and to me he was simply invaluable. Villiers had to chew his moustache and glower discontentedly at Andreas.

I had some good couriers for the conveyance of despatches back across the Danube to Bucharest, whence everything was telegraphed to London; but they were essentially fair-weather men. The casual courier may be alert, loyal, and trustworthy he may be relied on to try his honest best, but it is not to be expected of him that he will greatly dare and count his life but as dross when his incentive to enterprise is merely filthy lucre. But I could trust Andreas to dare and to endure, to overcome obstacles, and, if man could, to "get there," where in the base-quarters in Bucharest, the amanuenses were waiting to copy out in round hand for the foreign telegraphist the rapid script of the correspondent scribbling for life in the saddle or the cleft of a commanding tree while the shells were whistling past. We missed Andreas dreadfully when he was gone. Even Villiers, who liked good cooking, owned to thinking long for his return. For in addition to his other virtues, Andreas was a capital cook. It is true that his courses had a habit of arriving at long and uncertain intervals. After a dish of stew, no other viands appearing to loom in the near future, Villiers and myself would betake ourselves to smoking, and perhaps on a quiet day would lapse

s 2

into slumber. From this we would be aroused by Andreas to partake of a second course of roast chicken, the bird having been alive and unconscious of its impending fate when the first course had been served. No man is perfect, and as regarded Andreas there were some petty spots on the sun. He had, for instance, a mania for the purchase of irrelevant poultry and for accommodating the fowls in our waggon tied by the legs, against the day of starvation, which he always, but causelessly, apprehended. I do not suppose any reader has ever had any experience of domestic poultry as bedfellows, and I may caution him earnestly against making any such experiment.

I do not know whether it is a detraction from Andreas's worth to mention that another characteristic of his was the habit of awaking us in the still watches of the night, for the purpose of imparting his views on recondite phases of the great Eastern question. But how trivial were such peccadilloes in a man who was so resolute not to be beaten in getting my despatch to the telegraph wire that once, when a large section of the bridge across the Danube was sunk, he swam nearly half across the great river, from the right bank to the island in mid-stream whence the bridge to the left bank was passable! Andreas became quite an institution in the Russian camp. When Ignatieff, the Tzar's intimate, the great diplomatist who has now curiously fizzled out, would honour us by partaking sometimes of afternoon tea in our tent, he would call Andreas by his name and address him as " Molodetz!" the Russian for "Brave fellow!" In the Servian campaign Dochtouroff had got him the Takova Cross, which Andreas sported with great pride ; and Ignatieff used to tell him that the Tzar was seriously thinking of conferring on him the Cross of St. George, badinage which Andreas took in dead earnest. MacGahan used gravely to entreat him to take greater care of his invaluable life, and hint that if any calamity occurred to him the campaign would *ipso facto* come to an end. Andreas knew that MacGahan was quizzing him, but it was exceedingly droll how he purred and bridled under the light touch of that genial humorist, whose merits his countrymen, to my thinking, have never adequately recognised. The old story of a prophet having scant honour in his own country!

After the long strain of the desperate but futile attack made by the Russians on Plevna in the early part of the September of the war, I fell a victim to the malarial fever of the Lower Danube, and had to be invalided back to Bucharest. The illness grew upon me and my condition became very serious. Worthy Andreas nursed me with great tenderness and assiduity in the lodgings to which I had been brought, since they would not accept a fever patient at Brofft's. After some days of wretchedness I bécame delirious and of course lost consciousness; my last recollection was of Andreas wetting my parched lips with lemonade. When I recovered my senses and looked out feebly, there was nobody in the room. How long I had been unconscious, I had no idea. I lay there in a half-stupor till evening, unable from weakness to summon any assistance. In the dusk came the English doctor who had been attending me. "Where is Andreas?" he asked. I could not tell him. "He was here last night," he said—"you have been delirious for seven days." The woman of the house was summoned. She had not seen Andreas since the previous night, but, busy about her own domestic affairs, had no suspicion until she entered the room that Andreas was not with me still.

Andreas never returned. It appeared that he had taken away at least all his own belongings.

I saw him once again before I left Bucharest, but he seemed to shun me. I believed at the time that there were grave reasons why he should do so; but it is possible that he did not deserve the suspicions I could not help entertaining. Anyhow I never can forget that he saved my life among the pine trees of Djunis.

JOHN.

GoA is a forlorn and decayed settlement on the south-west coast of Hindustan, the last remaining relic of the once wide dominions of the Portuguese in India. Its inhabitants are of the Roman Catholic faith, ever since in the sixteenth century St. Francis

Xavier, the colleague of Loyola in the foundation of the Society of Jesus, baptised the Goanese *en masse.* Its once splendid capital is now a miasmatic wreck, its cathedrals and churches are ruined and roofless, and only a few black nuns remain to keep alight the sacred fire before a crumbling altar. Of all European nations the Portuguese have mingled most with the dusky races over which they held dominion, with the curious result that the offspring of the cross is darker in hue than the original coloured population. To-day the adult males of Goa, such of them as have any enterprise, emigrate into less dull and dead regions of India, and are found everywhere as cooks, ship-stewards, messengers, and in similar menial capacities. They all call themselves Portuguese and own high-sounding Portuguese surnames. Domingo de Gonsalvez de Soto will cook your curry and Pedro de Guiterrez is content to act as dry nurse to your wife's babies. The vice of those dusky noblemen is their addiction to drink.

The better sort of those self-expatriated Goanese are eager to serve as travelling servants, and when you have the luck to chance on a reasonably sober fellow no better servant can be found anywhere. Being a Christian he has no caste, and has no religious scruples preventing him from wiping your razor after you have shaved, or from eating his dinner after your shadow has happened to fall across the table. In Bombay there is a regular club or society of those Goanese travelling servants ; and when the transient wayfarer lands in that city from the Peninsular and Oriental mail-boat, one of the first things he is advised to do is to send round to the " Goa Club " and desire the secretary to send him a travelling servant. The result is a lottery. The man arrives, mostly a good-looking fellow, tall and slight, of very dark olive complexion, with smooth glossy hair, large soft eyes, and well-cut features. He produces a packet of chafed and dingy testimonials of character from previous employers, all full of commendation and not one of which is worth the paper it is written on, because the good-natured previous employers were too soft of heart to speak their mind on paper. If by chance a stern and ruthless person has characterised Bartolomeo de Braganza as drunken, lazy, and dishonest, Bartolomeo, who has learnt to read English, promptly destroys the "chit" and the stern man's object is thus frustrated.   But you must take the Goa man as he comes, for it is a law of the society that its members are offered in strict succession as available, and that no picking and choosing is to be allowed.   When with the Prince of Wales during his tour in India, the man who fell to me—good, steady, honest Francis—was simply a dusky jewel.   My comrade Mr. Henty, the boys' friend, rather crowed over me because Domingo his man, seemed more spry and smarter than did my Francis.   But Francis had often to attend on Henty as well as myself, when Domingo the quick-witted was lying blind drunk at the back of the tent; and once and again I have seen Henty carrying down on his back to the departing train the unconscious servant on whom at the beginning he had congratulated himself.

In the summer of 1878 Shere Ali, the old Ameer of Afghanistan, took it into his head to pick a quarrel with the Viceroy of British India.   Lord Lytton was always spoiling for a fight himself, and thus there was every prospect of a lively little war.   If war should occur it was my duty to be in the thick of it, and I reached Bombay well in time to see the opening of the campaign.   Knowing the ropes, within an hour of landing I sent to the "Goa Club" for a servant, begging that if possible I might have worthy Francis, who had fully satisfied me during the tour of the Prince.   Francis was not available, and there was sent me a tall, prepossessing-looking young man, who presented himself as "John Assisis de Compostella de Crucis" but who was quite content to answer to the name of "John."

John seemed a capable man, but was occasionally muzzy. After visiting Simla the headquarters of the Viceroy, I started for the frontier where the army was mustering.   On the way down I spent a couple of days at Umballa to buy kit and saddlery.   The train by which I was going to travel up country was due at Umballa about midnight.   I instructed John to have everything ready at the station in good time, and went to dine at the mess of the Carbineers.   In due time I reached the station accompanied by several officers of that fine regiment. The train was at the platform; my belongings I found in a chaotic heap crowned by John fast asleep, who when awakened proved to be extremely drunk. I could not dispense with the man; I had to cure him. I gave him then and there a considerable beating. A fatigue party of Carbineers pitched my kit into the luggage van and threw John in after it. Next day he was sore but penitent; he was redeemed without resorting to the chloride of gold cure, and, in his case, at least, I was quite as successful a practitioner as any Dr. Keeley could have been. John de Compostella, etc., was a dead sober man during my subsequent experience of him, at least till close on the time we parted.

And, once cured of fuddling, he turned out a most faithful fellow. He lacked the dash of Andreas, but he was as true as steel. In the attack on Ali Musjid in the throat of the Khyber Pass, the native groom who was leading my horse behind me became demoralised by the rather heavy fire of big cannon balls from the fort; and he skulked to the rear with the horse. John had no call to come under fire, since the groom was specially paid for doing so; but, abusing the latter for a coward in the expressive vernacular of India, he laid hold of the reins and was up right at my back just as the close musketry fighting began. He took his chances through it manfully, had my pack pony up within half an hour after the fighting was over, and before the darkness fell had cooked a capital little dinner for myself and a comrade whose commissariat had gone astray. Next morning the fort was found evacuated. I determined to ride back down the pass to the field-telegraph post at its mouth. The general wrote in my note-book a telegram announcing the good news to the Commander-in-Chief; and poor Cavagnari the political officer, who was afterwards massacred at Cabul, wrote another message to the same effect to the Viceroy. I expected to have to walk some distance to our bivouac of the night, but lo! as I turned to go, there was John with my horse close up.

In one of the hill expeditions, the advanced section of the force I accompanied had to penetrate a narrow and gloomy pass which was beset on both sides by swarms of Afghans, who slated us severely with their long-range jezails. With this leading detachment there somehow was no surgeon, and as men were going down and something had to be done, it devolved upon me as having some experience in this kind of work in previous campaigns, to undertake a spell of amateur surgery. John behaved magnificently as my assistant. With his light touch and long lissom hands, the fellow seemed to have a natural instinct for successful bandaging. I was glad that we could do no more than bandage and that we had no instruments, else I believe that John would not have hesitated to undertake a capital operation. As for the Afghan bullets, he did not shrink as they splashed on the stones around him; he did not treat them with disdain; he simply ignored them. The soldiers swore that he ought to have the war medal for the good and plucky work he was doing, and a major protested that, if his full titles which John always gave when his name was asked by a stranger had not been so confoundedly long, he would have asked the general to mention the Goa man in despatches. John liked war, but he was not fond of the rapid changes of temperature up on the "roof of the world" in Afghanistan. During one twenty-four hours at Jellalabad we had one man killed at noon by a sunstroke, and another frozen to death on sentry duty in the night. On Christmas morning when I rose at sunrise the thermometer was far below freezing-point; the water in the brass basin in my tent was frozen solid and I was glad to wrap myself in furs. At noon the thermometer was over a hundred in the shade, and we were all so hot as to wish with Sydney Smith that we could take off our flesh and sit in our bones. John was delighted when, as there seemed no immediate prospect of further hostilities in Afghanistan, I departed therefrom to pay a visit to King Theebaw of Burma, who has since been disestablished. When in his capital of Mandalay, there came to me a telegram from England informing me of the massacre by the Zulus of a thousand British soldiers at Isandlwana in South Africa, and instructing me to hurry thither with all possible speed. John had none of the Hindoo dislike to cross the "dark water," and he accompanied me to Aden, where we made connection with a potty little steamer which called into every paltry and fever-smelling Portuguese port all along the east coast of Africa, and at length dropped us at Durban, the seaport of the British colony of Natal in South Africa and the base of the warlike operations against the Zulus.

There are many Hindoos engaged on the Natal sugar plantations, and in that particularly one-horse colony every native of India is known indiscriminately by the term of "coolie." John, it was true, was a native of India, but he was no "coolie;" he could read, write, and speak English, and was altogether a superior person. I would not take him up country to be bullied and demeaned as a "coolie," and I made for him an arrangement with the proprietor of my hotel that during my absence John should help to wait in his restaurant. During the Zulu campaign I was abominably served by a lazy Africander and a yet more lazy St. Helena boy. When Ulundi was fought and Cetewayo's kraal was burned, I was glad to return to Durban and take passage for England. John, I found, had during my absence become one of the prominent inhabitants of Durban. He had now the full charge of the hotel restaurant—he was the centurion of the dinner-table with men under him to whom he said, "Do this," and they did it. His skill in dishes new to Natal, especially in curries, had crowded the restaurant, and the landlord had taken the opportunity of raising his tariff. He came to me privily and said frankly that John was making his fortune for him, that he was willing to give him a share in his business in a year's time if he would but stay, and meanwhile was ready to pay him a stipend of forty rupees a week. The wage at which John served me—and I had been told that I was paying him extravagantly—was twenty-two rupees a month. I told the landlord that I should not think of standing in the way of the man's prosperity, but would rather influence him in favour of an opportunity so promising. Then I sent for John, explained to him the hotel-keeper's proposal, and suggested that he should take time to think the matter over. John wept. " I no stay here, master, not if it was hundred rupees a day! I go with master; I no stop in Durban!" Nothing would shake his resolve, and so John and I came to England together.

The only thing John did not like in England was that the street-boys insisted on regarding him as a Zulu, and treated him contumeliously accordingly. His great delight was when I went on a round of visits to country houses, and took him with me as valet. Then he was the hero of the servants' halls. I will not say that he lied, but from anecdotes of him that occasionally came to my ears, it would seem that he created the impression that he had frequently waded knee-deep in gore, and that he was in the habit of contemplating with equanimity battle-fields littered with the slaughtered combatants. John was quite the small lion of the hour. He had very graceful ways and great skill in making tasteful bouquets. These he would present to the ladies of the household when they came downstairs of a morning, with a graceful salaam and the expression of a hope that they had slept well. The spectacle of John, seen from the drawing-room windows of Chevening, Lord Stanhope's seat in Kent, as he swaggered across the park to church one Sunday morning in frock-coat and silk hat with a buxom cook on one arm and a tall and lean lady's-maid on the other, will never be effaced from the recollection of those who witnessed it with shrieks of laughter.

In those days I lived in a flat, my modest establishment consisting of an old female housekeeper and John. For the most part my two domestics were good friends, but there were periods of estrangement during which they were not on speaking terms; and then they sat on opposite sides of the kitchen table, and communicated with each other exclusively by written notes of an excessively formal character passed across the table. This stiffness of etiquette had its amusing side but was occasionally embarrassing, since neither domestic was uniformly intelligible with the pen. The result was that sometimes I got no dinner at all. At other times when I was dining alone, the board groaned with the profusion, and sometimes when I had company there would not be enough to go round; these awkwardnesses arising from the absence of a good understanding between my two servants. I could not part with the old female servant, and I began rather to tire of John, whose head had become considerably swollen because of the notice which had been taken of him. It was all very well to be in a position to gratify ladies who were giving dinner-parties and who wrote me pretty little notes asking for the loan for a few hours of John, to make that wonderful prawn curry of which he had the sole recipe. But John used to return from that culinary operation very late, and with indications that his beverage during his exertions had not been wholly confined to water. To my knowledge he had a wife in Goa, yet I feared he had his flirtations here in London. Once I charged him with inconstancy to the lady in Goa, but he repudiated the aspersion with the quaint denial, "No, master, plenty ladies are loving me, but I am not loving no ladies!"

However, I had in view to spend a winter in the United States, and I resolved to send John home. He wept copiously when I told him of this resolve, and professed his anxiety to die in my service. But I remained firm and reminded him that he had not seen his wife in Goa for nearly three years. That argument appeared to carry little weight with him; but he tearfully submitted to the inevitable. I made him a good present, and obtained for him from the Peninsular and Oriental people a free passage from Bombay with wages besides, in the capacity of a saloon steward. I saw him off from Southampton; at the moment of parting he emitted lugubrious howls. He never fulfilled his promise of writing to me, and I gave up the expectation of hearing of him any more.

Some two years later I went to Australia by way of San Francisco and New Zealand. At Auckland I found letters and newspapers awaiting me from Sydney and Melbourne. Among the papers was a Melbourne illustrated journal, on a page of which I found a full-length portrait of the redoubtable John, his many-syllabled name given also at full length with a memoir of his military experiences; affixed to which was a facsimile of the certificate of character which I had given him when we parted. It was further stated that "Mr Compostella de Crucis" was for the present serving in the capacity of butler to a financial magnate in one of the suburbs of Melbourne, but that it was his intention to purchase the goodwill of a thriving restaurant named. Among the first to greet me on the Melbourne jetty was John, radiant with delight and eager to accompany me throughout my projected lecture tour. I dissuaded him in his own interest from doing so; and when I finally quitted the pleasant city by the shore of Hobson's Bay, John was managing with great success a restaurant in Burke Street. I fear, if she is alive, that his wife in Goa is a "grass widow" to this day.

XIV.

DISTINGUISHED CONDUCT IN THE FIELD.

ONE fine morning in August that dashing regiment the 13th Hussars, was marching from Exeter westward to take part in the Dartmoor autumn manœuvres of 1873. The regiment was trotting briskly along a sheltered valley trending up towards the moorland, the horses stepping out gaily after their comfortable night's rest. The colonel was riding at the head of his regiment, and I trotted along by his side on a smart Dartmoor pony. We had just passed a bend in the road, when there slowly upreared himself from behind a heap of stones, a bent, dilapidated man. He looked old before his time, he was round in the shoulders, he was set in the knees, on which were big leather caps for the man was a stone-breaker; but the bent back and the bowed legs straightened themselves after a fashion as the fellow squared himself to his front, and brought up his hand to his forehead in a smart salute. There was a sparkle in the eye of him, and I noticed the trembling of the lower lip as he let his arm fall by his side, while he continued to stand at attention as the regiment defiled past him. "An old trooper, I take it," remarked the colonel, "shouldn't wonder if he has served in the regiment; did you notice how his lip trembled?" "An old soldier, anyhow, sir," I replied, "for I noticed the dingy medal ribbons on his waistcoat."

Out of the saddle on to the stones, *facilis descensus;* nor is the trooper the only one of us whom the fate, too often self-inflicted, befalls. A man may have fought right gallantly for Queen and country yet still come to a parish job at last in this best of all possible communities of ours, while as yet the wrist, no longer supple for the sword-play, can at least wield the chipping hammer. I felt like having a talk with the old fellow, and so reined aside until the regiment had passed by.

There, opposite to me, he still stood at attention, the gnarled face all working, the tears running down the furrowed cheeks. The veteran—for veteran he clearly was, not of the barrack yard but of the battle-field, for his breast showed the Punjaub and Crimean ribbons, and by Jove! there too was the red ribbon of the "Distinguished Conduct Medal"—tried to pull himself together as he noticed me watching him. "Excuse me, sir," he said—"the old corps, the old corps, sir—never seen it since they invalided me fifteen years ago; and my heart swelled when I caught sight of the white plumes and the old buff facings. Why, sir, I was one of the dozen men that was all the regiment could muster when the remnant of us rallied behind the Heavies after the famous light cavalry charge you may have heard on! I little thought when I came up out of the valley that day, that I'd ever come to stone-breaking on the roadside. However, there was ne'er a one to recognise me, except it might have been the colonel who was lieutenant of my troop in the Crimea, or old Dr. Shipton who gave me the devil's own dose of physic the night of the Tchernaya."

It is not every day that one finds a man who has earned the medal for "Distinguished Conduct in the Field" breaking stones on the roadside, and I had a great desire to hear the old soldier's story. There was a little beer-house quite close, and I asked the ci-devant light dragoon to come and drink a pint with me and tell me something about himself. He was nothing loath, and presently we were seated on the bench outside the pot-house with a couple of mugs of Devonshire cider in front of us. Then I asked him how he had come by the Distinguished Conduct Medal; whereupon he delivered himself of the following yarn :—

"About the middle of October the cavalry division was pushed on to what you may call the rear front of the allied position before Sevastopol, and was lying in two separate but contiguous brigade camps out on the plain, some little distance beyond Kadikoi. It was an awkward position for a camp, for we had nothing in front of us but the Johnny Turks in the redoubts on the ridge; but that was not our affair. The two brigades had a bit of a make-shift commissary depôt between them, and a few handy men were picked out from the various corps to act as butchers. I was always ready for work, and volunteered all the readier for the butchering service because I knew that an odd tot of rum came one's way on commissary duty. If you should ever come across any fellows of the old Crimean Light Brigade, just you ask if they remember 'Butcher Jack' of the 13th Light, and you are sure to get your answer. I was as well known in the brigade as old Cardigan himself, and in my way was quite a popular character. I'd have had the stripes again and again if I had only kept straight; but there was too much rum going about for that. About once a week on an average I would be carried shoulder-high to the guard-tent, and over and over again I escaped being tied up to the wheel of the forage-cart, only because I was known for a useful, willing fellow when sober.

"The 24th of October was killing day. Slaughtering was finished and most of us were half-seas over, for there had been extensive transactions between us and the commissary guard—so much beef for so much rum. Paddy Heffernan of the Royals and I had got glorious before we had found time for a wash after our work, and a commissary officer dropped on us and had us both clapped in the guard-tent before you could say 'Knife.' For the time the guard-tent was about as good a place for us as anywhere else; so we did a fair allowance of sleep, wakening up occasionally for a drink out of a bottle which thirsty Paddy had contrived to smuggle in. It was well on for daylight when we fell into a heavy sleep, out of which Cardigan himself could not have roused us. I have a vague remembrance of having been hustled about in a half-awakened state, and of somebody saying, 'Well, let 'em lie, and be hanged to 'em.'

"It must have been past ten o'clock when we were roused by the noise of a heavy cannonade, which had been

going on Lord knows how long. Paddy and I were both
half muzzy still, for commissary rum, as you would
find if you ever tried the experiment, is not easy
tipple to get sober off; but I pulled myself together
a bit, opened my eyes, and sat up. To my surprise
the guard-tent had been struck, the guard was gone,
the camp was levelled and partly packed, and the
whole brigade had disappeared. Were we veritably
awake, or was all this a crazy dream? We rubbed our
eyes, sprang to our feet, and gazed around. What a sight!
The slope above us was covered to the ridge with a huge
mass of Russian cavalry, the front of which had just been
struck by part of the Heavy Brigade—some squadrons of
the Greys and Inniskillings. As we stared in bewilderment the Royals came thundering by us on the left at a
gallop, heading straight for the Russian mass with loud
shouts of 'Gallop, gallop! the Greys are cut off!' and
trying to form line on the move. A moment later two
squadrons of the 5th Green Horse with Captain Burton
at their head, came dashing through the Light Cavalry
camp in loose order, tripping over obstacles, caught by
tent-ropes and picket-ropes, and unable to get the pace on
until clear of the camp. Heffernan and I were both
knocked down by the rush; when we reached our feet
again, blest if there were not a lot of Cossacks down in
the Heavy Brigade camp on our left, hacking away at the
sick horses which had been left in the lines. We had
already tried to mount ourselves from the sick horse lines
of the Light Brigade, but had found there only two poor
brutes, one with a leg like a pillar letter-box, the other
down on his side and didn't seem much like rising any.
more.

"'Let's have a go at thim Cossacks!' cried Heffernan,
and you may be sure I was quite agreeable. I shouldered
an axe for my weapon, he found a sword somewhere; and
in our shirt-sleeves, just in the state we had left off killing
overnight and by no means quite sober, we doubled across
the interval and went at the Cossacks with a will. There

T

were some nine or ten of them, and they were having what I suppose they thought the amusement all to themselves, for there was not a man left in the camp of the Heavies. Some were jobbing with their lances at the poor wretches of sick horses, others had taken to their swords and were cruelly trying to hamstring the animals. They did not notice Heffernan and myself till we were right on them, and taken unawares they made quite a poor fight of it. I managed a brace of 'em right and left with my axe; Heffernan killed two more with his sword, but got a lance thrust through his sword-arm and was good for nothing more. But the Russkies had enough of us, and what were left of them galloped back to their own mass. I got what I wanted—that was a mount. He had been ridden by the Russian corporal, who I don't think was a Cossack; for the horse I fell heir to was a handsome, compact little iron-grey, and the saddle was much like our own, not the high-perched cushioned concern on which the Cossacks cock themselves. The Russian trooper must have ridden very short, for until I let the stirrups out ever so many holes my knees were almost up to my nose.

"The moment I got my seat on the little grey nag, I was after the Cossacks a cracker; but their little low-necked cats galloped like the wind, and I only got the axe to bear on one fellow before they mingled with the mass of their fellows. It was just at the moment that the great body of close-packed Russian cavalry began to break up and shirk back out of the hand-to-hand fighting with our chaps. I expected that they would have been pursued, for in a few minutes they were right on the run; and I rammed forward to have a share in the chase. But I suppose the word had been given to stand fast, and let them go and a good riddance. I heard no such order, however—I took deuced good care not to listen; and dodging round the left flank of our people, the rum still fresh in me—for Paddy and I had a refresher after we awoke—I darted right into the thick of the retreating Russians and went to work with the axe in the liveliest way. You see, sir, I had lost all the fun the rest of our fellows had been having, and was bound to make up my leeway somehow or other. I had a rare time, and, believe me, in a crowd the axe is twice the weapon a sword is; but ultimately I got so wedged and jammed among the Russkies that I could not help but be carried along with them, and quite expected to be made a prisoner. But just then came a cannon-shot from a troop of horse artillery of ours which had come into action on the flank of the flying Russians. It made quite a lane through them on my right, and plumped slap into my little grey horse, which dropped like a stone and I with him. After I had been ridden over by a couple of squadrons of Russian cavalry—the broken tail of the mass—I picked myself up and found no bones broken, although what between swords and horse-hoofs I was chipped a good deal about the head, and what between old and new blood and dirt must have looked rather a ruffian. I had still my axe but was now dismounted, and had to walk back towards where the Heavy Brigade was getting into order again. In trying to keep out of sight, who of all men should spot me but old Scarlett himself, the brigadier.

"'Who the deuce are you?' he asked, with a twist of his long white moustache.

"The rum was still lively in me, and I answered boldly—

"'Private ——, of the Thirteenth Light, sir, butcher to the Light Brigade.'

"'Where the devil have you come from?'

"'I've been pursuing the Russian cavalry, sir, and had my horse killed.'

"'Well, I don't wonder now that they ran; you'd scare the dead, not to speak of Russians. Be off, and give your own brigade a turn!'

"I don't wonder that Scarlett turned his nose up at me. I never was a great beauty, and I certainly now showed to disadvantage. I was bare-headed, and my hair must have been like a birch-broom in a fit. I was minus a coat, with my shirt-sleeves rolled up to the shoulder; and my shirt, face and

T 2

bare arms were all splashed and darkened with blood picked up at the butchering of the day before, to say nothing of the fresher colour just added. A pair of long greasy jack-boots came up to the thigh, and instead of a sword I had the axe over my shoulder at the slope as regimental as you please.

" I caught and mounted a Russian horse but could not see anything of the Light Brigade, so I coolly formed up on the flank of the old Royals. The men roared with laughter at my appearance, and I had not been in position a couple of minutes when up came Johnny Lee the adjutant on his old bay mare at a tearing gallop, and roared to me to 'Go to —— out of that !' So I was 'nobody's child,' and hung about in a lonely sort of way for more than an hour. I was dodging about the top of the ridge, looking down into the further valley in which the Light Brigade was formed up with the Heavies a bit to their right rear, when I saw an aide-de-camp come galloping down from the headquarter staff on the upland, and deliver an order to Lord Lucan who commanded the cavalry division. Then Lucan went to Cardigan who was in front of the Light Brigade ; and a few minutes later I heard Cardigan's loud word of command, ' The line will advance !' and saw the first line of the brigade follow him at a sharp trot. That line consisted of the 17th Lancers and my own regiment, the latter being the right regiment, nearest to myself. Hurrah ! I was in for another good thing. Shooting down the gentle slope at speed, I crossed the front of the Heavies and ranged up on the right flank of the right squadron of the old 13th—front rank, you may take your oath. The flanking sergeant stared at me as if I were a ghost, and Captain Jenyns looked over his shoulder at me with something between a scowl and a grin. No doubt I'd have been ordered to the rear promptly enough, only that there was more serious work in hand than disciplining a half-screwed butcher.

" We were under fire from front and both flanks before we had ridden down the valley two hundred yards. You may have heard of Captain Nolan, of the 15th ? He was the aide-de-camp who brought down the message ordering our charge from the headquarters staff to Lord Lucan ; and now, cavalry officer as he was, I suppose he was keen to take a share in the fun. Little fun it turned out for any of us, sir, least of all for him. He was out to the front, galloping athwart the right front, and waving his sword and shouting something over his shoulder—Lord knows what it was, or what the poor fellow meant—when a shell lit and burst right before him. A splinter struck him on the left side, his sword dropped from his still uplifted right arm, and the reins fell on his charger's neck. Such an unearthly yell came from the man's lips that the very blood turned in my veins. I believe the life went out of him then and there; but, dead or alive, he still sat straight in position, and the limbs kept their grip of the saddle. The scared horse whisked round and galloped to the rear through the interval I made between the sergeant and myself—the rider with his upraised arm, his ghastly set face, and the blood pouring from his torn chest, yet still square and upright in the saddle. It was the weirdest sight I saw all that day of blood.

"A few horse-lengths more, as it seemed, brought us right into the infernal cross-fire which was tearing our ranks to pieces. Men and horses went down at every stride, and as they fell the survivors closed in and rode straight, burning to have this one-sided devilry ended, and get stroke at an enemy before we were all killed. Men swore bitterly at the measured pace set and kept so obstinately by the chief, cantering along steadily on the thoroughbred chestnut with the white stockings, and neither giving order nor so much as looking over his shoulder since he had uttered the words, 'The line will advance!' 'By God, he's a wooden man!' the sergeant next me muttered. A squadron leader ranged up alongside of him only to be repressed by the flat of the brigadier's sword laid across his chest. But resolute as he was not to let his command out of hand, there was some human nature in him after all, and as the blasts of shot and shell from the guns in our front struck fiercer and fiercer in our faces, he relented and gradually quickened up to charging pace. Then along the ragged ranks there ran a sort of grunt of satisfaction; the spurs went home and the swords came to the 'right engage.' As for myself, what with the drink in me and the wild excitement of the charge, I went stark mad and sent the Russian horse along at a speed that kept him abreast of the foremost.

" Nearer and nearer we came to the batteries that were vomiting death on us, till I seemed to feel on my cheek the hot reek from the cannon-mouths. The air was full of grape. My sergeant went down with a groan, he and his horse struck at the same moment. At last—thank God !—at last we were there ! Cardigan shot forward out of sight in the smoke, head still well up, and heels down as if on parade. With a shout and a wave of his sword Captain Jenyns followed, and right on his heels half-a-dozen of us on the right flank leaped in among the Russian gunners, burning to get satisfaction. I will say for them that they stood manfully to their work. With a blow of my axe I brained a gunner just as he was clapping the linstock to the touch-hole of his piece; with another sweep of it I felled an officer who was trying to rally some men in rear of the guns ; and then what of us were left went slap through the stragglers, cutting and slashing to right and to left, and riding straight at the face of a mass of grey-coated cavalry on their grey horses, in solid formation in rear of the tumbrils and gun-teams. And what happened then, you ask ? Well, sir, I know this—that my comrades and I drove right in among the Russian cavalry, and kept thrusting and boring forward through the dense mass. They were round us like a swarm of bees, hustling and stabbing ; and we—so far as I could estimate not above a couple of dozen of us to the fore—were hacking and hewing away our hardest, each individual man the heart of a separate fight. I can say this—that I never troubled about guards myself but kept whirling the axe about me, every now and then bringing it down to some purpose ; and as often as it fell the Russkies gave ground a trifle, only to crush thicker the next moment. Still, barring a flesh wound or two from the point of a sword or lance, I suffered no harm. They funked coming to close quarters with their blunt old toasting forks, for the axe had a devil of a long reach ; and they dursn't use their pistols lest they should hurt one another.

"I have no notion how long I was at this close-quarter business, fighting hard and boring forward steadily; faith, I half think I might have been there now had I not heard, a little to my right, the word of command, 'Threes about!' Thinks I, if an officer considers it time to go about, a private man like myself has no special call to stop any longer among them grey-coated gentry, the reverse of civil as they are! So I pushed slowly through till I came out on a bit of an open space, where I found a small squadron of the 8th Hussars and a handful of the 17th Lancers in line with the busby-bags. Presently a few fellows of my own corps rallied under Captain Jenyns, and the little force moved off towards the rear. I was sober enough by this time, take my word for it; but the chances of getting back to our own end of the valley did not seem lively, for right in our track three heavy squadrons of Russian Lancers were forming up. So broad was the front they showed that we could not well pass them on either flank if we had a mind to, which we hadn't. Colonel Shewell of the Hussars gave the word and rode straight at their centre, sending their commander to grass and riding over him. Tired as were our horses, we went slap through their ranks as if they had been tissue-paper, and we routed the three squadrons completely at the cost of a few lance-wounds and a slain horse or two.

"The Hussars and Mayow's men of the 17th Lancers kept their ranks fairly unbroken as they rode up the valley unmolested after this last encounter; but we fellows of the 13th were in worse plight, since, having been of the first line, our horses were more beaten, and of men and horses alike most were wounded more or less severely. So we had to crawl home as best we might through the dead and dying of the advance, the Cossacks hanging viciously on our skirts, and the word being, 'Every man for himself, and God help the hindmost!' A lad of my troop and myself hung together, coaxing along our blown and jaded horses; but at last his horse dropped dead, and he lay wounded and bade me go on and leave him. Poor chap! he was little more than a boy, and I had a mother myself once. Dismounting, I raised him across my pummel, scrambled back into my seat, and was just able to boil up a trot and leave the Cossacks behind. He was a rare plucked one was that little Russian horse; right gamely did he struggle under his double load. And, hurrah! here were the Heavies at last, and we were safe.

"I dropped the lad where the surgeons were at work, and then went and formed up with the poor remnant left of the old 13th; but I wasn't allowed to stay there, such a black-guard as I looked, I suppose, and was ordered off to help shift the camp to a less exposed spot on the upland. The same night a sergeant made a prisoner of me for the crime of breaking out of the guard-tent when confined thereto — a mighty serious military offence, I can tell you. I was neither shot nor flogged, though; for next day I was brought up in front of Lord Lucan, who told me that although he had a good mind to try me by court-martial, he would let me off this time because of the use I had made of my liberty, and perhaps he would do more for me if I'd promise to keep sober. And that is how, sir, I came by the medal which is the soldier's reward for 'distinguished conduct in the field.'"

XV.

Twenty-two Years Afterwards—The New Frontier—For a Handful of Cigars—
Tracing the Old Movements—Vosges-Land—German Failings—Alsace-
Loraine—Want of Tact and of Manners—French Everywhere—The
Emperor William's Speculation—A Vast Graveyard—St. Privat to-day—
The Monuments—The English Dead—Concentrated Hatred—Where the
Old King Slept—The Battlefield of Sedan—The Weaver's Cottage—The
Ossuary at Bazeilles—"La Dernière Cartouche."

1. *August*, 1892.

IT is rather a sorry business for an invalid in quest of health
to find himself reduced to dodder about a mineral spring
in the self-same region where two-and-twenty years ago in the
full heyday of vigour, he was watching the greatest battles of
the century, a spectator of the making of history. To the
spot where I write the roar of Gravelotte came faintly on the
wind, and yesterday I changed trains at that beautiful Nancy
into which rode the three audacious Uhlans of whom Leland
has written. Looking eastwards, I can discern on the sky-line
the "long waving line" of the Vosges range, along whose
summits runs the new frontier which alienated Alsace from
France. There is scant traffic now along the fine roads built
by the last Napoleon through the passes and over the ridges
of the mountain-chain; indeed, there never has been much
since that second week of August, 1870, when MacMahon's
army, routed at Wörth, came pouring in disorder over the
Vosges by every road and hill-track from the "Englisch-
Berg" in the north, over the shoulder of the "Schnee-Berg,"
and southwards as far as the dominant "Schlucht." One
detachment took the picturesque hill-road commanded by the
old mountain-fortress of Lutzelstein, which, commanding
though its position was, made no attempt to stand a siege, and
where the French accuse a fellow-countryman of having pointed
out to the victors for a handful of cigars, the guns which the
garrison had buried. Most of MacMahon's own corps after

its first panic-flight from Reichshofen, rallied about Saverne, climbed therefrom to Phalsburg by the famous "Steige," up whose toilsome zigzags had toiled, some sixty years before, an earlier race of French soldiers commemorated in the pages of Erckmann-Chatrian; and thence down into the hither low country by Saarburg, Dieuze, and Blamont. By Urmatt and Schirmeck another body crossed the shoulder of the Donon, the mountain of sacrifice of the ancient Celts; and yet another through Markirch—a town so near the old provincial frontier-line that it used to be said of the Markirch people that they "kneaded in Alsace and baked in Lorraine"—over the Riezouard and down on St. Dié. The broken troops who marched through this neighbourhood in disorderly and un-disciplined fashion belonged mostly to the 5th Corps—De Failly's. They were passing from a temporary halt in Charmes across country to Chaumont, whence they were conveyed by train to Châlons there to join the ill-starred army which surrendered at Sedan. To this day the country-folk tell shudderingly of the disorder and indiscipline of the demoralised troops who, their arms and packs thrown away, their uniforms torn and befouled, their features haggard, straggled over the face of the quiet region plundering and devastating as if in hostile territory.

Apart from its natural beauties of lakes, of shaggy woods climbing the abrupt mountain-faces, of sweet sequestered valleys in which the villages nestle among the foliage; apart, too, from the old-world towns abounding in interesting speci-mens of mediæval architecture, and from the numerous picturesque and placid little watering-places which shelter themselves in the green recesses of the mountain range, the Vosges country is so full of historical associations as to deserve greater attention on the part of the British tourist than it has hitherto received. There is no region of Europe which will better requite a visit, made with Mr. Henry Wolff's charming book, "The Country of the Vosges," in the wayfarer's hand. It will guide him to spots which come directly into the history of his native land. Up in the northern Vosges are the ruins of the old castle of Trifels where Richard Cœur-de-Lion was imprisoned; and farther south, within the quaint old city of Hagenau, stood in the fork of the Moder the hoary palace of the Hohenstaufens, in the hall of which the Lion-hearted was put on his trial for alleged "misdeeds;" and where Cœur-de-Lion's nephew, Richard of Cornwall, held his court as "King of the Romans"—in that self-same moated and turreted palace in which for a time his uncle had been treacherously confined as a prisoner. The rugged and primitive "Hanauer Land" among the foothills between Bitche and Saargemünd—a region which is a rolling mass of woodland intersected by green valleys, bright with glittering lakes, and on every peak and bluff the ruin of a castle of the Middle Ages—was centuries ago the appanage of those masterful Counts of Leiningen who were the maternal ancestors of Queen Victoria. In Metz to this day there are traditions of Richard de la Pole the last "White Rose" claimant to the throne of England, who lived there in exile for several years. In the casemates, cells, and hospital of the eyrie-like citadel of Bitche are graven the names of numerous English prisoners of the Napoleonic wars, sent thither from Verdun and other less rigorous places of internment because of turbulent conduct and attempts at escape.

2.

The Germans are a masterful people. They can conquer with a meteoric swiftness; they can hold the conquered region in a vice; they can annex it. Everything that can be done by dint of force and domination they can do. But they strangely lack tact, possessing which they could incorporate and assimilate; and with the best intentions in the world, and the most anxious desire to weld into the German Empire the inhabitants of Alsace and Lorraine, they are to-day farther away from the attainment of their object than when grim but genial old Manteuffel—a Prussian indeed of the Prussians, but an innate gentleman and one who if firm was tactful and considerate—ruled over the conquered provinces as their first Stadtholder. The wise measures which Manteuffel initiated have been zealously carried on by the administrators who have succeeded him; but unfortunately they and their subordinates have substituted the Prussian manners in their most peremptory and rugged methods of expression, for the velvet glove which wise old Manteuffel wore over that iron hand of his. If the Alsatians and Lorrainers had no memories, no prepossessions, no prejudices, no emotions; if in short they were mere soulless chattels, then it might be admitted that the German administration of the two conquered provinces has left nothing to be desired. It may be said with truth that the German Government in Alsace and Lorraine has done and is doing more towards the advancement of the material welfare of the provinces which were torn from France in 1871, than the British rule in India has ever done towards the amelioration of the condition of the native population of that great Empire.

If the Hindoos do not bless us for what we have done in their material interest, the Alsatians and Lorrainers spurn and repudiate every effort on the part of the Germans to benefit them in spite of themselves. The harsh, dictatorial, suspicious Prussian gendarme dominates every scene. The Prussian " blood and iron " is in evidence everywhere. Metz is dragooned into a dumb, lurid, sullen silence by a whole Army Corps of German soldiers, whose massive tramp is constantly sounding by day and by night in the thoroughfares of the old capital of Lorraine, and whose officers with rattling sword-scabbard and jingling spurs hold the " crown of the causeway," and hustle the Messins into the gutter. You may visit any of the quaint little towns of Alsace and Lorraine at fair time, when the venerable old-world place is crammed with the surrounding villagers, trafficking, gossiping—always now in glutinous French—hurrying into and out of the amusement booths, or sitting under the pollards drinking great mugs of beer. Suddenly the brazen clash of military music rises above the miscellaneous din of the fair, and brows knit, hands are clenched, and eyes glare furtively. For the music comes from the band of a Prussian regiment, and the genial and apposite strains it has selected are " Ich bin ein Preusse," or " Die Wacht am Rhein." This is an illustration

among many of the tactful and graceful methods resorted to
by the Germans in the conquered provinces.

Such an incident as this is a sample of the manner in
which the Germans madden the Alsatians and Lorrainers
against them, and destroy much of the impression which
else might be wrought by their efforts to benefit the
provinces in a material sense. But for such things the
amalgamation of the provinces would probably have been
complete ere now, instead of being apparently more remote
than when the new frontier-line was drawn. For conquerors
and conquered are of the same Teutonic stock. The Alsatians racially are Swabians, the Lorrainers Bavarians of the
Palatinate. It took the French more than a hundred
years of repression to stamp out the German language in
Lorraine. Their efforts in the same direction in regard to
the Alsatians were arrested by ecclesiastical influence, and
German remained the language of Alsace until its annex-
ation to Germany. It may be broadly said that, in spite of
identity of race, and in spite of every effort on the part
of the Germans to discourage the use of it, the language of
Alsace is to-day French, so far as speech in public is concerned—in their homes the people still talk in the familiar
language. In the words of Mr. Wolff, the Alsatian speaks
French, reckons in French money, reads French papers,
affects French dress, French habits, a French style of living,
takes an interest in French events, warns you that there
are spies about; and on July 14, the day of the National
Fête you may see him crossing the frontier, denationalised
now though he be, to keep the French festival on French
soil. Half at least of the guests at the watering-places in
the French Vosges are Alsatians. At a glance one recognises
their prevalence at Vittel and Gérardmer. Yet in the
casinos and *buvettes* one never hears a word of German.
The unwritten *mot d'ordre* among them is to speak French.
But to right and to left of you, through the thin partitions
between the bedrooms you may overhear a wife administer-
ing a curtain lecture to her spouse in guttural Swabian
German, and a husband in the same accents grumbling

over the depreciation of landed property in Alsace since the
German sway came into force in that once prosperous
region.   And it is significant of the uncertainty of the
future in men's minds, that the land-speculator hesitates to
take advantage of the depreciation. The local resident has
neither the heart nor the means. But the corn-slopes, the
bright meadows, and the rich vineyards, one would imagine,
might surely tempt the wealthy Berliner who has made his
pile in finance. Yet the only German who has evinced the
courage of his opinions in investing in real estate to any
great extent in the conquered provinces is the Emperor
William, who recently bought cheap—for 100,000 marks—
the fine estate of Urville in German Lorraine, the previous
owner of which purchased it in 1854 for the eightfold
price of a million of francs.

3.

On the 18th of August, 1870, the day of the battle of
St. Privat-Gravelotte, the French defensive line from north
of St. Privat to a point a few hundred yards southward of
the village of Rozérieulles, had a front of about seven miles
in length.   This front the German assailants before the
lurid night closed in on the bloody day, overlapped by a
considerable distance on both flanks.   Roughly speaking,
then, there is an area of about nine miles in length by
about two in breadth which with scarcely a strain on
words, may be said to be one great graveyard, wherein rest
peacefully side by side the French and German combatants
who perished in the long-maintained and bitter strife of
that memorable day.   Hard by this area constituting at
once the battle-ground and the graveyard of Gravelotte,
there lies a little distance to the south-west another battle-
field with its resultant wide-stretching graveyard — the
theatre of that stubborn and desperate struggle fought on
August 16th, which is known in history as the battle of
Vionville-Mars-la-Tour. The area of this earlier battlefield
is more circumscribed, since the fighting was closer and
the combatants were fewer; but the slaughter was yet

proportionately greater than that of the succeeding battle, and on the rolling fields of Vionville, Flavigny, Mars-la-Tour, and Tronville the dead lie thicker than on the broader face of the later battlefield. All the village church-yards are filled high with the dead of the two battles: but it was given to comparatively few to rest in consecrated ground. Yet in a sense the whole wide stretch of the battlefields is consecrated ground—for what holier conse-cration can ground receive than from the life-blood of gallant men ·who died fighting in their country's cause? Plain and slope, ravine and copse, hold everywhere those sacred grave-mounds—some populous with multitudinous dead, others the resting-places of but two or three. All the graves of the battles are maintained decently and in order, their slopes and flat summits trimly sodded, the wild flowers luxuriantly nurtured by what lies below, blooming around the neat white crosses that tell in black letters what brave enemies in life and brothers in the grave moulder side by side. After the war the German authorities entered into an arrangement with the peasant-farmers in whose lands the dead of the battles were buried, that the graves should be maintained for a period of twenty-five years dating from August, 1870, after which the owners of the soil should be entitled to plough them in. This compact will run out in 1895*, and if the arrangement for their maintenance be not renewed, the mounds, the en-circling hedges, and the white crosses will disappear, and much of the vitally pathetic interest of the Metz battlefields will fade. It is true that the interest in a measure will be commemorated by the monuments of corps, divisions, brigades, and regiments which stud the fields to the number of sixty-four, and also by the separate graves of some of the fallen officers whose relatives have bought in perpetuity the patches of ground which hold their loved ones. And the numerous tombstones of officers and soldiers in the village churchyards will not let fade the vivid memory of those two days of desperate fighting when the parched soil

* I do not know whether this arrangement is being acted on. June, 1895.

drank in French and German blood, and when the blue sky was dimmed by the smoke of the strife and lurid with the blaze of a hundred raging conflagrations. The Germans insisted on the frontier-line running in a curiously zigzag fashion, so as to include almost the whole theatre of the battle of Gravelotte-St. Privat and the most important section of the battle of Vionville-Mars-la-Tour; but they left within French territory the vicinity of Mars-la-Tour and Tronville. By an amicable arrangement, German monuments have been erected on French soil, and French monuments on the German side of the frontier; but the French monuments on either ground are comparatively few. There is, indeed, one comprehensive and striking French monument at Mars-la-Tour, at the foot of which on each anniversary of the battle of August 16 solemn religious services are held, attended by old soldiers from every part of France who participated in the fighting, as well as by a vast assemblage of the population of the neighbourhood.

In the massive village of St. Privat the northern extremity of the French line, in which Canrobert maintained himself so tenaciously, the children are playing to-day in the lanes and open spaces where on that lurid evening two-and-twenty years ago, Prussian Guards, soldiers of Saxony, and Canrobert's staunch infantrymen clashed together in the furious hand-to-hand struggle that virtually ended the battle so far as Prince Frederick Charles's army was concerned. The shell-fire made an utter wreck of the place, strongly built as it was. When I saw St. Privat the day after the battle it was one ghastly blood-bedabbled ruin, amid the smouldering *débris* of which were heaps of dead and a litter of broken and battered weapons and accoutrements. St. Privat smiles again, yet not with wholly unknit brows. For every wall in the place shows where the shell-holes have been plastered up; many of the tombstones in the graveyard where stood the venerable church, remain as they were shattered by the shells, and the old church which the villagers loved was so shattered and riven by shot and fire that it could not be restored. Handsome new churches, both here and lower down at Amanvillers where the old church endured the same fate as that of St. Privat, have been built; but the spick-and-span new structures are not to the conservative habitants what their old holy places were.

Northward of St. Privat, between that village and Roncourt, on ground watered by the blood of the gallant and genial fighting men who had followed the Crown Prince of Saxony in the great turning movement, and who on the afternoon of the great battle struck St. Privat on the flank, stands the monument erected by the Saxon Army Corps to their fallen comrades. It is so ugly as to suggest that Saxon valour is of a higher order than Saxon taste; yet its monstrosity is more than half redeemed by the appropriate legend graven on its pedestal: "Be thou faithful unto death, and I will give thee a crown of life." Within a stone's throw of the southern end of St. Privat is the not ineffective monument to the fallen of the Prussian Guard Corps. From its summit the eye can sweep the whole face of the northern battlefield, from the Orne to Vernéville on the southern skyline. Over against us yonder, on the face of the gentle slope gliding down into the nearer gentle hollow, on that awful afternoon of this day twenty-two years ago (I am writing on the spot on the anniversary of the great battle), there thundered incessantly on St. Privat and Amanvillers the long line of German cannon stretching from Vernéville through Habonville, St. Ail, and on beyond St. Marie-aux-Chênes almost to Aboue. And the hither slope at our feet, where the tell-tale hillocks and mounds are so frequent and on whose face so many white crosses gleam in the sunlight, is none other " than the bare, smooth glacis gently rising up to the fortress-like village of St. Privat " —the stretch of terrain on which 6,000 of Prussia's finest soldiery went down in less than twenty minutes. Than that advance there has been nothing more heroic since the day of Fontenoy, when Cumberland's army, heedless of the gunfire doubly enfilading it, pierced Saxe's front. Both efforts were reckless and mistaken; neither quite succeeded; but those conditions no whit detracted from the steadfast heroism of the fighting-men.

U

Amanvillers, the French centre of the northern battle, was all but ground into powder by the fire of Manstein's cannon on the swell in front of Vernéville. At Amanvillers, now mostly rebuilt, and discernible far and wide because of the flaring new church which the Germans have built to replace the quaint old edifice which their shell-fire destroyed, is the railway station of the battlefield. From it the road, leaving the French for the German front, slants through a close succession of grave-mounds across the shallow hollow to Vernéville. Yonder on the left is that shoulder of the swell whither the over-ardent Manstein hurried his batteries; in the graves, ranged almost symmetrically in rear of the line of gunfire, lie the staunch gunners who endured unto death the hurricane of cross-fire that swept the Prussian batteries from Amanvillers and Montigny-la-Grange. Vernéville, picturesquely nestling among its foliage on the slope of the ridge, is a veritable Aceldama. It has for people of our nation a touching interest. Not a few of our countrymen fell on either side in the course of the great war between France and Germany. Britons gave their lives for an alien cause as volunteers in the improvised cohorts of Chanzy and de Paladines. English Winsloe, a lieutenant of Würtemberger cavalry, was the first man slain in the war. Argyleshire Campbell miraculously survived the shattering wounds he received in Bredow's historic "Todtenritt;" the gallant Douglas perished in the cavalry *mêlée* between Mars-la-Tour and Bruville; and "Kit" Pemberton of the Guards, to know whom was to love him, went down with a bullet through his brain on the red field of Sedan. And at least one woman of our race sacrificed her life in the sacred cause of humanity. In the village graveyard of Vernéville, among the dead of both nations whom while they lived she had tended in the adjacent château wherein were huddled 1,200 wounded men, there sleeps a devoted Englishwoman under the plain stone on which are chiselled the simple words: "In Memory of Henrietta Clarke, Deaconess, from Chiswick, Cumberland, England; Born December 24, 1837; Died October 26, 1870."

From Vernéville the road winds downward through

Malmaison, and past the great barn of Mogador, in which during the battle two hundred wounded Frenchmen were burnt alive, into the straggling village of Gravelotte. Tourists are drinking coffee outside the Cheval d'Or, the hotel in front of which on the day before Mars-la-Tour stood the haggard Napoleon, while his troops defiled past him "melancholy and beaten out, without a single shout of 'Vive l'Empereur!';" and whither on the following morning Bazaine brought him a posy of wild flowers as a souvenir of the broken man's fête day. Across the way, in a little room of the house which is now the German post-office, Napoleon spent the night before August 16, on the early morning of which day he drove away to Châlons to yet severer suffering and to the utter wreck at Sedan. About Gravelotte now, the people hate neither the Empire nor the memory of Napoleon —they concentrate their hatred on the Germans. "They dragoon us," said to me an old villager; "they tax us; they are harsh and brutal; but, thank God, monsieur, they cannot deprive us of the privilege of hoping for better days." After two-and-twenty years one's memory of localities grows dim, and it was in vain that I searched on the outskirts of the village for the place where, on the day of Gravelotte, I saw the dead of both sides built up into barricades from behind which fired the Prussian marksmen. "Voilà, monsieur!" replied to my question a peasant with a wave of the hand; and lo! what I recollected as a great ghastly shamble is now a green and shaded space, where blossoming creepers grow over the crosses above the 3,000 soldier-dead who rest in this now peaceful scene.

From Gravelotte to the field of Mars-la-Tour the high road goes due west through Rézonville, outside of which King Wilhelm sat in suspense as to the issue of the fighting on the right flank, until Moltke brought him at a gallop the tidings of final victory. Farther on the hamlet of Flavigny is seen on the left, the scene of the most desperate fighting of August 16th; and directly in front is the village of Vionville, whence Bredow's devoted charge sped along the green hollow to crash through rank after rank of French infantrymen, and onward and yet on up the gentle slope to the French cannon on the old Roman road on the sky-line. That long, broad, parallelogram on the northern edge of the road holds all that was mortal of the noble troopers who rode to their death for " King and Fatherland " on that momentous afternoon. Vionville is a long dunghill village, in a poor house of which King Wilhelm slept on the night after the battle of Gravelotte. There were better houses in the place, but they were all crammed with the wounded of the battle; and the old king was content to occupy a little upper chamber partitioned off from a granary whose wall and roof were full of shell-holes.

Returning through Gravelotte towards Metz the traveller, following the *chaussée*, plunges down into the ravine of the Mance, and then ascends to the great open slope on which occurred the fiercest fighting of the southern battle. Time after time did the soldiers of Steinmetz attempt to crown that slope, to be crushed back time after time by the fire of Frossard's resolute infantrymen. Not even darkness ended the strife, and hand-to-hand struggles broke out at intervals until daylight. The battered farmhouse of St. Hubert is now rehabilitated, but there are only a few ruins where the houses at Point-du-Jour stood before the battle. There are Prussian monuments right up to Point-du-Jour testifying to the daring and determination with which the Germans pushed onward, and not less to the dauntless reso-lution of the French on the defensive, who over and over again hurled their assailants back from the very lips of their shelter-trenches.

4.

A strange fate has overtaken the battlefield of Sedan. The battle itself, in its phases, and yet more in its results, must rank as the most memorable of European events since Waterloo. In many respects the intrinsic interest of the great struggle around Vauban's old fortress in the Ardennes equals that of the earlier contest in which British valour and constancy shone with so great an effulgence. To this day the field of Waterloo is the most frequented of

European battle-grounds. More than three-quarters of a century have elapsed since Wellington and Napoleon confronted each other in the historic arena between Mont St. Jean and La Belle Alliance, and still the Waterloo coaches with full complements of passengers start daily from Brussels. On the other hand, within ten years after the momentous clash of arms around the hoary defences of Sedan, the wide-ranging battlefield around that obsolete fortress had been almost entirely denuded of any visible relic or memento of the struggle which was fought out to the bitter end on its slopes on September 1st, 1870. The graves of the fallen had been ploughed down and sown over in some cases; in others the remains of the dead combatants had been exhumed and removed into the graveyards of the local villages, where their resting-places are unmarked by any memorial.

To-day the pilgrims to the scene of the ruin of French Imperialism are strangely few. "Germans never come," say the innkeepers, and the casual French visitors who do come content themselves with a visit to Bazeilles, which has risen from its bloody ashes and now again is a pretty and prosperous village. The once famous "Weaver's Cottage" on the Donchery road, where in the early morning of September 2nd the broken and dispirited Emperor had the historic interview with Bismarck, is to-day uninhabited and in dilapidation. Its door is locked, and the key is in the possession of the proprietor, a farmer of Carignan. There is no access now to the upstairs room with its windows in the gable, in which Napoleon and Bismarck had their conference. Madame Fournaise, the weaver's widow, is dead years ago. The Château Bellevue, the pretty bourgeois residence of the Sedan wine-dealer to which Bismarck and the cuirassiers escorted Napoleon from the "Weaver's Cottage," is to-day daintier and more picturesque than ever; but it has changed hands, and it is no longer shown to the few applicants who desire to look at the drawing-room where Napoleon and King Wilhelm had their interview, and at the panelled dining-room at the table in which with bitter tears de Wimpfen signed the capitulation of the "Army of Sedan." The present inhabitants of the house profess, indeed, not to know for certain in which apartment it was where the unfortunate French general subscribed that melancholy document, after which "sad and painful duty" he rode back to Sedan "la mort dans l'âme," to quote his own touching words. One, however, would have more sympathy with Wimpfen but for the circumstance that his ruin was wrought by his own rather self-seeking ambition.

The awful tragedy of Bazeilles is commemorated by a tall monument in the graveyard of that village, erected amicably by Germany and France in combination. Underneath the obelisk is a vaulted ossuary, on each side of the central alley in which are stacked and heaped the skulls and bones of the 3,000 German and French soldiers, who fell in the desperate and prolonged combat that raged in and around Bazeilles from daybreak until late in the afternoon of the great battle, and in the course of which the village became a burnt and bloody wreck. The dead of the two nationalities, now mere bones, rest in the same crypt, but they are not intermingled. The bones of the dead French are built up on the right of the central alley, those of the Germans on the left—a weird and ghastly spectacle. Bazeilles has been long ago rebuilt, and the hum and whirr of its weaving-shuttles are heard along its tortuous lanes. On the outskirt of the village nearest to Sedan is the little wayside cabaret bearing the sign of " La Dernière Cartouche," in and around which was the last fight of the day. It is maintained in the actual condition of dilapidation it presented on the evening of the battle; and is the actual original of De Neuville's famous picture of the same name. This little place—pierced and ragged as it is with shot and shell, its furniture riddled as are its ceilings, walls, and floors, and its rooms so full of interesting relics as to constitute a real museum —is perhaps the thing of most interest now extant in connection with the battle-field of Sedan.

XVI

SOLDIERS' WIVES.

I CANNOT say that I have had any success in gathering details as to the early history of the wife of the British soldier—when she first became a recognised institution in the Service, and what was the nature of the first privileges accorded to her. So I leave to some one else with better opportunities, the task of dealing with the historical part of the subject, and confine myself to describing what has come under my own observation since I joined her Majesty's Service, with respect to the condition, habits, morality, and manner of life generally of the wife of the British soldier. I should add that it is some considerable time since I quitted the army, and that since then many changes for the better have been effected in regard to the welfare of the soldier's wife. I propose in the first instance to deal with the subject as I was personally cognisant of it; and then to tell of the amelioration in the conditions of the lot of the soldier's wife accomplished or in progress in more recent years.

It was before I became an unit in the muster-roll of Britain's defenders, that the women of the regiment who were married with leave—technically, "on the strength"—lived almost without exception in the barrack-room among the men. There were commonly a married couple in each room. To the couple, in virtue of long custom, was assigned the corner farthest from the door. No matter what the number in family might be, they were allowed but two single bedsteads and two men's space. No privacy of any kind was accorded the family save what they could contrive for themselves; but the married soldier was wont to rig up around his matrimonial bower an environment of canvas screening something over six feet high, and enclosing an extremely exiguous domain of floor-space in addition to that occupied by the two beds placed together. In most regiments the "woman of the room" cooked for her room-mates at the fireplace thereof, in return for which service it was customary for a "mess" to be allotted to her from the men's rations; for in the days of which I am telling, married couples were entitled to no rations. The married man was put out of mess, and he had wherewithal to maintain himself and his family nothing except his money pay, in addition to anything that the wife might earn.

The mere idea of a married couple living and sleeping in a common room with a dozen or more of single men partitioned off but by a flimsy curtain, is outrageously repulsive to our sense of decency. One may well be struck with wonderment, as certainly was the case with me, that the abominable arrangement should have been left uninterfered with for so long. When the soldier got married in those times if he were a good fellow he strained, it was true, every effort to acclimatise gradually his wife to the barrack-room when, as was the case in many instances, she was fresh from a quiet country cottage or from service in a respectable family. He was wont to take lodgings outside the barracks for the first week or so of the married life, so that at least the earliest quarter of the honeymoon might be invested with something of the privacy of which there was to be so little afterwards. But old soldiers have told me how they have seen a pure girl brought straight from the marriage service to the barrack-room corner, and the tremor of mortal shame that overwhelmed her. It wore off, as most compulsions of the kind mercifully lose their horror, under exposure to the chafe of custom and necessity; but the bride's blushes for herself fell to be renewed at an after period on the tanned cheeks of the mother.

Children, indeed, were rarely born in the corner; for the woman when her time was near at hand was removed to outside lodgings, where at her husband's charges she tarried for a few days; but in the corner daughters grew from childhood to girlhood with but the screen between them and the men outside of it. When a daughter fell out of place, all the home she had to come to was the corner; and it was nowise uncommon for a grown young woman to sleep therein, on the top of the chest alongside the bed of her parents. When the family was large, living, or at all events sleeping in the corner was mere pigging, strictly limited as the authorised sleeping accommodation was to the two narrow regulation bedsteads. It was true that the woman used to dispose of her boys in the vacant beds of soldiers who were on duty; but in the case of women-children there was nothing for it but close packing behind the screen.

Bad as all this was—disgusting in theory and repulsive in practice—there were in it, strange as it may seem, some compensatory elements of good. Although the woman had to reconcile herself with what contentment or endurance she might, to a life that perpetually violated almost every instinct of womanhood, she became blunted indeed, but not degraded, in our sense of the term. In proportion as she lived in public, she had the consciousness of being amenable to public opinion as represented by the little world of her room; and lowly as her sphere was, and rough as too often became her manners and her speech, underneath the skin-deep blemishes there mostly lay self-respect and discretion. She would take her share of a gallon of porter at the common table; but she durst not get drunk, conscious as she was of the critics of her conduct around her. And she made the barrack-room more of a home— of a family circle as it were—than it was later in my experience. The men of her room looked upon her in some such light as they would on a relative keeping house for them. On a change of quarters they always struggled hard to keep their coterie together, with the same abiding woman for its presiding spirit. She humanised the barrack-room with the wholesome influence of her true if somewhat rough womanhood. There was less profanity among the men than seems to exist now; and that habitual expression of obscenity which could not but startle and shock the visitor to the barrack-room of a later period, was almost unknown then, quelled by the fact of the woman being within hearing. Ruffians there were in the Service then as there are now; and an outbreak of foul language occasionally came from the lips of one of them. But he was sternly put down and silenced; if a word from an old soldier and a finger significantly pointed towards the screen did not suffice, a straight left-hander formed a prompt and very convincing argument.

The woman of the room was a kindly, motherly soul to the forlorn "'cruitie;" and she would cheer him up with homely words of encouragement as he sat on his bed-iron, mopingly thinking of his home. She was always obliging if you entreated her civilly, whether to sew on a button or lend a shilling. If she were anything of a scholar, to her fell the office of letter-writer-general for the fellows whose penmanship had been neglected in their early days; and thus she became the repository of not a few little confidences, which she loyally scorned to violate. Some-times, as an especial favour, she would allow a man to bring his sweetheart on a Sunday afternoon to a modest tea behind the screen in the corner; and if friends came from a distance to see one of "her men," the married woman was always ready to do her best for the credit's sake of the hospitality of her room. There can be little doubt that fewer scandals were current in those days of the comparatively dark ages about the wives of soldiers than one has known in later periods; and I question much whether, accepting the roughness of the husk as an inevitable element of their situation, the married women who dwelt in the barrack-room corners were not more genuine at the core than are the ladies who more recently have been in habitation in the married quarters.

Besides the evil alluded to there was another that must not be forgotten. Soldiers are very fond of children, but are apt to regard them in the light rather of monkeys than of creatures with souls in their little bodies. So the imps of the period grew up tutored in all manner of precocious evil and mischief — developing a weird precocity in tossing off a basinful of porter, smoking the blackest of pipes, and addicted to fancy swearing of the ugliest kind. Mostly the youngsters either joined the band of the regiment, or went into one of the military schools, where bad habits were sternly dealt with to good purpose; and thus, under the old long-service *régime*, the country had to some extent an hereditary soldiery, not a few from the ranks of which, born at the foot of the regimental ladder, contrived to climb up it no inconsiderable distance.

In the days I am now telling of there were scarcely any railways except the great trunk lines. When a regiment went on the line of march the women rode in the accompanying baggage waggons, with their brats stowed away in odd corners among the other miscellaneous goods and chattels; and at the halts they shared their husband's billets if the local people were willing to accept them, as, to their credit, they for the most part were. When they were not, the husband had to find quarters .for his wife somewhere else. When the funds were low it was customary for married women to be smuggled into the hay-loft above the troop-horses, and sometimes they had even to bivouac on the lee-side of a hedge. To some extent the railways entailed an additional charge on the married soldier's slender purse. He had always to pay for his baggage, for the chest or two, the flock bed—if the couple had got that length of prosperity—and the few feminine belongings which the wife could call her own; but now the husband had to pay for the warrant under which his wife and family were conveyed by rail. Later, however, "baggage funds" were formed in most regiments, the proceeds of which went to meet the travelling charges of the women and children. In the days I refer to, if women had to live outside the barracks because of lack of room inside, there was no allowance in the shape of lodging-money. The first grant of this was made, I think, in 1852, and consisted of one penny a day paid quarterly. It was gradually increased, until now, I believe, the allowance is fourpence a day.

The above may be taken as a rough epitome of the condition of the soldier's wife up to the end of 1848 or the beginning of 1849. About that period, I think because of some troubles in the financial world, an exceptional number of better-class men joined the service. Because of the indecency of the barrack-room arrangements then in force, a number of anonymous complaints were sent in to the authorities. Other complaints through the press stimulated public opinion to demand a change, and the authorities in their sluggish fashion gradually complied. The reform was not carried out with any great promptitude, for I knew of women living in the barrack-rooms after the Crimean war. But the change was made in the cavalry regiment to which I belonged so early as in 1849. It was, in effect, a change very little for the better. Into one attic in Christchurch barracks seven families were huddled pell-mell. No better arrangements in the direction of privacy were made than had existed in the common barrack-rooms. Each separate family was curtained off by what may be called private enterprise. There was but one fireplace in the long, low attic, and the women scrambled waspishly over their turns for cooking, and were often forced to have recourse to the fires in the men's barrack-rooms.

The moral and social tone was visibly deteriorated under this arrangement, even below that which had characterised the common barrack-room. The women, congregated as they were and with a weakened check upon them, were too prone to club for drink; and convivialities were occasionally chequered with quarrels into which the husbands were not unfrequently drawn. There was a perceptible growth of coarseness of tone among both the women and the men, that became actual grossness; and I question if a young woman with some of nature's modesty still clinging to her did not have it more violently outraged in this congeries of married couples, than would have been the case in the old corner-of-the-barrack-room arrangement. Of this at least I am certain that with ominous rapidity she learned to talk, and would submit to be jeered, on subjects which were ignored under the old system.

The overcrowding also, which was all but universal, was physically injurious to both adults and children. The latter did not count in the allotment of quarters. I have known ten families in one long room in Weedon barracks. Eight families in a hut in the North Camp at Aldershot was nothing uncommon. But later an era of improvement and civilisation set in, and before long the majority of barracks contained married quarters in which each family had a room to itself. The inception of this system was due to our gracious Queen; and the rapidity with which married quarters became all but universal was owing, in the main, to her womanly sympathy with her sex. Still, however, those married quarters in many instances did not afford sufficient accommodation, and the surplusage had to fall back on the old system. So late as in the summer of 1867 more than one troop-room was occupied by four families; and later still it was estimated that about one-third of the married strength of the home forces was still unaccommodated with separate rooms. In civilian estimation a single room for a man and wife with their family—day-room and bed-room in one— seems no great boon; but the soldier and his wife had been so little used to mercies of any kind that they learned to be thankful for very small ones. In my day a married non-commissioned officer of the highest grade had to put up with a single room. A troop-sergeant-major is a person of importance and responsibility in the little world of his regiment—his position certainly equal to that of the super-intendent of a particular branch of a factory. But how would the latter relish having to pay the hands, the head of the concern sitting at the pay-table along with him, while his recently-confined wife lay in bed in the same room, seques-tered only by a curtain? I have signed accounts in the Royal barracks in Dublin when my troop-sergeant-major's domesticities were in the condition alluded to, the .captain of the troop being present.

The soldier does not very often go to his own native place for a wife. He forgets the sweetheart of his pre-soldiering .days, and finds another where he may chance to be quartered. Most soldiers' wives have been servant girls, with whom the gentleman in uniform has picked up acquaintance casually in his evening strolls. But there are many exceptions, and some of these of rather a remarkable character. I have known a soldier's wife who had been the daughter of a clergyman, another who had been a vocalist at a leading music hall, and a third who had been the widow of a captain in the navy. Since the relaxation in the rigour exercised in regard to marriages without leave—to which I shall presently advert— soldiers have been rather addicted to marrying women of no character. Repulsive as such connections are, fairness demands the admission that such women, with few exceptions, turn out well-conducted wives. Probably they are so weary of their previous life that to be a wife at all, no matter how humble the sphere, is a haven of refuge too deeply appreciated to be lightly forfeited.

So prone were soldiers to take their wives from among the daughters of the region in which the regiment might be stationed that an experienced hand could mark by the strata, so to speak, of married womanhood in a corps the track of its successive stations throughout the kingdom. Let me give an example from my own old regiment, as I knew it. The seniors of the married women were of the south of England— Christchurch and Brighton extracts—decently inclined, self-respecting, rather masculine dames, who had followed the kettledrums many a year and had got tanned and travel-worn, but were honest, cleanly, and fairly pure of heart. Then came a layer of canny Scots lasses recruited during the regiment's tour of service in the north country, clannish to the last degree, grasping and greedy, most of them; "wearing the breeches" as regarded their "gude men," but good wives, nevertheless, and excellent mothers; fond of a "drappie" when somebody else paid for it; mostly with a nest-egg in the regimental savings-bank, and willing to do a little bit of usury on the quiet; very unpopular with the other women, horribly quarrelsome, and scrupulously clean. Then followed an infusion of the Irish element, resulting from the corps having been quartered for some years in various stations of the sister isle. According to my experience, Irish women, with few exceptions, do not make good soldiers' wives. They are too ready to accommodate themselves to circumstances, instead of striving to make circumstances bend to them. Thus, in the unfavourable phase of life in which they find themselves through marrying a soldier, they are prone to go with the swim, to become slovenly and slatternly, to say "sufficient for the day is the evil thereof," and to be heedless if to-morrow's pot portends emptiness so long as the pot of to-day " boils fat."

When the soldier falls a prey to matrimonial longings, he obtains an interview with his colonel in the orderly room, and asks permission to get married. If he has some length of service and a good character, permission may be granted him, subject to the occurrence of a vacancy in the married roll of his class in the regiment. If he is a sensible man he waits for this; then he marries, and his wife is taken "on the strength" and becomes entitled to a share in what privileges may be available. A certain number of men are assigned her to "do for," in washing their quota of very dirty clothes. In some cavalry regiments she has in addition the task of keeping clean the room of her men. In this case she scrubs the floor, tables, and forms daily, washes the crockeryware after each meal, and generally is responsible for the cleanliness of the apartment. In other cavalry regiments the men perform these duties in rotation, and the woman has only the clothes-washing to do. In either case, I believe, each of her men pays her a penny a day. The charge in infantry regiments is but a halfpenny a man, solely for the washing, and the men are invariably their own housemaids. In most regiments of the latter branch of the service, the married women are prohibited altogether from entering the barrack-rooms.

Those women who do not have a certain number of men assigned to them, mostly have, in the cavalry, each an officer to attend to his room and do his washing, at the remuneration of a shilling a day; but this is an employment which falls chiefly to the wives of non-commissioned officers. Non-commissioned officers' wives to whom may be allotted the washing of a certain number of men, are no longer allowed to farm out the work, as until recently was the case. In the infantry an officer's soldier-servant attends to his room. A married couple in a cavalry regiment do not fare badly when the husband is an officer's servant with a wage of ten or fifteen shillings a month besides perquisites, or when he earns ten shillings a month for looking after a sergeant's horse in addition to his own; and when the wife has the washing of a dozen men or thereabouts. The joint income may in such a case amount to about a pound a week, with free quarters and the right to draw a daily ration of three-quarters of a pound of meat and a pound of bread for 4½d.—about one half the retail price in the open market.

Hitherto I have been writing of soldiers' wives who have become so in a strictly constitutional and regimental manner. But for one soldier who marries "with leave," at least half-a-dozen do so without leave. In the majority of cases circumstances render the formality of asking for leave a needless farce, and he marries without troubling to make the application. Rules affecting men married without leave vary according to the dispositions—severe or lenient—of commanding officers. In my early soldiering days I knew a man who had been married for twenty years, a man with an excellent character and holding non-commissioned rank, whose wife was never taken on the strength of the regiment at all, because the marriage had been "without leave." In some regiments a probation, or rather a purgatory, of eight years had to be undergone before the offence of getting married without leave was condoned, and the wife admitted to privileges. In later years a more lenient policy came into operation. As a special favour a suitable applicant was occasionally permitted to marry with the promise that his wife should be taken "on the strength" on the occurrence of a vacancy, and meanwhile some work was assigned her to ease the hardship of her lot. Prior to this it was not uncommon for the soldier and his wife to be married twice over, the second marriage taking place when leave was granted, in order to meet the necessity of the registration of the marriage lines in the orderly-room record, when the production of the record of the first marriage would have exposed the disobedience of orders, and led to a retractation of the permission. I remember a critical legitimacy question once arising out of a double marriage of this kind.

To get married without leave, even although it be accompanied by no other infraction of discipline, is a military crime coming under the head of disobedience of orders, and I have known a man severely punished for this offence alone. But most frequently marriage without leave used to be aggravated by the crime of concurrent absence, and the offender was punished nominally for the latter offence, but in reality for the former also. Thus I have known a man get seven days' cells, involving the loss of his hair, for a couple of hours' absence in the morning for the purpose of getting married. It is not pleasant, it must be confessed, to meet your bride with not so much hair on your head as would furnish a locket. Sometimes, in the stern wrath of the commanding officer, the woman's name is "put on the gate," that is, she is prohibited from entering the barracks. Her plight is very sad. She had left her service or her home, and it is with her *nulla vestigia retrorsum.* She lingers wistfully about the barrack gate, pitifully asking the men as they walk out what punishment her husband has got, and when it will be over. She gets a room somewhere near the barracks, her husband half starves himself that he may share his rations with her, and his sympathising comrades cut him the bigger mess because they know that it has to feed two mouths. With few exceptions the man acts very loyally by the woman with whom he has formed a rash union. Sometimes, it is true, things do go wrong. The woman gives up the hard battle in despair and enters on a yet more wretched campaign, with

V

sure defeat as its sad inevitable close; or the husband rebels against the prolonged self-denial and shirks his responsibility. But much oftener the twain cling together with a piteous, yet proud mutual devotion. The compassionate matrons who are on the strength may give the woman a job on washing days, or she picks up some employment about the officers' mess kitchen, or among the wives of the non-commissioned officers.

A change of station is a heavy blow to the struggling couple. There is no " warrant " for the woman married without leave, and it is seldom that her husband can meet the railway fare. I have known a soldier's wife married without leave, foot it all the way from Aldershot to Edinburgh, marching day for day with her husband's troop, sometimes getting into his billet at night, sometimes quartered in the hay-loft. Long ere she crossed Kelso Bridge her boots had given out; but her heart was stouter than her boots, and she triumphantly reached Piershill Barracks only a few hours behind her husband. Shorter journeys of this kind used to be common enough, not only with soldiers' wives married without leave, but also with females having no such tie with the men they followed.

A time, however, may come sooner or later, to the woman married without leave, when her courage is of no avail; when the regiment is ordered on foreign service and she is left straining her eyes through bitter tears after the receding troopship. Now she is, indeed, alone in the world. But she turns instinctively barrack-ward—there is consolation, seemingly, in the colour of the cloth. There is hardly a barrack of any size in the kingdom where there are not as hangers-on some of those compulsory grass-widows, picking up a precarious livelihood by the merciful consideration of soldiers' wives better circumstanced. Such an one, as she wrestles with the hard world, is counting longingly the years and the months, till her husband's term of service shall expire. It may be that one day a letter arrives from his chum, or a discharged soldier of her husband's regiment strolls into barracks with the tidings that Bill or Joe is dead of cholera at some unhealthy inland station, or that death took him in some march in the Afghan hill-country. But again, Bill or Joe is back himself with his discharge in his pocket and love in his heart; and her horizon glows very bright to the poor barrack-drudge.

But a very much married army has many encumbrances in the shape of women and children; and among its other advantages short service has all but abolished soldiers' wives whose husbands belong to the rank-and-file. In the cavalry and artillery the limit of married soldiers is now but 4 per cent.; in the infantry only 3 per cent. Matrimony in the British army of to-day at home, apart from its officerhood, is almost entirely confined to the non-commissioned ranks. All warrant officers are entitled to be married; as also are the three superior classes of non-commissioned officers. Fifty per cent. of non-commissioned officers of inferior grade may be included in the married roll. The private soldier of the period is barely adolescent, when at the age of twenty— occasionally somewhat short of that age—he is sent out to India; and for the couple of years or so prior to that deportation he is so assiduously growing in bulk and stature as the result of his consumption of the Queen's rations and so engrossed in learning the rudiments of soldier-craft, that he can find little leisure for precocious thoughts of love, far less of matrimony, whether with or without leave. Thus a soldier's wife married without leave is now very much more rare than in earlier times.

To-day there is no such abomination in the army as the crowding of more than one family in the same room. There is no family of the lowest military grade which is not entitled to at least one separate room. The advance, or rather indeed the revolution, of late years in the accommodation afforded to military married people and families, is simply surprising, especially at Aldershot. A married warrant officer in that station enjoys two very good sitting-rooms, two good bedrooms, kitchen and scullery, with yard, garden convenience, coal and washhouse. The family of a staff-sergeant has for quarters an excellent sitting-room, two good bedrooms, kitchen, and scullery. Married sergeants and rank-and-file are accommodated in two rooms and a kitchen, or one big room and kitchen: in the case of a large family, two bedrooms are allowed. Twenty years ago the regimental sergeant-major of a cavalry regiment, the man of highest non-commissioned rank in the regiment and a married man with a family, had to content himself and his with a single room of no great dimensions.

XVII.

OUR rural and primitive parish-school in the far north of Scotland was as I remember it, some five-and-forty years ago, a democracy tempered chiefly by vigour of biceps muscle. Whether inside the grim old building on the brae-face, or on the heather-bordered playground in the midst of which it stood, no distinction was recognised between the "classes" and the "masses." The master was at once impartial and indiscriminate in his frank and free use of his tough leathern "tawse." Was he gentleman's son from the mansion among the trees beyond the burn, or was he the cottar's son from the sour muirland of the foothills, the cock of the school and of the playground was the youngster who was smartest with his fists. The school was a microcosm of the parish. The laird who owned a large proportion of its acreage sent to the parish school his son and heir, who later became a Cambridge Wrangler. The manse was represented by my brother and myself, destined later for the north-country University, meanwhile seldom free from a black eye or two, and exceptionally frequent victims of the "dominie's" tawse. The local farmers, a prolific race, contributed whole families of both sexes indiscriminately. The ditcher down by the cross-roads educated his twins by the expedient of sending the boy and the girl on alternate days for a single fee. Besides the ordinary run of pupils whose ages varied from seven to about fourteen, the school was generally attended by some three or four full-grown young fellows, who were taking a half year at home away from farm work, that they might revive or increase the knowledge acquired in boyhood. The country lasses used occasionally to do the same, and I remember to have often seen a buxom girl of twenty and a stalwart ploughman of about the same age standing up courageously in the same class with youngsters of nine and ten. In the winter time our school fire was maintained by the daily contributions brought from the home stack by each scholar of a peat or a turf under his or her arm. Defaulters in this duty were punished by being exiled to the cold corners of the schoolroom.

In my young days, as is still the case, the lowlands of northern Scotland were singularly free from crime, but then—nor, I fear, is there to-day much improvement in this respect—they were affected by a moral taint, the results of which manifested themselves in our little school-community in the shape of some half-dozen strapping young fellows of great physical vigour and of considerable force of character. Our rustic Dunois from the Craighead was, like his prototype, both *jeune* and *beau*. Our local Falconbridge from the hovel at the back of the wood was so handsome that he might well have had "a trick of Cœur-de-Lion's face." Our sturdy William of the Ardoch promised in mental force and physical thew and sinew to take after the famous son of Arlotte of Falaise. Our herd laddie Maurice was no less successful in his warlike encounters on the school-green than was the son of Aurora of Königsmark in his wider sphere of action. Our Edmund of the Burnfoot might well have claimed, in the words of the "Edmund" of Lear, that—

> "My dimensions are as well compact,
> My mind as generous, and my shape as true,
> As honest madam's issue."

To those youths the taint of their origin was no secret, and it must be added that for them it had no shame, neither did it attach to them any stigma. Far from shrinking into the background, they carried their heads high among us; like the "little Jock Elliot" of the Border ballad they would "tak dunts frae naebody," but on the contrary were always on the alert to bestow those aggressive commodities.

The universal pet of the school was a beautiful child named Willie Stuart. As I write, after many long years

I still can recall the little man's long flaxen curls, his wistful blue eyes, the delicate complexion that flushed and paled with each passing emotion, the winsomeness of the whole little figure. The roughest of us was tender with Willie. He would participate eagerly in our sports, and we could not say him nay; but one of us always quietly undertook to watch, lest in the hurly-burly of rugged horse-play any mischief should befall the child. He was an apt scholar, but, sweet-tempered as he was, and grateful for the love that was lavished on him, he had a vein of mild sarcasm, and would sometimes in a light and airy way make game of a dunce. We knew of him, in a casual way, as the only son of a decent woman who lived a quiet lonely life in a cottage near the Kirkton, and who was spoken of as having been a lady's-maid in a nobleman's family whose seat was in an adjoining parish. Her neighbours called her Mrs. Stuart and it was understood that her husband was abroad, making money in some unhealthy region whither he would not bring his wife and child. Country folk of the lower orders up in the north, some half century ago, were not much addicted to prying into the affairs of their neighbours. The opportunities for gossip were comparatively few in a region where distances were great, and where there were no breeding-places of scandal in the shape of villages.

One forenoon the only dull-witted one of the base-born contingent of our schoolfellows had fallen into some ludicrous blunder, which, in spite of the stern discipline maintained, had kindled the class into an irrepressible roar of laughter, and had brought upon himself condign and severe punishment from the stinging tawse. During a momentary absence of the master from the schoolroom, Willie Stuart amused himself by chaffing the perpetrator of the blunder. The latter, sore and resentful, took the little fellow's badinage very ill. At length, to the utter amazement of all, he grimly retorted—

"Ye cock yer head gey crouse, my bonny little man: you that's naething but a bastard, like mysel!"

"It's a lee, a lee!" cried the child, flushing scarlet,

and bursting into a passion of tears as he flew at the throat of the other. We dragged him off just as the master returned, and the little scene ended—Willie sitting white and trembling over his dictionary.

During the mid-day play hour the boy who had aspersed Willie, and myself, had an encounter which improved the appearance of neither of us. The same evening I related to our old nurse what had occurred in the school. To my utter astonishment, she told me that the stigma which had been cast on Willie Stuart was warranted by the facts. She had been told the whole story by her sister, who for years had been in service at —— Castle. Mary Stuart had been the countess's own maid. She had been courted by a farmer's son of the neighbourhood, and she had accepted him. But subsequently they had quarrelled bitterly, on what account nobody seemed to know, and had parted in hot anger. The girl had soon to realise that the rupture had not been on even terms. Yet such was the stiffness of her nature, that she preferred to undergo shame rather than sue to the man with whom she had quarrelled. Her ladyship had sent her away, but had settled a small pension on her. Soon after her child was born and christened she had migrated into our parish, where her story was not known, and had lived there in good repute ever since. Our old nurse, kind and wise soul as she was, had held her tongue, and she believed that none other in the parish, save my father the minister, knew the story. But now she remembered that Bell Black, the mother of the fellow who had opened upon Willie, had been a kitchen servant at the castle about the time of Mary Stuart's misfortune.

For days little Willie moped about, pale and sad, all the young life seemingly dead in him. The story had begun to spread, and I fancy he had heard some kind of confirmation of it. He had been shunning me; but one afternoon the poor child came to me with his sorrow. " I believe it's a lee," said he wearily; " but God kens. I canna bring mysel' tae speer o' my mither—I wad suner droon mysel'! But, whether or no, I'm no like thae loons—it kills me tae doobt that I'm an honest-born laddie." I took the little fellow by the hand, led him down the brae to the manse, and brought him in by the side-door into the little room which belonged to my brother and myself and in which we were wont to con our lessons. Leaving him there, I went and found the old nurse, told her whom I had brought to see her, and begged of her to come into our room and give the child what comfort she might.

Good old Elspeth's heart went out to Willie at first sight of him. She smoothed with her hands his flaxen curls, and brought colour into his pale face by kissing the shy and unnerved little chap. As she talked it seemed at first as if, far from giving him any consolation, she was about to plunge him into utter despair. For she thought it the truest kindness to tell him all that she had told me and that I have already recorded, thus dashing from him any hope that he was other than he had been so abruptly characterised by his coarse and angry schoolfellow. But the good old soul had kept in reserve some balm of Gilead for the wounded spirit. And it presently appeared that she was somehow conversant with the kindly principles of Scottish law, in regard to the legitimation of offspring born before wedlock by the subsequent marriage of the parents.

" You're no honest-born, my bairn," said Elspeth, " but the guid auld law o' Scotland will mak' ye honest-born if your faither an' mither can be persuadit tae come thegither an' be marriet like wise an' dacent folk. I've heard they were baith dour an' bitter, but time often solders feuds. It's no true that yer faither is abroad. He is the auld farmer's son o' the Mains o' Drumfurruch, in the Enzie, no ten miles awa'. My counsel tae ye, laddie, is that ye gae an' see yer faither, an' plead wi' him for tae gie ye a guid name in the warld by marryin' yer mither. Ye're a bonny boy, an' ye hae a winsome face; he may weel be prood o' ye. If ye gain him, surely yer mither will no be obstinate for her ain sake, forbye yours. Ony gate, it's but tryin', and it's surely weel worth tryin'; it's a noble an' a holy endeavour, an' a' guid folk maun pray that it may succeed!" And Elspeth kissed the child, and their tears mingled as the good old Presbyterian woman blessed him and prayed that Heaven might prosper so worthy an effort.

Willie, comforted and heartened, would fain have started on his errand that same afternoon. But this was not to be thought of. He knew nothing of the road to the Enzie; he was quite unequal to so long a journey afoot and alone; his sudden absence would alarm his mother.

It was the season of peat-carting from the moss of Forgie, which is within three miles of the Enzie; and my suggestion was that next morning he should accompany the manse carts to the moss, then go on to Drumfurruch which was visible from the moss, and return therefrom in the afternoon in time to be carried back on one of the loaded carts. I advised him that he should not tell his mother of his project, and I undertook to furnish the schoolmaster with a reason for his absence.

This programme the resolute little man duly carried out. He brought back the tidings that he had seen his father, who had readily and affectionately owned him, had taken him to his grandfather now bedridden and very old, and had accompanied him most of the way back to the moss. But he had been stern and silent when the child, with piteous sobs and tears, had besought him to make the son he had owned an " honest-born " boy, and he had curtly told the little lad not to appeal to him on that point any more. But Willie, nevertheless, was not utterly disheartened, for his father had said that he should look forward to seeing him again. There was courage and resolution in the little fellow beyond his years, and Elspeth and I agreed in recommending that he should repeat his visit to his father occasionally—at all events, while the peat-carting season lasted.

The father, with each successive visit of his son grew more and more affectionate, and Willie, as he told us of this, increased in hopefulness of ultimate success. The colour had come back into the child's face, his head was no longer on his breast, the glint had returned to the soft blue eyes under the long lashes. I never saw him so beautiful as on the last morning he started with the peat-carts. In the gloaming of that same shortening day the carter came home without him. He had waited, he said, for some time after the usual hour of starting homewards. A dense fog, with a heavy flurry of snow, then set in, and the carter had left in the full belief that the bitter weather had detained Willie at Drumfurruch for the night.

. This was quite probable; but, again, it was possible that the child had been well on his way to the moss before the weather thickened. So the groom and I started immediately in the manse gig, intending to drive to Drumfurruch; keeping as we went on, a keen look-out along the road and on both sides of it. We carried blankets and a whisky-flask in case of need. The road was bad; the fog and snowdrift thickened, and so slow was our progress that we were traversing the moss only in the small hours of the following morning. It had lightened a little just as we were passing the manse plot of moss-land, and the sudden idea occurred to me to alight and glance over that spot. It was a fortunate impulse, for there, just under the peat-bank, on the sparse fodder left by the horses, lay Willie, partially snowed over and asleep. We promptly wrapped him up warmly and administered restoratives. I drove him straight to his mother's cottage, while the groom walked on to tell his father of what had happened. By nightfall Willie was in peril of imminent death from inflammation of the lungs, and he was all but unconscious for days. When he came to himself he found his father and mother bending anxiously over him. A common apprehension, a common solicitude, had united the dissevered parents. He rallied under the inspiration of a great happiness, but the doctor shook his head and talked ominously of rapid wasting of the lungs. It was not long ere the child knew that he was doomed; but he piteously entreated that his parents would gratify him by enabling him to die, as he pleaded, " an honest-born boy." The banns of marriage between John McPherson and Mary Stuart were duly proclaimed on three successive Sundays for the first, second, and third times. On the fourth Sunday, which fell on New Year's Day, the couple were made man and wife by my father in the old barn-like church.

During their absence I was sitting with Willie, whose weakness
and fragility were painfully visible through the hectic flush
of excitement. As his parents, now united in wedlock,
entered the cottage, he started up into a sitting attitude,
and with extraordinary eagerness and extended arms, he
pathetically begged his mother to give him the " marriage-
lines." He devoured the certificate with ardent, hollow eyes,
gave one great panting sigh of gratification, clasped the paper
to his heart with the exclamation, " Oh, faither an' mither,
this is a New Year's gift frae Heaven itsel' !" and then he
turned his happy, wasted face to the wall. Ten minutes later
I touched his forehead. The " honest-born boy " was dead.

XVIII.

THE late summer sunshine was irradiating the broad undulating expanse of the Tempelhoferfeld, the historic
parade-ground of the troops forming the garrison of the capital
city of the German Empire. It was the 1st of September,
the anniversary of the battle of Sedan; and athwart the
green face of the Tempelhoferfeld were drawn up the long
straight lines of the Prussian Guard Corps, ready for its
inspection by the venerable soldier-monarch to whom, on
the afternoon of Sedan, Napoleon III. sent his sword
and his surrender. The guns of the salute rang out their
greeting as a brilliant cavalcade, gay with plumes and glittering in gold and silver, cantered on to the parade-ground. At
the head of the *cortège,* a horse-length out to the front, rode
a square-shouldered white-haired chief, stricken in years,
yet still lusty and stalwart. KAISER WILHELM I. was in his
eighty-first year, yet the glance of the keen blue eye was
undimmed, his form was erect, and he rode the strong black
charger with strength and skill. Old Marshal Wrangel, of
whom it was said that "he had forgotten to die," had at
length at the age of ninety-four remembered that duty;
and now the venerable warrior-king was the oldest soldier
of all that Germany the unity of which he had lived to
see accomplished under his sway. What to us was history
were memories with this hale octogenarian! He could
remember the catastrophe of Jena; for that stroke befel

Prussia in 1806 and he was then nine years of age. His latest campaign had been in 1870–71; his earliest in 1814, which he made as aide-de-camp to Blücher, when old "Marshal Vorwärts" in the early months of that year marched his Prussians from the Rhine to the heart of France, stormed the heights of Montmartre, and occupied Paris in conjunction with the Russian and Austrian armies.

Four times, so far as I know, Wilhelm met the Napoleon who surrendered to him at Sedan—the nephew of that Napoleon who had insulted his mother. The first time was at the end of the campaign of 1814, when with his father he visited the Château of St. Leu, near Paris, where Queen Hortense dwelt apart from her husband with her two boys, the younger of whom lived to be Napoleon III. The second time was in September, 1861, the year of his accession, when he paid a visit to the Emperor Napoleon at Compiègne. During his stay there occurred a military parade, which Napoleon chose to witness in civilian costume. To wear uniform when his host was in plain clothes was impossible; and so Wilhelm, for the only time in his long life, had to appear on a parade-ground in a black coat and a tall hat. Sedan was avenged in anticipation. The third time was in 1867, the year of the great Paris Exposition, when he was the guest in the Tuileries of that child of Hortense who, after a life of strange vicissitudes, was now the Emperor of the French. The fourth time—and of their memorable meeting then I was a witness—was on the morning after the battle of Sedan, when that Emperor was a prisoner and his throne was crumbling into wreck Napoleon, familiar already with exile, was to die in exile. Wilhelm died in the purple, but he too had known exile; for in the Red Year of 1848 political troubles at home forced him to take refuge in England for a time; reputed— it has long ago seemed incredible—the most unpopular man in Prussia!

Wilhelm was not a heaven-born general, but he was a thorough soldier. Brave to recklessness, his staff had always difficulty in keeping him outside the range of hostile fire, nor were they always successful. He had an aide-de-camp killed by his side at Königsgrätz. At Gravelotte I saw him sitting on his horse among the bursting shells; and later in the same afternoon belabouring fugitives with the flat of his sword, while he swore fine racy German oaths at them for disgracing themselves in a momentary panic. For the rest he was only a grand simple old gentleman, with a very soft heart and a very hasty temper. In regard to politics he did the bidding of Bismarck, and Bismarck often had very sharp tussles with the sturdy old opinionated Trojan in the effort to conquer his prejudices or to restrain his impulses. In his personal life Wilhelm was simplicity itself. He dined at four o'clock, and the chief joys of his palate were sauerkraut and lobster salad. His campaigning equipment was almost Spartan in its plainness, and contrasted curiously with the elaborate train that followed Napoleon out of Sedan. Of all the family of which he was the head— a family which in all its ramifications he ruled with a strong yet kindly hand—his greatest favourites were the wife of his son, our English Princess Royal, and her eldest son, who was one day to be himself German Emperor, and who meanwhile was a hardworking officer in the Imperial Guard.

I saw Wilhelm in the shell-fire of Gravelotte. I witnessed the greeting between him and the Emperor Napoleon at the foot of the steps of the Château Bellevue on the morning after the battle of Sedan. I saw him standing on the daïs of the Galerie des Glaces in the Château of Versailles, when, amidst a tempest of cheering, amidst waving of swords and of banners, he was hailed German Emperor, as with eyes streaming with tears he received the homage of princes, dukes, and lords of the Empire. I saw him on the great day of the triumphal entry into Berlin after the Franco-German war, as he rode down the Linden between a double row of captured French cannon. Before him rode abreast Bismarck, Moltke, and Roon, "the makers of history;" behind him the "combined battalion," whose ranks were made up of men of every German nationality, escorting the eagles, colours, and standards that had lately belonged to the French armies. But, to my thinking, none of those spectacles vied in human interest with that presented by the simple cordiality and tenderness of Wilhelm's home-coming immediately after the ending of the Franco-German war, the most memorable and most colossal conflict of the century. Long before the time named for the arrival of the royal train, the platform of the Potsdamer railway station was thronged with notabilities. There were Bismarck in his white cuirassier uniform, and Moltke and Roon, and other principal personages of the great head-quarters staff. There was the venerable Marshal Wrangel, a still older soldier than his venerable sovereign. There, too, were Vogel von Falkenstein, grim and grey, and old Steinmetz, come from his distant Posen governorship. Of ladies and children of the royal house the name was legion. In a siding opposite the platform, whether by accident or design, had been shunted a hospital train, from the windows of which pallid faces looked out on the brilliant scene. Upon the carriage roofs clustered convalescents; and a little squad of fellows maimed at Spicheren and Borny gave Steinmetz a cheer—old "Immer Vorwärts," as they styled him; and so with gossip and endless kindly greetings the moments of expectancy passed.

At the sound of a distant whistle, from out the waiting-room stalked Bismarck. Wrangel doffed his plumed helmet; a stream of ladies and children followed Bismarck's stalwart form. In two minutes more a near rumble, and the train rolled up to the platform. Then rose a mighty shout of cheering; and there, at the carriage window, stood the Emperor, looking out on his family and servants. A moment later, and he was down the steps, and kissing the Dowager Queen Elizabeth. It seemed as if the women of his race were mobbing him as they crowded round him for his kisses, while grandchildren hung about his knees. The old man was brushing his shaggy eyelashes with the back of his hand as he struggled through the women-folk about him. In his path stood "Papa" Wrangel, a beam from the setting sun flashing on his snow-white hair. The soldier-patriarch raised his hand and tried to utter a welcome, but his voice failed him, and the tears rolled down his face. His master, not less moved, kissed his aged servant on both cheeks. The two old soldier-comrades embraced, and Steinmetz's wounded fellows on the carriage roof cheered the mutual greeting. Then the Emperor grasped Bismarck by the hand and kissed him too, and old Steinmetz as well—forgiven for his waste of men on the slope over against Gravelotte; he kissed his way right through out into the waiting saloon, hand-in-hand with the Empress who was shedding quiet tears. The scene was like an April day—showers and sunshine, tears and smiles; all state and ceremony were swept away in the gush of homely affection. When his Majesty had reached the Palace, the cheers of his Berliners kept him long lingering on its threshold; over and over again he had to come out on to the balcony with the Empress; and his final appearance was at the accustomed corner window, at which he had shown himself when the declaration of the war was announced. That war was now triumphantly finished, and Wilhelm had come home from his last campaign.

In the forefront of the *cortège* which Kaiser Wilhelm headed as he cantered on to the Tempelhofer parade-ground, rode three men whose names, then as now, were familiar to the world—Moltke, the Imperial Crown Prince, and Prince Frederick Charles. MOLTKE was the lean man with the slight stoop of the shoulders, and the fleshless, strong-lined face out of which the keen blue eyes looked with quiet alertness. You might have taken him for a professor of mathematics, but he was the greatest strategist of the age. Made Chief of the Prussian General Staff in 1858, there thenceforward devolved upon him the duty of planning the successive campaigns in which the Prussian armies were subsequently engaged; and in which, thanks in great measure to his strategical genius, they were uniformly successful.

Moltke was a singularly quiet and unostentatious man. It was quaintly said of him that "he could be silent in seven

w

languages," and he was nearly as great a linguist as he was a strategist. Seated at his desk in Berlin, with his maps and plans on the wall before him, he directed by telegraph the opening operations of both the Prussian armies engaged in the invasion of Austria in the summer of 1866; and on the battlefield of Königsgrätz he watched, with calm assurance of the result, the bloody and desperate struggle which culminated in the decisive victory his bold and shrewd strategy had brought about. He was in the field from the first in the Franco-German campaign of 1870–71; and it was intensely interesting to discern how, as if by intuition, he penetrated the designs of the French commanders, and had taken measures to thwart them before the attempts had been begun to carry them out. Moltke's fighting motto was "Erst wägen, dan wagen"—"First ponder, then dare"; and the keynote to his strategy may be summed up in his maxim: "Separate for the march, concentrate for the battle." Frequently he took what seemed startling liberties with the enemy. Over and over again, trusting to his own genius, he disregarded what are commonly called "the rules of the art of war," and ventured on operations which, according to those rules, he had no right to risk. This, no doubt, was simply because he had taken the measure of the commanders who were his antagonists, and had recognised their capacity, or rather their incapacity.

The notion was general that Moltke, Bismarck, and Roon, the three men who were the chief makers of the German Empire, were on the most friendly and most intimate terms with each other. In reality they had by no means mutually cordial relations. Bismarck had a standing umbrage with Moltke, because the great strategist was resolute in withholding from the great statesman the military information which the latter insisted he ought to share. Moltke has roundly disclosed in his posthumous book his conviction that Roon's place as Minister of War was at home in Germany; and not on campaign, embarrassing the former's functions. Roon, again, envied Moltke because of the latter's more elevated military position ; and he disliked Bismarck, because that outspoken man made light of Roon's capacity. I have happened to know the headquarters staff of a British army whose members were on bad terms with each other ; and the result, to put it mildly, was unsatisfactory. But those three high German authorities, each with bitterness in his heart against his fellows, nevertheless co-operated zealously and loyally in the service of their Sovereign and for the advantage of their country. Their common patriotism had the mastery in them over their mutual dislike and jealousy. Arndt's line: "Sein Vaterland muss grösser sein!" was the watchword of all three, and dominated their discordances.

Moltke was not a man to spare bloodshed in the accomplishment of given ends. In the first month of the campaign the German losses in killed and wounded were well on to 80,000 men. With him the end justified the means. But the private life of the iron soldier was worthy and beautiful in all its relations. He was a man of singularly varied accomplishments, and his tastes were at once simple and refined. He had no children, but his family affection was full of warmth. I once saw the tears in his eyes, as I gave him the message of love and duty entrusted to me by one of his nephews who lay in danger from a wound received in a forepost skirmish on the east of Paris. All Germany idolised the quiet, silent, self-contained soldier-sage, to whom the Fatherland owed so much. Full of years and honours, he had the euthanasia for which he had prayed when his time should come.

The IMPERIAL CROWN PRINCE, afterwards, during a short period of nobly-borne suffering, the Emperor Frederick, was an imposing and soldierly figure. Never have I seen a face which expressed more vividly calm serene strength of command. He looked taller on horseback than he really was ; and upright, broad-shouldered, and deep-chested, he was every inch a man. He hated war, yet it was his fate to take part in three great wars, and to command in several momentous and bloody battles. He was thoroughly conversant with the art of war, and there was no readier chief in the field of

w 2

battle. The most urbane of men while no fighting was in hand, the Prince's manner wholly altered when the bullets were flying. Then the Hohenzollern temper rose in him; his face flushed; there was a sparkle in his eye; he spoke but to command; and when he had cause to chide, he who was rebuked did not soon forget the reproof. But he was the most humane of the fighting race of which he was a member. Like his father, he thought of the wounded the moment that the victory was won. Unlike his father, he was always averse from extreme measures. He held out long against the bombardment of Paris, and his voice was ever in favour of the introduction into the beleaguered city of medical comforts for the sick and wounded, and for permitting the exit of helpless women and children.

The great day of the Crown Prince's life was that momentous ceremony in the Château of Versailles, when the princes and potentates of the great Teuton nation hailed his father with the crowning dignity of that august historic title, the "German Emperor"; and when the Prince on bended knee was the first to kiss the hand of his father and Emperor. The Crown Prince's public life in peace-time was full of steady usefulness; his private life was good and beautiful in every relation. I remember hearing him say that on campaign there never passed a day on which he did not write to his wife. In those times they were quite poor, according to our notions of the appanage of the heir-apparent to a great throne; and they lived within their modest and somewhat precarious income. Their Berlin mansion was a small palace on the Linden; and any morning when they were living in the capital one might have met the Prince and Princess strolling quietly in the avenues of the Thiergarten, with some of their children walking by their side. She was as proud of him as he was fond of her; it was a love match at the beginning, and it continued to the sad premature ending of the noble and devoted husband an alliance of tender and beautiful mutual affection.

Prince Frederick Charles, the nephew of the old

Kaiser, and the cousin on both the father's and the mother's side of the Imperial Crown Prince, was a man of quite another stamp from the latter. The Red Prince was a soldier to the core; and I question whether he was ever quite happy in peace-time. And I think that, although he had his faults in a military sense, yet, take him all in all, he was one of the greatest soldiers of modern times. He was a very stern and unlovable man; his private life was the reverse of creditable; and he could be, and indeed generally was, more roughly ill-bred than any commander with whom I ever had personal relations. But in the field on campaign there was a certain bluff good comradeship in his manner, which earned him the devotion of his soldiers. He was severity itself as regarded discipline; he exacted from his men the hardest of hard work; but he shared with them their dangers, privations, and exposure, and they ever followed him and believed in him with unfaltering and enthusiastic zeal. When condemned to peace, Prince Frederick Charles employed himself chiefly in the elaboration of improved methods in the art of man-killing, and he wrote several works of high authority on this interesting and humane subject. But his joy was to be in the heart of a great battle. When still young he was a dashing cavalry officer, and he was severely wounded in a hand-to-hand *mêlée* in the Baden insurrection of 1849, in the somewhat quixotic effort to storm earthworks at the head of his squadron of hussars. Düppel, Königsgrätz, Vionville-Mars-la-Tour, Gravelotte, Beaune-la-Rolande, Orleans, and Le Mans were among the great battles which Prince Frederick Charles made victories for the Prussian arms.

When I think of Prince Frederick Charles, there ever recurs to my memory the daybreak of Gravelotte. On that morning he was stirring early to give rendezvous to his corps commanders that they might receive his instructions as to the setting of the battle in order. What a subject for a great painter, this daybreak gathering of the German leaders under the poplar trees on the highway between Vionville and Mars-la-Tour, with the Red Prince in the centre, brusque, curt, and emphatic! Around the group conning over a new slaughter, lay the ghastly evidences of a past, in the heaps of the dead of the battle of the 16th of August, still awaiting interment. Keen-eyed, handsome-faced Prince of Saxony; puffy, phlegmatic August of Würtemberg; Alvensleben the aristocrat, with his thin, clear-cut features and bright hawk-eye; Voights-Rhetz, with the keen shrewd look of a lowland Scot; Manstein, grim, grey, and determined — these stood in a roughly defined semi-circle with their horses' heads turned inwards; and there addressed them in a few short crisp sentences, the square upright man on the powerful bay. The Red Prince let his hand drop on his thigh with an audible blow, for he was very heavy-handed in every sense, this stalwart man with the massive hair-clad jaw, the strong, wide mouth, cruel in its set resoluteness when the features were at rest, the well-opened piercing eye under the high arched forehead, broad, square and knotted. A man this, in the tight red tunic, cast surely by nature in her special mould for a great military leader. He did not detain his generals long under the poplar trees. One of them afterwards gave me his laconic parting words:—"Your duty is to march forward, find the enemy, prevent his escape, and fight him wherever you encounter him!" And Alvensleben the pious added in his quiet tones—"In the name of God!" as the generals wheeled their horses' heads outwards, and the little council scattered.

During the siege of Metz one could not but admire how Prince Frederick Charles threw himself into the comparatively routine duties of the weary toilsome drudgery with as much relentless energy as if he had been engaged in a campaign when every second day furnished a stirring battle. Within a fortnight after the siege began, he had enclosed Metz in an environment of field-fortifications against which Bazaine might beat his head to no purpose. The moment that the capitulation was settled, he was off by forced marches towards the Loire country, there to combat with and thwart Chanzy and Aurelles de Paladine. In the deep snow and bitter frost of that terrible winter, he marched and fought, and fought and marched again, with a ruthless energy that stimulated the reluctant admiration of the world. "If," said a distinguished neutral soldier in my hearing after the Prince's arduous success at Le Mans—"if I were called upon to define Prince Frederick Charles in two words, I should style him a 'disciplined thunderbolt.'"

I have dwelt over long, I fear, on the principal German chiefs of the Franco-German campaign; and my excuse must be that it was with the German armies I witnessed many events of that stupendous struggle. With French warriors I have had but little intercourse, and that only of a casual kind. It was the day of the formal capitulation of Metz. A vast throng of infuriated citizens and of French soldiers not yet formally surrendered, was fermenting boisterously on the Ban Saint Martin road, on the opposite side of the Moselle from the city. Suddenly an open carriage dashed down the road, scattering the crowd to right and to left. In it sat a short fat man with a heavy determined face, in the lines of which it seemed to me that there lurked some scorn. It was Marshal Bazaine who, having completed the surrender of the no longer virgin fortress, and of the still formidable French army which had lain in and around that fortress, was now on his way to Prince Frederick Charles' headquarters at Corny, *en route* for Germany as a prisoner of war. At the sight of him there rose from the crowd a wild unanimous yell of execration. "Down with the traitor!" "Curse him!" "Kill him!" were the angry cries; and infuriates dashed at the carriage and the horses' heads only to be hustled aside by the cavalry escort. Bazaine's face never changed or blenched, and he looked down upon the people who were clamouring for his blood as if they had been dirt. When again I saw Bazaine, he was undergoing his trial by court-martial for treason to France because of his surrender of Metz. He had not to all seeming a dozen friends in all France, as he stood there in the great salon of the château of the Trianon, arraigned on a capital charge before a tribunal that could scarcely dare to acquit him even if he should prove his innocence; yet he confronted fate here with the same impassive phlegm as he had faced the populace of Metz.

I never believed in the accusations of treachery hurled against him so vehemently.   I hold Bazaine to have been a heavy, unenterprising, plodding, fairly honest style of man, who should indeed have held out longer than he did, but who believed that in surrendering when he did he was doing the best possible for France, for his master, for his army, and *perhaps for himself.*   The court-martial formally sentenced him to death, but the sentence was commuted to degradation and imprisonment for life.   After a few months' confinement in the fortress of the Île Ste. Marguerite he effected a not very difficult escape, and when I saw him last he was living in retirement and poverty in Madrid.   I had subsequently written something in the way of a vindication of the unfortunate man, as the result of which I received from him the following letter:—

"Madrid, 2, Calle Argensola, 18th November, 1883.

"Dear Sir,

"I feel that I must express to you my gratitude for your article on my iniquitous trial.   It certainly is very late to attempt to influence public opinion, purposely prejudiced as it has been by all parties, in order to save the national vanity, as well as the several responsibilities of the Governments of the Empire and of that of the National Defence.   But truth always prevails in the end, and your conscientious article should have a great effect.

"There are many things I could say, not to defend myself—my conscience as General-in-Chief has no reproaches to make to me; but to enlighten upright men and to open their eyes to their own shortcomings at that epoch.   A scapegoat was searched for, who offered himself up; and the French nation, reckoned so generous, relieved itself of all responsibility by transferring it to the head of the soldier, a self‑made man, who having spent forty years of his life in campaigning in the four quarters of the earth, had no personal friends among the politicians in power; and who had no supporters, once the Empire was overthrown and the Republic took its place.   Again thanks, and a hearty clasp of the hand.

"MARSHAL BAZAINE.

"Mr. A. Forbes."

Twice only did I have speech with the late MARSHAL MACMAHON; once soon after the battle of Sedan, when in the village of Pourru‑les‑Bois, in the vicinity of that place, he was slowly recovering from the shell wound which struck him down on the morning of the battle; and again the day after the Versaillist army, as it was called, which he commanded, had carried the ramparts of Paris and driven the Communard hordes back to fight to the death along the boulevards, in the narrower cross streets, and ultimately into the great dead-pit in the cemetery of Père-Lachaise. MacMahon, in the Crimea, in Africa, and in the Italian War of 1859, had achieved a brilliant reputation before the Franco-German War brought doubt on his capacity in high and quasi-independent command. In the disastrous expedition which began amid distraction at Châlons and ended in the wholesale surrender at Sedan, he was simply obeying political, as contra-distinguished from military considerations. He went then on the forlornest of forlorn hopes. A heaven-born general might perhaps have snatched success out of the untoward conditions; but MacMahon lacked the inspiration and failed. His wound at Sedan was in a sense opportune, for it saved him from signing the capitulation; and France to this day has a sort of half-belief, which is quite unwarranted, that had he not been struck down that humiliation might have been averted. So MacMahon retained, or rather indeed increased his popularity. It was not impaired because he crushed the Commune with an iron hand, pursuing in regard to it the ruthless policy of extermination. He, the servant of an empire whose shallow foundations were laid in military glory and prestige, was scarcely in place as the President of a Republic whose motto was utilitarianism; and he lived out his long life in dignified and unambitious retirement, with the respect of all who could honour an honest soldier and a well-intentioned patriot.

GENERAL TROCHU was the mock and gibe of frivolous, spiteful Paris during the latter part of the long, strange, weary, exciting months, when that capital was environed by the German hosts. Trochu and his plan—that plan of which he was ever talking and which he never was executing—have been all but forgotten long ago by swift-living Paris; and it is hardly to be expected that the rest of the world remembers of him and of it much more vividly. Yet Trochu was the notable man of surely a signally notable period. He was Governor of Paris and Commander-in-Chief of its vast garrison during the long, memorable siege. And, in spite of his quaint pragmatic ways and utterances that excited the badinage of the Parisians, he deserved infinitely better of his country than many men who have occupied high places in its temple of fame. When hurriedly despatched from Châlons to his thankless duty in Paris, he found the capital alike bewildered and defenceless. Trochu restored calm and hope; and he organised a defence so efficient that Paris held out for as many months as the Germans had expected weeks. Not only did he save the honour of Paris, but he also achieved for her the attribute of heroism. And because he was simply a plain, upright man, whose sole aspiration was just to do his duty unostentatiously and conscientiously, it is in the natural course of events that his name has drifted almost into oblivion. If he had swaggered, struck attitudes, and perpetrated epigrams, Paris would have raised a statue in commemoration of his exploits, and would have named streets after him.

In the spring of 1861 there was living a shabby life in a dingy town in the American State of Illinois, a middle-aged man, who to all appearance had got the chance of a career and had failed to grasp it. An obscure tanner now, he had been an officer in the regular army of the United States; but he had left that profession, or rather it might perhaps be said that profession had left him. Four years later this obscure tanner of Galena had climbed to the highest pinnacle of military position and fame. He had crushed the most colossal and most stubborn rebellion of modern times. His grateful country had raised him to a military rank higher than that enjoyed by George Washington himself. Four years more and he was to fill the Presidential chair of the Great Republic. Among all the strange turns of fortune's wheel, was there ever a stranger revolution than this? Luck, or fate, or chance might have had some small share in the swift, wonderful mutation; yet no man can truly aver that ULYSSES SIMPSON GRANT did not fairly earn every step of the marvellously abrupt elevation. Ungifted with the arts to court popularity, he put his foot in the ladder a friendless man —a man, indeed, under a cloud; and he carved his way to position and fame by sheer dint of his innate attributes. And what were those? A dauntless honesty, a sturdy common sense, a perfect self-reliance, a will as strong as fate itself, a total exemption from all inconvenient emotion, an uncommon faculty of calmly mastering all the bearings of a situation in the midst of a chaos of distractions, an indomitable taciturnity, and occasional but opportune flashes of military inspiration. Grant was not a heaven - born soldier; of that rare wonder the great American Civil War produced but one example in the gifted Stonewall Jackson. Robert Lee was Grant's master in the science of strategy as in the art of tactics; but Lee lacked certain of the attributes that went to the making up of Grant's greatness. Lee had not Grant's imperturbability. Lee was a rapier, bright, keen, adroit. Grant was a Nasmyth's hammer. Lee knew when he was beaten; Grant never would own himself beaten—and it is strange what surprises of good fortune come to the man who has this resoluteness of incredulity. Think of the terrible evening of the battle of Shiloh! The Union lines had been driven back, dyeing the ground with Northern blood at every step; back, in many places back almost to the very verge of the river. From the most sanguine, hope of all save disaster had fled. Buell, arriving at sundown, wasted no words in questions as to the maintenance of the struggle; his queries were solely as to the expedients for retreat. Grant's calm response was, " I have not given up the idea of beating them to-morrow." And with the morrow he renewed the battle; ay, and he won it; and this by sheer dint of his dogged refusal to own that he was worsted. Grant's tactics ever were simple; he began the attack, he persevered in the attack, he conquered by the attack. The grand stroke that ended the rebellion was the outcome of one of Grant's rare flashes of inspiration. Sheridan with his cavalry had been sent out with orders to cut loose from Grant's main force, and to operate independently. But the same evening the inspiration fell upon Grant; and he sent counter-orders out to Sheridan to strike the Confederate flank and rear; for that he, Grant, "felt like ending the matter this time before going back." Then Sheridan replied that "He saw his chance were he to push things." Grant's laconic reply was simply, "Push things!" And things were so pushed that ten days later the noble Lee and his gallant remnant of an army had succumbed to fate; the impassive Grant had accorded to him and his men terms of magnanimous generosity, and the Great Rebellion was at an end.

The career of the late GENERAL SHERMAN, Grant's successor in the headship of the Army of the United States, was scarcely less strange than that of his great predecessor. A graduate of West Point Military Academy, he was sent to California on military service before the discovery of gold in that great province. When the golden shower fell on the Pacific slope, Sherman left the army and took to banking in San Francisco. He was not entirely a success as a banker. Then he was a lawyer in Leavenworth, and failed to earn a living even in this avocation. He could not thrive as a farmer, and, when Secession loomed close, he had to relinquish the position he had acquired as principal of a military academy down in the South. When at length the war-cloud burst, he was in the service of a tramway company in the city of St. Louis. In the earlier days of the war Sherman did not make much head. He dared to prophesy, and he shared the fate of most true prophets, in that he was scouted as a crazy lunatic. Ere long he was able to smile at the imputation on his sanity. He and Thomas helped Grant to win the great battle of Chattanooga. Then, when Grant was called to the Eastern theatre of war to take the supreme command of all the Union forces in the field, he left Sherman in the West to achieve renown by carving a bloody path from Chattanooga to Atlanta, and by the comparatively bloodless, but more sensational, march " from Atlanta to the sea "—from the heart of Georgia to the Atlantic at Savannah ; thence northwards through the Carolinas, through the flames and over the ashes of Columbia, till at length he gave terms at Raleigh to the last Confederate army that remained in the field. When Grant was made President, Sherman succeeded him in the command-in-chief of the army, from which he was super-annuated a few years before his lamented death. Grant and Sherman, the opposites of each other in character, yet were the closest friends. Grant was a silent man ; Sherman was a witty and voluble man — vivacious, excitable, and, indeed, electric. For the rest, he was a friendly, unaffected, genial person, with a quaint dash of cynical humour, and an abiding conviction, which he frequently expressed to me with great heartiness, that all war-correspondents ought to be summarily hanged, and that he, personally, would have no objections to perform the operation.

The face of the late General Philip Sheridan was emphatically the face of a fighting man. Nor did the face belie the character, for between May, 1861, and April, 1865, this trenchant little warrior took part in about seventy battles and combats, not to speak of minor skirmishes. In that short period, without interest, without special good fortune, he had raised himself from the rank of lieutenant to that of full major-general — he had sprung from the profoundest obscurity to the highest pinnacle of military fame. When I first made Sheridan's acquaintance he was watching from the hill-top of Frénois the battle of Sedan, attached to the head-quarters staff of the Prussian King in the capacity of Military Commissioner from the United States. He steadily noted the crushing repulse of Margueritte's cuirassiers as they charged headlong to ruin down the slope of Illy ; and when, closing his glass, he quietly remarked, "It is all over with the French now!" the members of King Wilhelm's staff shook him by the hand for the word, for they knew well it came from the lips of a past-master in practical warfare.

The story of Sheridan's "Ride from Winchester" has been told in burning verse, but the stern prose of it is more thrilling than any lyric can be. Suddenly called from his command to attend a council of war at Washington, he left his army camped in a strong position along Cedar Creek in the Shenandoah Valley, twenty miles in front of Winchester. General Early, at the head of a Confederate army, was confronting it at no great distance; but no battle seemed imminent; and before his departure Sheridan had taken careful precaution to make its position safe. On his return journey from Washington he spent the night in Winchester. Riding out from that town on the following morning towards the front, he met fugitives from his beaten army. Galloping headlong forwards, pressing black "Rienzi" to his utmost speed, he rallied to him the fugitives as he met them. They were no longer beaten runaways; he inspired them with the magnetism of his own enthusiastic heroism; they fell into order as they rallied and followed their impetuous leader back at the double to the field of honour. He rode along his retrieved lines bareheaded, blazing with the ardour of battle; and then he led them to the attack like a whirlwind. The enemy, already plundering in his camp, he assailed and routed; he hurled him back across Cedar Creek; he retook all his positions, and, not content with this, he pressed the broken foe with inveterate fury, routed him, horse, foot, and artillery, and chased him for miles. It was an electrical exploit, savouring rather of the fighting of the Middle Ages than of the methodic warfare of modern times. Homer might have sung the deed, only that it was wrought by a little man wearing a frock-coat and trousers, and using trenchant modern oaths instead of Greek polysyllables.

After the great war Sheridan made campaign after campaign against the Indians of the West and South-West, until, in course of time, he succeeded Sherman in the command-in-chief of the Army of the United States. When scarcely beyond middle age he died suddenly of heart-mischief, the malign result of his ceaseless and arduous exertions on active duty. A few days before his sudden and premature ending I spent a long evening with him in his pleasant Washington house, while he gossiped over the tumultuous war times in a low soft voice that had no note in it of the battle-field. But, as I watched the strong, earnest face while he talked, I could discern the flush rising on it and the sparkle of the eye that told of the stirring of the fighting spirit. Better soldier than Phil Sheridan never trod the earth.

Shortly before his lamented death, my father-in-law the late General Meigs, for many years Quartermaster-General of the United States Army, sent me a very interesting letter from General Sheridan to General Grant, in which he gave his estimate of the German and French troops who fought under his eye at Gravelotte, Beaumont, and Sedan :—

"In seeing these battles" (wrote Sheridan), " I have had my imagination clipped of many of the errors it had run into in its conceptions of what might be expected of the trained troops of Europe. There was about the same percentage of sneaks and runaways, and the general conditions of the battles were about the same as were our own in the war between North and South. One thing was especially noticeable—the scattered condition of the men in going into battle, and their scattered condition while engaged. At Gravelotte, Beaumont, and Sedan the men engaged on both sides were so scattered that the affair looked like thousands of men engaged in a deadly skirmish without any regard to lines of formation. These battles were of this style of fighting, commencing at long range ; and it might be called progressive fighting, closing at night by the French always giving up their positions or being driven from them in this way by the Germans. The latter had their own strategy up to the Moselle, and it was good and successful. After that river was reached, the French made the strategy for the Germans, and it was more successful than their own.

"The Prussian soldiers are very good brave fellows, all young—scarcely a man over twenty-seven in the first levies. They had gone into each battle with the determination to win. It is also especially noticeable that the Prussians have attacked the French wherever they have found them, be the numbers great or small ; and, so far as I have been able to see, though the grand tactics of bringing on the engagements have been good, yet the battles have been won by the good square fighting of the men and junior officers. It is true that the Prussians have been two to one, except in one of the battles before Metz (Vionville-Mars-la-Tour), the battle of 16th August ; still the French have had the advantage of very strong positions. Generally speaking, the French have not fought well. This may have been because the poor fellows were discouraged by the trap into which their commander had led them; but I must confess to have seen some of the tallest running at Sedan I have ever witnessed; especially on the left of the French position all attempts to make the men stand seemed unavailing. So disgraceful was this that it caused the French cavalry to make three or four gallant but foolish charges; as it were, to show that there was at least some manhood left in a mounted French officer.

"I am disgusted. All my boyhood's fancies of the soldiers of the Great Napoleon have been dissipated, or else the soldiers of the Little Corporal have lost their *élan* in the pampered parade-soldiers of the Man of Destiny. The Prussians will settle, I think, by making the line of the Moselle the German frontier, taking in Metz and Strasburg, and exacting an indemnity for their war-expenses. I have been most kindly received by the King and Count Bismarck, and all the officers of the headquarters of the Prussian Army. I have seen much of great interest, and especially have been able to observe the differences between European battles and those of our own country. There is nothing to be learned here professionally, and it is a satisfaction to learn that such is the case. There is much, however, that Europeans could learn from us: the use of rifle-pits, the use of cavalry, which they do not employ to advantage; and, for instance, there is a line of communication from here [Sedan] to Germany, exposed to the whole south of France, with scarcely a soldier on the whole line, and it has never been molested. There are a hundred things in which they are behind us. The staff departments are very poorly organised; the Quartermaster's Department specially wretched, etc. etc.

" Your obedient servant,

" P. H. Sheridan, Lieutenant-General.

" General Grant, Washington."

Nearly seventy years ago the late Lord Napier of Magdala went out to India a stripling, friendless cadet, with his sword for his fortune; and the good weapon served him well, although he had no opportunity of using it until he had served for nineteen years. Nor did promotion come to him very promptly, for he was only a colonel thirty-five years after receiving his first commission as second lieutenant in the Bengal Engineers. But once he drew his sword on the afternoon of Moodkee, the scabbard knew it thenceforth only occasionally. He fought all through the Sutlej campaign at Moodkee, Ferozeshah, and Sobraon; in the Punjaub war he was wounded—he was always being wounded—at the siege of Mooltan; and he was in the thick of the fighting at the decisive battle of Goojerat. He rode and fought with Havelock and Outram on that heroic enterprise, the first relief of Lucknow. The rebel Sepoys might well execrate his name, for his skill as an engineer opened for stout old

Colin Campbell his conquering way into the heart of the great stronghold of the Kaiserbagh. He commanded with skill and vigour a brigade under Sir Hugh Rose in that chief's swift, ruthless campaign in Central India. He was Sir Hope Grant's second in command in the expedition to China in 1859, and was hit five times at the storming of the Taku forts. Then, eight years later, his great opportunity came to him as the organiser and commander of the Abyssinian expedition. As regarded mere fighting, that was not a very stupendous affair; but it was perhaps the neatest and cleanest piece of military work Britain had accomplished since the days of the Peninsular War; and the chief credit of it belonged to the sagacious and painstaking leader who left nothing to chance, and who was strong enough to have his own way in everything. It was in Abyssinia that Napier earned his peerage; and he had acquired so good a repute for steadfast careful soldierhood, that when in 1878 war between England and Russia seemed inevitable, he was named for the command of the British army whose services fortunately were not actively required. Lord Napier was in chief command of the great peace manœuvres on the plains near Delhi, at which the Prince of Wales was present in the course of his Indian tour. On the first day of the operations I saw his collar-bone broken by his charger falling under him; but the staunch old warrior was up and in the saddle again immediately, kept it throughout the day, and for the week during which the sham campaign lasted, never went sick an hour; but wore his uniform and rode his horse with no trace of the accident save that his arm was in a sling. They somehow don't make men nowadays like modest, sterling, genial old Lord Napier of Magdala!

In a work called "The Soldier's Pocket-Book," which, although now somewhat obsolete, is still deservedly highly appreciated in the British Army, the author genially refers to the profession of which I have had the honour to be a humble member, as "the curse of modern armies—I mean war-correspondents"; and again he writes: "Travel-

x

ling gentlemen, newspaper correspondents, and all that race of drones, are an encumbrance to an army; they eat the rations of fighting men, and they do no work at all." This is not the place to discuss the question whether the harm which the war-correspondent may do, is counter-balanced or not by the useful ends which his presence with an army in the field equally unquestionably may subserve. I am not sure that the point is one upon which I have quite succeeded in making up my own mind. But, at all events, my mind is fully made up as regards this, that there is some inconsistency in writing slightingly and opprobriously of a profession, and at the same time in making assiduous endeavour to be well-spoken of by that profession. For-tunately war-correspondents are for the most part men who bear no malice, and who are too catholic in their readiness to recognise merit where it exists to allow any personal feeling to rankle in their bosoms. Further, they are phi-losophers, and when they find a man who has abused them vehemently in print, nevertheless sedulously anxious to have them with him, and to afford them every opportunity to recognise and promulgate his merits, why, they smile good-humouredly, and are quite content to allow the hatchet to lie buried.

The author of "The Soldier's Pocket-Book," I proceed to observe, is FIELD-MARSHAL LORD WOLSELEY. Lord Wolseley is a man of whom it has been the habit on the part of those who do not like him to say that he has had exceptionally good luck. Well, he has had some good luck; and on the other hand he has had not a little bad luck. But for the latter, he might have had the supreme command of the latest operations in Afghanistan, or might have conducted the Zulu campaign instead of merely cleaning up after Lord Chelmsford. But what good luck has befallen him—the charge of the Red River expedition, the conduct of the Ashantee expedition, and the leadership of the Egyptian campaign (I say nothing of his Transvaal experiences nor of the Nile expedition)—he has proved himself thoroughly worthy of. Success in all those affairs demanded fertility of resource, strength of purpose, self-reliance, and administrative skill. All these attributes belong to Lord Wolseley, and it was in virtue of them that he achieved success. For example, from the landing of the Ashantee expedition on the pestilential shore of the Gold Coast till the day he led his troops back victorious from Coomassie, Wolseley was the heart and soul of the enterprise, its moving and master spirit, its strong backbone. He never faltered or lost his head when repeated hindrances threatened to baulk him; harassed by a depressing and almost deadly climate, his buoyant courage never deserted him.

It has been said of Lord Wolseley by his detractors that he is self-reliant to a fault, but it is to be observed that those who thoroughly believe in themselves have a strong tendency to make others believe in them also; and Lord Wolseley's frank self-reliance and self-confidence have ever reacted favourably on all around him. He is an almost ruthlessly practical man; he has risen superior to pipeclay, and has dared to despise red-tape. Very much of Lord Wolseley's success has been due to his faculty of intuitive discernment of character. With this skill in selection for his guide he gathered around him a band of devoted adherents, in each one of whom he recognised some special and particular attribute of which when the occasion occurred he made astute and purposeful use. The "Wolseley Gang," as I have heard this following called by angry outsiders, were not by any means one and all men of exceptional general military capacity. Some of them, indeed, might have been called dull men. But never a one of them but had his speciality. You might wonder what Lord Wolseley saw in this man and that that he had them always with him. If you watched events long enough, time would furnish you with the answer and justify the Chief's insight into individual character. His coterie of adherents he was ever on the alert to recruit without regard, for the most part, to interest or position, and acting simply on his perception of character. And he has constantly and exclusively employed his own men, arguing with great force and good reason, that what may be set him to do he can accomplish more efficiently and smoothly with instruments whom he has proven, and between whom and himself there is a mutual familiarity of methods, rather than with new and unaccustomed men, of whom, however good, he has had no experience. It remains to be proved—it may probably never be proved—whether Lord Wolseley has the capacity for successfully conducting war on the grand scale, with skilled experienced commanders and trained civilised troops for his antagonists. His record, say his detractors, scarcely warrants the repute in which we, his countrymen, hold him. Be this as it may, his record is a record of almost unvarying success. He has been set to do almost nothing that he has not done, neatly, cleanly, adroitly, and without apparent strain. It seems no unfair deduction from that past to which he has been so often equal, that Lord Wolseley is likely to prove equal to any future that may come to him.

It happened to me to be engaged in journalistic duty in Tirhoot, a vast district of northern Bengal, during a famine which was ravaging that region in the winter of 1873–74. It soon became apparent to me that the relief operations were being skilfully conducted by a functionary who must be drawing on his military experiences; and presently I had the honour of being introduced to a brisk, dapper little man, whom I soon learned to admire as Colonel Frederick Roberts, then Deputy-Quartermaster-General of our Indian army; and who is now FIELD-MARSHAL LORD ROBERTS, at home here among us after long and brilliant service as Commander-in-Chief of her Majesty's forces in India. Roberts—he was then, and probably still is, familiarly known all over India as " Bobs "— had seen no small amount of fighting before I had the good fortune to meet him. He had distinguished himself greatly in the siege of Delhi; he had won the Victoria Cross by a feat of brilliant gallantry later in the mutiny; and he had done fine service all through that bloody, tumultuous time. He had been with Chamberlain in the heart of the hard fighting in the Umbeyla campaign, and won his C.B. in the Lushai expedition; and he had so distinguished himself under Napier in Abyssinia that that chief had sent him home with the despatches announcing his crowning success. Still there was something of a growl among the sticklers for seniority when Roberts, at the outbreak of the Afghan War in the beginning of the winter of 1878, got the independent command of one of the columns of invasion; for, although as quartermaster-general he held the local and temporary rank of major-general, his substantive rank was simply that of major in the Bengal Artillery. But Roberts soon proved himself abundantly equal to the occasion. His capture of the Afghan position on the Peiwar Kotal was as brilliant in execution as skilful and daring in conception. And after the gallant Cavagnari was treacherously slain in Cabul, Roberts's avenging march on that capital was prompt, dashing, and successful.

The nation at large, and India in particular, had already grown proud of Roberts as not less a fine commander than a valiant soldier, when the chance came to him to make for himself a world-wide reputation. It was a moment of imminent peril and intense anxiety. An Anglo-Indian army had been defeated and crushed at Maïwand, a few marches west of Candahar. The safety of that place, the capital of southern Afghanistan, was in grave hazard; the British prestige and supremacy all over Afghanistan were trembling in the balance. Stewart and Roberts at Cabul, three hundred miles from Maïwand and Candahar, realised that it was only from Cabul that the blow of relief and retribution could be struck. So Roberts started on that long, swift, perilous march, the suspense as to the issue of which grew and swelled until the strain became intense. For the days passed, and there came no news of Roberts and of the 10,000 men with whom the wise, daring little chief had cut loose from any base, and struck for his goal through a region teeming with enemies. The pessimists held him to be marching on ruin. The Afghans, said they, inspired by their success at Maïwand and strengthened by hordes of hill-men, would dog every step he took and finally mob him in the

open. If not to the sword, surely he would fall a prey to
famine, for Candahar was thirty marches distant from Cabul
not counting rest-days, and Roberts had marched out with
supplies that would last him barely a week. But Roberts
knew the country, knew himself, knew the gallant men whom
he commanded, and knew the enemy he might have to
confront. He marched light; he lived on what the country
supplied; he gave his enemies no time to concentrate against
him. And lo! two days in advance of the time he had set
himself he had relieved Candahar, he had shattered into
wreck the Afghan army which had been threatening it, and
had made his name famous among the nations.

There must be few Britons who are not familiar with Sir
Evelyn Wood's achievements; how, for instance, at Kambula
he held his own with a handful against many thousands of
brave Zulu warriors. A singular combination of the *suaviter
in modo* with the *fortiter in re*, Wood's soldiers have ever
loved and respected him with an almost unique personal
fidelity. Of a compact and nervous build, a man somewhat
under the middle size, his body is seamed with wounds; yet
he can endure fatigue and privation with the toughest.
There is command in the clear blue eye; the sweetness of his
smile goes to your heart, and stays there. A man of singular
modesty, it is not from himself that one can hear a word of
Wood's conduct under fire. But when I first visited his
camp in Zululand, some of his soldiers took me up on to the
bare ridge of Kambula, where, out in the open, up against the
sky-line, he stood directing the fighting, while the Zulu
attacks surged in front and on flanks, and while a storm of
bullets whistled about him. Wood has been a fighting-man
from his boyhood. He received his first wound when a
midshipman in a battery in front of Sevastopol. Then he
went into cavalry; and in the Mutiny time he won the
Victoria Cross in command of a corps of wild irregular
horsemen which he had himself recruited. He fought in
China, and a little campaign all to himself in Africa with
Lord Wolseley. As poor Colley's successor on the border of

the Transvaal, he proved himself as wise in council as he had shown himself valiant in war. A many-sided man, he found time in an interval of peace to become a barrister; he was the most purposeful, the most thorough, and the most unresting divisional commander that Aldershot has ever known; he is habitually at the War Office from 9 a.m. to 5 p.m.; he is in the first flight in the hunting field; and he has published a volume of Crimean reminiscences which is more enthralling than any fiction. A veteran of many wars, Evelyn Wood, now serving as Quartermaster-General, is among the foremost military figures of our nation.

A yet more notable commander than Sir Evelyn Wood is his friend and comrade, SIR REDVERS BULLER. Like Wood, Buller was one of Lord Wolseley's men. He took service first under that able leader in the Red River expedition, was with him in Ashantee, served under him throughout the Zulu War, served with him in the Egyptian campaign, and was his chief-of-staff in the Nile expedition. When I first visited Wood's camp in Zululand, I found Buller there in command of some 800 volunteer irregular horsemen—or perhaps rather mounted infantry; a strange, wild, heterogeneous band, whom Buller held in sternest discipline, and made do wonders in fighting and marching, by sheer force of character. A stern-tempered, ruthless, saturnine man, with the gift of grim silence not less than a gift of curt, forcible expression on occasion, Buller ruled those desperadoes with a rod of iron. Yet, while they feared him, they had a sort of dog-like love for him. Buller's advancement has been exceptionally rapid; but almost every step of rank he gained in face of the enemy, just as he won the Victoria Cross by a sequence of deeds of all but unique heroism. Routine men grumbled that Wolseley should have sent him out to the eastern Soudan to command a brigade in Sir Gerald Graham's first short expedition. Amply did Buller vindicate the choice. It is not too much to aver that by his cool, skilful handling of his brigade in the crisis of the fight of Tamai he averted a disaster that but for his conduct was inevitable, retrieved the all but desperate situation, and buttressed the tottering fortunes of the British arms. Again, later, on the Nile, it was he who with characteristic abruptness snatched the dishevelled remnant of the column which he found at Gubat out of the very jaws of imminent peril, and reconducted it, with a cool promptitude that was all his own, back into a region of comparative safety. He shares with the Duke of Devonshire the by no means unserviceable attribute of "you-be-damned-ness." I have watched Redvers Buller's career with the closest attention and the profoundest admiration. I regard him as the strongest soldier of the British army to-day; and if he remains in the service and there be hot work again in our time, I predict for Buller a great fighting career.

It is not possible for me to write without emotion of poor SIR HERBERT STEWART, for we two had been close friends ever since we lived together in the same tent on the Zululand veldt. That was in 1879; Stewart was then a simple cavalry captain with little expectation of speedy or rapid promotion. Before the life had gone out of him by the wells of Jakdul, he knew that the Queen had promoted a colonel of scarce two years' standing to the rank of major-general for distinguished service in the field. But the honour came, alas! to a man who in performing that service had got his death hurt; and we had lost at the premature age of forty-one a soldier who if he had been spared would have covered himself with yet more glory. I count among my treasured souvenirs the last letter I received from him, just before he marched from Dongola to Korti. It thus concludes:—"If with 1,500 as good soldiers as ever breathed I cannot do something creditable to them and to me should the chance offer, then, old friend, I give you full permission to invest in the heaviest procurable pair of boots to kick me wherewithal when I return to England."

Stewart had been a staunch Wolseleyite ever since the Transvaal; and another of Lord Wolseley's adherents was

Sir George Colley, who met a soldier's death on the Majuba Hill on the 27th February, 1881. Colley was an officer of wide experience and great ability. I knew him well, and because of what I had seen of him I should have named caution as one of his principal attributes. But had this been so he probably would have been alive now. Indeed, had he cared greatly to live, I do not think he need have died. Some day, perhaps, the true story of that strange futile campaign in which Colley met his fate may come to be written.

Not less than the Hohenzollerns of Prussia, are the Romanoffs, the Imperial family of Russia, a fighting race. Of that family, besides its then existing head the Emperor Alexander II., no fewer than twelve members took part in the Russo-Turkish War, occupying positions from Commander-in-Chief to Captain on the Staff. The Grand Duke Nicholas, a younger brother of Alexander II., had the command-in-chief of the Russian forces in Europe. Nicholas was a fine soldierly chief, but not a great general. He was the heartiest and bluntest of soldier-men when in a good humour; when in the opposite temper he exemplified graphically the adage—"Scratch the Russian and you will find the Tartar." He had his settled likes and dislikes; I suppose that I ranked among the former, for "Monseigneur" was always civil enough to me, and occasionally curiously frank. When I rode into the Imperial headquarters at Gorni Studen with the earliest tidings of the desperate struggle in the Schipka Pass, the Emperor sent me across the valley to his brother the Grand Duke to repeat to the latter the intelligence which I had brought to him. The Grand Duke asked me what I thought of the situation I had left behind me on the Schipka. I replied that in my humble opinion the safety of that important position could not be assured, unless a whole army-corps were permanently allotted for its defence. "An army-corps!" cried the Grand Duke, as he tossed down a glass of wine—"Good God, what is the use of talking of an army-corps when I don't know where to find a spare battalion!" Nicholas was recklessly outspoken; but he was a strong man who would enforce the line of action he regarded as most advantageous. It was he who, backed only by Skobeleff and Gourko, insisted on the winter crossing of the Balkans after the fall of Plevna, and so converted a virtual failure into a remarkable triumph. Nicholas would have gone further if he had got his own way; he would have occupied Constantinople, and the occupation of Constantinople must have brought about war between England and Russia. But the Grand Duke loyally obeyed the injunctions of the Tzar that he should refrain from this extremity; and so, but by a hair's-breadth, was averted a conflict so much to be deplored. After the war the Grand Duke Nicholas fell into disgrace on account of his peculations. So discreditable a discovery was not to be allowed official promulgation. The inquiry was quashed, the court engaged in the investigations was dissolved, and the Grand Duke was ordered to retire to his estates in the country, where for the most part he lived in seclusion until his death.

When Russia was at her wits' end how to reduce the Plevna fortifications, so sublimely defended by Osman Pasha and his gallant, stubborn Turks, she fell back on an old soldier who had served her right well in a long-gone-by campaign. It was GENERAL TODLEBEN'S skilful and energetic exertions in the defence of Sevastopol that had kept English and French soldiers for so many long weary months toiling, fighting, and dying in front of that fortress. He had been summoned to the seat of war in Bulgaria in the autumn of 1877, so hurriedly that he arrived in Bucharest with a single aide-de-camp, and was destitute of any provision for taking the field. Bucharest had been so depleted of horseflesh that he found himself unable to obtain even a single charger up to his weight. I happened to be in Bucharest for a few hours during Todleben's short stay there, and I was the possessor of a powerful grey stallion which was a very disagreeable mount and took a great deal of riding. He was bucking, rearing, and generally " playing up " along the Podo-Mogosoi, when General Todleben hailed me and asked me whether I would sell the horse. I ventured to observe that he was rather a handful for me, and certainly scarcely an elderly gentleman's horse; but Todleben insisted on trying him, and to my surprise and, I confess, relief, an hour later he rode the big grey into the courtyard of Brofft's Hotel, on excellent terms with the animal. The circumstance that the general was some four stone heavier than I, no doubt weighed with the grey. He promptly changed hands, and General Todleben did me the honour to desire that I should dine with him the same evening. It passed only too quickly, for the general's conversation was full of varied interest, and I could have listened to him for a week on end. He asked with great solicitude after Mr.— now Sir—William Howard Russell of the *Times*, with whom of old, he said, he had had sundry controversies which he was sure did not at all interfere with their mutual friendly relations. Next morning Todleben started for Plevna on the big grey, which traversed Bucharest mostly on his hind legs. Todleben was a singularly handsome and stalwart man, exceptionally young-looking for his years. In Sevastopol he had to resist a siege; now, before Plevna, he had the converse duty of conducting a siege. He promptly seized and recognised the situation, adopting the policy of refraining from all further offensive, and of that slow, sure, scientific starvation which was inevitably successful in the end.

SKOBELEFF, take him all in all, was the most remarkable man I have ever known. We lived in considerable intimacy during the earlier days of the Russo-Turkish campaign, and in my haste I set Skobeleff down as a genial, brilliant, dashing—lunatic. Presently I came to realise that there was abundant method of a sort in the superficially seeming madness; and I ended in holding, as I still hold, that

Skobeleff came nearer being the heaven-born soldier and
inspired leader of men than any chief of whom I have had
personal cognisance. I have seen him do many things
which, on the face of them, looked mad enough and to
spare. I have seen him swim the brimming Danube
on horseback with his handful of personal escort at his
back. I have seen him go into half a dozen actions wearing a white coat and riding a white charger. I have seen
him, apparently quite wantonly and needlessly, stand alone
for an hour at a time under a heavy fire. All this looks like
a species of madness; but it was simply intense, if reckless,
devotion to a purpose—that purpose being to gain prestige,
to instil his soldiers with confidence to follow wherever
he should lead, to inspire them with daring by the force of
his own example. I remember Skobeleff on the morning
of the crossing of the Danube. General Dragomiroff, who
commanded, had never been under fire before, and was not
sure whether it would be wise to land in the face of the
Turkish force which was firing on us from the bank and
slopes above. He asked advice of Skobeleff. "Attack without delay and let me lead!" was that officer's curt reply;
and away he went up the steep slope at the head of a
torrent of men. In the July attempt on Plevna, Skobeleff
forced his way with the handful of soldiers which he commanded right up to the environs of the town; and when
Schahoffskoy was crushed, his skilful diversion saved that
general from utter annihilation. It was his audacious but
skilful bravery that drove the Turks out of Loftcha, and
gave to the Russians that important place of arms. In the
September assaults on Plevna he commanded the extreme
left wing of the Russian army, when he made that series
of desperate onsets which has gone into history as the
hardest fighting of modern times. In obeying his orders
and trying to accomplish all but impossibilities, he lost
nearly one-half of his command and made good a name
for all but fabulous bravery. The soldiers said of him that
they would rather fight and die under Skobeleff than fight
and live under another general. There is nothing in war-

correspondence more luridly vivid than poor MacGahan's description of Skobeleff as he returned from that two days' deadly paroxysm of strife, foiled of success because denied reinforcements:—"He was in a fearful state of excitement and fury. His uniform was covered with mud and blood; his sword broken, his Cross of St. George twisted round on his shoulder. His face was black with powder and smoke; his eyes were haggard and bloodshot, and his voice was quite gone. He spoke in a hoarse whisper. I never saw such a picture of battle as he presented."

From first to last of the Russo-Turkish War Skobeleff was its most shining figure. His bravery and his personal recklessness were not more conspicuous than the assiduous care which he bestowed on his men, in marked contrast to the conduct of other commanders in this respect. Skobeleff had a very comic father, an old gentleman of the now obsolete school of officers, who commanded a combined division of mounted Cossacks. When riding to the telegraph wire after the passage of the Danube, I met Skobeleff senior at the head of his division, jogging on towards Simnitza. I was able to tell him of the safety and conspicuous valour of his son. He deliberately dismounted, kissed me on both cheeks, hugged me vehemently, excoriating the back of my neck with a huge diamond he wore on his thumb, wept aloud, and finally blew his nose copiously on my moustache. He and his son were always having droll quarrels about financial affairs. The old gentleman was rather a miser; Skobeleff junior was a reckless spendthrift. So long as the father ranked his son, the latter had to take what the father chose to give him. But by-and-by young Skobeleff became a lieutenant-general while his father remained a major-general; and then the old man was at the mercy of his son, who compelled him to furnish him with money, with half-comic, half-serious threats of putting his parent under arrest unless he opened his purse. Once the son actually did put his father under arrest, on the pretext that the old gentleman had the impertinence to report himself in undress instead of full uniform; and he held his parent in that ignominious condition until, with tears and sobs, Skobeleff senior produced an adequate amount of rouble notes. But there was no real ill-will between the father and the son; the father had a great simple pride in his heroic son, and the son loved his father very dearly.

Skobeleff, at the premature age of thirty-six, died a wretched death, the incidents of which cannot be told. Had he lived, and been wise, there was no future to which he would not have been equal.

GENERAL GOURKO, though not so striking a military figure as Skobeleff, attained a well-deserved reputation in the Russo-Turkish War. He it was who, immediately after the crossing of the Danube, headed an adventurous raid across the Balkans into Roumelia, which, had the Russians been in position promptly to support him, would probably soon have ended the business. After the fall of Plevna he led 80,000 men across the Balkans a second time, in weather so cruel that he actually lost many more men from frost than by the bullet. It was a stupendous march, and in accomplishing it he achieved what the world had believed impossible. Gourko fought as stoutly as he marched swiftly, and he displayed great tactical skill in the disposition of his forces. Personally, in war time he was a cold, stiff, saturnine man who regarded his men as mere machines, and who failed, therefore, to inspire them with any personal warmth of feeling towards him, although they thoroughly believed in him as a commander.

I had some experience in the Servian war of 1876 how hard a fighter was OSMAN PASHA, the heroic defender of Plevna, a year before his name had reached to the ends of the earth as the man who for five long months defied from behind his earthworks the whole strength of the Muscovite empire. Strangely enough that position of his at Plevna was all chance—a mere fluke. In the earlier days of July he had left the up-stream fortress of Widdin with some 15.000 men, on the mission of succouring Nicopolis, a Turkish fortress threatened by the Russians. He learned that Nicopolis was already taken by the enemy; so he bent inwards to Plevna and proceeded to entrench himself there. With the intuitive eye of a fine soldier, he discerned how the Plevna position loomed on the flank of the Russian main line of advance towards the Balkans, and how important it was to hold on to · it with tooth and nail. A Russian force attacked him before he had begun his spade work. That force he summarily smashed and went on building earthworks. On the last day of July Schahoffskoy and Krüdener struck at him again with all their might, only to be driven back with the loss of more than a third of their strength. Still he went on digging and building earthworks. In September the Russians attempted the enterprise yet once again, this time more systematically and in immensely greater force They rained on him a storm of missiles from their great siege guns for five long days and nights. Osman, under cover of his earthworks, took no more heed of the shell-fire than if it had been a display of fireworks. On the sixth day they assailed his positions furiously with 80,000 men. Osman was ready for them; he slew them in thousands and tens of thousands, and sent them reeling back upon their supports. Then the Russians realised that they had endured enough of fighting with this masterful indomitable Turk and his stubborn army of 45,000 men. So they set themselves systematically to starve him into surrender, suspending meanwhile all other operations. Not till three months later, when hunger and sickness were eating out the hearts of his gallant soldiers, did Osman relinquish his hold of the positions which he had defended so stoutly in accordance with his orders. And even then, there still remained fight in the obstinate Moslem. Not, like Bazaine, would he tamely surrender in his trenches; he would strike one last fierce blow for extrication from the toils which had been woven around him. It was a wild-cat furious sortie that the Turks made on the serried Russian lines on the snowy morning of December 10th—a sortie that cut through rank after rank and filled the ground with dead and dying. Osman, blazing at its head, received the wound of honour; and then came the end. He surrendered to brave antagonists, who chivalrously admired the indomitable gallantry he had displayed. I had speech with him in Bucharest, when on his way to captivity in Russia. "I did my best," was all the comment this noble warrior would make on his historic defence. If Turkey had owned two Osmans that autumn of bloodshed, the Russians never would have crossed the Balkans!

THE END.

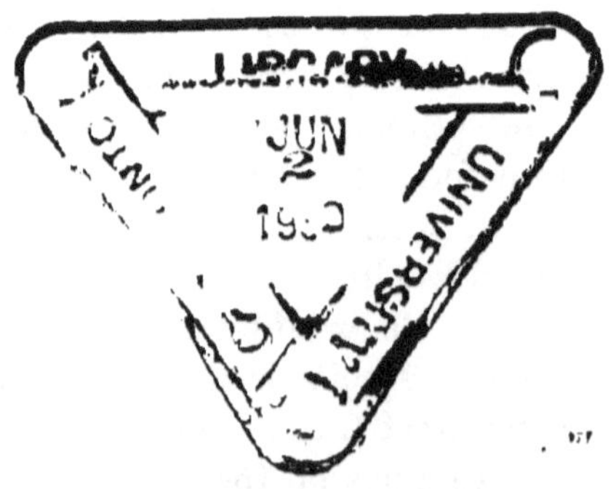

PRINTED BY CASSELL & COMPANY, LIMITED, LA BELLE SAUVAGE, LONDON, E.C.